I0754754

Christiane Hadamitzky

Heroism in Victorian Periodicals 1850 – 1900

HELDEN – HEROISIERUNGEN – HEROISMEN

Edited by

Ulrich Bröckling, Barbara Korte, Ralf von den Hoff

Published on behalf of the Collaborative Research Center
SFB 948 at the University of Freiburg

Volume 15

ERGON VERLAG

Christiane Hadamitzky

Heroism in Victorian Periodicals 1850 - 1900

Chambers's Journal – Leisure Hour – Fraser's Magazine

ERGON VERLAG

a.t.: Diss., University of Freiburg, 2016
Original title: "Homely, Easy and Attainable for All".
The Representation of Heroism in Victorian Periodicals 1850 – 1900:
Chambers's Journal – Leisure Hour – Fraser's Magazine

Funded by the Deutsche Forschungsgemeinschaft
(DFG, German Research Foundation) –
Project-ID 181750155 – SFB 948

Cover illustration:

Unknown artist: The Tenby life-boat proceeding to the rescue of the crew
of the "Nuevo Torcuvato", The British Workman, No. 27, 1857.
With kind permission of the Working Class Movement Library,
Salford, United Kingdom.

The Deutsche Nationalbibliothek lists this publication in the
Deutsche Nationalbibliografie; detailed bibliographic data
are available on the Internet at http://dnb.d-nb.de.

First published 2020
© Ergon – ein Verlag in der Nomos Verlagsgesellschaft, Baden-Baden 2020
This work is subject to copyright. All rights reserved. No part of this publication
may be reproduced or transmitted in any form or by any means, electronic or mechanical,
including photocopying, recording, or by any information storage or retrieval system,
without prior permission in writing from the publishers.
Printed on age-resistant paper
Cover design: Jan von Hugo

www.ergon-verlag.de

ISBN 978-3-95650-723-6 (Print)
ISBN 978-3-95650-724-3 (ePDF)
ISSN 2365-886X

For my father

Table of Contents

Acknowledgements

This study was written in the DFG Collaborative Research Center 948 (SFB 948) "Heroes – Heroizations – Heroisms. Transformations and Conjunctures from Antiquity to the Modern Day" at the University of Freiburg. Thanks are due to Ralf von den Hoff and all the members of the research center for the inspiring exchange of ideas.

I would like to thank my supervisor Barbara Korte for introducing me to the research field of periodical studies, and for giving me the opportunity to be part of this project. I am grateful for her continuous advice and support. I would also like to thank my second supervisor Ronald G. Asch for his historian's perspective in the finalisation of this study. I am also grateful to Margaret Beetham for sharing with me her love for periodical and gender studies and for her encouragement.

I would like to acknowledge the staff at The British Library, the Working Class Movement Library and especially the archive staff at The National Library of Scotland for helping me hunt for truffles in the vast amount of uncatalogued materials.

I am grateful to have been part of the first group of junior researchers at SFB 948 and would like to thank all of my colleagues for the time we shared in the research group and beyond. Special thanks are due to our coordinator Ulrike Zimmermann who advised us with a perfect mixture of patience, insistence and warmth. I would also like to thank my colleagues at the English Department, especially Doris Lechner who had the courage to immerse herself in periodical studies before me and for whose work and advice I am grateful.

Thanks are due to the SFB 948's former coordinators Jutta Schloon and Andreas Friedrich for their support as well as to the current coordinator Sebastian Meurer and research assistant Philipp Multhaupt for their work in the publication process of this book.

Through the ups and downs of writing a dissertation, Mark Kermode, Simon Mayo and their "Kenneth Branagh & Tom Courtenay's Chuckle Off" have kept me in good spirits.

My thanks for their support well beyond academia go to Christiane Hansen, Carolin Hauck, Christine von Lossau, Andreas Schlüter and Ulrike Zimmermann. They have read (sections of) this book and I am grateful for their valuable suggestions, their support and their friendship. My deepest thanks go to my parents Renate Schobner-Hadamitzky and Bernhard Hadamitzky for always assuring me that I can achieve anything I set my mind to. I am grateful to my partner Christina Rosenfeld for her unconditional support and encouragement in life – and in turning my dissertation into this book.

Part 1:
Heroism and the Periodical Press of Nineteenth-Century Britain

1. The Cultural Importance of Heroism in Victorian Britain

In June 1864, the satirical periodical *Punch* (1841–1992) published a note that read

> Universal Hero-Worship Company (Limited).
> Incorporated under the Companies' Act, 1862.
> [By operation of which the liability of each shareholder will be limited to the amount of cheers, or other manifestations of enthusiasm (including banners, dinners, subscriptions to memorials, &c. invested).] (Universal Hero-Worship Company, *Punch*, 4 Jun 1864, 236)

This short comment points to the omnipresence of the heroic in Victorian culture. From biographies of 'great men' to mass events such as the Duke of Wellington's funeral, from programmatic texts like Thomas Carlyle's *On Heroes, Hero-Worship and the Heroic in History* to commemorative flasks in the shape of parliamentary reformer Lord Brougham: heroes and public hero-worship were a characteristic of the Victorian age. Worshipped through public attention and "other manifestations of enthusiasm", heroism was a public and media phenomenon. At the time of a developing mass consumer culture, as the note in *Punch* makes clear, heroes were also a commercial commodity and their groups of admirers potential consumers. Thus, these few sentences reveal significant details about heroism in the public (and popular) culture of the nineteenth century. They recognise the widespread fascination with heroes and heroic acts, but at the same time profess unease about their massive presence in contemporary culture.

The ubiquity of the heroic in Victorian culture also shows that heroism was an answer to a general societal demand. At a time of transformation, diversification and rapid change in professional and private life, charismatic leader figures as well as role models became simultaneously both more desirable and more disputed. Referring to the thinkers of the age, to Thomas Carlyle, Matthew Arnold, Alfred Tennyson and John Ruskin and their ideas of guidance through a superior individual, Walter Houghton identifies hero-worship as a key characteristic of the *Victorian Frame of Mind*.[1] However, while some "lost in the maze of ideas [...] loo[ked] to a savior",[2] others felt that prophet-like hero figures had been rendered anachronistic by the ideas of evolution and a growing democratisation movement. Hence, competing concepts of the heroic were negotiated, justified and defended among intellectuals as well as in popular culture catering to all seg-

---

1 As Juliette Atkinson puts it, "venerating great men provided a means of reaffirming faith in the individual at a time when scientific advance and the successive blows dealt to religious institutions threatened to reduce human action to a set of impersonal laws." Juliette Atkinson: Victorian Biography Reconsidered, Oxford 2010, p. 47.

2 Walter Houghton: The Victorian Frame of Mind 1830–1870, New Haven 1957, p. 310.

ments of society. While most of the scholarship on the heroic in Victorian culture has centred on individual historical actors and thinkers[3] or specific works of literature, the competing concepts of the heroic and their particular functionalisations in popular culture have not been examined yet.[4]

---

3 As the most influential nineteenth-century voice on heroism until today, most scholarly work has been conducted on Thomas Carlyle and his ideas on heroism. See for example James Eli Adams: The Hero as Spectacle. Carlyle and the Persistance of Dandyism, in: Carol T. Christ / John O. Jordan (eds.): Victorian Literature and the Victorian Visual Imagination, Berkeley 1995, pp. 213–232; Ulrich Broich: On Heroes and Hero-Worship, Especially in English Romanticism, in: Anglistik 16.2, 2005, pp. 49–62; Rainer Emig: Eccentricity Begins at Home. Carlyle's Centrality in Victorian Thought, in: Textual Practice 17.2, 2003, pp. 379–390; Mark Engel: Collating Carlyle. Patterns of Revision in Heroes, Sartor Resartus, and The French Revolution, in: Davis R. Sorensen et al. (eds.): The Carlyles at Home and Abroad, Aldershot 2004, pp. 240–247; Ranjan Ghosh: Carlyle's "Hero as Poet" and Sri Aurobindo's Poetic Theory. Reconfiguring Few Dimensions of Creativity, in: Angelaki 11.1, 2006, pp. 35–44; Monroe Z. Hafter: Heroism in Alas and Carlyle's On Heroes, in: MLN 95.2, 1980, pp. 312–334; Charles H. Haws: Carlyle's Concept of History in Heroes and Hero-Worship, in: John Morrow (ed.): Thomas Carlyle 1981. Papers Given at the International Thomas Carlyle Centenary Symposium, Frankfurt am Main 1983, pp. 153–163; Geraldine Higgins: Heroic Revivals from Carlyle to Yeats, Basingstoke 2012; Paul E. Kerry: The Outsider at the Gates of Victorian Society. Thomas Carlyle's On Heroes, Hero-Worship, and the Heroic in History, in: Steven Wright (ed.): The Image of the Outsider in Literature, Media, and Society, Pueblo 2002, pp. 369–373; Karina Momm: Der Begriff des Helden in Thomas Carlyles On Heroes, Hero-Worship and the Heroic in History, Freiburg 1986; Ian Ousby: Carlyle, Thackeray, and Victorian Heroism, in: Yearbook of English Studies 12, 1982, pp. 152–168; Morse Peckham: Victorian Revolutionaries. Speculations on Some Heroes of a Cultural Crisis, New York 1970; Branwen Bailey Pratt: Carlyle and Dickens. Heroes and Hero-Worshippers, in: Dickens Studies Annual. Essays on Victorian Fiction 12, 1983, pp. 233–246; Richard Salmon: Thomas Carlyle and the Idolatry of the Man of Letters, in: Journal of Victorian Culture 7.1, 2002, pp. 1–22; id.: "The Unaccredited Hero". Alton Locke, Thomas Carlyle, and the Formation of the Working-Class Intellectual, in: Aruna Krishnamurthy (ed.): The Working-Class Intellectual in Eighteenth- and Nineteenth-Century Britain, Surrey 2009, pp. 167–193; David Sonstroem: The Double Vortex in Carlyle's On Heroes and Hero Worship, in: Philological Quarterly 59.4, 1980, pp. 531–540; Ilia Stambler: Heroic Power in Thomas Carlyle and Leo Tolstoy, in: European Legacy. Toward New Paradigms 11.7, 2006, pp. 737–751; John S. Tanner: When God Is Hero. Worshipping God as Hero in Carlyle and Hopkins, in: The Hopkins Quarterly 10.4, 1984, pp. 145–163; Michael Timko: Thomas Carlyle. Chaotic Man, Inarticulate Hero, in: Carlyle Studies Annual 14, 1994, pp. 55–69; Jane Wright: Sincerity's Repetition. Carlyle, Tennyson and Other Repetitive Victorians, in: Timothy Milnes / Kerry Sinanan (eds.): Romanticism, Sincerity, and Authenticity, New York 2010, pp. 162–181.

4 Valuable exceptions are John Price's study on *Everyday Heroism* which considers the growing public importance of acts of lifesaving by civilians and their public recognition (cf. John Price: Everyday Heroism. Victorian Constructions of the Heroic Civilian, London 2014) and Christine MacLeod's *Heroes of Invention* which traces the ascription of hero-status to inventors and engineers before and after the industrial revolution (cf. Christine MacLeod: Heroes of Invention. Technology, Liberalism and British Identity 1750–1914, Cambridge 2007).

Periodicals as a Site for Negotiating the Heroic

As the defining mass medium of the Victorian era, periodicals constitute a source situated within the everyday life of British society in the nineteenth century. The Victorian print market underwent enormous growth and diversification, with periodicals, journals and newspapers for every political and religious orientation or private interest being established and widely read. As a site for the negotiation and dissemination of current ideas, periodicals provide rich ground for the examination of the heroic. Heroism materialises in the periodical press as a cultural construct and product shaped by the worldviews of its producers, the expectations of the readers and regulation of the market.

As a means of communication between reader and periodical, heroes represent different worldviews and identities which producer and consumer can be presumed to agree upon in the act of consumption. Periodicals as a publishing genre "within capitalist economies in which class, gender, and other differences"[5] play a crucial role have not yet been analysed with regard to the heroic. Though some scholars have taken examples from the periodical press to support a more general argument, there are no studies of the heroic which take periodical texts and the cultural practices around them seriously as "an object of enquiry in its own right".[6] Over the last decades, due to some extraordinary pioneering scholarship on Victorian popular print culture,[7] the periodical has been established as an object worthy of analysis in itself rather than "as an empty vessel, a neutral medium for content that can be extracted and often analysed in a misleadingly decontextualized form".[8] Thus, this study is not only situated in literary and cultural studies research of the heroic, but is equally a contribution to the study of Victorian periodicals and their social and cultural functions. It will examine how and by which stylistic and formal means heroes and heroic acts are constructed, designed and presented in selected periodicals of the second half of the nineteenth century[9] intended for specific readerships. For this purpose, three period-

5 Margaret Beetham: Time. Periodicals and the Time of the Now, in: Victorial Periodicals Review 48.3, 2015, p. 324.

6 Matthew Philpots: A Return to Theory, in: Victorian Periodicals Review 48.3, 2015, p. 207.

7 Among those scholars I would like to pay special tribute to Margaret Beetham. I have not only profited from her ground-breaking work on periodicals as a publishing genre and a gendered space, but am grateful for the support and advice she has provided in the realisation of this study.

8 Ibid.

9 From mid-century, the periodical is considered a mass medium, with the flood of affordable (family) magazines entering the market after the abolition of the 'Taxes on Knowledge' (cf. chapter 3.2). This assertion determined the beginning of the period of examination in 1850. The end of the period in 1900 was chosen for the more practical reason that the periodicals are only digitised up until 1900 in the ProQuest *British Periodicals* database. To account for specific events of cultural significance, such as the Boer War (1899–1902), issues from 1901 and 1902 were consulted in the National Library of Scotland.

icals have been chosen for close investigation: *Chambers's Edinburgh Journal* (1832–1956), *Leisure Hour* (1852–1905) and *Fraser's Magazine* (1830–1882).

These periodicals offer a rich basis for analysis and comparison. *Chambers's Edinburgh Journal*, the main focus of this study, was published weekly and sold at 1½d, and was thus affordable even to the lower ranks of society, which the editors Robert and William Chambers explicitly wanted to address. The publication attempted, as stated in the editor's address to the readers in the first issue in February 1832, to be free of all religious and political bias and opinion and tried to instruct and educate the broadest possible audience. Wanting to appeal to the whole of the family, the journal published a broad range of genres, from informative reports, travel writing, history and biographical articles to fiction, poetry, popular science, practical advice and contributions for children. Although *Chambers's Journal* was written and produced for the lower classes, it also had a large middle- and upper-class readership, which the editors themselves commented upon in their disappointment at the fact that more educated than uneducated readers consumed their product (cf. Address of the Editors, *CJ*, 25 Jan 1840, 8). Within *Chambers's Journal*, a distinct didactic functionalisation of the vocabulary of the heroic becomes obvious. Coinciding with a growing general societal emphasis on personal progress, as for example propagated by Samuel Smiles in his influential work *Self-Help* (1859), the periodical used heroism as a validation for norm-conforming moral behaviour rather than extraordinary transgressive acts. Influenced by the publishers' location in Edinburgh and the Scottish tradition of Presbyterianism, a clear heroic profile[10] emerged, which foregrounded values such as selflessness and perseverance applied for the benefit of the community rather than for individual gain.[11] In positive as well as negative ascription, the heroic was utilised in *Chambers's* as a means to negotiate and mediate cultural values and norms.

The analysis of this publication will be complemented by a comparative discussion of *Leisure Hour* and *Fraser's Magazine*, which were chosen for their distinct orientations. *Leisure Hour*, a weekly published by the Religious Tract Society, aimed at a similar market as *Chambers's Journal*, but with a religious focus, while *Fraser's Magazine* was a monthly periodical that catered to a very specific educated conservative upper-class audience. Quite distinct in their orientation, intended readership, and institutional background within the commercial marketplace, the three periodicals form a suitable basis for a comparative study of heroic representations.

---

[10] For the idea of a discursive heroic profile of periodicals see Barbara Korte: Viele Helden für viele Leser. Das Heroische in viktorianischen Publikumszeitschriften, in: Ronald G. Asch / Michael Butter (eds.): Bewunderer, Verehrer, Zuschauer. Die Helden und ihr Publikum (Helden – Heroisierungen – Heroismen 2), Würzburg 2016, pp. 93–114.

[11] As will be elaborated in chapter 2.1 in greater detail, the idea of individual progress could be integrated with the idea of selflessness and work for the common good, since any personal progress was considered as directed at the betterment of society as a whole.

The main focus in the study of heroes often lies on their polarity, their ability to make boundaries visible by transgressing them, their status as outsiders of the communities they inspire and their strong individual agency and charismatic attraction.[12] While heroic figures exhibiting these characteristics still circulated in Victorian society,[13] they are, in the framework of this study, mostly significant in their absence. Publications with a didactic orientation such as *Chambers's Journal* or *Leisure Hour* focused on the communal and socially integrative functions of the heroic and used its vocabulary to create a "collective emotional investment"[14] to bind its consumers to a specific identity. The likeness of heroic figures to the readership of the periodicals is stressed rather than their extraordinariness or transgressive potential. As will be shown in the main body of this study, the hero[15] acts as a projection screen for the periodicals and constitutes a "heroic totality"[16] of what is already present in each and every member of the intended readership.

---

12 For this strand of research see for example Maurice Blanchot: The End of the Hero, in: Maurice Blanchot (ed.): The Infinite Conversation, Minneapolis 1993, pp. 368–378; Josef Früchtl: Das unverschämte Ich. Eine Heldengeschichte der Moderne, Frankfurt am Main 2004; Bernhard Giesen: Triumph and Trauma, Boulder 2004; id.: Zwischenlagen. Das Außerordentliche als Grund der sozialen Wirklichkeit, Weilerswist 2010; Nikolas Immer: Der inszenierte Held. Schillers dramenpoetische Anthropologie, Heidelberg 2008; Albrecht Koschorke: Zur Funktionsweise kultureller Peripherien, in: Susi K. Frank et al. (eds.): Explosion und Peripherie. Jurij Lotmans Semiotik der kulturellen Dynamik revisited, Berlin/ Boston 2012, pp. 27–40; Jurij M. Lotman: Die Struktur literarischer Texte, Munich 1993; Christian Schneider: Wozu Helden?, in: Mittelweg 36. Zeitschrift des Hamburger Instituts für Sozialforschung 18.1, 2009, pp. 91–102; Ralf von den Hoff et al.: Heroes – Heroizations – Heroisms. Transformations and Conjunctures from Antiquity to Modernity. Foundational Concepts of the Collaborative Research Centre SFB 948, in: helden. heroes. héros. E-Journal zu Kulturen des Heroischen, special issue 5: Analyzing Processes of Heroization. Theories, Methods, Histories, 2013, pp. 9–16, DOI: 10.6094/helden.heroes.heros./ 2019/APH/01.

13 Within the Victorian print market, transgressive hero-figures (often coinciding with a focus on physicality) can especially be found in publications which aimed at entertainment through sensational stories, for example in the so-called Penny Dreadfuls or adventure literature especially designed for boys.

14 Geoffrey Cubitt: Introduction, in: Geoffrey Cubitt / Allen Warren (eds.): Heroic Reputations and Exemplary Lives, Manchester 2000, p. 3.

15 Following Lee Edwards, this study will not refer to heroes and heroines, but will refer to both male and female actors who are assigned heroic attributes as heroes: "Not heroines, tamed and subordinate, without identity except in relation to male hero, but independent *heroes*." Lee R. Edwards: Psyche as Hero. Female Heroism and Fictional Form, Middletown 1984, n.p. Almost exclusively associated with works of fiction, the heroine, Edwards argues, can only ever exist in relation to a hero, whereas "a hero can theoretically exist in a narrative without a heroine" (ibid., 5). The texts analysed in this study are by no means forward-thinking in their portrayal of gender roles and women's agency, and female heroism is often exercised in relation to male actors. However, the decision to examine female heroes rather than heroines is a deliberate one in order to shed light on such practices of power: "The hero dances in the spotlight. The heroine is eclipsed, upstaged, in darkness." Ibid, p. 6.

16 Ibid.

In differentiation from the extraordinary hero figure, as for example designed by thinkers such as Carlyle, a second dominant type of hero emerges over the course of the nineteenth century, which substitutes the distance between a group and their heroes inherent to many other conceptualisations with proximity.[17] In this line of thinking, identification is a key characteristic in the relationship between heroic figures and their audience. The audience has to be able to find their own identity in that of the hero. When Walter Houghton emphasises the "Victorian tendency to think of men in two categories, heroes and ordinary mortals",[18] this separation is not as clear-cut as Houghton makes it out to be. As an answer to a "collective need",[19] the heroic could be adopted by collectives and imbued with their own meaning: "It was because the heroic image could serve so ambiguously as message and as compensation that it won so conspicuous a place in the Victorian imagination."[20] Being "[i]ncarnations of abstract ideals and ineffable desires",[21] heroes provided a projection screen for virtues without having to be exactly defined. Informed by the idea of a social imaginary, the heroic can thus be cast into a "form that allows us to conceive what it is towards which the sign points"[22] without having to make it explicit.[23]

Given the diverse landscape of popular print culture, the heroic as a projection screen was attractive for most publishers: "The flexibility of the terms 'hero' and 'hero-worship' meant that there were opportunities to celebrate new kinds of heroes."[24] Due to the openness of the concept, the heroic could be utilised by all kinds of different groups for the purpose of identity affirmation and stabilisa-

---

17 For the idea of closeness and distance see also chapter 2.2 of this study. On adoration and admiration see Ines Schindler et al.: Admiration and Adoration. Their Different Ways of Showing and Shaping Who We Are, in: Cognition and Emotion 27.1, 2013, pp. 85–118 and Veronika Zink: Von der Verehrung. Eine kultursoziologische Untersuchung, Frankfurt am Main 2014.

18 Houghton: Victorian Frame, p. 306.

19 "When understood as personal figurations, heroic figures represent an individual, 'Gestalt-like' offer to societies, a reaction to a collective need." Von den Hoff et al.: Heroes, p. 9.

20 Houghton: Victorian Frame, p. 340.

21 Edwards: Psyche, p. 4.

22 Wolfgang Iser: The Fictive and the Imaginary. Charting Literary Anthropology, Baltimore 1993, p. 2.

23 Iser emphasises the importance of the imaginary in relation to fiction and the different functions of fictional genres as compared to more factual texts will become apparent in the specific analyses (cf. for example chapter 4.2). On the idea of a heroic imaginary see also Mohr, who emphasises the potential which lies in the opaque quality ("Unschärfe", Jan Mohr: Männer mit Äxten. Heroismus in der Populärkultur, das Imaginäre und Hard Rock. Ein Versuch, in: KulturPoetik. Journal for Cultural Poetics 12.2, 2012, p. 231) of the imaginary, or Lucien Braun: Polysémie du concept de héros, in: Noémie Hepp / Georges Livet (eds.): Héroïsme et création littéraire sous les règnes d' Henri IV et de Louis XIII, Paris 1974, pp. 19–28, who situates the hero in a culture's imaginary.

24 Atkinson: Victorian Biography, p. 50.

tion.[25] In that way, prophet heroes to be adored from afar could exist simultaneously with everyday heroes mediated as exemplars to be emulated. A diverse set of heroes with different possibilities regarding autonomy and agency, with different values, morals and limitations were represented under the same vocabulary.

In the analyses of these differentiated representations of the heroic within the periodical marketplace, this study – in a discourse-centred approach – follows a number of intersecting guiding questions:

- Which kinds of figures, qualities and acts are labelled heroic in the different publications?
- Can dominant domains of the heroic be identified?
- Is the vocabulary of heroism imbued with a specific meaning, is it appropriated and re-interpreted by the periodicals or used with reference to a preconceived notion of heroism?
- How are issues of class, age, education, gender, ethnicity, space and individual agency discussed in the context of heroism, and how do these relate to the intended readership?
- To what extent are larger societal issues linked to the representation of the heroic?
- Does the vocabulary of the heroic and its functionalisation coincide with specific genres?
- Which stylistic and formal means are employed in the construction of the above?

The first part of the study will offer an overview of the contemporary competing models of heroism in Victorian society and the social functions they imply. It will locate the periodical material within the print culture of the nineteenth century and provide a theoretical framework for its examination. Part two will be concerned with the representation of heroism in *Chambers's Journal.* As dominant domains of the heroic, it considers the representation of heroism in military contexts, in relation to processes of civilisation, and in everyday life. To complement these findings, it will compare other selected publications of the Chambers publishing house and consider whether the heroic profile was exclusive to the periodical or could also be found in publications for other readerships. The third and last part of the study will, in a comparative analysis, consider the representation of the same domains of heroism in *Leisure Hour* and *Fraser's Magazine.* It will elaborate how the different political and religious perspectives are reflected in the publications' portrayal of the heroic before coming to an assessment of the representation of heroism on the periodical market for different readerships.

25 Atkinson notes that "[i]n effect, hero-worship could be appealed to in order to justify an astonishing range of ideals". Ibid., p. 48.

The following study would not have been possible without the large amount of digitisation work done over the last decades. All three periodicals examined are available as full text until their 1900 editions on the ProQuest *British Periodicals* database. As an entry point into the corpus, I chose a semantic approach by searching the database for keywords from the semantic field of heroism.[26] This search resulted in around 2,400 results for *Chambers's Journal* for the examination period of 1850 to 1900, in more than 2,200 results for *Leisure Hour* and over 2,900 results for *Fraser's Magazine*. As this corpus would have been too large to handle, I examined alternate years, later selectively adding years of particular cultural significance for heroism, such as times of war.

The remaining texts were fed into a customised database in which they were categorised according to different parameters. I recorded the general data for each text, that is issue number, title of publication, page numbers, and, if available, author. Additionally, I grouped the articles according to their genre, the time the texts were set in and their domain of heroism; this last category constituted a first broad qualitative categorisation of the represented heroism. It soon became clear that the discourse of heroism was predominantly negotiated in the context of the military, the idea of progress and civilisation and in the realm of everyday life. These domains also serve as the structure of the case studies and as axes of comparison in the main part of this study. As a last step within the database, I excluded those articles which only used the word 'hero' or 'heroine' as a synonym for 'protagonist' in a literary text. These preliminary measures resulted in a body of around 1,000 texts from the three periodicals for the examination period. However, the quantitative figures only served as a first access to the corpus and cannot be considered a meaningful analysis on their own. They point to tendencies yet are necessarily reliant on contextualisation and relativisation through the qualitative analysis which this study provides. It is important to keep in mind the semantic and discursive approach. When referring to a hero or heroic act, the study is not drawing on a preconceived notion of the heroic, but referencing a fictional or historical person being labelled as heroic in the periodicals. Through close readings, the study analyses the vocabulary of heroism in the different publications and examines the discourse around what is called heroic. Following this approach, the analyses are not actor-centred, but focus on the discourse around heroism. While specific historical actors might feature in the discourse as heroic figures, it is the representation, negotiation and functionalisation of the heroic in its context which stands at the heart of this study.

[26] As search terms I used 'hero', 'heroes', 'heroine', 'heroines', 'heroic' and 'heroism' as well as 'hero*', meaning all words beginning with the root 'hero-'.

2. Discourses on Heroism in Nineteenth-Century Britain

Heroism and hero worship are present throughout the Victorian period and it is not surprising that Walter Houghton devotes a whole subchapter in his seminal study *The Victorian Frame of Mind* to the examination of Victorian attitudes towards hero worship.[1] As he puts it,

> when the Victorian period began, all the prerequisites for hero worship were present: the enthusiastic temper, the conception of the superior being, the revival of Homeric mythology and medieval ballad, the identification of great art with the grand style, the popularity of Scott and Byron, and the living presence of Napoleonic soldiers and sailors.[2]

This environment not only sparked a high tide of literary and artistic representation of heroic conduct, but also encouraged a more abstract discussion on hero figures and heroism. This chapter will first explore and compare a number of conflicting and competing concepts of heroes and heroism and then extract general theoretical considerations as a foundation for the examination of nineteenth-century representations of heroism.

2.1 Contemporary Theoretical Considerations on Heroes and Heroism

As Houghton's quote illustrates, heroic characters and actions were omnipresent in nineteenth-century artistic works. On a theoretical level, high standards were not only applied to heroism within the texts, but also to the writers of epics, ballads and other material stages of heroic conduct. Thus, thinkers such as Matthew Arnold or John Ruskin called for a Grand Style, which Arnold related back to Homer. Following his example, a writer of the Grand Style should make sure

> that he is eminently rapid; that he is eminently plain and direct; both in the evolution of his thought and in the expression of it, that is, both in his syntax and in his words; that he is eminently plain and direct in the substance of his thought, that is, in his matter and ideas; and, finally that he is eminently noble.[3]

The quality of authors' writing is here directly connected to their personality. It results from a state of mind and seems to only be explicable through abstract concepts such as 'nobility'. Therefore, Arnold's and Ruskin's idea of Grand Style[4]

---

1 Cf. Houghton: Victorian Frame, pp. 305–340.

2 Ibid, p. 310.

3 Matthew Arnold: On the Study of Celtic Literature and On translating Homer, New York 1970 [1861], p. 162.

4 For Grand Style see for example George P. Landow: Aesthetic and Critical Theory of John Ruskin, Princeton 1971; Edward Alexander: Matthew Arnold and John Stuart Mill, London 2010 [1965]; id.: Matthew Arnold, John Ruskin, and the Modern Temper, Columbus 1973;

is rather an expression of the artist's genius in the romanticist sense than of knowledge of style or technique. According to Arnold, Grand Style arises "when a noble nature, poetically gifted, treats with simplicity or with severity a serious subject"[5] and grand artworks, as Ruskin claims, are "produced by men in a state of enthusiasm. That is, by men who feel *strongly* and *nobly*"[6] and show the artist's "human character and form in their utmost, or heroic, strength and beauty".[7] Underlying these ideas is a clear conception of a genius artist superior to others. This superiority not only expresses itself in artistic quality, but in a moral nobility, as well as in the strength and earnestness of the writer or painter. Thereby, the Grand Style as proposed by critics such as Ruskin and Arnold already exhibits two central qualities which reoccur in other considerations of heroism in the nineteenth century: sincerity and nobility of character.

However, a period as eventful and transformative as the Victorian age could not have produced one consistent idea of heroism; as technological, scientific, religious and social changes occurred, different and conflicting opinions on heroes, their constitution and relation to the rest of society arose. The following chapter will identify and discuss two larger strands of thought regarding the heroic by elaborating upon the theories of their two primary representatives: Thomas Carlyle and Samuel Smiles.

"The History of the World is but the Biography of Great Men" – Carlyle's On Heroes, Hero Worship and the Heroic in History

Thomas Carlyle's ideas of hero worship and heroism are present throughout his oeuvre from his biographical work on men such as Frederick the Great to his literary pieces and his social criticism. The theory finds its most explicit form in a series of lectures which Carlyle delivered in London in 1840. In these lectures, he designs a general concept of heroism and hero-worship and develops six different categories of heroes, devoting one lecture to each and providing representatives for each type of hero. Carlyle structures the lectures chronologically, beginning with ancient Paganism and concluding the lectures with Napoleon and the nineteenth century.[8]

Amrollah Abjadian: Ruskin and the School of "Grand Style", in: Etudes Anglaises. Grande-Bretagne, Etats-Unis 29, 1976, pp. 15–26 or Jason Camlot: Style and the Nineteenth-Century British Critic. Sincere Mannerisms, Aldershot 2008.

5 Ibid., p. 289.

6 John Ruskin: Modern Painters, New York 1863 [1860], p. 14.

7 Ibid., p. 15.

8 The following is not an attempt at a critical evaluation of Carlyle's concept, but a summary of the characteristics which are relevant for the analysis of the material in this study. Evaluating Carlyle's concept from a present day perspective would not be effective, but rather obstructive for that purpose. For a critical analysis of the lectures see for example Eric Bent-

The hero that Carlyle introduces in his lectures is someone with a special insight into the world; a man[9] who can see the reality behind idolatry and superficiality, a man who has a direct connection to the divine presence of god and who goes about his life with a genuine sincerity and truthfulness. In some way, be it through literature, song or direct action, the hero will try to mediate his insight into the world to others, will try to make them see what he sees and thus has the possibility of changing and shaping the world. A true hero proves his sincerity and genuine earnestness through selfless dedication and devotes his life fully to his cause.

Carlyle describes the development of heroism as a descending movement, a kind of devolution, throughout his lectures. Beginning with the *Hero as Divinity* and the example of Odin in his first lecture, Carlyle depicts the heroes as a direct representation of the divine. He depicts Odin as mediating between the divine and the world and thus providing guidance for his followers. Through developing and passing on runes, he further shows Odin as a mediator of a way of thinking, thereby creating a legacy for his ideas that reaches beyond his immediate presence.

The following lectures, *Hero as Prophet* and *Hero as Poet*, can then already be seen as an increasing removal from the divine. Had Odin been a god himself, the prophet, described by Carlyle through the example of Muhammad, is merely god-*inspired* and the poet, examples for which are Dante Alighieri and William Shakespeare, already stands completely outside the divine realm. Nevertheless, Carlyle believes them to possess a "seeing eye" which "discloses the inner harmony of things" (*OH* 94). Though he still functions as a mediator between the "inarticulate" (*OH* 101) and society, the poets does not want to convey a "heavenly message" (*OH* 100). With the *Hero as Priest*, Carlyle enters the realm of practicality even further. The heroic priest, though again more closely linked to the divine, is the first one to consciously *utilise* his heroism. Carlyle emphasises the role of reformers, of priests fighting for a cause (cf. *OH* 105) and bringing about change.

With the *Hero as Man of Letters*, Carlye then turns to a form of heroism which is directly linked to the "new ages" (*OH* 138). The Man of Letters in his opinion is facing the fragmentation of life, the "Machine-Sceptics" (ibid.), and is shown as trying to convey the beauty and mystery of nature, to bring god back into men's hearts. This changed environment, however, already hints at the fact that the Man of Letters is a different kind of hero for Carlyle; although the character-

---

ley: The Cult of the Superman, Gloucester 1969; Stambler: Heroic Power, or Higgins: Heroic Revivals.

9 Carlyle in his lectures only ever refers to male heroes and does not explore the possibility of female heroism. In my summary of his ideas I will therefore use 'he' and 'man' when referring to the representatives of Carlyle's concept.

istics developed before – genuineness, sincerity, truthfulness, faith – still apply to him, he is not a bringer of light anymore, but himself a seeker.[10]

Though Carlyle attributes so much importance to the Man of Letters, a crucial change can be perceived in this "new" (*OH* 138) form of heroism, one which Carlyle does not reflect upon: this hero, so the characterisation, still wants to convey the mystery of the world, wants to mediate the divine presence he himself is still struggling towards. Nevertheless his heroism, through the connection with print media, has become something marketable, something which is commercialised, bought and sold, a quality which does not necessarily fit the scheme of the genuine, sincere hero.

Carlyle's lectures close with the *Hero as King*, who for him constitutes the quintessence of all heroic figures:

> Priest, Teacher, whatsoever of earthly or of spiritual dignity we can fence to reside in a man, embodies itself here, to *command* over us, to furnish us with constant practical teaching, to tell us for the day and hour what we are to *do*. (*OH* 175)

Styling the Hero as King as the epitome of all heroes seems to be somewhat inconsistent. Keeping in mind that Carlyle sees the development illustrated over the six lectures as a devolution, a step-by-step departure from the immediate impact of the divine, it is surprising that a secular King, and with the example of Napoleon an ultimately failed King and Emperor without institutionalised religious blessing, should rank higher than a priest or a prophet. As a political figure, this hero *actively* guides people towards order and his importance thus exceeds or moves away from the recognition of the divine in the world. It is he, says Carlyle, who sees the flaws in the existing order and thereby is able to establish a new and better one, fighting a "war of Belief against Unbelief" (*OH* 182) in search of a new, true form of society. In Oliver Cromwell and Napoleon, Carlyle chooses two well-known figures, both of whom were not only known for their political success and the establishment of a new order, but primarily associated with the destruction of previously existing structures. Presenting Cromwell and Napoleon in a favourable light could thus have been perceived as a provocation to many. A large part of Carlyle's last lecture is devoted to Napoleon, whose sincerity, ambition and faith he praises.[11]

---

10 Carlyle perceives Goethe to be an exception to this, considers him to be the most important Man of Letters, a "true Hero; heroic in what he said and did" (*OH* 141), but does not discuss his example in greater details, since he believes him too far removed from the audience's life and fears that his arguments would "to the great majority of you, remain problematic, vague" (ibid.).

11 Keeping in mind Carlyle's enormous dislike for the eighteenth century and the fact that throughout his life he remained an advocate of a patriarchal society, monarchy and strong hierarchies, he re-interprets the French Revolution to fit his concept. He presents the revolutionaries' claim for liberty and equality as a sign of frustration with existing heroes and he interprets the revolution as a search for the truth, which for Carlyle was equivalent to the search for a hero (cf. *OH* 181). Thus, Carlye focuses on Napoleon restoring order

Significantly, Carlyle denies Napoleon the status as hero at the end of this life. Since he, according to Carlyle, "parted with Reality" (*OH* 217), he could not be considered a true and sincere man anymore and, in his last years, only remained "a great implement too soon wasted [...] our last Great Man" (ibid.). Thus, Carlyle closes his lectures with a hero who is both supposed to belong to the highest category of heroism, but at the same time already constitutes a compromise of Carlyle's concept, since he lacks the faith in a divine presence and eventually ends up without sincerity and consistent principles. Having put an ultimately failing hero at the end of his remarks on heroism, the bleak outlook for heroism became apparent to the listeners and readers. Thus, the development described by him from the Pagan hero-worship of Odin to Napoleon can be perceived as a diminishing one; the hero changes from god to a godlike and finally to a god-inspired person.

Carlyle's lectures and the subsequently published book were very popular at their time and were received positively by both critics and the general public. For example, John Sterling wrote to Carlyle's wife saying that he could now "see many things more clearly than before. It is a sublime Book, – the best in all English prose so far as I know".[12] Joseph Barrett wrote in the *Monthly Review* (1749–1845) in 1841, after the lectures were published, that

> thousands will read and re-read them with ever-increasing delight and profit; for there is more thought, strength, and strangeness in the duodecimo than in all the books put together that have come under our notice for months. [13]

And indeed, the lectures were suitable for "thousands"[14] of the general reading public, despite Carlyle's poor reputation for his complicated style (which Matthew Arnold called 'Carlylese') that seemed hard to comprehend for many readers, highly abstract and too strongly influenced by his intensive study of the German poets. Similarly, the case studies about the great men of history seemed to be more easily comprehensible than the more complex theoretical parts to the visitors of his lectures: "attention was keenest when he touched on the career and personal character of the man of whom he happened to be speaking, and flagged when he went off into disquisition of literary criticism."[15] Although the attention "flagged" during the theoretical parts of the lecture, Carlyle reached his audience and, through the frequent use of repetition of the main requirements of the hero, may well have succeeded in imprinting his concept on his listeners. The same can be presumed for the printed work, which was published by James

---

rather than on the revolution itself. This enables him to read the movement as one longing for orientation and order given to the people from above.

12 Quoted in Momm: Begriff des Helden, p. 67.

13 Quoted in D. J. Trela / Rodger L. Tarr: The Critical Response to Thomas Carlyle's Major Works, Westport 1997, p. 95.

14 Ibid.

15 Ibid., p. 70.

Fraser in 1841. By attaching his concept of heroism to anecdotes and biographical information about the heroic representatives, his audience was able to relate to his ideas and his view soon became part of common knowledge for the upper and middle classes.

Carlyle's theory remains one of the most enduring considerations of heroism until today. What is striking about it in comparison to other concepts is that Carlyle does not seem to require his heroes to be necessarily active or to perform an extraordinary act.[16] Thus, the heroism in Carlyle's sense rather shows itself in a messianic design than in 'mortal' expressions such as braveness or high moral fibre, which are often associated with heroic behaviour. Carlyle's reasons for calling somebody heroic thus were firmly rooted in a transcendental view of the world. A hero in the messianic sense could be understood as someone chosen by a divine power and equipped with special abilities. It is this *being chosen* and the connectedness to the divine that enabled Carlyle's heroes to perform extraordinary deeds – which manifest themselves in 'conventional heroic behaviour' such as braveness in the face of danger – but could, as illustrated by the examples given above, also come forward in other ways. Thus, Carlyle's theory creates a Pantheon of unattainable messiahs, of heroes that the average person can adore and worship, but cannot become like. Although Napoleon, the exception in more than one respect, shows a case of failed heroism, the concept would never allow somebody to all of a sudden *start* being heroic; in this line of thinking, one either *is* a hero or can never be one. Unlike others, Carlyle's concept does not mirror movements brought about by industrialisation and the societal changes of the nineteenth century. It remains, at its core, a transcendental and unmaterialistic theory that does not encourage its audience to better themselves or improve their condition but holds on to a hegemonic idea of improvement from above and propagates a hope for the coming of a saviour. Although Carlyle's idea of heroism was and remains popular, he did not only receive support but also sparked a counter-strand of the discourse on heroism. The most well-known representative of this other line of thinkers is Samuel Smiles.

Improvement through Role Models – Samuel Smiles's Self-Help

Like Carlyle, Smiles first put forth his considerations on heroism in the form of lectures. However, his ideas are fundamentally different both in content and regarding the impetus for the lectures. In 1845 Smiles was invited to speak at a Mutual Improvement Society, a group of men of different ages who wanted to exchange knowledge for the sake of self-improvement and education. As Smiles

[16] Ralf von den Hoff et al. note that the heroic is constituted in a two-fold performative way: "First, in the actual performance of a deed, and second, in the staging of the performance for (and by) others." Von den Hoff et al.: Heroes, p. 13.

puts it himself in the introduction to *Self-Help*: "Those who knew a little taught those who knew less – improving themselves while they improved the others; and, at all events, setting before them a good working example."[17] Contrary to the public lectures held by Carlyle, which were attended by an educated audience in a public event, the lectures held by Smiles were initiated by a group of men who were interested in improvement and instruction, but had not enjoyed formal education. Smiles, a Scot who originally trained as a surgeon, had turned to journalism and popular education in a professed attempt to show people how to best take advantage of the changes brought about by the industrial revolution. Thus, lectures in Mechanics' Institutes or Improvement Societies, which were attended by workers and middle-class businessmen, were the ideal ground for Smiles to plant his seed. The spirit of the events was described as industrious, sincere, yet friendly. The introduction to the first edition of *Self-Help* states that Smiles

> could not fail to be touched by the admirable self-helping spirit which they had displayed; and, though entertaining but slight faith in popular lecturing, he felt that a few words of encouragement, honestly and sincerely uttered, might not be without some good effect. And in this spirit he addressed them on more than one occasion, citing examples of what other men had done, as illustrations of what each might, in a greater or lesser degree, do for himself; and pointing out that their happiness and well-being as individuals in after life, must necessarily depend mainly upon themselves – upon their own diligent self-culture, self-discipline, and self-control – and, above all, on that honest and upright performance of individual duty, which is the glory of manly character. (*SH* v)

In the same vein, Smiles envisaged that the printed version of his lectures, which he "leaves in the hands of the reader; in the hope that the lessons of industry, perseverance, and self-culture, which it contains, will be found useful and instructive as well as generally interesting" (*SH* vi). Thus, the introduction to the book already declares its purpose. It is to be seen as a guidebook for men to make something of themselves, to better themselves and be useful for society. As if advertising the worthiness of the following elaborations, the introduction states that the members of the self-improvement classes taught by Smiles came "to occupy positions of trust and usefulness" (*SH* v). Thereby, the lessons given by Smiles are proven successful before they even begin.

The main body of the printed version of the lectures, which was not published until 1859,[18] is divided into thirteen sections, some of which show a specific character trait (e.g. "Application and Perseverance"), while others present "Leaders of Industry" or look at "Facilities". All chapters are united in their structure,

---

17 Samuel Smiles: Self-Help, London 1997 [1859], p. iv. In the following, I will cite from this work by using the abbreviation *SH* and the page number in parentheses.

18 In the early 1850s, Smiles had negotiated with Routledge about the publication, but had been rejected in the end. It was not until 1859 that he decided to publish it independently from his own funds.

they present the audience with biographical sketches of 'heroes', of role models who exemplify specific virtues or disciplines.

The first of the thirteen chapters is headed *Self-Help – National and Individual* and deals with the very character of self-help and the condition of the individual within English society: "[A] State depends far less upon the form of its institution than upon the character of its men. For the nation is only the aggregate of individual conditions, and civilisation itself is but a question of personal improvement" (*SH* 2).[19] Smiles breaks down the condition of the state to the individual and turns his concept of self-help into a private as well as a political one. Thereby, he values the 'common man' whom he finds equally important, if not even superior, to famous men: "Though only the generals' names may be remembered in the history of any great campaign, it has been mainly through the individual valour and heroism of the privates that victories have been won" (*SH* 4). By valorising persons just like the very men he was addressing, Smiles tries to give appeal to the idea of self-help, creating a remuneration that is outside the realm of fame, glory and public recognition.[20]

However, Smiles also points out that the way towards becoming such a hero is arduous and that – although he provides them with instructions – anyone who wants to better themselves has to achieve this improvement on their own: "There is no power of law that can make the idle man industrious, the thriftless provident, or the drunken sober, though every individual can be each and all of these if he will, by the exercise of his own free powers of action and self-denial" (*SH* 2). Real improvement for individual and society therefore can only be gained by the one virtue which Smiles regards as the highest: perseverance. If acted out continuously, perseverance could, so Smiles argues, teach people from humble birth special competences and even make them rise the ranks: "The facts of nature are open to the peasant and mechanic, as well as to the philosopher, and by nature they are alike capable of making a moral use of those facts to the best of their powers" (*SH* 11–12). Thus, he does not only stress that men from lower ranks of society can make something of themselves,[21] but also that every humble knowledge or skill can be of use to society in its immediate effect on the individual's environment. Hard labour is not only necessary in order to rise in society – be it the micro-society of one's neighbourhood or the national macro-society – but, as Smiles points out, has to be kept up continuously. As examples of this, Smiles points to successful men like Robert Peel, Edward Bulwer-Lytton or Benjamin

---

[19] Similar to Carlyle, yet not as exclusively, Smiles mostly talks about men in his work, therefore I am going to use male pronouns apart from the rare cases in which he includes women into his concept.

[20] Interestingly, the many biographical sketches he uses as examples only show public figures, which reveals a tension between the propagation of humility and the necessity of external incentive.

[21] As proof for this, he points to men like Richard Arkwright, Lord Tenterden, William Turner, William Shakespeare, James Cook, Robert Burns or Ben Jonson (cf. *SH* 4).

Disraeli who, so his argument, only remained in their positions, and thereby useful to society, through their never-ending efforts to become better persons. Thus, the first chapter sets the tone for the whole of the work and already stresses the recurring demand for perseverance and hard work of men of all ranks.

Under the headline of *Leaders of Industry – Inventors and Producers*, Smiles shows how self-help and perseverance were applied in English industry to the benefit of the nation as a whole. And although the call for hard work remains the same, Smiles in this chapter adds an additional quality by stressing not only the fact that each individual is decisive for the whole, but that every person has a responsibility towards society at large as well. Thus, he condemns fame as a motivator but calls for a higher cause to work for. This idea he sees exemplified in the lives of inventors, whose discoveries often were "effected step by step – one man transmitting the result of his labours, at the time apparently useless, to his successors, who took it up and carried it forward another stage, – the sentinels of the great idea answering each other across the heads of many generations" (*SH* 25). With that, Smiles not only demands perseverance, but also a high tolerance of frustration on the way to personal and societal improvement. However, not only "great ideas" (ibid.) are propagated, but the practical side of inventions is also emphasised. Thereby the subject was brought closer to the specific audience, the middle and working classes; avoiding abstract theoretical elaborations, he stresses the importance of workers, who actually implement and use inventions. As one example, Smiles recalls the steam engine which "was nothing, however, until it emerged from the state of theory, and was taken in hand by practical mechanics; and what a noble story of patient, laborious investigation, of difficulties encountered and overcome by heroic industry, does not that marvellous machine tell of!" (*SH* 25). Significantly, Smiles thereby transfers the importance of the individual to the influence of whole groups or classes of people involved in a process. In that line of thinking, workers and producers were just as important as thinkers and inventors and only jointly constituted an industry, which for Smiles was at the heart of English national identity:

> Men such as these are fairly entitled to rank among the heroes of England. Their patient self-reliance amidst trials and difficulties, their courage and perseverance in the pursuit of noble aims and purpose, are no less heroic of their kind than the bravery and devotion of the soldier and the sailor, whose duty and whose pride it is heroically to defend what these valiant leaders of industry have heroically achieved. (*SH* 45)

Here, it is decidedly the sailor and the soldier, not the captain or the general, whose actions are regarded as heroic; those who *do* are put in the centre of attention. Thus the factory workers whom Smiles was addressing in his lectures are promoted to the rank of "leaders of industry" (ibid.) alongside inventors such as James Watt or James Hargreaves. The ordinary converges with the exceptional, since "the greatest results in life are usually attained by simple means, and the exercise of ordinary qualities" (*SH* 46).

Continuing his praise of the ordinary, Smiles in the chapter on *Application and Perseverance* explicitly puts the ordinary hero in opposition to the genius. It was "not so much men of genius" (*SH* 50) which he finds have "moved the world" (ibid.), but "men of intense mediocre abilities, untiring workers, persevering, self-reliant, and indefatigable; not so often the gifted […] as those who apply themselves diligently at work, in whatever line that may lie" (ibid.). This phrase, a quasi-demonisation of talent, is a call for mediocrity which in turn is valorised. Here, the didactic purpose of Smiles's work becomes prominent; the reader can presume that Smiles is *not* addressing geniuses but 'ordinary' people whom he wants to motivate to work hard. However, in order not to exclude anyone, he then seems to redefine genius, when he says that "all men have an equal aptitude for genius; and that what some are able to effect under the influence of the fundamental laws which regulate the march of intellect, must be within the reach of others who, in the same circumstances, apply themselves to like pursuits" (*SH* 48). Thereby, the idea of genius is turned from something innate to something which one can aspire to and achieve through perseverance, the only possible hindrance being unequal opportunity. As an example, Smiles uses the most obvious realm of genius – the arts – and explains that musicians and dancers can only ever be artistic at their best through hard and continuous work (cf. *SH* 51–52).

For an average man to become a hero, Smiles not only requires him to embody certain values and be determined, but also to achieve a balance between body and mind. Under the heading of *Self-Culture*, he thus asks for "the education or training of all parts of a man's nature; the physical and moral, as well as the intellectual. […] It is only by training all three together that the complete man can be formed" (*SH* 240). He goes on to explain that lack of physical exercise not only leads to health problems, but also affects the intellectual capacities. The remarks on physical education are, in comparison to the long and often repetitive arguments about perseverance and mental discipline, rather short and this again illustrates the target audience which Smiles addresses:

> The chief disadvantage attached to the calling of the laborious classes is not that they are employed in physical work, but that they are too exclusively so employed, often to the neglect of their moral and intellectual faculties. While the youths of the leisure classes, having been taught to associate labour with servility, have shunned it […]. (*SH* 244)

Wanting to reach working- and middle-class men, he was speaking and writing for an audience which was engaged in physical labour on a daily basis. Therefore, he did not have to convince his listeners or readers that they should do physical work, but seemed to have felt that his emphasis should lie on the intellectual side for the lower social ranks. By quoting examples such as Newton, Watt or Stephenson, all of whom engaged in manual labour early in their life and then complemented this physical exercise by intellectual training, Smiles again suggests that careers such as theirs can be repeated by young men of a lower social background and gives them role models they could aspire to.

The realm of politics being relatively unattainable for active involvement by the general public, politicians only feature in one chapter of *Self-Help*. Here, the value of courage, in addition to perseverance and discipline, is foregrounded and positive as well as negative examples provided. The latter is exemplified by Napoleon, whom Smiles at first attests good 'self-help material': "Napoleon, he would have the word 'impossible' banished from the dictionary. 'I don't know,' 'I can't,' and 'impossible,' were words which he detested above all others. 'Learn! Do! Try!' he would exclaim" (*SH* 157). Napoleon thereby shows determination, discipline and will to work hard for the sake of improvement. What makes Napoleon a warning example though is the way in which he utilised his qualities, since "power, […] without beneficence, is fatal to its possessors and its subjects" and "knowledge, or knowingness, without goodness, is but the incarnate principle of evil" (ibid.). Thus, Napoleon was, in the author's view, too concentrated on fame and personal gain and thus gave the wrong outlet to his qualities. As the positive counterexample, he establishes an Englishman, the Duke of Wellington: "Napoleon's aim was 'Glory;' Wellington's watchword, like Nelson's, was 'Duty'" (ibid.). Wellington, in Smiles's depiction, embodies all of his ideal characteristics, he is "resolute, firm, and persistent", "self-denying, conscientious, and truly patriotic", he possesses "the patience, the firmness, the resolution" (ibid.) to go through difficult situations. Interestingly, Wellington's peninsular campaign is the only military political action which Smiles mentions. Apart from that, he exclusively refers to civilising missions and to representative men such as Robert Livingston, John Williams or William Carey, whose mission was not military, but scientific or didactic.

The closing remarks of *Self-Help*, which Smiles leaves to historian Thomas Fuller and his description of Francis Drake, sound like practical advice to the audience:

> Chaste in his life, just in his dealings, true of his word; merciful to those that were under him, and hating nothing so much as idleness; […] always condemning danger, and refusing no toyl; he was wont himself to be one (whoever was second) at every turn, where courage, skill, or industry, was to be employed. (*SH* 334)

Smiles's concept can be seen as an inclusive one, which touches every aspect of the life of those who attempt to follow it. Though it does not require anything to begin with, thereby enabling any individual to identify with it, it calls for hard mental and physical work, for a high tolerance of frustration and a self-denying attitude. In valorising the hard-working yet socially not necessarily high-ranking man, Smiles creates a heroism of 'the common man' and attempts a re-evaluation of what is heroic and desirable. By comparing established great men such as Wellington or Nelson to common workers, Smiles uses heroism as a didactic tool, turning the hero into a role model.

The concepts offered by Thomas Carlyle and Samuel Smiles not only represent different strands in thinking about heroes, but thereby design different views of Britain and its people. What Carlyle attributes to genius and divine presence, Smiles attributes to hard work and self-denial. Where Smiles wants an active people who try to shape the world themselves, Carlyle wants a people for whom the world is shaped and who follow an all-knowing leader. However, not only Smiles and Carlyle were publicly debating heroism; they were the most prominent and sometimes even omnipresent representatives of different ways of thinking, but their positions were supported, ingested and developed further by other thinkers as well.

In search of a grand leader, the American poet and philosopher Ralph Waldo Emerson, whose writings were widespread in Britain as well, adopts Carlyle's general assumption. Emerson is of the conviction that "nature seems to exist for the excellent. The world is upheld by the veracity of good men: they make the earth wholesome" and he believes that "the search after the great is the dream of youth and the most serious occupation of manhood".[22] Man's great aim, he believes, is not trying to become a "good"[23] man nor striving for excellence, but finding a great man to follow whose excellence one can venerate. Thus, Emerson, like Carlyle, advocates that the majority of the population be inactive, their only activity being the search for a guiding figure which can lead them in their passivity. This great man then "inhabits a higher sphere of thought"[24] and has a "mental and moral force"[25] which exceeds that of 'normal' men. These chosen leaders, Emerson believes, "can, without aid from the eyes, or any other sense, proceed to truth and to being".[26] As examples he chooses Shakespeare, Plato, Napoleon, the Duke of Wellington and Johann Wolfgang Goethe. His ideas mirror those of Carlyle. However, Emerson believes in an evolution of heroes where Carlyle sees a devolution: "Yet, within the limits of human education and agency, we may say, great men exist that there may be greater men. The destiny of organized nature is amelioration, and who can tell its limits?"[27] Thus, there can always be a new and 'better' hero, who can teach the majority of people and give them guidance.

In a similar vein, the British scholar William Linwood gave a lecture on "Great Men" on the occasion of the American Unitarian preacher Reverend Channing's

---

22 Ralph Waldo Emerson: The Collected Works of Ralph Waldo Emerson, vol. 4: Representative Men. Seven Lectures, Cambridge 1987 [1850], p. 3.
23 Ibid.
24 Ibid., p. 5.
25 Ibid., p. 8.
26 Ibid., p. 10.
27 Ibid., p. 20.

death in 1842 and proclaimed that "greatness is greatness, wherever found or however exercised; and when it appears, it is the TRUE inspiration from Heaven, rendering its possessor an Emanuel, a god with us".[28] Thus, the religious Linwood not only draws a direct connection between great men and god, but also reaffirms the belief in one deeper truth behind reality. Further, he is not only sure that great men or heroes have existed in every age, but also that they are essential for society:

> No age, no country of the world, has ever been left entirely destitute of great men and benefactors, who have guided the enquiries, assailed the prejudices, and *aided the progress of the popular mind.* It is a false notion which pervades men that truth has been kept wholly from humanity, or that a period has ever existed when no *prophet* appeared to champion and expound it. All times and ages have had their truth and its teachers.[29]

These "saviours, prophets, heroes"[30] live "to alter, to push forward, to expand, the opinions and habits and laws he [the "Great Man"] finds at work when he enters the lists of Providence, and wages war with the social and political defilements of his times".[31] Although in a more religiously charged institutional context, heroes are here again used as a means of guiding people, of giving a leader, a prophet to the "popular mind". Thus, this strand of concepts of heroism is strongly class-oriented. The belief in a majority of people possessing a "popular mind" who do not need to be educated to think for themselves, but who need to be guided by a messianic saviour, thereby keeping the hierarchy in place, is common to all conservative, traditional theories on extraordinary men. The great men constructed in these theories have a number of common features: all of them have a religious, supernatural side; they all possess superior knowledge, insight or intuition over their contemporaries and can uncover a truth which others would not be able to see. Where the various ideas and associated examples differ is in the actual active involvement of the representatives. Whereas some examples, such as the ever-returning Shakespeare, give insight through the mediary of their works only, other examples are in close contact with a group of people, literally teaching and educating them. These examples, however, mostly come from the religious realm. The level of activity of these hero-prophets thus does not seem to be a qualitative criterion for their greatness. They can be active, in a didactic, a political, even a military sense, but do not necessarily have to, as long as they share their higher insight. Furthermore, there seems to be a consensus that heroism is something that transcends time: "Errors and delusions

---

28 William Linwood: Great Men, Their Characteristics, Influence and Destiny. A Lecture Occasioned by the Death of the Rev. E.W. Channing, London 1843, p. ii.

29 Ibid., p. 9, emphasis mine.

30 Ibid., p. iii.

31 Ibid., p. iv.

pass away, but truth endures; heroes pass away, but heroism endures; fogs and mists pass away, but heaven's lights endure; ages pass away, but god endures".[32]

In summary, one can see that there is a strong conservative, even elitist, tendency in this strand of theories on heroism. The hero is understood as a saviour-figure with superior abilities, who not only gives guidance and orientation to a group of people who are perceived as less gifted, but thereby also ensures the power-balance in a society which is perceived as justly hierarchical.

In contrast to the above concepts rooted in religious or spiritual beliefs and in a strong notion of social hierarchy, another approach to dealing with the public at large and extraordinary figures emerges. Alongside Samuel Smiles's works, the temperance movement, utilitarianism and self-improvement societies produced a number of texts directed at large audiences from working-class men to children, which have a different take on heroes. The 'great man' is here reinterpreted as an improved version of the common man, the sacrality of the messiah-hero is exchanged for the moral conduct of the everyday hero. Thus, the texts which can be associated with the promotion of role-model heroes, apart from *Self-Help* such texts as Kingsley's *The Heroes*, Charlotte Yonge's *Book of Golden Deeds* or later in the century Comte's *Calendar of Great Men*,[33] focus much more on practical examples than on theoretical considerations:

> The chief use of biography consists in the noble models of character in which it abounds. Our great forefathers still live among us in the records of their lives, as well as in the acts they have done, and which live also; [...] furnishing examples for our benefit, which we may still study, admire and imitate. (*SH* 303)

In this vein, many of the above-named texts had a clear didactic purpose, they wanted to educate and support middle- and working-class men, women and children in their development and thus also mirrored their audience in the way they were constructed. The great variety of examples that most of the texts provided gave the listener or reader the opportunity to identify themselves with the lives described.[34] As seen in Smiles's text, the audience was supposed to find themselves in the beginnings of the later successful and extraordinary persons and

---

32 Ibid., p. 41.

33 Though not a British thinker, Comte's idea of positivism influenced Britain strongly. Not only intellectuals like Harriet Martineau and George Henry Lewes propagated a positivist worldview, but its ideas also entered the lectures of Mechanics' Institutes. "In fact, by the 1860s, [...] the social and religious aspects of Comtean positivism, including its scientific celebration of the new ideal of 'altruism' were becoming much better known." Thomas Dixon: The Invention of Altruism. Making Moral Meanings in Victorian Britain, Oxford 2008, p. 63. Significantly, as Dixon's quote shows, Comte's ideas were used as a way to negotiate science and religion in a world in which the two were increasingly mutually exclusive.

34 The didactic value of biographical sketches becomes even more apparent when keeping in mind the statements by attendees of Carlyle's lectures who thought that his description of exemplary men were the parts of his talks at which – in contrast to the theoretical parts – everybody paid attention. Cf. Trela / Tarr: Critical Response, pp. 18–19.

thereby feel encouraged to tread a similar path, to work hard and become role models themselves.

However, as the contrast between Carlyle and Smiles has already shown, the ideas of the more utilitarian approach to heroism differ greatly from the more conservative concepts. Whereas the latter relied on the innate grandness of a person, the former placed a much greater emphasis on the possibility of every person to evolve and improve themselves. Thus, the focus in this line of thinking was much more on the individual's attempt to become a better person and on the core values and virtues which a 'common hero' should possess. The examples given therefore often showed hard-working people who, through self-denial, endurance and diligence, made a good living and came to be respected role models of their environment. Many other texts focus on a specific event in the life of sometimes fictional but often factual well-known figures, in which they perform an extraordinary deed which exemplifies specific qualities. This combination of showing virtues 'in action' and assigning them to specific heroes was used particularly in texts for the working classes and in works directed at children.

Since children were in the early stages of their development and were often considered still uncorrupted, they were a popular target audience for texts describing popular everyday heroes. The texts were supposed to give them guidance and role models which they could aspire to and the range of didactic material displaying heroic behaviour addressed to children was enormous. Thus, for example, Charles Kingsley in 1856 dedicated a book on *The Heroes, Greek Fairy Tales* to his "dear children"[35] which reiterates stories about Perseus, the Argonauts and Theseus, Greeks "who were brave and skilful, and dare do more than other men".[36] Kingsley had written the stories for his own children as a Christmas present in 1855 and the preface gives an appropriate Christian background for the occasion. He stresses that great things can only come from god and claims that the Greeks' wisdom and hunger for knowledge was given to them by god. The preface also shows quite clearly that the stories have a strong didactic facet; when he states that the "kings and heroes" and the "queens"[37] did household work and other chores themselves and how they were valued and respected because of these abilities and talents, he immediately draws a connection to the present, saying that this is "as it is now at school".[38] Thus, the extraordinariness of the presented heroes is domesticated in order to turn them into role models for diligent behaviour for children in nineteenth-century Britain. Being a hero is connected to hard work, to strength and, at the end of the preface, also to love for one's country. Kingsley tells his children that heroes have to "do good for [their]

35 Charles Kingsley: The Heroes, Hildesheim 1968 [1856], p. vii.
36 Ibid., p. xix.
37 Ibid., p. xviii. It is important to note here that a man can be both king and hero, women, however, are only referred to as queens.
38 Ibid.

fellow-men" and leave their "country better than they found it".[39] The preface already gives a guideline for reading the book – as a collection of tales about role models for honest work, love for god and one's fellows. The actual stories which follow always have telling headlines such as "How Perseus slew the Gorgon" or "How the Argonauts were driven into the Unknown Sea" which evoke the action displayed in the story and also hint at related virtues. Thus, one can assume that the story of Perseus slaying Medusa will focus on manly strength and the story about the Argonauts at sea will be about bravery in the face of the unknown. Although the represented figures could just as well be examples of transgressive hero figures, the way in which the narratives are framed by Kingsley leads to a didactic domestication of their heroism.

Similarly, Charlotte Yonge's *Book of Golden Deeds* has a didactic purpose. However, apart from some well-known examples such as Florence Nightingale, the book presents incidents in the lives of 'common' men and women, sometimes even children. Thereby, the narratives can be related to the readers' lives even more easily and the preface already points out what the audience is supposed to learn from the book:

> What have been here brought together are chiefly cases of self-devotion that stand out remarkably, either from their hopelessness, their courage, or their patience, varying with the character of their age; but with that one essential distinction in all, that the dross of self was cast away.[40]

Again, the headlines of the short chapters either foreshadow what is going to happen in the story (e.g. *The Heroes of the Plague*) or indicate the actors involved, so that readers can pick chapters which they might identify with (e.g. *The Shepherd Girl of Nanteree* or *The Housewives of Lowenburg*). Apart from self-devotion, it is enthusiasm, "united with the utmost tenderness of heart [and] the very appreciation of suffering"[41] which for Yonge enables heroism. The examples in her book were therefore intended to make "the young and ardent learn absolutely to look upon danger as an occasion for evincing the highest qualities".[42] Thus, Yonge wanted to teach children to become fearless, but in a moral way, since only "fearlessness for a good cause is heroic!"[43]

After the 1860s, a flood of books like Yonge's and Kingsley's appeared on the popular print market. Titles like *Clever Girls of Our Time Who Became Famous Women, Clever Boys of Our Time and How They Became Famous Men* or books "Dedicated To Youths and Young Men as a Stimulus to Earnest Living"[44] presented

39 Ibid., p. xx.
40 Charlotte M. Yonge: A Book of Golden Deeds, London 1864, p. 17.
41 Ibid., p. 12.
42 Ibid.
43 Ibid., p. 14.
44 Joseph Johnson: Clever Boys of Our Time and How They Became Famous Men, London 1879 [1860], title page.

easily digestible biographical sketches with a moral lesson for young readers to turn to and adapt to.[45]

However, not only children were given guidebooks for moral conduct and self-sacrificing work ethos, but there were similar works for adults as well. August Comte's *Calendar of Great Men*, which was first proposed in 1849,[46] can be seen as one of the most prominent examples of such works. Although 'Comtism', as the movement came to be called, was in large parts an intellectual trend, the Comtists "did not ignore the working class".[47] According to Comte, the pioneer of positivism and one of the fathers of the discipline of sociology, "the proletarians were closest to the condition of altruism and hence to the positive state, being the least tainted by liberal individualism".[48] One means of spreading his belief in humanity's ability to govern itself was through his solar calendar. It consisted of 13 months of 28 days in which the months were named after great figures in Western European history in the fields of science, religion, philosophy, industry and literature and were aligned in chronological historical order. Each day was named after a figure in history and each week and month had a patron which exemplified the field of human progress depicted in it. Since Comte believed that knowledge about the past would lead to further progress in the future, 559 persons were "selected as types of the general advancement of civilisation".[49] However, not only great men who brought about progress were treated in the calendar, but also 'villains of history' were shown as warning examples. The men selected for the calendar were to be considered as substitute "Saints and Heroes" of humanism, "as men to be remembered for effective work in the development of human society as society existed in Western Europe about the beginning of the nineteenth century".[50] Thus, their aim, as depicted in the biographical sketches of the 559 men, was not to impose their superior knowledge on others in a self-centred manner, but to bring progress to society. Thus, the main moral of the calendar for the reader is a notion of working hard towards an improvement of society as a whole; thus, the work of the individual is placed into a larger scheme and the achievements are important in their relevance for a

45 A commented bibliography of gift and prize books with a focus on the heroic from the Victorian and Edwardian era for a range of different readerships has been compiled, cf. Christiane Hadamitzky / Barbara Korte (eds): Hero Books on the Victorian and Edwardian Print Market. Commented Bibliography, 2016, www.heroic-as-gift.uni-freiburg.de/, 22 January 2020.

46 The earliest English edition of the positivist calendar I could identify was published in 1891; it is however possible that earlier editions exist. However, positivism was being discussed widely in the British public from the 1850s onwards (cf. Fn. 33).

47 Christopher A. Kent: Higher Journalism and the Promotion of Comtism, in: Victorian Periodicals Review 25.2, 1992, p. 54.

48 Ibid.

49 Auguste Comte: The New Calendar of Great Men. Biographies of the 559 Worthies of All Ages and Nations, London 1920 [1849], p. v.

50 Ibid., p. vi.

common greater good, not because of personal success. Additionally, with Comte's emphasis on scientific developments, the Comtists' popular print products provided a way to conceptualise unsettling concepts, such as Darwin's theories, in a broader setting and view them as something enriching in a long historical line of succession.

It has thus become clear that the second strand of works on heroism, with representatives like Smiles, Yonge, Johnson or, in some of his publications, Comte, has a completely different target audience than the more conservative writings. They focus on the working and middle classes, for whom the books were intended to be a guideline. However, the examples were constructed as an encouragement for the readers, as role models for their own development and a call for active involvement in working on one's own personality for a greater good (be it a religious or a secular, humanist moral one).

A diagnosis which opens John Stuart Mill's *Utilitarianism*[51] can be seen as a motivation for both lines of work discussed above:

> There are few circumstances among those which make up the present condition of human knowledge, more unlike what might have been expected, or more significant of the backward state in which speculation on the most important subjects still lingers, that the little progress which has been made in the decision of the controversy respecting the criterion of right and wrong.[52]

Both the more hierarchy-oriented concepts of heroism and the approaches centred on the 'common man' want to offer an answer to the question of what is right and wrong and found answers in different worldviews.

The Missing Female Hero

Though the different lines of thinking about heroism were very dissimilar in the roles they assigned to heroes, they were united in their limited acknowledgement of the role of women within the public sphere. Although thinkers like Carlyle and Emerson might have been more extreme in their habit of ignoring the existence of accomplished women, Smiles, Comte and Kingsley followed the same pattern. Thus, female heroes seemed to be impossible in the works of the conservative writers. Although not explicitly stated, the conservative concepts of heroism implied that heroism was not considered a field for women. This was, for one, mediated by the complete lack of female examples for heroic behaviour. The only women to be mentioned in Carlyle's *On Heroes* are Muhammad's wives and their description rather discredits female agency. They are described as being

51 Significantly, the text had first been published in *Fraser's Magazine* in 1861 before appearing as a volume in 1863.

52 John Stuart Mill: Utilitarianism, Oxford 1998 [1861], p. 49.

driven by jealousy and thus not possessing the vision and rational perspective which is a precondition of Carlylean heroism.

Although Smiles's *Self-Help* was not as exclusively masculine as the conservative works, the great majority of exemplary persons shown in the work are male. The few women who are depicted are presented in a way that emphasises their subordinate status. Smiles, for example, mentions Madame de Genlis and "her charming volumes" (*SH* 83); this description of her achievements almost ridicules her literary merits and implicitly shows that women were expected to be "charming", not clever, witty or intellectual. Similarly, in Smiles's later works such as *Brief Biographies*, a publication with biographical sketches of didactic purpose, only six of the thirty-six biographies were of women. These six biographies are grouped together and thus explicitly marked as a gendered 'other' in the paratext. The women, Elizabeth Barrett Browning, Frances Brown, Sarah Margaret Fuller, Sarah Martin, Harriet Martineau and Caroline Chisholm, all had an artistic or philanthropic background and lack the transgressive qualities often held to be essential for masculine heroism. Thus, female heroism was, if at all possible, always a passive one, one which was located in high arts or distinguished by extraordinary altruism. Female heroism was, in theoretical considerations, however never physical or norm-transgressing, but mostly oriented to the existing passive role commonly designated to women in Victorian society.

The only exceptions to this lack of representation of female heroism seem to be didactic books directed at girls. Works such as Joseph Johnson and William Pairman's *Clever Girls of Our Time Who Became Famous Women* described extraordinary women but avoided references to the heroic paradigm. The field of action of these women was, again, quite limited and mostly included artists such as George Eliot, Elizabeth Barrett Browning, Angelica Kauffman, Frederica Bremer, Frances Brown or Mary Thornycroft. Apart from artistic talent, philanthropy was brought forth in these didactic writings, especially through the examples of Sarah Martin and Florence Nightingale. Additionally, it was mostly the childhood of the "clever girls" which was described and not their extraordinary adulthood. Thereby, the narratives foreground their behaviour and values at a relatively ungendered age and can serve as role models for the young female readers. In other works for children, such as the above mentioned *Book of Golden Deeds*, which was intended for children of both sexes, women or girls again play a subordinate role and those persons who were actually doing 'golden deeds' remained to be boys or men in the majority of cases.

It can thus be stated that the nineteenth-century discourse on heroism exhibits a void regarding female heroism. Female heroes were missing from the theoretical considerations on heroism, both from conservative and more didactically oriented thinkers, thereby reflecting the general role assigned to women in Victorian life.

2.2 Heroism and Social Identity

Though the different strands of thinking about heroism are united in their exclusion of women from the heroic sphere and the attempt to provide orientation, they differ in the way they deal with the individual and the community. The first group is looking for a heroic individual who has an innate ability which sets him apart from the community. It is this ability then which enables him to lead the community and to show them what is right and wrong. This can happen in different ways, through political action, through religious guidance or in writings. In these concepts, the community's main action is the acknowledgement and worship of the hero, followed by subordination to his 'truth' and 'reality'. "It is true", writes Mill, that "confusion and uncertainty, and in some cases similar discordance, exists respecting the first principles of all the sciences" and regarding "the trustworthiness of the conclusions of those sciences".[53] The messiah-like hero is an answer to this confusion and uncertainty of people who may turn to such a figure for orientation. Especially for men and women with religious beliefs, the solution of leaving one's mental and spiritual fate, one's view of the world, in the hands of a prophet-like representative of god, may have been appealing.

Furthermore, the different conceptions of what a hero is and which kind of hero should be worshipped also fall back on the admirers' ideas of themselves, since hero worship necessarily creates a relation between worshippers and worshipped. Heroes in the vein of Carlyle rank high above those who admire them and are unreachable in their messiah-like features. Thus, they can only ever be worshipped and, since their heroism is presented as innate, never seriously be emulated. Thus, the concept can be utilised as one that established order and control and can only be effectively empowering for a small minority.

Writers like Smiles or Comte tried to answer questions of right and wrong as well, but went in a different direction. They did not see great men as chosen ones marked by a divine aura – and their concepts are much less religiously charged – but wanted to provide the opportunity for everyone to aspire to extraordinariness. Of course, this effort always has to be viewed in the context of the existing class structures: the writers of such guidebooks or didactic biographical works did not completely do away with hierarchies and were only in a position to advise the lower ranks of society on what was important because of their higher education and status. Nevertheless, they attempted to prompt action among their readers. They did not produce an abstract theory, but provided biographical sketches on which the readers could model their own values and actions. Though embedded in a system of power relations, thinkers like Smiles tried to create the image of an everyday hero whom their audience could aspire to, who would val-

53 Ibid.

orise their career and general being and motivate them to work hard for more than their own personal gain. Accordingly, the selected biographies in works like *Self-Help* tend to be less political and grand than the examples in *On Heroes*, and focus more on the virtues behind the actions and the benefit they constitute for society at large.[54]

Following Schindler et al.'s considerations on admiration and adoration, the main difference between the concepts on an abstract level can be seen in the relation between heroes and their group of followers. While the heroism as described by Carlyle or Emerson is shaped by a distanced adoration or worship, the idea of heroism in the context of self-help relies on the idea of admiration. It supposes a much smaller distance between hero and admiring group, even relies on the likeness between the two. This also points to different utilisations of the heroic as represented through the opposing concepts:

> [A]dmiration motivates the internalisation and emulation of ideals embodied by an outstanding role model. Adoration motivates adherence to the teachings and expectations of a meaning maker and benefactor perceived as superhuman or sacred. Thus, the primary function of admiration is to promote individual learning and change, whereas adoration primarily serves to bind communities together.[55]

The concept of a messiah-like[56] hero figure relied heavily on the idea of the hero being other than his group of admirers and aimed at creating a situation of social adherence "to maintain social cohesion",[57] in which the majority of people followed a small group of leaders. The hero in the vein of Smiles, however, was designed with the idea of emulation in mind. Through the object of a hero in the likeness of the admiring group, admiration aimed to "enhance one's own agency in upholding ideals".[58]

One can see that the works of Samuel Smiles and Thomas Carlyle exemplify two main directions of thinking about heroes and heroism. Carlyle was addressing an educated audience and arguing for a messiah-like hero to 'save' and instruct the masses – and thereby also to keep hierarchies in place or establish new ones. By contrast, the ideas directed at the working classes are more universal and inclusive. By stating that everyone can become a great man and do heroic deeds and stressing the likeness between audience and presented hero rather than

54 In comparing the two lines of work, the example of Napoleon is especially interesting. Though some of the representatives of heroic men, such as Wellington or Shakespeare, are given as examples for both notions of heroism, Napoleon is considered one of the greatest heroes by men like Carlyle and a villain by Smiles and Auguste Comte.

55 Ines Schindler et al.: Admiration, p. 85.

56 In *Von der Verehrung*, Veronika Zink emphasises the distance which adoration entails and further characterises it as always having a sacral element: "Bei der Verehrung handelt es sich um ein genuin sakrales Phänomen." Veronika Zink: Von der Verehrung. Eine kultursoziologische Untersuchung, Frankfurt am Main 2014, p. 59.

57 Schindler et al.: Admiration, p. 89.

58 Ibid.

creating distance, writers like Samuel Smiles were trying to educate and train untaught workers and children into becoming more ambitious and diligent.

Significantly, these lines of thought did not succeed each other, but emerged at roughly the same time[59] and existed alongside each other. As pointed out above, they can also be seen as different ways of answering the questions posed by scientific and technological changes and their effects on society. While both give orientation to people, the competing concepts do not only construct characteristics of hero figures but indirectly represent different concepts of the individual and their possibilities and duties in society.

Thus, there seem to be certain abstract features that unite those considered heroes and the way they are venerated. Heroes can be seen as representatives of specific views of the world. They are personified versions of societal values and norms as perceived by a specific group. It is this group that, in a reciprocal process, both receives and creates a heroic figure as an epitomisation of their perception of the world. They can be perceived as marking a collective's values, but also its hierarchies, structures and rules. Heroes can only become relevant in their function for a given group of admirers. Thus, they can be actual individuals, but also fictional, imaginary or historically distant, as long as they fit the habitual profile of the group and perform a social function. If one thinks of heroic figures in this way, the fundamentally different concepts of thinkers like Carlyle and Smiles can be united on a theoretical level: for both, heroes embody their view of the world, their habitus. Their heroes differ in the way the admirers relate to them, the hierarchies and structures they are embedded into are different, but both perform a social function. They both act as a medium of assurance – be it through more distant forms of adoration or through identification – for the members of a group.

As Cubitt writes, heroes are "endowed by others, not just with a high degree of fame and honour, but with a special allocation of imputed meaning and symbolic significance – that not only raises them above others in public esteem but makes them the object of some kind of collective emotional investment".[60] Thereby, heroes represent a certain group and its ideals and norms and also fulfil a social and cultural function in that they stabilise the society of their admirers. As a cultural construct, heroes are necessarily mediated. Although many heroes and heroines, as the nineteenth-century examples above have shown, are persons of historical influence, they always need someone who labels them or their actions heroic. Thus, a hero is always part of a group's communicative processes. Range and media contribution of these processes may vary, but they need to both affect the actors in the communicative act personally – the actions or

---

59 The idea of the common hero comes up mid-century, whereas the idea of a divine hero is formulated by Carlyle in the early 1840s.

60 Cubitt: Heroic Reputations, p. 3.

values of a hero have to be relevant for their individual life – and have a normative power for the group.

Thus, heroes can act as an assurance of values, norms and concepts of life, both on an individual as well as on a collective level:

> In the history of Europe since antiquity, certain heroisms have defined the self-understanding, self-portrayal, and imagination of social groups – especially those in power – sometimes in distinction from each other, sometimes in reference to one another. The orientation towards heroes as human models is extremely important for the formation of heroisms as habitus patterns.[61]

As Cubitt states, heroic figures perform significant community-building functions as "products of the imaginative labour through which societies and groups define and articulate their values and assumptions, and through which individuals within those societies or groups establish their participation in larger social or cultural identities".[62] Accordingly, heroic figures are not defined by their 'real' actions, but by the meaning which is given to them through others.

Both the liminal heroes of Carlyle as well as the exemplary heroes of Smiles can be understood as defining and contouring collectives. While the latter type embodies a norm and defines what is appropriate *within* the boundaries of a society, liminal heroes such as Cromwell or Napoleon mark social and cultural boundaries by transgressing them. Thus, heroes have the potential to stabilise social order, but at the same time can threaten existing structures.

The Victorian era has been described as a time of growing distance from a heroic "ideal that served their forefathers long and faithfully".[63] In this context, the identificatory potential of heroic figures grew in importance, both the individual's relation to heroes as well as the public utilisation of heroism's potential to stabilise hierarchical structures. Stuart Hall notes that identity – individual as well as collective – "is constructed on the back of a recognition of some common origin or shared characteristic with another person or group, or with an ideal, and with the natural closure of solidarity and allegiance established on this foundation".[64] Societies thus rely on their members' identification with a collective interpretative system. This includes things such as (religious or other) belief, moral guidelines or regimes of power (e.g. between social classes, genders, profes-

---

61 Von den Hoff et al.: Heroes, p. 11.

62 Cubitt: Heroic Reputations, p. 3. Cubitt also notes the tension that arises with the idea of an exemplary hero, which will emerge in many of the analyses in the main body of this thesis. As John Price summarises, "Heroes, according to Cubitt, are both 'representative', in that they embody values with which others can identify, and 'exceptional', in that they live or behave outside of normal rules or conventions. This, it is argued, is a particular problem in the use or construction of 'great heroic' individuals as exemplars." Price: Everyday Heroism, p. 6.

63 Ian Ousby: Carlyle, Thackeray, and Victorian Heroism, in: Yearbook of English Studies 12, 1982, p. 152.

64 Stuart Hall: Questions of Cultural Identity, London 2002, p. 2.

sions) as a frame providing meaning. However, identification needs "material and symbolic resources",[65] groups need symbols in order to maintain their bonds and avoid worries about the future stability of a society. Thus, the common ground of a group can only become effective when it is mediated through symbolic material or actions, since identification "is grounded in fantasy, in projection and idealization".[66] Heroic figures as representatives of a group form an integral part of its identity, constitute the projected ideal of what a group believes or aspires to. Identities, individual or collective, are about "the process of becoming, rather than being"[67] and it is not about "'who we are' or 'where we came from', so much as what we might become, how we have been represented and how that bears on how we might represent ourselves".[68] Identification through heroes thereby becomes both an active and passive process: on the one hand, a society is passively represented and thus perceived from outside through the selected heroes; on the other hand, the selection – at least for parts of the group – is an active and conscious process, a decision about the identity for the whole group, who also internally use their representatives as a reference point for their view of the world.

Thus, heroes both encourage and control groups through their identificatory function. They are used as a part of a society's repertoire of symbolism and embody a group's values. They can be used as guiding figures in times of inner or outer turmoil, but they can also be used for didactic or ideological purposes to keep members of a group 'in line'. A heroic figure for a group both constitutes what is ideal and implicitly marks out those who are different. Heroes, as symbols, can be seen as a bridge between the personal and the social. Since they embody the ideal, and thus the expectations of a group, the personal relation to them and their values can be used as a marker for one's place within society. Consequently, heroic figures and the representation of heroic actions are part of the symbolic repertoire of societies and also part of what constitutes identities. Since "the inner core of the subject [is] not autonomous and self-sufficient, but [is] formed in relation to 'significant' others, who mediate to the subject the values, meanings and symbols – the culture – of the world he/she inhabit[s]",[69] personal identity is always connected to cultural identity and one's conception of oneself is "formed out of a common history, ancestry, and set of symbolic resources".[70] Those regarded as exceptional or exemplary are necessarily an integral part of this conception.

65 Ibid.
66 Ibid., p. 3.
67 Ibid., p. 4.
68 Ibid.
69 Stuart Hall (ed.): Modernity and Its Futures, Cambridge 1992, p. 275.
70 Chris Barker: Cultural Studies. Theory and Practice, London 2012 [2000], p. 231.

Although the idea of heroes as symbols for the stabilisation of society and their selection as a continuous re-negotiation of a society is plausible, it also implies questions of hierarchies, power and agency. One always has to be aware of the fact that heroes are cultural constructs, are consciously selected and only surface in medial representation through others. Thus, the question of who selects those representative of and for a specific group is crucial. Though the heroes of Carlyle and Smiles differ greatly in their characteristics and the function they are supposed to fulfil for their audience, they share the fact that they were selected by the authors as prototypes for a specific ideal and embody this ideal only through the act of representation. Although the intended effect is fundamentally different, they both aim for a form of identification. Therefore, heroes as represented in media are always embedded in a system of power relations and, if used didactically or even ideologically, take away agency from those who adopt them as symbols of meaning-making.

It can thus be summarised that heroic figures, though they may refer to living acting human individuals, are always cultural constructs that only exist through medial communication. They constitute an important part of the habitus, the identificatory repertoire of a community, and are part of the cultural and personal identity of its members. Heroes offer a sense of belonging and significance for groups and, though also possessing disruptive potential, often have a stabilising function. Thereby, they are formed by those creating their image and are always also instruments for the exertion of power.

Having established that a hero can only become an object of cultural reference and worship through materiality, the following chapter will deal with the medium which will stand at the heart of the main part of this study. In order to be able to analyse the heroic as materialised on the pages of popular periodical publications in the second half of the nineteenth century, it will provide an overview of the history and functionality of Victorian periodicals.

3. Periodical Culture in Nineteenth-Century Britain

> Perhaps there is no single feature of the English literary history of the nineteenth century, not even the enormous popularisation and multiplication of the novel, which is so distinctive and characteristic as the development [...] of periodical culture.[1]

The periodical, as George Saintsbury's analysis in his 1896 *History of Nineteenth Century Literature* illustrates, was the defining medium of the nineteenth century. The increase in the number of periodical and newspaper publications[2] between 1800 and 1900 and subsequent increase in readership was enormous; they seemed to have been, as Richard Altick put it in his groundbreaking 1957 study *The English Common Reader*, the media "best adapted to the needs of a mass audience".[3] Thus, the periodical press of the nineteenth century is today widely acknowledged as a mass medium.[4] But why were periodical publications so popular and successful in the nineteenth century, what was their political, cultural and societal role and how did the players in this Victorian *circuit of culture* influence each other? This chapter will give an overview of the development of the periodical press in nineteenth-century Britain, a short account of those publications

---

1 George Saintsbury: A History of Nineteenth Century Literature 1780–1895, London 1896, p. 166.

2 Although it has often been discussed whether periodicals and newspapers can be dealt with as separate entities, whether they are separate – to borrow Margaret Beetham's expression – publishing genres (cf. Margaret Beetham: Towards a Theory of the Periodical as a Publishing Genre, in: Laurel Brake et al. (eds.): Investigating Victorian Journalism, New York 1990, pp. 19–32), and whether newspapers are not themselves periodicals, I will maintain this distinction between the two formats.

3 Richard Altick: The English Common Reader, Columbus 1998 [1957], p. 318.

4 On the periodical as a mass medium see Altick: Common Reader, Patricia Anderson: The Printed Image and the Transformation of Popular Culture 1790–1860, Oxford 1991; Scott Bennett: Revolutions in Thought. Serial Publication and the Mass Market for Reading, in: Joanne Shattock / Michael Wolff (eds.): The Victorian Periodical Press. Samplings and Soundings, Leicester/Toronto 1982, pp. 225-257; Frank Bösch: Zwischen Populärkultur und Politik. Britische und deutsche Printmedien im 19. Jahrhundert, in: Archiv für Sozialgeschichte 45, 2005, pp. 549–584; Simon Eliot: Some Patterns and Trends in British Publishing 1800–1919, London 1993; John Feather: A History of British Publishing, London 2005 [1988]; Ian Haywood: The Revolution in Popular Literature. Print, Politics and the People 1790–1860, Cambridge 2004; Martin Hewitt: The Dawn of the Cheap Press in Victorian Britain. The End of the "Taxes of Knowledge" 1849–1869, London 2014; Andrew King / John Plunkett (eds.): Victorian Print Media. A Reader, New York 2006; E. M. Palmegiano: The First Common Market. The British Press on Nineteenth-Century European Journalism, in: Media History Monography 11.1, 2009, pp. 1–44; Beth Palmer / Adelene Buckland (eds.): A Return to the Common Reader. Print Culture and the Novel 1850–1900, Farnham 2011 or John Plunkett: Queen Victoria. First Media Monarch, Oxford 2003.

which will be discussed in the main body of this study, their influence in the first half of the century and a description of their role between 1850 and 1900. Finally, a theoretical framework for dealing with periodical publications will be introduced.

3.1 *The First Half of the Nineteenth Century*

There were only a few periodicals with high circulations on the market at the beginning of the nineteenth century,[5] the leading ones being *The Quarterly Review* (1809–1967) and *The Edinburgh Review* (1802–1929). This was for one due to the fact that publishing a journal in the first decades of the century was an expensive undertaking. For example, "printing-house compositors were the best-paid skilled workers in London; [...] Newspaper compositors made even more – 40s. in 1801 and 48s. in 1810 – which accounts in part for the high prices of newspapers at this period".[6] Furthermore, material costs were significant and many book – but subsequently also periodical – publishers had to regulate their print runs according to paper availability. The price of paper increased rapidly since the government had to find ways to fill the treasury, which had been considerably emptied by the ongoing war with France. Thus, the Excise Duty on paper was doubled in 1801.[7] General availability also became a problem in the early years of the nineteenth century, as publishers not only had to compete with one another for paper, but with other tradesmen as well: "The Industrial Revolution brought with it a demand for paper; the expanding printing industry needed paper and there was no substitute for paper for wrapping grocery items such as sugar, tea or small quantities of flour."[8] But even with paper at hand, publishing a periodical was an expensive undertaking, since taxes on publications were constantly rising as well. The potential of serial publications as a source of tax revenue was high and thus the Stamp Act of 1819 tried to close all potential loopholes that publishers had used before. Although tax evasion had been possible before the passing of the act by a declaration that the newspaper or magazine published opinion only and no news, this option was removed in 1819, with the result that all publications had to be stamped and paid for before they could be sold. The new legislation had been aimed at the radical press, which the government was concerned about for publishing anti-religious and anti-governmental opinions;

5 Altick: Common Reader, p. 318.
6 Ibid., p. 262.
7 Cf. ibid.; also, when running short in Britain, paper was often imported from the European mainland. However, the customs duties were very high and in any case exceeding the excise duty within Britain. For a detailed account of the development in paper prices see H. Dagnall: The Taxes on Knowledge. Excise Duty on Paper, in: The Library 6.4, 1998, p. 348 and Hewitt: Cheap Press.
8 Dagnall: Taxes, p. 348.

however, the act not only affected radical publications, but all those with low circulation numbers, small funds and financial difficulties. Thus, all publications appearing at least once a month and costing less than 6d were subject to a tax of 4d, a measure which made many small and cheap publications disappear from the market altogether. This led to protest among intellectuals like Leigh Hunt as well as social reformers such as Sir Edwin Chadwick, one of whom eventually coined the term 'Taxes on Knowledge' for the taxation on printed goods.[9] This name was soon adopted by all opponents of the policy, as it could be seen as a political statement and a description of the effects of the taxation. As Henry Parnell, former Treasurer of the Navy, put it in his 1830 *On Financial Reform*:

> The duty on paper has an injurious effect on many other trades beside that of the paper maker. [...] The greatest evil of all is the high price of books which it gives rise to. This places a great obstacle in the way of the progress of knowledge, of useful and necessary arts, and of sober and industrious habits. Books carry the productions of the human mind over the whole world, and may be truly called the raw materials of every kind of science and art, and of all social improvement.[10]

The taxes not only had consequences for the publishers, who had to invest more money into their business or sometimes even had to stop publishing their journals, but subsequently for the readers as well. Cheap periodicals became rarer after the act. Those that were still affordable for the even middle ranks of society were mainly subsided by religious organisations and thus were mostly comprised of didactic religious rather than informative content. William Chambers, whose *Chambers's Edinburgh Journal*[11] was to become one of the first affordable periodicals at a low price of 1d, described the cheap publications in the first half of the nineteenth century as papers containing "disjointed and unauthorized extracts from books, clippings from floating literature, old stories, and stale jocularities".[12] This was mostly due to the fact that, apart from publishing and selling illegally, the only way to avoid taxation after the Stamp Act was to reprint text which had already appeared in books or was out of copyright. Thus, the non-religious cheap periodicals tended to consist of collections of reprints of old tales.[13] The leading publications, however, were still quite expensive, *Blackwood's* (1817–

---

9 The question of who coined the term has not been answered conclusively. Both Finer, Chadwick's biographer, as well as Holyoake, who wrote about Hunt's life, claim that their 'subject' invented the phrase. Cf. S.E. Finer: The Life and Times of Sir Edwin Chadwick, London 1952, p. 35; George Jacob Holyoake: Sixty Years of an Agitator's Life, London 1892, p. 293.

10 Henry Parnell: On Financial Reform, London 1830, p. 37.

11 A more detailed profile of *Chambers's*, *Fraser's* and *Leisure Hour* can be found at the beginning of the corresponding text corpus analysis chapters.

12 Quoted in Altick: Common Reader, p. 319.

13 This loophole of the taxation laws also led to a revival of gothic fiction. Cf. Altick: Common Reader, p. 321.

1980) and *Fraser's* were sold at 2s6d, and the *Edinburgh Review* and the *Quarterly Review* were even as expensive as 6s.

Still, not being able to afford a weekly or monthly periodical on one's own did not mean not being able to read one. After the 1819 act, many subscription reading rooms were established in which one could access a variety of publications for a yearly subscription fee. This fee would have been lower than the cost of regularly buying a publication oneself and the reading room had the additional advantage of offering more than one periodical or newspaper and subscribers could choose according to their taste. Furthermore, coffee houses would have had newspapers and some monthly publications in stock and the practice of 'hiring out' newspapers and journals was common, albeit illegal:

> A London newsman might make seventy or eighty lendings of the morning's *Times* in a day, at a penny an hour, after which he would post the used copies to subscribers in the country who paid him 3d. for a copy mailed the day of publication and 2s. for one mailed the day following.[14]

Once it had arrived in the countryside, the publication would have continued to travel from hand to hand in the village and might even have been sold off to travellers the following day.[15] Also, sometimes several families would jointly subscribe to a magazine or a newspaper together and would then share it. As Horn describes in his study *Victorian Pleasures and Pastimes*:

> Often papers were handed round from one family to another, as the Revd J.C. Atkinson remembered of mid-century Danby in the North Riding of Yorkshire. He claimed that only about three newspapers were brought into the whole areas. "I myself remember the *Yorkshire Gazette* passing on from one farmer to another, and its circulation hardly ceasing until it was three or four weeks old."[16]

A writer in the *Monthly Magazine* (1796–1843) was sure that "not less than 5,000 [of these informal subscription groups were] serving with mental food at least 50,000 families".[17] This calculation may be slightly optimistic, but nonetheless it is clear that, even in the first half of the nineteenth century, periodicals reached a wider middle-class audience than the circulation numbers can account for and might even have had a small working-class readership.[18] In terms of content, the periodicals of the first half of the century were primarily marked by informative

---

14 Ibid., p. 323.

15 Cf. ibid.

16 Pamela Horn: Pleasures and Pastimes in Victorian Britain, Stroud 1999, p. 209.

17 Quoted in Altick: Common Reader, p. 323.

18 This was further intensified by the emergence of lending libraries. On the importance of lending libraries in Victorian Britain see for example Altick: Common Reader, Chris Baggs: "In the Separate Reading Room for Ladies Are Provided Those Publications Specially Interesting to Them". Ladies' Reading Rooms and British Public Libraries 1850–1914, in: Victorian Periodicals Review 38.3, 2005, pp. 280–306; Alistair Black: Lost Worlds of Culture. Victorian Libraries, Library History, and Prospects for a History of Information, in: Journal of Victorian Culture 2.1, 1997, pp. 95–112; Guinevere L. Griest: A Victorian Leviathan.

and news articles. Richard Altick points out that the population was, in the wake of the Napoleonic wars, keen on staying up-to-date on political events and saw newspapers and periodicals as a necessary source for this type of information.[19]

However, as the mid-century drew closer, the British print market moved towards mass production and periodicals became one of the first mass media. The various factors which contributed to the rise of popular reading material are extremely difficult to bring into a linear or causal framework. Historical research long focused on cultural and educational developments and connected the rise of literacy with the growing market for reading matter. Contemporary publishers such as Newes and Northcliffe also "perceived that the spread of elementary schooling had created a new class of consumers"[20] and thus the growing number of educated middle- and working-class readers were the reason for the growth in edition and circulation numbers. Nevertheless, Altick observes that

> viewed in long perspective, the relationship between the development of a mass audience in the 19th century and the rise of the cheap periodical was simple: the growth in the number of readers made periodical publishing an increasingly attractive commercial speculation, the more reading habit spread. But examined more closely, the process proves to have been no clear circle of cause and effect.[21]

Following this assumption, historians like Harold Perkin have argued that the impact of rising literacy rates on the popular press was far smaller than originally thought, amounting in the, as Perkin terms it, "egregious truism"[22] that people would obviously have been required to be able to read if they were to consume a newspaper or journal. However, there would have been publications for people with limited reading abilities as well, although many were of ill repute, such as the so-called Penny Dreadfuls.[23] Illustrations could make an article or a story more accessible and could, for example, draw the attention of children towards a

---

Mudie's Select Library, in: Nineteenth-Century Fiction 20.2, 1965, pp. 103–126; ead.: Mudie's Circulating Library and the Victorian Novel, Bloomington 1970; Bob Nicholson: Counting Culture; Or, How to Read Victorian Newspapers from a Distance, in: Journal of Victorian Culture 17.2., 2012, pp. 238–246; Lewis Roberts: Disciplining and Disinfecting Working-Class Readers in the Victorian Public Library, in: Victorian Literature and Culture 26.1, 1998, pp. 105–132 and id.: Trafficking in Literary Authority. Mudie's Select Library and the Commodification of the Victorian Novel, in: Victorian Literature and Culture 34.1, 2006, pp. 1–25.

19 Cf. Altick: Common Reader, p. 321. Reading rooms and coffee houses thus would not only have been places of information but also spaces to discuss the news.

20 David F. Mitch: The Rise of Popular Literacy in Victorian England, Philadelphia 1992, p. 71.

21 Altick: Common Reader, p. 318.

22 Harold James Perkin: The Origins of the Popular Press, History Today 7.7, 1957, p. 429.

23 For scholarship on this periodical genre see for instance Patrick A. Dunae: Penny Dreadfuls. Late Nineteenth-Century Boys' Literature and Crime, in: Victorian Studies. A Journal of the Humanities, Arts and Sciences 22, 1979, pp. 133–150; Robert J. Kirkpatrick: From the Penny Dreadful to the Ha'penny Dreadfuller, London 2013; Rohan McWilliam: The Melodramatic Seamstress. Interpreting a Victorian Penny Dreadful, in: Beth Harris (ed.):

publication which could only be fully consumed by their parents.[24] However, the possibilities which an enlarged readership offered to the publishers could not have been taken up had it not been for technological developments. Amongst those, "the printing machine may have been the most dramatic of the technical changes in the printing trade".[25] But it was not only this most obvious technological change that dramatically affected the whole publication process: "it was accompanied by the arrival of machine-made paper, stereotype plates and edition bindings, and several new techniques for reproducing illustrations."[26] At first, especially newspapers and journals with weekly circulation profited from these technological advances; the usage of steam-presses and stereotype plates equalled an enormous gain in time since publications could be produced closer to the publishing deadline. Thus, more recent news could be published using a steam-press than when running multiple hand presses. Furthermore, through printing from stereotype plates, reprints could be produced more easily. The growing railroad network connected the industrial areas of Britain and readerships outside the urban centres would be reached in a speed unheard of before.

Famine and Fashion. Needlewomen in the Nineteenth Century, Aldershot 2005, pp. 99–114; Elizabeth Penner: "The Squire of Boyhood". G. A. Hutchison and the Boy's Own Paper, Victorian Periodicals Review 47.4, 2014, pp. 631–647 or John Springhall: "A Life Story for the People?" Edwin J. Brett and the London "Low-Life" Penny Dreadfuls of the 1860s, in: Victorian Studies. A Journal of the Humanities, Arts and Sciences 33.2, 1990, pp. 223–246; id.: "Pernicious Reading?" The Penny Dreadful as Scapegoat for Late-Victorian Juvenile Crime, in: Victorian Periodicals Review 27.4, 1994, pp. 326–349 and id.: "The Mysteries of Midnight". Low-Life London "Penny Dreadfuls" as Unrespectable Reading from the 1860s, in: Martin Hewitt (ed.): Unrespectable Recreations, Leeds 2001, pp. 160–175.

24 On periodicals and illustrations see for example Laurel Brake / Marysa Demoor (eds.): The Lure of Illustration in the Nineteenth Century. Picture and Press, Basingstoke 2009; Simon Cooke: Illustrated Periodicals of the 1860s, London 2010; Paul Goldman: Beyond Decoration. The Illustrations of John Everett Millais, London, 2005; Katherine Haskins: The Art-Journal and Fine Art Publishing in Victorian England 1850–1880, Farnham/Burlington 2012; Brian Maidment: Comedy, Caricature and the Social Order 1820–50, Manchester/New York 2013 or Brian Maidment / Aled Jones: Illustration, in: Laurel Brake / Marysa Demoor (eds.): Dictionary of Nineteenth-Century Journalism in Great Britain and Ireland, Ghent/London 2009, pp. 304–305.

25 Aileen Fyfe: Steam-Powered Knowledge, Chicago 2012, p. 5. The first steam-printing machine was used by the *Times* as early as 1814; however, the technology only affected a larger market from the 1830s onwards and only percolated through the whole printing industry at the beginning of the second half of the nineteenth century. For more information on new printing technologies and their influence on society see Richard Altick: The Presence of the Present. Topics of the Day in the Victorian Novel, Columbus 1991; Elizabeth L. Eisenstein: The Printing Press as an Agent of Change, Cambridge 1982; Lee Erickson: The Economy of Literary Form. English Literature and the Industrialization of Publishing 1800–1850, Baltimore 1995; Robert Escarpit: Book Revolution, London 1966; Feather: British Publishing; David Finkelstein: Publishing and the Materiality of the Book, in: Kate Flint (ed.): The Cambridge History of Victorian Literature, Cambridge 2012, pp. 13–33 or John Sutherland: Victorian Fiction. Writers, Publishers, Readers, New York 2005.

26 Fyfe: Steam-Powered, p. 5.

It was through these developments that, despite the high taxes on publications, the 1830s and 1840s saw the rise of several cheaper publications which were the forerunners of the flood of periodical publications to hit the market after 1850. Thus, "Bible and tract societies [...] were using both steam printing and stereotyping earlier than might have been expected".[27] It was by employing those means that organisations such as the Society for the Diffusion of Useful Knowledge (SDUK) were able to distribute high circulation numbers as early as the 1830s. However, this was only possible due to ideological commitment, which above all meant that the organisations were not interested in maximising their profits. As charities, these publishing societies were of course somewhat removed from the traditional commercial marketplace and publishers like Charles Knight, who published the *Penny Magazine* (1832–1845) for the SDUK, but nevertheless was an independent businessman, were struggling to make their work profitable. This was even more so true for the Edinburgh-based brothers William and Robert Chambers, who attempted to publish easy, readable, educational and entertaining information for the masses and whose business was independent. In the case of Chambers, profitability was achieved by keeping the printing presses running all week long. After having been successful with their *Chambers's Journal*, they filled the time in which the printing presses were not occupied by the periodical with other publications and began to establish a whole range of informational and educational books, thus making the most of their resources.[28]

It was these two journals then that paved the way for affordable mass-market periodicals. Unlike other publications before, Knight's and the Chambers's periodicals offered a more holistic programme which neither included only information, nor resorted to serialised tales which were out of copyright. In the "Address to His Reader" of the first issue in 1832, William Chambers describes his weekly as one which would offer something to everyone; it would contain – among other things – practical information, essays on education, science, finances, articles on gardening, farming, observations on the building of roads and bridges, information on technological development and literature (cf. Address to the Reader, *CJ*, 4 Feb 1832, 1). Though the educational imperative is quite obvious from this short collection of topics to be included in the journal, the last item – literature – was especially important since its entertaining qualities had the potential of enlarging the magazine's readership.

Furthermore, Knight and the Chambers brothers were also the first among publishers of cheap papers to employ professional writers. Unlike the other contemporary publishers of penny papers, they did not merely stick together snippets from books but printed articles which were written specifically for publica-

27 Ibid., p. 7.

28 A more in-depth characterisation of the Chambers's printing and publishing establishment will be provided in chapter 4.1.

tion in their journals. Thereby, an enormous difference in quality could be observed between these new cheap journals and those magazines which selected their contents with tax evasion in mind.

Thus, the first two prominent cheap periodicals can be seen to have started what would later become almost a convention among popular family magazines and which was arguably one of the formulas for success: professional writing, fiction and illustrations. It was therefore not surprising that almost all family papers published in the second half of the century opened their issues with large images illustrating the serialised fiction, which was regularly the first text in the periodical.

3.2 The Second Half of the Nineteenth Century

After the Repeal of the Stamp Act in 1855 and the abolition of the last of the 'Taxes on Knowledge', the Paper Duty, in 1861, circulation numbers were going through the roof. By the end of the 1850s the first periodicals had "attained a circulation of more than 100,000".[29] These numbers grew even more in the sixties, for which Altick gives circulation numbers of monthly "London publications"[30] which range from 250,000 to 1,500,000. The market that had grown so rapidly did not merely supply the upper and upper-middle classes, but predominantly consisted of middle and lower-middle class audiences.[31] "Obviously, the greatest increase in periodical-buying occurred among the lower-middle class and the working class",[32] and this was a readership which did not simply want to be informed about the occurrences in parliament and court, but also wanted to be

29 Ibid., p. 357. On the mid-century as a time of transition for periodicals see also Margaret Beetham: Magazines, in: Laurel Brake / Marysa Demoor (eds.): Dictionary of Nineteenth Century Journalism in Great Britain and Ireland, Ghent/London 2009, pp. 391–392; Graham Law / Amy Loyd: The Leisure Hour, in: Laurel Brake / Marysa Demoor (eds.): Dictionary of Nineteenth Century Journalism, Ghent/London 2009, pp. 356–357; Maidment / Jones: Illustration; James Mussel: New Journalism, in: Laurel Brake / Marysa Demoor (eds.): Dictionary of Nineteenth Century Journalism in Great Britain and Ireland, Ghent/London 2009, p. 443 or Jennifer Phegley: Educating the Proper Woman Reader. Victorian Family Literary Magazines and the Cultural Health of the Nation, Columbus 2004.

30 Altick: Common Reader, p. 358.

31 This can be assumed from the fact that those periodicals which were addressed to an upper-middle- and upper-class audience did not undergo a massive increase in circulation. Cf. ibid.

32 Ibid.

entertained in the little leisure time they had.[33] Periodicals therefore offered much more than the mere supply of information.[34]

They included reports on current events in the region, the country and the world and thus would, for example, inform the readers about decisions being made in London, but also about developments in the colonies or on the American continent. Informative articles, however, went far beyond mere political information but covered a broad variety of topics from, depending on the orientation of the periodical, gardening to history of the arts, from hints on cooking, household management and education to notices of concerts or recitals coming up in the region. Some of the publications also contained sections such as "Answers to Correspondents" which give answers from the writers to questions posed by readers. Thus, the periodical also provided information on Victorian readers' lives, since the readers often sent in questions regarding issues in their everyday lives. But apart from instruction and information, the publications offered entertainment and distraction from everyday work life. The publications often contained short tales, poems, essays on societal events, short anecdotes and even stories especially designed for children. Among the entertaining content, the serialised novel, published in weekly or monthly instalments, came to be one of the most popular forms of publishing and reading fiction.[35] Accompanied by illustrations, the serialised novels appealed to the whole of the family.[36] They were read, often out loud, by the parents or older children and gave the younger children pictures to look at and thus an opportunity to experience the story as well. The publication in instalments not only had the advantage of drawing the readers into the story and ensuring that they would buy the next issue of the periodical as well, but also benefited those in the audience for whom reading still was an exhausting task. Though literacy was constantly rising throughout the cen-

---

33 An orientation of many popular weekly periodicals towards the middle and working classes can also be presumed from the fact that they usually appeared on Saturday in order to be consumed during the working population's leisure time on Sunday.

34 This remained the domain of the daily newspapers, which also experienced an increase in circulation after the Repeal of the Stamp Act and Paper Duty, which lead to the emergence of newspapers in the countryside and local journalism.

35 On serial publication of fiction in Victorian periodicals and subsequent book publication see for example Catherine Delafield: Serialization and the Novel in Mid-Victorian Magazines, Farnham 2015; Jennifer Poole Hayward: Consuming Pleasures. Active Audiences and Serial Fictions from Dickens to Soap Opera, Lexington 1997; Linda Hughes / Michael Lund: The Victorian Serial, Charlottesville 1991; Graham Law: Serializing Fiction in the Victorian Press, Basingstoke 2000; David Payne: The Reenchantment of Nineteenth-Century Fiction, Basingstoke 2005; J. Don Vann: Victorian Novels in Serial, New York 1985 or Deborah Wynne: The Sensation Novel and the Victorian Family Magazine, Houndsmill 2001.

36 Wynne notes: "Although features occasionally appeared which were more likely to appeal to one gender or age group than another, they were usually presented in such a way as to be intelligible to other family members." Wynne: Sensation Novel, p. 16.

tury,[37] there were still many people, especially among the lower ranks of society, who, while literate, would still not have been able to read a whole book at a time. Thus, the serial novel was a way of enjoying literature without becoming too frustrated with one's own ability. The value of this kind of reading practice not only applied to the serial novel but to the periodical as a whole. With its many short articles and stories, it was not only suitable for people with limited reading skills, but the reading could also be done over the whole of the week or month in short intervals. By giving people a successful reading experience, the periodical itself also contributed to the creation of a mass audience; without requiring sustained attention and perfect reading skills, the periodical offered information and entertainment, to which the inclusion of literature contributed immensely:

> Particularly after 1850 I see their relation [of literature and periodicals] as symbiotic, productively mutual, and interdependent. Rather than claiming credit for the greater importance of periodicals on the basis that they 'carried' literature, as Saintsbury and other scholars do (and of course the periodicals carried much else), I want to suggest that the widespread incorporation of the novel into mainstream periodicals in the 1850s and after helped to assure the proliferation and economic viability of the periodical press. Consumers of popular culture, attracted to fiction, supplemented those arguably graver readers of the miscellany of articles on history, philosophy, and science to make journals viable and sustainable; the greater inclusion of fiction, its appropriation, crucially broadened readership, and arguably advertising as well. Basically, I am arguing that the novel 'made' the periodical press in these 50 years as much as the press fostered and 'carried' the novel (as well as other literature), legitimizing it in the admixture of a "miscellany" context.[38]

Serialised fiction thus not only amused the masses, but was also a clever business transaction, since "there was less risk all round for [...] the author and the publisher".[39] If readers liked the first parts of a novel, they were likely to buy the following ones. As Margaret Beetham points out, "the consumer of the periodical is not so much satisfied as stimulated to return at regular intervals to buy the next number of the product. [...] [Thus, t]he periodical was designed to both ensure rapid turnover and to create a regular demand".[40] Furthermore, serialised novels presented publishers with the additional opportunity of earning money twice, since most of the novels were published in book form after they had appeared in a periodical.

Similarly, the medium was an opportunity for writers to make their living. Being employed at a periodical would ensure regular income for writers and

---

37 In the 1830s, only 50 per cent of the population were able to read and write; by the end of the century, almost universal literacy was accomplished. Cf. King / Plunkett: Print Media, p. 12.

38 Laurel Brake: The Advantage of Fiction. The Novel and the "Success" of the Victorian Periodical, in: Beth Palmer (ed.): A Return to the Common Reader, Farnham 2011, pp. 11–12.

39 Ibid., p. 12.

40 Margaret Beetham: A Magazine of Her Own?, London 1996, p. 21.

make publication of larger works, for example in a series, easier than finding a book publisher outside the periodical realm.[41] Since most of the articles were published anonymously[42] or sometimes even written collaboratively, the contributors were able to voice controversial opinions in their pieces, since those could not be traced back to them with certainty. Therefore, many of the most eminent figures of Victorian literature started off as periodical writers. The most well-known example is of course Charles Dickens who, before publishing his own periodicals *Household Words* (1850–1859) and later *All the Year Round* (1859–1895), worked as a journalist for several different newspapers and periodicals. He was, however, not the only prominent literary figure who became known through periodical writing. John Stuart Mill first wrote for magazines, as did Leslie Stephens, James Knowles as well as Thomas Carlyle, Walter Pater and William Thackeray. The periodical "made authors",[43] and some of them, such as Thackeray, even followed Dickens's example and founded their own periodical. 'Journalist' was not as yet a fully defined profession and there was often little separation between journalism and literature.[44] But it was not only the quality of literary contributions to the periodicals that was of a high standard, the medium also attracted eminent figures from all of the other significant fields. Scientists like Charles Lyell or Thomas Henry Huxley, economists like John McCulloch, church representatives like Cardinal Manning and J. H. Newman or politicians like Benjamin Disraeli were frequent contributors to various periodicals. In short: "all the major novelists, generals and captains in the army and navy, diplomats, judges, bishops, travellers, [...] African explorers"[45] were writing for magazines. The brightest minds of the age voiced their opinion through the medium of the periodical at a time which was full of transformation and doubt, which saw great changes in technology through urbanisation and technological progress, but also in frames of mind. One need only mention the most prominent shift in Victorian thought, Charles Darwin and his theory of evolution, to recall the destabilisation of people's beliefs, not knowing how to relate religious

41 Especially novels published as serials provided a solid income for authors. Contributors for *Chambers's Journal*, for example, received an average sum of £10 to £15 for an instalment of a novel from the 1870s to the 1890s (cf. payment records in the publishing house's archive, "Payment Records" NLS Dep 341/368, 370 and 371). Rarely, an author would receive a substantially larger amount of money per instalment, the most notable example being James Payn, editor of the periodical from 1858 to 1874, who received £70 for each instalment of several novels during the time of his editorship (Payment Records 1871–1879, Dep 341/368: unnumbered, National Library of Scotland, Edinburgh). Significantly, his name was not recorded in full in the ledger, but only his initials.

42 Up until today, even articles by the most well-known Victorian writers often cannot be attributed with certainty.

43 Laurel Brake / Marysa Demoor (eds.): Dictionary of Nineteenth-Century Journalism in Great Britain and Ireland, Ghent/London 2009, p. v.

44 Matthew Rubery: Journalism, in: Francis O'Gorman (ed.): The Cambridge Companion to Victorian Culture, Cambridge 2011, p. 179.

45 Houghton: Victorian Frame, p. 3.

traditions to new scientific findings and where to place oneself in this matrix.[46] Therefore, the fact that important figures from all fields of interest wrote for the masses functioned as orientation and security for many. As Cardinal Newman put it, periodicals "instructed audiences what to think and what to say".[47]

The periodical thus had various functions for the readers: it served as a means of information and entertainment, but also as a medium in which they sought guidance through a world which had become increasingly complicated.[48] As such, the periodical was a suitable medium to create role models and represent and shape values and standards. In 1842, Thomas Carlyle wrote to John Sterling: "there is at present no preaching in England, and a visibly growing appetite (the sternest *necessity* there has long been) to have some: [...] the Printing Press is the only, or by far the chief, Pulpit in these days."[49] Accordingly, writers and publishers early on saw the potential of periodicals to educate children and adults from the lower ranks of society through cheap print publications. Especially after schooling was made compulsory for children between the age of five and thirteen in the Education Act of 1870, the market for children's periodicals grew considerably.[50] This, however, also shows that the educational goal that publishers seemed to pursue was always linked to their own financial interest.

This interest was also strongly tied to technological developments. Railways hastened the pace of business transactions and passenger trains created a new

---

46 For the conflict between science and religion in Victorian Britain, see Dennis R. Alexander: The Implications of Evolutionary Biology for Religious Belief, in: Kostas Kampourakis (ed.): The Philosophy of Biology, Dordrecht 2013, pp. 179–204; Peter J. Bowler: Evolution. The History of an Idea, Berkeley 1989 (especially pp. 218–245); John Hedley Brooke: Religious Belief and the Content of the Sciences, in: Osiris 16, 2001, pp. 3–28; Colin Campbell: The Romantic Ethics and the Spirit of Modern Consumerism, Oxford 1987; Gary B. Ferngren: Science and Religion. A Historical Introduction, Baltimore 2002; Aileen Fyfe: Science and Religion in Popular Publishing in 19th-Century Britain, in: Peter Meusburger et al. (ed): Clashes of Knowledge Dordrecht 2009, pp. 121–132; Peter Harrison: "Science" and "Religion". Constructing the Boundaries, in: The Journal of Religion 86.1, 2006, pp. 81–106; David C. Lindberg / Ronald L. Numbers: Beyond War and Peace. A Reappraisal of the Encounter between Christianity and Science, in: Church History. Studies in Christianity and Culture 55.3, 1986, pp. 338–354; James Moore: The Historiography of Science and Religion, in: Gary B. Ferngren (ed.): Science and Religion. A Historical Introduction, Baltimore 2002, pp. 208–218; Ronald L. Numbers: Science and Religion, in: Osiris 1, 1985, pp. 59–80; Colin A. Russell: The Conflict of Science and Religion, in: Gary B. Ferngren (ed.): Science and Religion. A Historical Introduction, Baltimore 2002, pp. 3–12 or David Sloan Wilson: Darwin's Cathedral. Evolution, Religion, and the Nature of Society, Chicago 2010.

47 Quoted in Rubery: Journalism, p. 181.

48 This complexity of life and diversification of views is also reflected in the variety of journals on the market at the time which provided publications for every possible political, religious or ideological orientation and a vast range of special interests.

49 Quoted in Walter Houghton: Periodical Literature and the Articulate Classes, in: Joanne Shattock (ed.): The Victorian Periodical Press. Samplings and Soundings, Leicester/Toronto 1982, p. 9.

50 Cf. King / Plunkett: Print Media, p. 14.

space for reading; steam print and stereotype plates made production in larger quantities possible and products less expensive; and the telegraph link between Dover and Calais in 1851 considerably enlarged the region from which news could be reported. With telegraph links between Europe and India in 1865 and the transatlantic cable in 1866, business deals could be made more easily on a larger scale. Furthermore, the content of periodicals was enriched, since, for example, news from the colonies would reach the reader much faster.[51]

As this short overview has shown, the relation between publications, their publishers and readers is quite complex and it is not easy to determine what was decisive in the creation of demand and supply. It has become clear that the success and importance of the periodical press in Victorian Britain was due to the interplay of various factors: The technicalisation and urbanisation of city life gave rise to the possibility to produce print products fast and relatively cheaply, especially after the abolition of the 'Taxes on Knowledge', effectively turning periodicals into a mass medium for a mass audience. At a time of transition, transformation and growing fragmentation of everyday life, readers sought entertainment as well as information and guidance, which the publications could provide, employing some of the best and most prominent representatives of many fields of interest as contributors. The weekly and monthly periodicals, other than the daily newspapers, appealed to people from all kinds of social backgrounds and also included children or adults with poorer reading skills in the consumption process. As a form, the medium was both open and closed, since it on the one hand always was a "self-contained text"[52] and on the other hand always already implied the following issues. Also, it was open in regard to audience participation. As Beetham puts it, the periodical

> engages with its readers across time. This means it involves them not just in the production of their own individual readings, but actually in the development of the text. [...] Reader response is fed back to the producers by sales figures but in addition many periodicals invite readers to intervene directly, by writing letters, comments and contributions. This may help to account at once for the immense resilience and popularity of the form and for its intractability in terms of theories which think of texts as results simply of authorial activity.[53]

---

51 For information on communication technologies in Victorian Britain and their cultural importance see for instance Asa Briggs: Victorian Things, London 1988; Charles Frederick Briggs / August Maverick: The Story of the Telegraph and a History of the Great Atlantic Cable, Ann Arbor 2006 [1958]; Anthony Burton: The Railway Empire, London 1994; Jack Simmons / Gordon Biddle: The Oxford Companion to British Railway History. From 1603 to the 1990s, Oxford/New York 1997; Tom Standage: The Victorian Internet. The Remarkable Story of the Telegraph and the Nineteenth Century's Online Pioneers, London 1999 or Roland Wenzlhuemer: Connecting the Nineteenth-Century World. The Telegraph and Globalization, Cambridge 2015.

52 Beetham: Magazine, p. 29.

53 Ibid.

Thus, there developed a periodical culture from which all actors involved profited: the readers were provided with entertainment, education and information, many writers had found a relatively easy way to publish their work and earn their living, and publishers had found a mass market in which the readership and thus sales were predictable and stable.[54]

As the emphasis above on the political, technological and economic backdrop to publishing a periodical already suggests, an analysis of Victorian periodicals has to be strongly contextualised; production and consumption have to be kept in mind as well as general societal and political influences. A study of the heroic in British periodicals thus cannot be conducted by only looking at the representation of heroes, heroines and heroic deeds, but necessarily also has to include the constructedness of these persons and acts. Thus, this study intends to approach its material with regards to both representation with its literary and medial aspects as well as the field within which it is constructed and produced.

Assuming that all publications, whether books, periodicals, ephemera or pamphlets, are cultural products which are produced and received within a cultural process, the *circuit of culture* seems an appropriate tool for analysis. The model,[55] developed by Paul du Gay together with Stuart Hall, Linda Janes, Hugh Mackay and Keith Negus, does not focus on specific product stages such as the printing or manufacturing of a book, but identifies *cultural* processes which, due to their level of abstraction, can be applied to all cultural artefacts, to all products which produce or bear meaning.[56] For them, cultural artefacts develop

> a distinct set of meanings and practices. [...] We talk, think about and imagine it. It is also 'cultural' because it connects with a distinct set of social practices [...] which are specific to our culture or way of life It is cultural because it is associated with certain kinds of people [...]; with certain places [...] – because it has been given or acquired a social profile or identity.[57]

---

54 For further reading on the Victorian print market and the rise of the periodical see for example Anderson: Printed Image; Bösch: Printmedien; Eliot: British Publishing; Feather: British Publishing; Haywood: Revolution; Hewitt: Cheap Press; John O. Jordan / Robert L. Platten (eds.): Literature in the Marketplace. Nineteenth-Century British Publishing and Reading Practices, Cambridge 1995 or Beth Palmer / Adelene Buckland (eds.): A Return to the Common Reader. Print Culture and the Novel 1850–1900, Farnham 2011.

55 Cf. Paul du Gay et. al.: Doing Cultural Studies. The Story of the Sony Walkman, London 1997.

56 In contrast to traditional book history approaches, the circuit of culture accounts better for the complexity of cultural processes and the cultural significance of specific products. Robert Darnton's *Communications Circuit* is rather production-centred and provides a "model for analysing the way books came into being and spread through society" (Robert Darnton: What Is the History of Books, in: Daedalus 111.3, 1982, p. 65) and Adams and Barker in an already more context-oriented approach place the production within "the whole socio-economic conjuncture". Thomas R. Adams/Nicolas Barker: A New Model for the Study of the Book, in: Nicolas Barker (ed.): A Potencie of Life. Books in Society, London 1993, pp. 5–43.

57 Du Gay: Circuit, p. 10, emphases mine.

When relating this to the Victorian periodical, it becomes clear that the periodical also has its distinct culture, its own set of practices around it. This is already apparent from the name; 'periodical' instantly invokes regularity, it will appear in periodic intervals and thus has an element of stability, reliability, even companionship to it. Therefore, the term itself has a cultural practice inscribed into it: the periodical is understood to be consumed in regular intervals. Thus, the periodical is cultural in du Gay's sense; it is not only a meaningful object which can and could be talked about, but it is also clearly rooted within the Victorian "culture or way of life".[58] "Meaning-making lies at the interface between cultural and technology"[59] and the periodical's identity and its meaning become apparent with changing technology. As the previous chapters have shown, the rise of periodical publication was closely interconnected with technological, scientific and social developments of the time and can be seen as a sign for the industrialised, urbanised and increasingly educated British society. Considering the "kinds of people" and "places" mentioned in the above quote, however, also shows how multi-layered an analysis of cultural practices necessarily is. Since there is not, of course, 'the Periodical' with a capital p, these "certain kinds of people" and "places" cannot be fixed in relation to a nonspecific periodical. For the readership, one would have to look at specific periodicals and at which groups they would have been targeted; as for the "places" one needs to not only look at specific periodicals, but also at the periodical market in the course of the Victorian age. Where periodicals, in terms of production and immediate accessibility for readers, had been associated with an urban environment, especially London and maybe Edinburgh as well, this would have changed with acceleration of travel, which would have made periodicals more easily available in rural areas and would have lessened their association with specific urban capitals.

With the circuit's focus on influences and relationships, it offers a possibility to analyse Victorian periodicals, their materiality, production and consumption within their network of power-structures. Thus, its five poles – representation, identity, production, consumption and regulation – will guide the analysis of the heroic in *Chambers's Journal, Leisure Hour* and *Fraser's Magazine* throughout this study.

58 Ibid.
59 Ibid., p. 23.

Part 2:
Tradition and Transformation? – Charting Heroism in *Chambers's Journal*

4. Charting Heroism in *Chambers's Journal*

4.1 Chambers's Journal

Venturing into Publishing: The Early Careers of William and Robert Chambers

When *Chambers's Edinburgh Journal*[1] appeared for the first time in 1832, its editors were already well-known in Edinburgh's publishing scene. Both brothers had ventured into the book trade in 1820 when each rented a bookstall on Leith Walk. William, the older brother, had just completed his apprenticeship at a bookseller's shop and started his own venture and Robert, who, due to the family's circumstances, had not been able to learn a profession, opened a bookstall with the family's books as stock. The same year, William Chambers acquired his first printing press, an old hand press, and started his career in publishing with an edition of 750 copies of the first sixteen pages of *Songs of Robert Burns*. He taught himself the manual production processes of printing: composing type and printing the individual pages, one at a time. Though this was a slow process and the quality of the print was lacking, William Chambers was able to sell all copies at a shilling each and claimed to have earned £9 over his original purchases of paper and ink.[2] With this, William Chambers saw his future profession set, not only because he was soon commissioned with printing small pamphlets for "Friendly and Burial Societies",[3] but because he felt an emotional connection to the task:

> I think there was a degree of infatuation in my attachment to that jangling, creaking, wheezing little press. Placed at the only window in my apartment, within a few feet of my bed, I could see its outlines in the silvery moonlight when I awoke; and there, at the glowing dawn, did its figure assume distinct proportions. When daylight came fully in, it was impossible to resist the desire to rise and have an hour or two of exercise at the little machine.[4]

Robert Chambers, who had successfully enlarged his bookselling business, had started to write literary texts in his leisure time and in 1821 the brothers first went into business together in an attempt to publish a popular periodical. *Kaleidoscope*, an octavo, appeared fortnightly from October 1821 onwards and its production was a family effort. The contents, "a miscellany of poetry, sketches of

---

1 The publication, which was later called just *Chambers's Journal*, will in the following be referred to as *CJ*. Excerpts from the periodical will be cited in the text by referencing the author (if known), the title of the article, its date of publication and page number.

2 The account of this first endeavour is taken from William Chambers: Memoir of William and Robert Chambers, Edinburgh 1883.

3 Ibid., p. 142.

4 Ibid., p. 140.

authors, historical tales, and musing or satirical essays",[5] were exclusively composed by the brothers, with Robert Chambers writing the largest amount of text and William contributing to "only three or four papers".[6] William, with the help of their younger brother James, did the typesetting, printing and stitching of the journal. Already in this early publication, the brothers' will to bring education to the lower ranks of society and their self-perception as having come from and still being part of this class becomes obvious. As William Chambers recollects in his memoir: "This little periodical also contained a few articles descriptive of a wayward class of authors in the lower walks of life, written from personal knowledge, and marked by that sympathy for the unfortunate which characterized my brother throughout life."[7] Though the *Kaleidoscope* only existed for four months, it had given the brothers something to aspire to, "a trial of one's wings, and encouraged to higher flights in more favourable times and circumstances".[8] Only a short time later, both of their careers picked up; Robert Chambers became acquainted with Sir Walter Scott and began to write more and more and both brothers exchanged their bookstalls for more permanent premises in the city.

"The Universal Appetite for Instruction Which at Present Exists" – Chambers's Journal, *a Publication for the People*

Throughout the 1820s, both brothers enlarged their reputations – Robert as a writer, William as a bookseller – and with the increase of cheap(er) publications on the print market, they decided to try their hand at a periodical publication again. Especially William Chambers, who "had occasion to deal in these cheap papers", was "greatly against them".[9] He felt that they appeared too irregularly, papers from London often arrived long after their date of publication, were "conducted with no definite plan [...] but to furnish temporary amusement" and were "the perversion of what, if rightly conducted, might become a powerful engine of social improvement".[10]

These thoughts then gave rise to the desire to establish a periodical themselves, and the first issue of *Chambers's Edinburgh Journal* (later *Chambers's Journal of Popular Literature Science and Art*, then *Chambers's Journal*) was published on 4 February 1832 and appeared weekly. Naturally, the periodical, which from the

---

5 Fyfe: Steam-Powered, p. 17. Aileen Fyfe's excellent study *Steam-Powered Knowledge. William Chambers and the Business of Publishing 1820-1860* is the only major monograph which analyses the early endeavours of Chambers's publishing house and offers access to a vast amount of archival material.

6 Chambers: Memoir, p. 147.

7 Ibid.

8 Ibid.

9 Ibid., p. 208.

10 Ibid., pp. 208–209.

beginning was issued in around 30,000 copies,[11] could not be produced as a family endeavour on one or even several hand presses. In this respect, Edinburgh proved a business disadvantage since "there were obstructions as regards both paper and printing".[12] These involuntary regulations regarding production led to the work being contracted out to a printer in Edinburgh whose workers, "toiling night and day", produced the first numbers of *CJ*.

Once printed, *CJ* was sold for one and a half pennies[13] and the publishers had a clear target audience in mind which is articulated in the "Editor's Address to His Readers":[14]

> The grand leading principle by which I have been actuated, is to take advantage of the universal appetite for instruction which at present exists; to supply to that appetite food of the best kind, and in such form, and at such a price, as must suit the convenience of every man in the British dominion. Every Saturday, when the poorest labourer in the country draws his humble earnings, he shall have it in his power to purchase, with an insignificant portion of even that humble sum, a meal of healthful, useful and agreeable mental instruction. (Editor's Address to His Readers, *CJ*, 4 Feb 1832, 1)

A right to education and knowledge is thus established as a basic right, just as basic a need as food; the example of the "poorest labourer in the country" shows that the publication wanted to provide information and instruction for less educated readers of the lower-middle classes and wanted to reach them by keeping prices low. The magazine's identity as a paper for instruction and information was also reflected in its representation. With its double crown octavo size[15] it was small enough to be held in one hand and read in a comfortable pose, yet not small enough to be carried around in one's pocket and was clearly intended for domestic consumption. Its serifed fonts and especially the narrow margins between the two columns and small side margins told the prospective reader that

---

11 The *Waterloo Directory of English Newspapers and Periodicals: 1850–1900* for the remainder of the nineteenth century gives circulation numbers up to 90,000 copies (in the late 1840s) and between 60,000 and 70,000 copies after 1860. However, it is unclear whether these numbers include circulation in the whole of Britain or only in England. For the highest circulation number of 90,000, it specifically refers to circulation "including Scottish, English, and Irish editions" ("Chambers's Edinburgh Journal", n.p.). Ellergård gives circulation numbers of 70,000 for 1865 and 60,000 for 1870. Cf. Alvar Ellergård: The Readership of the Periodical Press in Mid-Victorian Britain. II. Directory, in: Victorian Periodicals Newsletter 13, 1971, p. 21.

12 Chambers: Memoir, p. 238.

13 From 1855 onwards, the price was reduced to 1d a week or 7d for buying all issues of one month. Cf. "Chambers's Edinburgh Journal", n.p.

14 Robert Chambers had only been involved as a contributor for the first fourteen issues of *CJ* and only thereafter became its second editor. Thus the first article of the journal is entitled "Editor's" in singular, not "Editors' Address".

15 The periodical was printed in this size from 1844 onwards. Cf. Laurel Brake: The "Popular Weeklies", in: Bill Bell (ed.): The Edinburgh History of the Book in Scotland, vol. 3, Edinburgh 2007, p. 363. In its initial years, the periodical had been printed in a larger broadsheet size and in three columns. For the examination period of this study, however, the later smaller size is relevant.

the periodical wanted to make the best possible use of the space at hand. Thus, the periodical's size and layout told a story of its intended consumers as much as the address to the readers.

The editor's reference to "every man in the British dominion" also makes it clear that *CJ* was not only intended for consumption in the Lothians or Scotland, but in Britain as a whole. William Chambers in his address therefore creates the imagery of an educationally starved British readership that is not 'fed' adequately. However, when speaking of the "meal of healthful, useful and agreeable mental instruction" (ibid.), an implicit opposite is present within the text. Chambers wanted to provide good reading material for the uneducated, but at the same time intended to keep them from consuming other material. In particular, he seems to have had the Society for the Diffusion of Useful Knowledge's *Penny Magazine* in mind here when he says that the "scheme of diffusing knowledge has certainly more than once been attempted on respectable principles [...]. Yet the great end has not been gained" (ibid.). Chambers thus expressed the desire to perform a "service to mankind at large" (ibid.).

How did *CJ* differ from other journals for the lower and middle classes such as Charles Knight's *Penny Magazine*? According to William Chambers: through independence. In his opinion, all other endeavours had failed because they had been institutionally – both politically and religiously – bound to certain positions and attitudes. Although, of course, the aim of educating less educated people and the process of selection and mode of presentation involved were in themselves political, Chambers believed that he was taking "a course altogether novel" (ibid.). He wanted to take as many people as possible upon the "path of moral responsibility", whether "the highest conservative" or "the boldest advocate of universal democracy", whether an "Irish Roman Catholic" or a "more highly cultivated Presbyterian cotta[r] of my native land".[16]

This was, of course, also a commercial consideration. The less specific the ideological orientation of the periodical, the more it would appeal to a general readership and the more copies would be sold. Thus, the only obvious ideology in the "Editor's Address" seems to be the idea of self-improvement. Chambers continues to explain to whom different parts of the journal would be dedicated

16 Ibid. In a 40-page pocket sized publication celebrating the *Jubilee Year of Chambers's Journal* in 1882, William Chambers reaffirmed this professed neutrality: "Political topics have been studiously avoided, or more properly left to the acknowledged organs of public opinion. So, likewise, matters of religious nature have been resigned to their appropriate exponents." William Chambers: Jubilee Year of Chambers's Journal. Reminiscences of a Long and Busy Life, Edinburgh 1882, p. 18. Furthermore, the archive material suggests that contributions were edited in that respect as well. In a letter to Canadian author Grant Allen, for example, Charles Chambers in 1885 asks the author to "omit" certain passages from the upcoming novel *In All Shades* because they are "relating to Politics + Religion" which *CJ* "carefully avoided". Charles Chambers: Letter to Grant Allen, 1885, Dep 341/165: No 822, National Library of Scotland, Edinburgh.

and the benefits the different readerships would gain from it – all of which include individual improvement. Those people living in rural parts of the country would gain education in topography, geography, statistics and moral instruction; artisans would receive information on new inventions relevant for their industry; housekeepers would be able to improve their "domestic and cottage economy" and even the "poor man" unable to continue a life in Britain would find "valuable and correct information for his guidance" on how to emigrate (ibid.). Additionally, Chambers also wanted to address young women[17] and boys. The former, he believed, would benefit from "traditional anecdotes" and "nice amusing tale[s]" (ibid., 2) which would be more suitable for them than the popular gothic tales. Those he described as "the ordinary trash about Italian castles, and daggers, and ghosts in the blue chamber, and similar nonsense" (ibid.). The household was the field of instruction in which Chambers wanted to cater for the girls, whom he wanted to provide with "a thousand useful little receipts and modes of housewifery, calculated to make them capital wives" (ibid.).

Boys, however, seemed to be one of the most important addressees for William Chambers. He talks about his own youth, his unwillingness to be educated due to bad teaching and his eagerness to learn once things were explained to him in a way he could understand. Accordingly he wants to explain the world to the boys, tell them stories about other continents, how society and economy work, how to build "rabbit-houses on scientific principles" and to "inform them about matters which their papa does not think of speaking to them about because he is so busy" (ibid.). It is a plea to the boys then with which the address ends:

> Finally, I shall give some accounts of men who were at one time poor little boys like themselves, but who, on paying a daily attention to their studies, and being always honest, and having a great desire to become eminent, and not be mere drudges all their days, gradually rose to be great statesmen, and generals, and members of learned professions, and distinguished authors, and to have fine houses and parks; and that at last they even came to be made kings or presidents of powerful nations. (ibid.)

William Chambers in his opening address thus established high expectations for his publication: he wanted to inform and instruct all parts of the middle and lower classes, wanted to publish appealing articles for all different classes and professions and situated his journal as both teacher and parent of the uninformed. Thus, the ultimate claim of *CJ* was to create an improved society and consequently an improved nation.

---

17 Nicola Thompson notes: "*Chambers's Journal* explicitly included women and children [...] in its prospectus: 'With the ladies of the "new school," and all my young countrywomen in their teens, I hope to be on agreeable terms [...] I will also inform them of a thousand useful little receipts of housewifery, calculated to make them capital wives.'" Nicola Diane Thompson: Reviewing Sex. Gender and the Reception of Victorian Novels, New York 1996, p. 122.

Hints towards the actual readership of *CJ* can be found in the publishing house's archive material held at the National Library of Scotland in Edinburgh and show that the journal succeeded in reaching a broad public,[18] although it can be presumed that their goal to cater to the uneducated reader on a large scale did not succeed.[19] Thus, one can find letters by readers like that of a Mr Hawke of London, who in 1854 complains about the serial novel "Wearyfoot Common" for being too sentimental for *CJ*'s audience, since the "readers are not generally women and children but practical utilitarian men of business who hate a love story (if nothing else) as they do a lazy or useless servant neither being worth the space they occupy".[20] Letters from readers such as this give evidence of a readership which was educated and perceived the printed material they consumed as being intended for them and their peers. Also, the archive material illustrates that readers responded especially well to topics which they recognised from their own lives. For example, after an article on "Some Curious Superscriptions" in 1854 had presented the readers with entertaining and odd addresses on letters, many readers wrote in to the journal in order to share their own curious experiences with superscriptions.[21]

On the other hand, correspondence with authors on prospective articles in the journal show that much material was written with the very purpose of education in mind:[22] The translator and author Charles Martel wrote to the editors in the same year with the proposal of adapting Michel Eugène Chevreul's *The Principles of Harmony and Contrast of Colours* for a more broad audience. He had pub-

---

[18] Chris Baggs notes that *CJ* was one of the most popular periodicals in libraries. For the Aberdeen Public Library, which "collected figures [for individual loans] between 1884/5 and 1899/1900. [...] *Chambers's Journal*, *Cassell's Family Magazine*, *Windsor* and *Pearson's Magazine* were the most consistently popular titles, along with the *Boy's Own Paper*." Baggs: Reading Rooms, p. 281. It is worth noting that among these most popular periodicals, *CJ* was the only one without illustrations.

[19] In the issue of 25 January 1840, Robert and William Chambers write that "this paper is read, we believe, by a class who may be called the *élite* of the labouring community, those who think, conduct themselves respectably, and are anxious to improve their circumstances by judicious means. But below this worthy order of men, our work, except in a few particular cases, does not go. A fatal mistake is committed in the notion that the lower classes read. There is, unfortunately, a vast substratum in society where the printing-press has not yet unfolded her treasures." Address of the Editors, *CJ*, 25 Jan 1840, 8. The text goes on to state though that *CJ* "is now, as before, framed chiefly for that large department of society, who, being engaged in the duties of the counting-house, the shop, the workroom, or those of their private dwellings, have little leisure for the cultivation of their minds". Ibid.

[20] Hawke: Letter to Chambers's Journal, 1854, Dep 341/129: unnumbered, National Library of Scotland, Edinburgh.

[21] Cf. Correspondence, 1854–1855, Dep. 341/129: unnumbered, National Library of Scotland, Edinburgh.

[22] It remains a problem that this part of the intended readership usually remains invisible in archival material as they would presumably not have written in. This, of course, does by no means indicate that there were no readers using the journal for their personal advancement.

lished the direct translation, which had not found a large readership; "[s]ince its publication however, I have observed that the book is too Scientific for the generality of readers".[23] Thus, Martel's hope was to publish Chevreul's theory in a new form in *CJ:* "a more popular form is required to insure that wide acceptance of the principles set forth, which their importance demands."[24] Although this proposed series of articles was never realised (though Chevreul and his theories feature in the journal), Martel's letter shows how *CJ* was perceived as a publication which popularised scientific material for a broad audience and would ensure the wide dissemination of material.[25] Since the majority of the archived readers' correspondence came from England, especially from London, the archive material shows clearly that *CJ* succeeded in catering to a Britain-wide audience, though the readers' identity – in the sense of du Gay et al. – is not as clear-cut as the editors would have wanted it to be in terms of class and education.

Unlike many other periodicals published at a similar price and aimed at a similar audience, *CJ* was not illustrated. This was, as William Chambers writes, a deliberate decision: "At no time was there any attempt to give pictorial illustrations of objects in natural history, the fine arts, or anything else. Without undervaluing the attractions of wood-cut engravings, the aims of the editors were in a different direction."[26] The objective to "cultivate the feelings as much as the understanding" was in his opinion best achieved through "the essay system".[27] This focus on written information rather than illustration is also evident in the general layout; at first it was printed as a folio publication with four pages and four columns of text per page; from autumn 1832 onwards it was published as a quarto with eight pages and three columns, and finally in 1844 changed to a double crown octavo size with two columns.[28] In all cases, a rather small font was chosen, the magazine's title banner was unembellished with only a small margin to the sides and between columns. Thereby, the layout itself suggests the emphasis on the written word. Though the decision not to include illustrations may well also have been a financial one, the programmatic focus on essays was

---

23 Charles Martel: Letter to Chambers's Journal, 1854, Dep 341/131, unnumbered, National Library of Scotland, Edinburgh.

24 Ibid.

25 *CJ*'s conception as a didactic periodical is acknowledged in much of the correspondence. The Irish writer Samuel Carter Hall under the pseudonym Anna Maria Hall (under which he later also submitted articles to *CJ*) calls it a "work in the highest repute as at once cheap and good" which contributes to "to their [its readers'] social and moral improvement" (Anna Maria Hall: Letter to Chambers's Journal., n.d., Dep 341/121: No 17, National Library of Scotland, Edinburgh). A reverend for example praises it as follows: "I know not better Journal than your Journal, and that I have for many years circulated it in my Parish" (Reverend: Letter to Chambers's Journal, 1883, Dep 341/139: unnumbered, National Library of Scotland, Edinburgh).

26 Chambers: Memoir, p. 240.

27 Ibid.

28 Cf. Brake: Popular Weeklies, p. 363.

also turned into a facet of the brothers' self-conception as middle-class men in retrospect. Robert Chambers writes in the preface to one of his essay collections:

> One ruling aim of the author must be taken into account: it was my design from the first to be the essayist of the middle class - that in which I was born, and to which I continued to belong. I therefore do not read their manners and habits as one looking *de haut en bas*, which is the usual style of essayists, but as one looking round among the firesides of my friends. For their use I shape and sharpen my apothegms; to their comprehension I modify any philosophical disquisitions on which I have entered.[29]

Thus, one can clearly see how important the middle class as a target audience was for the editors of *CJ*. They marketed their magazine as one being written *by* the middle class *for* the middle class and those from lower ranks aspiring to rise in society. Although the publishing house soon grew well beyond the limits of a mid-sized enterprise and the brothers became part of the intellectual circles of Britain (e.g. Robert Chambers was a member of the Royal Society of Edinburgh and the Athenaeum Club in London, William Chambers was Provost of Edinburgh from 1865 to 1869), they always emphasised the social responsibility of their work. This is also reflected in the way their magazine was produced.

Production Processes

Compared to the production of William Chambers's edition of Burns's poetry, the production of *CJ* was a highly modern, industrialised process. Given their intention to cater to "every man in the British dominion" (Editor's Address to His Readers, *CJ*, 4 Feb 1832, 1) and their – at least for this purpose – marginal location in Edinburgh, one can imagine that William and Robert Chambers had to overcome some obstacles to establish an efficient publishing company that operated nationwide. Although Edinburgh was the second centre of the British book trade and produced the main share of material for the Scottish market, it still was small compared to London and the number of paper making and printers' shops was considerably lower than in the capital. The first issues of the journal were printed by John Johnstone, a "genial old man",[30] and William Chambers had ordered a run of 30,500 copies.[31] However, this proved to be a difficult task for the printer and his workers, who were frequently unable to deliver the required number at the agreed-upon time. This led to problems in distribution: for the magazine to be available in the bookshops on Saturday, the copies had to be produced a considerable time in advance: several days for delivery by the journal's agents for the Scottish and North-England country and ideally several

[29] Quoted in Chambers: Memoir, pp. 240–241.
[30] Ibid.
[31] All of the following numbers are taken from Fyfe: Knowledge.

weeks for distribution of copies to London.[32] Although Chambers persuaded Johnstone to let the printing machines run throughout the night and add several work shifts, it proved to be nearly impossible to achieve.[33] Thus, other printers, in some cases as far away as Glasgow, were frequently contracted to cover the missing issues. Within the first year of publication, therefore, a decision was made to divide the printing of the paper: one part of it (approximately 22,000 copies) was published in Edinburgh, the other was printed by the company of Bradbury and Evans in London. Under the supervision of William Orr, the relationship to whom was a difficult one and ultimately led to the abandoning of the London department, the London edition was produced at low prices and on time, since Orr could rely on a greater number of printers and the most modern technology available. Seeing the advantages of modern printing techniques made William and Robert Chambers think about acquiring equipment of their own.

A first step in this direction was the switch to stereotype plates in the composition process. This made both the reprinting of issues as well as the production in London easier; when establishing the London edition, the procedure had been to send one printed copy of the complete journal to London where it would be typeset again. The use of stereotype plates thus made the composition process in London obsolete and printing could begin as soon as the plates arrived. However, this did not change the fact that the printing shops in Edinburgh, most of which were still working with hand-presses, were overwhelmed with the amount of copies they needed to produce. Chambers therefore made a far-reaching decision in 1833 which put them among the pioneers of modern technology in the printing trade: after having pondered the option of moving the whole of the printing to London, they decided to venture into the business of steam-printing themselves. Since there were no printing-machine makers in Edinburgh, Chambers commissioned Robert Gunn to build a printing machine which was installed on the company's premises in December 1833. The new equipment worked more than seven times faster than the hand-presses and was

---

32 The issue of distribution was an important factor in Chambers's initial decision to publish a periodical and not a newspaper. On the one hand, a newspaper had to reach the reader fast, as it contained current information that could well be old news after a couple of days, on the other hand, publishing a newspaper was more expensive. Sending news through the mail – e.g. from Edinburgh to London – "required the payment of 4*d.* in stamp duty, which would have more than trebled the price of the journal and put it far beyond the reach of [its] intended readers." Fyfe: Knowledge, p. 47. The decision to publish a periodical and thus a print product with no time-sensitive information gave the editors the time to print the journal several weeks in advance and thus also to pack and ship the copies to England, Ireland and the rest of Scotland.

33 Fyfe remarks that the night shifts produced a different set of problems since the work was often done sloppily because the workers were rarely sober. Cf. ibid., p. 56.

able to produce 900 sheets within an hour.[34] By 1840, "the Chambers establishment included workshops for the composition of type, the casting of stereotype plates, steam-powered printing, and a bindery"[35] and by 1846, the entire run of *CJ* (by then 60,000 to 80,000 copies) was again produced solely in Edinburgh. Since Edinburgh had by then been connected to the south through the railways, fast distribution to all parts of the country was ensured.

The new technology did not only bring economic advantages but, in Chambers' opinion, also social ones. On the one hand, *CJ* repeatedly published notes saying that the low price – and thus the accessibility for large parts of society – of the journal could only be maintained due to the fact that it was steam-printed (cf. e.g. Mechanisms of Chambers's Journal, *CJ*, 6 Jun 1835, 150). On the other hand, Chambers believed that the new technologies would also lead to societal changes for the better. This is expressed in various Chambers publications on printing technologies, such as an issue of *Information for the People* devoted to the topic which points out that the new machines require educated and specialised workers. Thus, Chambers believed that the innovations would affect society from two sides: the growing amount of cheap instructional publications would educate people without access to formal education and the growing demand on the job market would lead to more and more people acquiring skills for those more qualified manual jobs. To enhance the latter development they ran a library for their workers, hired teachers to educate the younger employees and from 1838 onwards held an annual soirée for their employees. This event, which was always reported on in an article in *CJ*, was thought to reward the workers of all classes and give them a sense of unity.

As this short overview of the establishment, production processes and content orientation of *CJ* has shown, the journal was unique in a number of ways: the publication was managed and produced in Edinburgh and remained there throughout its existence. In a distinctly Scottish tradition,[36] *CJ* had a firm didactic orientation and wanted to act as a moral guide to those parts of society who

---

34 As already mentioned in chapter 3.1, this innovation in production processes also lead to new publications from the house of Chambers. With the new speed of printing, *CJ* only occupied the press for half of the week and the brothers came up with additional publications, such as the pamphlets *Information for the People* and later also encyclopaedias and school books, to fill the empty time slots to keep the machines running and regain their investment of £500 which they had paid for the printing machine and the steam engine.

35 Fyfe: Knowledge, p. 90.

36 In a tradition reaching back to the reformation in the sixteenth century, Scotland until today perceives itself as having a distinct identity in relation to education. As Stephen Mark Holmes puts it: "It is a commonplace that 'The Scottish Reformation' of 1560, with its desire to enable people to read the Bible in their own language, led to the establishment of a system of education available to the whole nation in an extensive network of parish schools and headed by a unique system of universities." Stephen Mark Holmes: Education in the Century of Reformation, in: R.D. Anderson et al. (eds.): The Edinburgh History of Education in Scotland, Edinburgh 2015, p. 57. This Presbyterian approach to create education equality (both in terms of financial as well as spatial access and gender) influenced

were able to read yet unable to afford formal education. Its contents were focused on conveying as much information as possible, which is reflected in the layout of the publication and its omission of illustrations as well as in the predominant genre of the essay. By being in charge of all production processes involved in the printing of the journal and not being associated with any organisation, Chambers gained a degree of independence that most publishers would not have had and that allowed them, within the restrictions of the market place, free reign over their material.

Editors and Contributors

The *Waterloo Directory* lists a number of well-known authors under the contributors of *CJ*, for many of whom correspondence in the archival material held at the NLS can be found. Among them are – for the period this study is concerned with – men and women such as Grant Allen, Walter Besant, R. D. Blackmore, Arthur Conan Doyle, George Manville Fenn, Elizabeth Gaskell, Thomas Hardy, Mary Howitt, Harriet Martineau, Caroline E. S. Norton or Edmund Norton.[37] However, since the predominant amount of articles in *CJ* was published anonymously, even the names of these well-known authors would not have been acknowledged in the periodical.[38] It was mostly serialised fiction which was pub-

---

both education policy and the public climate regarding learning and instruction throughout the centuries. As Jane McDermid argues, the nineteenth century can be seen as "an attempt to revive the Presbyterian educational tradition [...] and to ensure common provision across the country." Jane McDermid: Education and Society in the Era of the School Boards 1872–1918, in: R. D. Anderson et al. (eds.): The Edinburgh History of Education in Scotland, Edinburgh 2015, p. 190. In an age of secularisation, the state increasingly took the place of the church in the execution of this goal (cf. ibid.) and the "educational debate and investigation, notably between the 1830s and 1860s, convinced many in Scotland that the continuation of common provision was essential for the social order" (ibid.). The launch of *CJ* and its didactic goals can be located in this context. For more scholarship on Scottish Presbyterianism and education see for example R. D. Anderson: Education and the Scottish People 1750–1918, Oxford 1995; id. et al. (eds.): The Edinburgh History of Education in Scotland, Edinburgh 2015; Heather Holmes (ed.): Scottish Life and Society. A Compendium of Scottish Ethnology, vol. 11, Edinburgh 2000; R. A. Houston: Scottish Literacy and the Scottish Identity. Illiteracy and Society in Scotland and Northern England 1600–1800, Cambridge 2002; W. M. Humes: Leadership Class in Scottish Education, Edinburgh 1986; id. / Hamish M. Paterson: Scottish Culture and Scottish Education 1800–1980, Edinburgh 1983 or James G. Kellas: Modern Scotland, London/Boston 1980.

37 Apart from the Chambers brothers themselves, contributors to the early periodical included Maria Edgeworth, Eliza William Green, Walter White, William Wilson or William Henry Willis.

38 This is especially interesting since many of those names would have been good advertising for selling to specific audiences. The National Library of Scotland holds notebooks giving the details of almost all articles published from 1839 to 1846 and 1871 to 1903 and to whom a payment was made (though sometimes only noting initials). Since this study is concerned with what readers would have encountered in the periodical, an analysis of

lished under authors' names, such as Grant Allen's series *Dumaresq's Daughter*[39](1891) or William Le Queux's spy novel *Of Royal Blood* (1899–1900).

CJ was a strongly editor-led periodical. In its early years, a majority of the content was written by Robert and William Chambers themselves. Although the brothers were succeeded as editors by Leith Richie in 1858 and James Payn later took over the editorship, the periodical was still strongly influenced by them. As the firm's correspondence in the National Library of Scotland indicates, the successive editors strongly relied on the advice and approval of the two founders.[40] In 1874, the editorship was taken into family hands again, with Robert Chambers Jr. taking over and he was subsequently succeeded by his son who remained the periodical's editor for the rest of the century.[41]

Unlike other periodicals, the profile of *CJ* did not significantly change with the different editors. The strong influence of Robert and William Chambers until their deaths and the continuation of their editorial ideals through their descendants ensured a stability in the periodical's identity as an entertaining and educating paper for the mass market.

4.2 Heroism in Chambers's Journal

The last paragraph of *CJ*'s opening address to the readers promised the periodical's younger readers accounts of "great statesmen, and generals, and members of learned professions, and distinguished authors, [who have] fine houses and parks" (Editor's Address to His Readers, *CJ*, 4 Feb 1832, 2). These were men whom the readers could aspire to and one day possibly become like. This promise offers a first glimpse at *CJ*'s mode of presenting the heroic. While not using the word 'hero', William Chambers points out in his address that every reader (or at least every *male* reader) could become an extraordinary 'great man' if he

whom specific articles might be attributed to would not have been productive to the argument.

39 This narrative will be discussed in greater detail in chapter 4.5. As was general practice in the day, not every instalment of the series referred to Grant Allen's name and in many of the parts he is referred to as "the author of" other serialised novels that had been published in *CJ* (specifically "In All Shades" which had been published in 1886 and "This Mortal Coil" which had appeared in *CJ* in 1888). This can not only be seen as a means of advertising the serialised novel the reader was currently consuming, but also an attempt at countering the ephemeral quality of the periodical publication by referencing the content of past issues.

40 Robert Chambers died in 1871 and was involved in the publishing house's proceedings until his death. William Chambers also remained active in the firm until late in his life; after his brother's death he became the principal shareholder in the firm. Robert Chambers's son, Robert Chambers Jr., became the publishing house's director and was assisted by William Chambers until his death in 1883.

41 Cf. G. A. Aitkin: Chambers, Robert (1832–1888), in: Lawrence Goldman (ed.): Oxford Dictionary of National Biography, 2014, DOI: 10.1093/ref:odnb/5080.

only received the right education and excelled in virtues such as honesty, diligence, ambition and discipline. In the context of the different contemporary ideals of heroism discussed in chapter 2.1, *CJ*'s address already shows a strong tendency towards Samuel Smiles's notion of each and every man having the ability to become a hero for his community through hard work and perseverance.

This part of the study will examine how a more distinct concept of the heroic emerges in *CJ*. Subsequently, it will analyse how this concept is functionalised for different target audiences at different points in time in the second half of the nineteenth century. The first section will discuss articles which explicitly – or ex negativo – define heroism on an abstract level as a basis of comparison for those articles which deal with heroism more implicitly or on a more specific level. It will outline the qualities and domains of the heroic which emerged as the most dominant ones in the corpus. The first section will analyse texts from *CJ* which explicitly define heroism for the readers before turning to the most prominent domains for which such qualities of heroism are evoked. In that, it will become clear that the periodical emphasises the identificatory potential for the readers in its usage of heroism, especially through the characteristics of selflessness and perseverance. As the first and one of the most significant domains of the heroic in *CJ*, one chapter will examine military heroism and illustrate the impact of ongoing wars on the periodical's display of heroic actions in military contexts. The next sections will turn to civil heroism and in particular focus on the way in which class and gender intersect with and complicate the representation of the heroic. With a focus on the Victorian ideal of progress and civilisatory advancement, the subchapter "Heroes of Civilisation" will analyse instances of heroism which are presented as part of a greater societal goal of improvement played out in the areas of science, medicine and education. As a last dominant domain, everyday heroism will be examined. Two types of heroism of everyday life will be identified: firstly, acts of lifesaving, the public recognition of which boomed from the 1860s onwards, and secondly, the idea of a heroism of ordinary everyday life, which was strongly connected to class membership and questions of gender, will be investigated. Each section will identify different themes or strands of the specific domain of the heroic and will discuss the associated articles in *CJ* in chronological order so that both a synchronic picture as well as an idea of the development over the examination period emerges. In order to substantiate if these findings were specific to *CJ*, "Different Heroes for Different Readers", will investigate how the Chambers brothers mediated heroism in their other publications, such as school books, encyclopaedias or biographies.

"What is Heroism?"

This programmatic question is posed in the title of an article which appeared in *CJ* on 9 May 1857. Just one year after the end of the Crimean War, an anonymous contributor tries to define heroic actions both on and far removed from the battlefield. The text aims at defining a heroism different from traditional notions and moves the hero closer to the readers' everyday lives, making the concept of heroism more easily available for individual identification.

In a historical perspective, the text starts its examination with the heroes of antiquity who "every tolerably forward school-boy is familiar with" as "illustrative of the heroic virtues, self-sacrifice and fortitude" (What Is Heroism, *CJ*, 9 May 1857, 297). The stories of these extraordinary men and women – "Leonidas and his three hundred", "Aristides" or "Arria, by her own death, encouraging her husband to brave a similar fate" (ibid.) – are taught in "dramatic episodes and tableaux" (ibid.) in school and form the basis of every schoolboy's notion of heroism. Emphasising the need for mediation of narrations of heroism, the text stresses that the stories "have been handed down from generation to generation, from the old civilisations to the new, and have challenged and received more or less admiration and applause" (ibid.). Though representing accounts of "mythic history" that "though ascribed to historical personages, are nevertheless fictitious" often only existed "in the imaginations of ballad-singers" (ibid.), the stories were passed down in oral and written tradition by historians and biographers because they carried cultural meaning regarded relevant for coming generations. Consequently, the authenticity of the heroic deeds is deemed unimportant as long as they carry a specific cultural meaning.

The opening paragraphs establish the importance of mediation, tradition and commemoration through exemplars for the concept of heroism. It is not Aristides, Leonidas and his men, or Arria who are of heightened importance, but their actions and most of their underlying motivations and values which are considered noteworthy for future generations. Heroism is thereby utilised as a medium of transmission for cultural or group-specific values which can best be remembered through narrative patterns. For example, the story of Leonidas and his three hundred men becomes a vehicle for the importance of bravery in the face of danger, for the importance of physical strength and selflessness and significantly also a model for the coming generations in the construction of their identity. From these stories of ancient heroism, the author constructs a profile of requirements for heroic figures: "we shall find them [the heroes] to be an enthusiastic abnegation of self, and a somewhat exaggerated development of a single virtue" (ibid.). Selflessness is presented as the underlying value required for all acts of heroism. However, the text suggests that the "human virtue" (ibid.) still needs an igniting spark, an "actuating motive" (ibid.), to result in the creation of a hero. Patriotism, honour and "domestic affection" (ibid.) are named as examples for this kind of enthusiasm-creating motivation, all of which are, notably, vague concepts which every reader could easily relate to. An act of heroism can finally occur when selflessness, another heightened virtue, and honourable motives come together in a specific situation "of time and place, or peculiar character of mind" (ibid.). Only if all of these requirements are met can real heroism be observed. Accordingly, a lack of any of the named requirements can turn a presumably heroic person into one of mere "quasi-glory" (ibid.).

The medial nature of heroism also entails that it is by definition always public. Therefore, the fame of heroism also attracts characters who do not fulfil the foremost heroic virtue of selflessness, but seek fame and public recognition:

> Every action, however praiseworthy and virtuous in outward seeming, may be accounted for, if we so incline, by consummate hypocrisy, far-sighted selfishness, or immoderate pride. By hypothetical assumptions, we may attribute the public life of Washington to his greed for glory, or of Wilberforce to a puerile love of fame. (ibid.)

Starting with these apparently attention-seeking heroes, the text goes on to elaborate on different kinds of heroism in modern times in relation to their presumed truthfulness. Presented as such, heroism almost appears as a skill which one can master at different levels. The article states that "it is obvious at once, that isolate acts, illustrating an impulsive virtue, and occurring at conjunctures of great emergency, are but doubtful guides to general character" (ibid., 298). In what can be called situational heroism, individuals are enabled by *specific circumstances* and courage to perform spontaneous acts which transgress their own (physical, mental, emotional, norm-given) limitations. This could be a single incident, such as a passer-by coming to the aid of a fellow pedestrian in peril; this act, however, would not necessarily be an accurate representation of the hero's character. In this case, much of the heroic impulse would have been, if one connects the arguments of the text, due to the "peculiar circumstances of time and place" (ibid., 297).

Similarly, the text argues that the military domain might produce heroism more easily than other areas of life, since "in order to create military heroes, we have only to provide a field of action" (ibid., 298). As all parties involved in a war effort are in a state of "excitement" (ibid.), they "after the first moments of the conflict customarily lose all sense of danger, are urged on by a wild agitation of the spirits, and make the final assault in almost a state of delirium. The foundation of heroism of this kind is physical courage and common manly sentiment" (ibid.). In contrast to this situational heroism, the text constructs "a higher kind, which is often not patent to the world, which requires no grand stage and no dramatic incidents to give its lustre" (ibid.). This "higher kind" then seems to be less dependent on specific circumstance and opportunity, but more related to a general heroic character, a moral disposition which allows for heroic actions without the external conditions brought up in the first part of the article. Most importantly, the necessity of medial presentation and recognition in a public forum (no matter how small it might be) is discarded for this kind of heroics: "the higher kind of heroism of which I speak, avoids rather than seeks the pomp and circumstance of war and the glare of publicity" (ibid.). Again, the heroics of wartime are given as an example of the less pure, more easily attainable kind of heroism, which is born out of a necessity, not out of a conscious decision of the hero, and which appeals to many men because it might entail public recognition:

> Enthusiastic British youth, moved by the recital of heroic deeds of ancient or modern times, yearn to become performers of similar exploits: they are filled with regret that their surrounding circumstances are commonplace, that they have no Thermopylae to defend and no Sebastopol to storm, that there is not the slightest occasion to imitate the Athenians under Themistocles, and embark their household gods. They crave the inducement of a tragic glory and opportunity to create an undying fame by a single effort. (ibid.)

Only one year after the Crimean War had ended, the text on the one hand compares the actions of British soldiers during the Siege of Sebastopol to the ancient legend of the Battle of Thermopylae; on the other hand, it states that opportunities for similar actions are scarce in the present day and ancient narratives as those of the Thermopylae are shown to inspire vain dreams of heroism in the British youth. The enthusiasm which was initially praised in the article seems to border on puerile eagerness in this description. The selflessness and implicit acceptance of one's own death inherent to any participation in combat then turns into selfishness symbolising a want for "tragic glory" and "undying fame" (ibid.).

Having established a negative image of glory-seeking heroism, the text contrasts this idea with the "truest heroism" (ibid.). It is neither bound by specific opportunities or situations, nor constituted by a singular incident but related to one's character. However, the text radically limits the possible properties for true heroism:

> The truest heroism requires for its exhibition calm reflection and deliberate will, rather than excitement. [...] [I]ts groundwork is a sense of duty able to contend with conflicting and baser motives. Patient uncomplaining endurance – steady perseverance in overcoming obstacles – conduct always upright in good and evil report, when no human eye may see with commendation and no human heart respond with sympathy – this is true heroism, and raises its possessor far beyond the ranks of those who plant the standard on a well-won breach. (ibid.)

This results in a form of heroism, "true heroism", which operates unseen and unheard of by the rest of society. This second definition of heroism directly contradicts the first definition given in relation to ancient heroes. The latter necessarily relied on the mediation of their deeds to others and in their afterlife only ever existed in tales and myths. "True" heroism, however, as described by the author, apparently exists without a medium and an audience and is never dependent on external acts of appreciation nor seeks glory.[42] This is further stressed throughout the text through the use of metaphors of light and darkness and through allusions to the stage. The heroism associated with the first definition possesses an "éclat", it is seen in the "light of an after-age" (ibid., 297) and is given a "lustre" (ibid., 298). The "true" heroism on the other hand acts in "the shade", it does not "need stage-effect or brilliant éclat", but is situated in the "private life" (ibid.). It is the private sphere which is identified as the realm of true heroes, in contrast to the public, attention-seeking, staged nature of the heroism considered more superficial by the text.

Thus, the text deprives heroism of its glamour and its fame. Instead, private acts of endurance which are not communicated to others are regarded as the highest heroic deeds. The didactic message of the text is obvious: in the private sphere, everybody can be a hero in moral terms, even those who do not enter cultural memory in its media. "Such heroism [...] lies as much within the reach of the man of peace as of the warrior, of the private citizen as of the statesman or sage" (ibid.). This call for private, silent, selfless heroism gives the first hints towards a tendency to turn the unattainable, out-of-reach hero into an obtainable role model that can be emulated. The text develops a concept of what Geoffrey Cubitt in *Heroic Reputations and Exemplary Lives* calls exemplary heroism:

> Exemplarity involves a perception not just of excellence, but also of relevance – and thus, in a sense, of similarity. Those whom we take as exemplars may be better than we are, but not than we might in principle become – not better in some absolute way that implies a difference of kind, but better relative to some common standard against which we hope to improve.[43]

In "What is Heroism", one can clearly recognise the attempt to motivate the readers to act more morally in general through creating an attainable form of silent heroism. Furthermore, it reflects the broad intended readership established in the first issue: it tries to appeal to as many groups of readers as possible. Although it establishes the two kinds of heroism as unequal, the text calls both of the types heroic and does not dispute that the actions of soldiers in battle constitute a form of heroism and are hence inherently regarded noteworthy. The short yet dense programmatic text clearly has a didactic purpose. However, it also

---

42 This idea of a heroic figure which exists without communication or medium is highly problematic. As Ralf von den Hoff et al. argue, the heroic only comes into existence through mediation ("The heroic only actually becomes present in a society through its representation and communication via different media." Von den Hoff et al.: Heroes, p. 12). Thus, the idea of an unmediated heroism within a public medium constitutes a conceptional clash which cannot be resolved. The specific text discussed above tries to negotiate this tension by not giving examples for the 'true' form of heroism, but rather by referring to the underlying values identified for humble heroics, such as perseverance and selflessness. However, on the whole, the call for an unmediated heroism within the medium of the periodical remains an inconsistency.

43 Geoffrey Cubitt: Introduction, in: Geoffrey Cubitt / Allen Warren (eds.): Heroic Reputations and Exemplary Lives, Manchester 2000, p. 11.

shows a fundamental contradiction: in admiring acts of silent "truest heroism", it is praising something which is – by its own definition – not supposed to be praised.

Thereby, the text shows a fundamental difficulty in the usage of the heroic for a didactic purpose. While a hero generally is considered a person who performs extraordinary actions which are unheard of in everyday life and needs a group of admirers who consider the actions heroic, this definition of heroism is ill suited for the purpose of motivating people. The publishers and contributors of *CJ*, similar to Samuel Smiles in his guide books and instructive biographies, aimed at educating people without formal training and at motivating them to better themselves and live after a certain code of values and morals. Since the readers' lives were far removed from conventional scenes of extraordinariness, anyone wanting to use heroism as a didactic tool would out of necessity have had to move the concept's definition closer to the intended audience and its environment. Precisely this effort can be seen where the text tries to fill the concept of heroism with new content. By defining it as something private, heroism is aligned with the life of the readership. What cannot be resolved, however, is that the heroic is appealing (and therefore potentially motivating) for the very fact that it is, in its traditional conception that was so dominantly present through the ideas of Thomas Carlyle in the nineteenth century, extraordinary, visible and a possible source of fame and worship. The struggle between extraordinariness and exemplarity is at the heart of the representation of the heroic in *CJ* and reoccurs in many of the texts examined in the following sections.

Thus, the idea of public hero-worship is at the centre of the tension between adoration and emulation of heroes. The *OED* gives two main definitions for "worship" which were in use in the nineteenth century: 1. "to honour or revere as a supernatural being or power, or as a holy thing, to regard or approach with veneration; to adore with appropriate acts, rites, or ceremonies";[44] and 2. "to regard with extreme respect or devotion".[45] Both definitions emphasise that anyone who is worshipped is considered greatly above the ordinary. The main definition with its description of the worshipped object as "supernatural" or "holy" is clearly a spiritual, even religious one and interestingly includes the practice of worship. By calling those acts "appropriate", the definition also implies that worship is not an individual behaviour, but the result of the negotiations of a group upon a set of appropriate "acts, rites, or ceremonies". Thus, the object of worship can constitute a community and the act of worship is a collective one. Furthermore, whether one worships religiously or, following the second definition, secularly regards someone "with extreme respect or devotion",[46] the worshipped is al-

44 This definition mirrors the view put forth by thinkers such as Thomas Carlyle.

45 Worship, in: OED Online, Oxford University Press, December 2019, www.oed.com/view/Entry/230345?isAdvanced=false&result=1&rskey=WORcPD&.

46 Ibid.

ways on a different level than the worshipper. In order to create heroes, they have to be elevated above the ordinary level so that they can be treated with heightened respect and devotion. However, if heroes perform the function of a role model at the same time, the difference in social stance becomes problematic as it reduces the chances of the worshippers following in the footsteps of the worshipped. This inherent difference in collective esteem of worshipper and worshipped is at the heart of the tension in the didactic utilisation of the heroic in *CJ*. In the following therefore, I will look at those articles in *CJ* which explicitly deal with the relationship between a hero and its audience, or express an opinion on the nature of hero worship in general.

Hero Worship

The ongoing debate about the necessity of the heroic, about the ideal properties of a hero, and about the function in relation to the worshippers that was taking place in Victorian intellectual circles from the 1840s onwards also appears in popular media such as *CJ*.

The article "Hero-Worship", published in September 1849,[47] puts the two different approaches to hero worship in direct contrast and explores which of the two is more easily adaptable to contemporary society. In the initial paragraph the text states that the history of the human race and its progress was "usually" influenced by "one great spirit brooding over the latent energies of the race" (Hero-Worship, *CJ*, 1 Sep 1849, 129). Strongly reminiscent of Carlyle's argument in *On Heroes*, the different stages of human progress are interpreted as the result of the efforts of different extraordinary individuals who influenced and guided the mass of the people in a "monarchy of mind" (ibid.). What is striking about these two short quotes is the level to which these extraordinary subjects are elevated. They are described as "great spirits", not as worldly human beings, and belong to an imaginary aristocracy which rules the mass. However, these guiding figures seem to have vanished from the present age, according to "a favourite speculation of the thinkers of the day. The great lights of the world, say they, are extinguished – our mighty men have passed away" (ibid.). This clearly alludes to contemporary intellectuals such as Carlyle who had diagnosed the Victorian age as lacking the proper environment for heroic figures (cf. *OH* 12).

After this diagnosis the text poses a leading question: "All present things show that there is a general interregnum [...]. Who, what, and where are the Coming Men?" (ibid.). Having up until this point followed the 'traditional line' of thinking about the heroic, the article afterwards departs from this. Instead of trying to compare the contemporary situation to that of the past, the author tries to relate

47 Though published before 1850, I have included this article into my corpus since it explicates many things which can implicitly be found in many other articles.

hero worship to present societal developments and comes to a more positive conclusion. Although still supporting the opinion that "[o]ur great men have indeed perished. In government, war, science, literature, we see only a crowd of individuals more or less capable, but none supreme" (ibid.), this is explained as a "natural progress of society" (ibid.). Just as "absolute governments, vested in a single person, are overturned", all other social duties are subject "to a wider diffusion" (ibid.).

Consequently, the text suggests that the fact that no "great spirit" has come forth from the mass of society in recent years is not a sign of its weakness, but rather of the growing strength of the collective. Concurrent with the growing importance of the middle classes threatening to replace the elite, the text replaces the extraordinary individual with one which is ordinary to the highest possible degree. The more traditional way of looking at hero worship – which presupposes distance – is further assessed as unsuitable for the present climate, which promotes an ultimate closeness with the hero being part of the collective. The question of distance and proximity between hero and collective then relates back to the different functions of admiration and adoration as stated by Schindler et al. By situating the hero *within* society rather than elevated from it, the aim is rather to enhance the readers' "own agency in upholding ideals"[48] than to present them with a messianic leader figure. The assertion that contemporary society relies on the "crowd of individuals more or less capable" (Hero-Worship, *CJ*, 1 Sep 1849, 129) further emphasises emulation and exemplarity rather than a distant form of adoration of one individual exceptional figure. The hero becomes part of a community rather than being a reference figure outside of it.

The present age is described as "not the age of originality, but appliance; not of theory, but experiment; not of discovery, but invention" (ibid.). In each instance of this enumeration, the former concept is one which has arisen from inspirational individuals and thus might better fit the concept of a messianic hero. Building on the achievements of the past, the text constructs a different form of societal progress that is not dependent on originality: "One man may pioneer; but the route being once pointed out, numbers may enter in, and pass far beyond the discoverer" (ibid.). The text which in the initial paragraph mourned the lack of extraordinary guiding figures in society subsequently turns this very fact into an asset of British society. Being so far advanced in its ideas and discoveries[49] that the execution of these ideas is its new focus, the workforce of society becomes more important than its leaders.[50] Consequently, the assumed inter-

---

48 Schindler et al.: Admiration, p. 86.

49 The text argues that "[i]t [contemporary society] knows more than the greatest of its predecessors, for it begins at the point where they ended". Hero-Worship, *CJ*, 1 Sep 1849, 130.

50 What the article fails to solve is the fact that each workforce needs a job description so that the individual workers of the mass know what their particular task is. Thus, logical thinking would still call for some people to "pioneer". Ibid., p. 129.

regnum is only an "imaginary" one: "in fact, the governing power of mind having reached a new stage of development, is merely distributed among a greater number – it follows that there is a wider scope for individual ambition" (ibid., 130). The article thus dismisses old attitudes towards hero worship which focused solely on the extraordinary individual as a guide for the greater mass of society and instead imagines a society in which heroic qualities are distributed among a larger number of people. The "monarchy of mind" (ibid.) is traded for a sort of efficiency of the working mass which values each individual in its contribution to the collective progress of its age.

Although the text criticises old forms of hero-worship, it is not declared unnecessary as a practice in general. It decidedly dismisses "the hero-worship which shuts our eyes" (ibid.) and "the hero-worship of the past" (ibid.), but through the definite article and the qualifying additions, it is only the specific kinds of hero-worship which are rated obsolete, not hero-worship as a whole. The statement which closes the article affirms this notion that the heroic still exists and is worth noticing in the present day: "there is no interregnum!" (ibid., 131).

The article epitomises how the practice of hero worship is utilised for a social diagnosis. The way in which society relates to heroes and what is expected from them becomes a measurement for society's present state and its relation to the past. This example from the mid-century shows how different notions of the heroic were competing due to societal developments around them. At the same time, the example also shows how traditional concepts are not replaced completely by new ideas, but remain rooted in collective thinking. The assertion that "there is no interregnum" (ibid.) shows a wish to retain continuity with traditional ways of relating to the heroic, but at the same time attempts to reinterpret the location of the heroic within society. Thereby, the article hints at several changes to the heroic in its public negotiation and representation: it acknowledges a need for heroes, however, the personnel of the heroic is changing, the properties of the hero do not remain the same and the societal function of the heroic becomes increasingly fluid.

The issue of worshipping someone as a hero remains a concern in the discussion of the heroic in *CJ* throughout the rest of the century. Contributors try to find a way of determining the appropriate amount of attention heroes should receive and what effect the interaction should have on the worshipping group. On the one hand, they criticise the fact that hard-working men often do not find recognition and are measured against the abstract ideal of "the coming man" whom "all look for" (The "Coming Man", *CJ*, 5 Apr 1851, 216). On the other hand, a different line of criticism, which became more and more pronounced as the century progressed, focused on a counter-phenomenon, namely the increasing glorification of heroes and, metaphorically speaking, "the universal tendency to canonise into a hero every one that rides a horse and robs" (Bushranging Yarns, *CJ*, 20 Sep 1890, 593).

The first line of criticism emphasises the fact that many people have preconceived expectations regarding the properties of a hero which are unrealistic and often cannot be met. In the 1850s and 1860s, these preconceptions are clearly still modelled after the idea of a messianic hero or 'the coming man' as proposed by a number of intellectuals in the first half of the century. The ideal of a coming man, who is extraordinary in all aspects of his being, is not only criticised but ridiculed, with contributors asking: "Is the 'Coming Man' yet born into the world? Is he an unruly brat, squalling for his porridge in some obscure hovel? [...] Supposing him to be arrived at manhood, whether does he flourish a pen or a sword?" (The "Coming Man", *CJ*, 5 Apr 1851, 216). These sentences reveal several preconceptions about a heroic figure for whom society seems to be waiting. First of all, it seems to be common sense that heroism is an innate gift which necessarily has to manifest from childhood onwards already. The profane image of a "brat [...] squalling for his porridge" clearly mocks this notion, declaring it to be unrealistic.

With regards to the recognition of the heroic, the tendency not to value "noble aspirations" (ibid.) is identified as particularly problematic by the author: "It may be argued that, ever since the world began, heroes have had to contend with peculiar difficulties before they established themselves in their respective shrines. Circumstances, however, change with times" (ibid., 217). The changed circumstances here refer to the greater volume of accumulated knowledge and consequently also the heightened stakes for any person to excel.[51] This can be seen both as an advantage, as a living sign of evolution, but also as a problem for any person seeking to have an effect on society as a whole.[52] Thus, the prospective hero who enters the public arena (politics is the chosen field of action in this article) is met with expertise from a number of different sides, the demands of which can hardly be met. To illustrate the obstacles and criticism the 'coming man' would have to overcome, the author poses ironic questions to the prospective hero, such as: "'Have you the constitution of a rhinoceros, the suavity of a courtier, the coolness and imperturbability of an iceberg?'", "'Can you submit to be called a fool, an idiot, a designing demagogue?'", or "'Can you bear to be hissed, laughed at, mimicked, caricatured; to have every action misconstrued; your deeds of benevolence ascribed to systematic bribery and corruption?'"

51 In reference to Thomas Carlyle's *On Heroes*, the author gives the example of Muhammad, one of Carlyle's prime examples to prove that the heroic is above the lines of time and religion. Were a person to do what Muhammad is said to have done, "he would readily find accommodation in Bedlam, and his case would be reported in the morning papers at the rate of three-halfpence a line". The "Coming Man", *CJ*, 5 Apr 1851, 217.

52 The aspect of evolution is exemplified through the antipodes of moral and physical courage. While a contemporary 'coming man' would have to possess the former, physical courage cannot elevate a person anymore: "Thousands of men may be picked up to face a storm of bullets for the poor guerdon of a shilling a day. But that is physical courage, a quality existing in the greatest force among the lower animals." Ibid.

(ibid.). If all those questions were met with a negative response then: "I am sorry to say you are not the 'Coming Man!'" (ibid., 218).

These pointed questions illustrate the text's view on the contemporary situation of public life in Britain: the climate is diagnosed as unfavourable for any person with "generous and noble aspirations" (ibid., 217) to make a career and gain a reputation. All of the questions, of which I have only quoted a selection, point to the fact that any candidate for becoming a hero needs to be, above all, self-denying and full of "moral courage" (ibid.) in order to face the criticism of others.

As the text exemplifies, there still seemed to be a quite specific preconception of what was and was not considered heroic in the middle of the nineteenth century, which demanded from the hero a universal extraordinariness. This resulted in an increased doubt and distrust towards those people entering the public sphere, which still seemed to be regarded the realm of heroes. The climate of a growing market place and its means of publicity seemed to have brought with it a fear of the abuse of public influence. It is striking that in face of these challenges the text demands a moral integrity from a prospective hero figure. Interestingly though, hero worship at this point in time nevertheless seemed to be a normality in people's lives. Although objects of adoration were said to be harder to find, the desire for a guiding figure for the collective good seemed unbroken. Despite the fact that the shift from physical and action-based to a more general moral heroism seemed to have taken place already,[53] the heroic was still firmly rooted in the public sphere as something that was influenced by public opinion and increasingly also the media.

This necessity of a heroic act to be disseminated through a medium and to be brought to public attention lies at the heart of the second strand of criticism regarding hero worship. This type of criticism comes from the opposite end of the spectrum and does not lament the fact that not enough heroes are recognised in society, but that too many heroes are admired. As an article from the year 1863 asserts, the age of the popular hero has arrived and there is only one uniting characteristic of their heroism: "fame" (Popular Heroes, *CJ*, 24 Oct 1863, 264). Otherwise "[t]he heroes themselves are of all sorts and sizes, and of all conceivable degrees of popularity. Some of them are very local as to fame [...]. Others have found their way so often into print as to be spoken of [...] from Bendigo to Blackwall" (ibid.). These "vague stars" (ibid.) could not go through "even a mild cross-examination with the remotest chance of leaving the court 'without a stain upon their character'" (ibid.). Rarely, specific examples of popular heroes of Brit-

[53] As Mary Beth Rose shows, a shift from physical heroism towards a more abstract – and distinctly gendered – heroism of endurance, which focuses on selflessness and the willingness to make sacrifices rather than physical courage can already be observed in the early modern period. Cf. Mary Beth Rose: Gender and Heroism in Early Modern English Literature, Chicago 2002.

ish (contemporary) society are given to the reader. The 1863 article criticises the romanticised notion of highwaymen among the British and gives men like Dick Turpin, Claude Duval or even Robin Hood as examples.[54] What seems to unite the popular heroes on an abstract level, though, is their lawlessness and a closeness to a "great deal of mischief" (ibid., 265). It might be the questioning of formal hierarchies and established order which makes these kinds of heroes attractive to the masses and problematic for the social elite.

However, it is not the fact that these popular heroes are admired despite their unlawfulness which seems to be the main point of criticism, but the fact that heroism, which in the opinion of many contributors to *CJ* should be about private ideals, is increasingly becoming a phenomenon of public honours and fame.[55] This differentiation between internal and external honour is frequently referred to in relation to hero worship. External honour is identified with acts of public recognition and fame and hence with an unfavourable kind of heroism which is motivated by a wish for glory and attention. Internal honour, on the other hand, is propagated as a private guideline which is evaluated as morally good and worthy of emulation.[56] The want for external honour is criticised strongly: "See how the craving for 'honours' as they are called betrays a man into faulty logic and false morality" (A Few Words About Heroes, *CJ*, 4 Oct 1856, 222). This becomes problematic for the contributors because the growing celebrity of heroes, which they consider "the worst of vulgar hero-worship" (Popular Heroes, *CJ*, 24 Oct 1863, 264), in their opinion does not refer to

54 However, the assessment of the men needs to be differentiated: while the heroisation of Duval and Turpin is criticised, Robin Hood is reaffirmed as hero and only the way in which the tales around him are overly romanticised is noted: "there seems to be an undercurrent through them all of the pleasant rustle of green bough, and the patter of deer's feet, as they dash down the glades, and the liquid notes of the mavis and merle, the stage-names of our homey friends the thrush and black-birds, as they carol overhead." Popular Heroes, *CJ*, 24 Oct 1863, 265.

55 I have discussed the idea of external public honours and internal honour elsewhere in greater detail. Whereas the former is "awarded in a public act which involves the active consensus of a group" and entails public forms of attention such as fame, the latter "is an act of private internal recognition of an individual which is *guided* by the rules of a specific group". Christiane Hadamitzky: Public vs. Private Honour. The Precarious Case of Victorian Modest Heroism in Chambers's Journal and The Leisure Hour, in: helden. heroes. héros. E-Journal zu Kulturen des Heroischen, special issue 2, 2016, p. 56. DOI: 10.6094/helden.heroes.heros./2016/QMR/10.

56 A similar distinction between public recognition and private reward can also be detected regarding chivalry. In the context of the medieval revival in nineteenth-century Britain (cf. Mark Girouard: The Return to Camelot. Chivalry and the English Gentleman, New Haven 1981), chivalric figures (especially in the type of the gentleman) were a dominant presence in British popular culture. In *CJ*, the depiction of chivalry is always connected to a notion of pastness. In some instances, the idea of medieval chivalry is criticised as too public and ritualistic and a modern form of chivalry is proposed as a more humble private concept. Cf. True Chivalry, *CJ*, 29 Jun 1850, 416.

achievements or values anymore, but is mostly due to the wide dissemination of stories with popular appeal and sensational potential. Heroes are now a product:

> But is this not the manufacturing age, and is there not a manufacture of heroes as well as of calico and railway bars? I for one am a hero-worshipper, and don't mind avowing the fact; but I have not yet been able to worship manufactured heroes, or to feel any sympathy with those who are always ready to come forward with their testimonial. (A Few Words About Heroes, *CJ*, 4 Oct 1856, 222–223)

With this interpretation of popular heroes as mass products, the function of the heroic changes: while the individual (as opposed to mass manufactured) hero evoked a sympathy in their admirers based on a common moral ground, the manufactured heroes seem to aim for mere sensation and entertainment. Periodicals, as products in the market place, had a commercial interest in publishing what sold best. Thereby, the criticism of the production of heroism is at the same time a criticism of the contemporary media which produce them.

Consequently the most popular heroes, who find "their way so often into print" (Popular Heroes, *CJ*, 24 Oct 1863, 264), are those that the editors and contributors calculate will sell most, not those whom they might consider worth emulating. The diagnosis regarding hero worship in *CJ* is a clear one over the course of the second half of the century: traditional hero worship with a group of people admiring a messiah or prophet figure whom they turn to for guidance is a thing of the past. However, a new, "appropriate" form of hero worship has not yet been found and a tendency towards the extremes can be perceived: either society is reluctant to avow themselves to heroes because of fixed preconceptions which the individual cannot meet, or a mass audience follows popular heroes who no longer perform a social function but are mostly a source of entertainment and sensationalism. Accordingly, the media coverage of historical heroes undergoes a change as well and the private life of historical personalities increasingly becomes the focus of public attention: "How much closer are we drawn to our favourite heroes in biography, when we know how they were loved and reverenced by their nearest relatives" (Stray Thoughts in a Library, *CJ*, 5 Jun 1880, 366).

As a possible solution for this dilemma of hero worship, *CJ* suggests, overtly in a number of meta-heroic reflections and more implicitly in a greater number of texts which will be discussed in later chapters, a turning away from celebrated heroes of history writing, song and literature and towards "unsung heroes" (Unsung Heroes, *CJ*, 27 Jul 1888, 464). It is this humble heroism that has no immediate audience which the magazine establishes as the only 'real' heroism worth worshipping:

> So long as the world and the heart are young,
> Shall deeds of daring and valour be sung;
> And the hand of the poet shall throw the rhyme
> At the feet of the hero of battle-time.

But nobler deeds are done every day
In the world close by, than in fight or fray.
There are heroes whose prowess never sees light,
Far greater than ever was ancient knight.
In many a heart lies a secret tale
That would make the Homeric legends pale:
And oft is a deed of valour untold
Which is meet to be written in letters of gold! (ibid.)

Many texts in *CJ*, as exemplified in this poem, aimed at telling stories of "unsung heroes", which mostly meant fictional heroes who could be contextualised in actual occurrences and historical events. This had the advantage that stories of unknown heroes could not contribute to the fame or celebrity of an actual person but would focus on the audience to "feel [...] sympathy" (A Few Words About Heroes, *CJ*, 4 Oct 1856, 223) for the characters depicted. Through this feeling of sympathy, the social function of the heroic as providing role models was stressed and the moral values and characteristics of the heroic became the focus of attention.

Precarious Heroicity

It has become apparent that *CJ* constructs a heroicity which is desirable and worthy of emulation. However, the periodical also shows cases of presumed heroism which are unworthy of imitation. Bearing in mind that heroism on the whole fulfilled an exemplary role in *CJ*, cases of heroism related to traits deemed undesirable were precarious. The most prominent form of this kind of precarious heroicity is the 'hero of romance'. The vocabulary of the heroic is, in relation to romance, seldom used to describe actions to be imitated by the readers. Nevertheless, the frequent usage of the words 'hero' and 'heroine', not merely as synonyms for protagonists, is striking in the context of romance tales. Like in the examples above, the semantics of heroism are used in these fictional narratives as a signifier for a set of socially established meanings.

In this context, hero, and especially 'hero of romance', often denotes a convention which is limited to fictional texts and appears in and relates to the genre of the novel. The 'hero of romance' is exclusively male and typically denominates a male object of projection for female affection. However, these heroes of romance are characterised by entirely different attributes than the usual heroic personnel in *CJ*. The 'hero of romance' seldom has a moral component but is rather judged by outward appearance, his conduct in society and his gentlemanliness.

This can for example be seen in a passage from the fictional text "Myself and My Relative". The serialised novel by an anonymous author had been advertised in two preceding issues of *CJ*[57]and was published in the journal from early July until late September 1861. In the first instalment, a young girl has just moved from London to the countryside with her family. The rural settlement into which she and her family have moved is populated by farmers whose manual labour is governed by necessity. This stands in stark contrast to the way she describes a young man of the village, whom she adores:

> but one youth particularly struck my fancy: his air was noble; his face beautiful as an ideal vision; his eyes soft, meditative, charming; his fair hair wavy and soft as a girl's; his figure faultless – at least so I thought at my discerning age of ten years. [...] I regarded him as one might have regarded a work of art. He was a poetic passage to me – a glimpse into a higher sphere. I invested him with marvellous attributes, and felt convinced that he would not more think of cheating Mr Horne with his lessons, or of robbing an orchard, than he would dream of flying. It was long before I could find out his name, for I shrank from asking any one respecting it. Having even at that tender age read more than one novel, I knew very well what falling in love was, and I thought I must surely have been in love with my hero, which made me afraid to breathe a word of him to mortal [...]. Strange infatuation! Yet I never dreamed of speaking to the object of my adoration; to think of him was enough. Long did his image remain engraven on my memory. (A Tale, Entitled Myself and My Relative, *CJ*, 6 Jul 1861, 3)

The description given by the young female protagonist remains solely on the surface; she describes his outward appearance but also the effect his looks have on her. Her words aestheticise the young man and make him appear more like "a work of art" (ibid.) than a human being. Although the girl is passive in the actual situation – she watches the boy and dares not talk to him – she is very active in the construction of her hero[58] since it is she who paints the canvas of the "work of art" she perceives. Although she uses his "beautiful" face, his "faultless" figure and his other visible attributes as inspiration, the girl then creates her hero in her fantasy, equips him with "marvellous attributes" and fictitious scenarios in which he acts according to her imagination. Different from the heroism seen above which focused on the similarities between a represented hero and the implied reader, the girl constructs her object of affection *in contrast* to herself and her surroundings. She herself describes her family repeatedly as poor and dreams of a higher social position. This is reflected in the description of the boy, whom she sees as "noble" and "faultless". She interprets the look in his eyes as "soft, meditative, charming" – three characteristics that do not fit the requirements of a farmer's household but rather point to leisure time and idle reflection. She thus constructs him as the embodiment of her dreams of "a higher sphere". The young girl draws further inspiration from literature and the world as represented in the novels she has read also serves as a reference for interpreting her own feelings.

This image of her hero can only be held up by retaining a distance between the object of description and the girl describing him, and thus it is only "his

57 Cf. A Tale, Entitled Myself and My Relative, *CJ*, 15 Jun 1861, 384 and 29 Jun 1861, 416.

58 The protagonist calls the young man "my hero" until she learns his name.

image" which she remembers and which her imaginations are based on. The fact that the protagonist speaks of the boy as "the object of my *adoration*" (emphasis mine) rather than of affection, desire or love underlines the necessity of distance for this notion of heroism as well.[59] The 'hero of romance' as represented in this text is not supposed to be emulated but to be adored from afar. This is for one due to conventions of romance narrative, of which emulation is no part, but is also rooted in the fact that the 'hero of romance' in most cases primarily functions as a space for the projection of the respective female's dreams of an ideal gentleman. As soon as adoring girl and adored young man actually interact, the latter loses his status as an imagined 'hero of romance', since he turns from object of projection into a subject which interferes with the girl's imagination.[60] In keeping the distance, the situation of romantic yearning, closely defined through social conventions and patterns presented in novels, a clear and insurmountable demarcation between the one admiring her hero and the heroic figure is maintained through gender: the 'hero of romance' in *CJ* is necessarily a man and the adoring and imagining subject is always a woman; one cannot take the other's position without violating conventions.

This specific notion of precarious heroicity can be found in many other fictional texts in *CJ* and seems to be stable throughout the second half of the nineteenth century. All the stories are connected through a distance between the female and male protagonists – either self-chosen as in the example above or through circumstance – and a strong female imagination. Kate, the protagonist of the story "Miss Winter's Hero", is, for example, separated from Laurence, the object of her adoration, through social restrictions. Having accompanied her father on a business trip to Scotland, she had immediately fallen for the young writer Laurence, "her hero, her poet" (Miss Winter's Hero, *CJ*, 30 May 1891, 345). However, Kate Winter's father "was an honest, comfortable, matter-of-fact-man of business" but "had never made any pretensions to finer feelings" (ibid., 344). In this manner, he had "expressed himself very freely [about Laurence] this morning, and Kate [resented] it accordingly" (ibid.). Although the young man is described by a local as "idle" and "over head and ears in debt" (ibid.), the young woman still meets Laurence in private and keeps adoring him – because her imagination turns him into a 'hero of romance'. This is illustrated by the first interaction the reader observes between the two, in which Kate relates the stories about him to Laurence but immediately adds that "if the whole world said so, what difference could it make to me? Even if I had never seen you, I should have believed in you from your poems" (ibid.). The reader is already assured through

59 This links up to the considerations of Ines Schindler, Veronika Zink et al. on admiration and adoration discussed before (cf. Schindler et al.: Admiration) and the ambivalent evaluation of hero-worship established in chapter 4.2.

60 This is supported by the fact that the protagonist only calls the young man "my hero" until she learns his name and receives 'actual' information on his life story and character.

Laurence's reaction – "he turned scarlet and white alternately" (ibid.) – that the rumours about him will turn out to be true, but Kate is trapped in her imagination of Laurence. Although the utterance is based on the man's poetry, it is again strongly motivated by Laurence's looks and his "being other" than people in Kate's everyday environment. As she approaches him, the reader sees him through her eyes as follows:

> There was a circular green bench round the staff, and on the bench sat a handsome young fellow in a brown velvet coat. His hair was a little longer than is customary in these close-cropped days; and that, or a certain rapt absent expression, would have stamped him at once as either poet or artist with most people. Kate, looking at him in the full flush of the warm sunset, felt that it was not light privilege even to know such a man; but having known him, that he – refined and cultivated to such a pitch of perfection – should have laid his fortune at her feet, should have counted her worthy to share his future, the fame that coming days were to bring him, passed all belief. (ibid.)

Laurence is described as a clear opposite to the young girl's father. The "matter-of-fact businessman" without "finer feelings" (ibid.) stands in the greatest possible contrast to the romantic young poet whose "absent expression" and "refined" nature do not comply with the world of business Kate is used to from her father. Interestingly, the artistic quality of Laurence is mostly conveyed by his outward features – his too-long hair, his expression, and possibly also the romantic location on a cliff in the "warm sunset" he has chosen for their meeting – rather than by his actual talent of writing, which the reader never gets an opportunity to sample. And although the female protagonist in this case interacts with her hero, her imagination as triggered by the young man's appearance and 'otherness' overshadows her actual experience with him and any doubts are erased by "another of Laurence's smiles" (ibid., 345).[61] In the course of the narrative, Kate elopes with Laurence and it is only by overcoming the distance demanded by her father and in the confined space of a ship that she finally seems to meet Laurence outside of her imagined world. Soon, she finds that her father "was very well justified in his opinion" (ibid., 346) and wishes herself back to him ("'Oh, if I was only at home with my father'", ibid.). Through the encounter (as opposed to the interaction overshadowed by the girl's imagination), Laurence's hero-status is revoked, and he turns into "her sometime hero" (ibid., 247). In line with Max Weber's idea of the routinisation of charisma,[62]

---

[61] Similarly, Mrs Gretton, a character in C. G. Furley's serial novel "The Ring and The Bird", points out that a "hero of romance" is firstly defined by his looks and the way he moves in society, when she states that "[t]he Colonel was not a hero of romance; he was a little, bad-tempered, red-faced man, who bolted his food and snubbed Mrs Gretton's attempts at civility". C. G. Furley: The Ring and the Bird, *CJ*, 7 February 1891, 91. The explicit use of the phrase "hero of romance" in this case also shows that Mrs Gretton's idea of an ideal gentleman is modelled after those she has encountered in romance writing.

[62] Cf. Max Weber: The Theory of Social and Economic Organization, New York 2009 [1947], pp. 363–373.

Laurence's appeal diminishes through proximity and the contact with everyday life.

Although in a different way, the relation between the female protagonist and her hero is shaped by literature in "Miss Winter's Hero" as well. Unlike in other texts, Kate is not described as a reader of novels, but the 'artistic air' she perceives around Laurence is the prime reason for her attraction and the fact that she judges him solely on the basis of his writing ("I should have believed in you from your poems", Miss Winter's Hero, *CJ*, 30 May 1891, 344) shows that she either is used to reading literature or is drawn to it. In relation to romantic imagination, the heroic figure seems to be chiefly – and doubly – informed by (romance) literature. On the one hand, the female characters' objects of fancy seem to be modelled on what they have read in novels; on the other hand, literature as a form of expression and realm of imagination functions as their general inspiration for creating the image of an 'ideal gentleman' in their minds.[63] Especially when paired with their naïveté, the female protagonists' dreaming up of a 'hero of romance' immediately evokes the contemporary discourse on female reading and its effects.[64] The general anxiety about (especially young) women reading has been discussed in detail, and it has been shown that in particular the activity of solitary – and hence not controllable – reading was considered a dangerous activity for young women since the content of the texts was likely to be romantic *and* could possibly stimulate the readers' imagination. As Margaret Beetham puts it, "the central subject matter of nineteenth-century fiction was ro-

63 In the case of "Myself and My Relatives", the connection to romance literature is additionally mirrored in the girl's surrounding since part of her imaginations take place in and around a park which reminds her of the "Gothic" (A Tale, Entitled Myself and My Relatives, *CJ*, 6 Jul 1861, 2). This indirectly relates her imagination to the realm of Gothic fiction which is, apart from its appeal through terror, also chiefly known for its imaginative settings and romantic sub-plots.

64 On this subject see for example Janet Badia et al. (ed.): Reading Women. Literary Figures and Cultural Icons from the Victorian Age to the Present, Toronto 2005; Margaret Beetham: Women and the Consumption of Print, in: Joanne Shattock (ed.): Women and Literature in Britain, 1800–1900, Cambridge 2001, pp. 55–77; Sarah Bilston: "It Is Not What We Read, But How We Read". Maternal Counsel on Girls' Reading Practices in Mid-Victorian Literature, in: Nineteenth-Century Contexts 30.1, 2008, pp. 1–20; Barbara Caine: Victorian Feminists, Oxford 1992; ead.: Feminism, Journalism and Public Debate, in: Joanne Shattock (ed.): Women and Literature in Britain 1800–1900, Cambridge 2001, pp. 99–118; Christina Crosby: The Ends of History. Victorians and "the Woman Question", London 1991; Kate Flint: Reading, Prohibition and Transgression, in: Robert L. Patten: Dickens and Victorian Print Cultures, Surrey 2012, pp. 249–258; Ruth Livesey: Reading for Character. Women Social Reformers and Narratives of the Urban Poor in Late Victorian and Edwardian London, in: Journal of Victorian Culture 9.1, 2004, pp. 43–67; Kenneth Morgan: The Birth of Industrial Britain. 1750–1850, Harlow 2011; Phegley: Woman Reader; Leah Price: How to Do Things with Books in Victorian Britain, Princeton 2013; Valerie Sander: Women, Fiction and the Marketplace, in: Joanne Shattock (ed.): Women and Literature in Britain 1800–1900, Cambridge 2001, pp. 142–161 or Joanne Shattock (ed.): Women and Literature in Britain 1800–1900, Cambridge 2001.

mantic love".[65] This kind of fiction, contemporaries feared, would create and perpetuate a longing in the readers that was feared to not only lead to "day-dreaming",[66] but eventually to undesired actions which would not conform with society's conventions.

Thus, the fictional texts representing the imagined 'heroes of romance' can be seen as both a result of and an answer to the perceived problem of female reading of romance literature. On the one hand, the girls' and young women's perception of their objects of affection seems to be informed by the conventions of romance fiction, on the other hand, the imaginative space of the novel encourages them to use their imagination. The texts thereby acknowledge the growing number of female readers and affirm, and to some extent perpetuate, the patterns of romance literature. At the same time, they can also be seen as an answer to the perceived danger fiction could pose since, on the plot-level, the imagining protagonist and the object of fancy rarely get the happy ending a romance might supply. The heroic status of the male object ends as soon as he turns into a subject and the distance or obstacles between male and female are removed. Going back to the previous examples, Kate Winter has to find out that "her hero, her poet" is indeed only a product of her imagination and although the young protagonist finally meets the object of her youthful adoration again and marries him, it is in a manner which is "sobered, subdued" (Miss Winter's Hero, *CJ*, 30 May 1891, 185) and with the insight that neither her future husband nor she are without flaws, as imagination would have had it in younger years. With the means of plot development, the narratives put the very patterns they themselves employ into perspective and try to show that the 'hero of romance' is only a product of an author's imagination and does not hold up to the 'real world'.[67]

As these examples have shown, the 'hero of romance' is employed with a didactic undertone in *CJ*. The behaviour patterns of social interaction between young women and men might have been applied because they appealed to the

---

65 Margaret Beetham: Women and the Consumption of Print, in: Joanne Shattock (ed.): Women and Literature in Britain, 1800-1900, Cambridge 2001, p. 66.

66 Colin Campbell: The Romantic Ethics and the Spirit of Modern Consumerism, Oxford 1987, p. 26.

67 This clash between a 'real world' and the world of fiction is presented in various texts with an emphasis on the fact that the latter – at least in relation to romantic social interaction – creates female expectations which cannot be met. This can for example also be seen in the text "My Coming Out" in which a girl is allowed to go to a social event. She dreams of getting to know a gentleman similar to the heroes of her novels but is disappointed and spends the entire night talking to a child. Cf. My Coming Out, *CJ*, 15 Dec 1860, 369–371. A further example is the narrative "A Strange Wedding" which again stresses the danger of distance and limited knowledge of the object of adoration and criticises the female protagonist for having "imbibed no doubt from the vast amount of fiction with which she filled her little brain." A Strange Wedding, *CJ*, 28 Aug 1880, 554.

intended readership – especially to girls the same age as the protagonists –[68] but the development of the individual plot lines also make it clear that the pining after a 'model hero' from romance fiction would not lead to a happy ending.

In a strict sense, one cannot speak of heroic *behaviour*; the young men to whom the term 'hero' is applied in this class of fictional texts do not actively contribute to their hero-status, which is assigned to them exclusively by the female protagonists. Thus, a striking tension in terms of gender roles emerges: on the one hand, the texts dealing with 'heroes of romance' allow the female characters an agency which is greater than in any of the texts discussed previously. The women are – within the frame of a fictional narrative – allowed to dream of and imagine whatever they want and to create a 'model hero' for themselves. The men, on the other hand, undergo an objectification, are mainly judged by their outward appearance and act as a projection screen for the women's fantasies. However, although the female as the 'imaginer' creates the respective hero figure in the narratives, they themselves are always outside of the heroic sphere, since they commonly construct 'their hero' as something desirably different from their everyday experience. Although the female characters are seemingly given complete freedom of imagination, the fact that they resort to the patterns and conventions of romance fiction to guide their imagination, and are thus depicted as only craving romance, undermines their agency again.

However, not only girls are shown as being misguided by their imagination and the influence of 'bad' literature. The essay "Boyish Freaks" presents a similar problem for boys who try to imitate – often violent – adventure stories. Having read too many of them, it is feared that they will follow "on a small scale the heroes of the boys' books" (Boyish Freaks, *CJ*, 21 Apr 1888, 252): "he looks with wondering contempt on any calling tamer than that of soldier, hunter, admiral, or pirate, in one of which exciting professions he will distinguish himself before long" (ibid.). One of the examples of the imitation of an undesirable hero figure is a young man who acts on his "romantic ideas" by buying a revolver "without which no hero is genuine" (ibid., 253). He then takes a ship to the Isle of Man to lead the life of a would-be Robinson Crusoe, which results in the death of a large number of sheep through his revolver. Though no human being is hurt through his act of imitation, the text condemns his actions and approves of his arrest (cf. ibid.). Subsequently, anecdotes of robbery, kidnapping and violence are given and especially the fascination of boys with weapons is emphasised of which "[t]he youth who lately provided himself with dagger, revolver, and bowie-knife, and commenced his journey Wild Westward by travelling from London to Liverpool, is another instance of this fascination" (ibid., 254). The undesirability of an attempt to imitate such false heroes is made even clearer by the fact that all of

---

[68] The essay "Beggar My Neighbour" which appeared in *CJ* in August 1861 actually criticises the "modern novel" for depicting characters which are too similar to their readers. Cf. Beggar my Neighbour, *CJ*, 10 Aug 1861, 81–85.

the anecdotes show boys who *fail* in their imitation. Neither is the Isle of Man a deserted island like that of Robinson Crusoe, nor does the journey from London to Liverpool come close to the American settlers' journey towards the Western Frontier. Thus, the adventure stories and their heroes are shown as a male version of the 'hero of romance' which can only exist in the boys' imagination.

On the whole, the examples of fictional heroes who were not deemed worthy of emulation have emerged as examples of precarious heroicity. As such, they represent the negative side of hero-worship in that they lead to a misdirected imitation of a form of heroism which can only exist in a person's imagination and necessarily relies on distance. If transferred to the adoring subject's own life – be it the girls trying to find a hero of romance or the boys trying to imitate the heroes of their adventure books – the heroism becomes destructive and anti-social. Accordingly, *CJ* wanted to provide examples more deserving of emulation for their readership and the following chapters will be concerned with the predominant representation of exemplary heroes and those features of the heroic deemed worth imitating.

4.3 Chambers's Journal*'s Heroic Imaginary*

Much more frequently than texts devoted to the explicit definition of the heroic, articles can be found in *CJ* in which heroism is defined indirectly. Often, a heroic status is attributed to characters in passing. It is often not defined overtly, but evoked through reference to a socially agreed-upon set of qualities which are deemed heroic and can be immediately recalled in the readers' minds without having to explicate them – a heroic imaginary. Heroes emerge as social figures which can both unite a collective imagination[69] and create a community by referencing an abstract set of values.[70] As a means to negotiate and mediate societal values through collective imagination, heroes thus act as constituents of symbolic values.[71] When Habermas describes the imaginary as a "massive background consensus"[72] for a group, this can also be identified in relation to the heroic. In

---

69 Mohr: Männer, p. 210. The German original reads: "[D]ie soziale Figur 'Held' [kann] Imaginäres auf sich bündeln."

70 For the idea of a group identity based on a social imaginary see Benedict Anderson: Imagined Communities. Reflections on the Origin and Spread of Nationalism, London 2006; Cornelius Castoriadis: The Imaginary Institution of Society, Cambridge, MA 1998; Jürgen Habermas: Between Facts and Norms. Contributions to a Discourse Theory of Law and Democracy, Cambridge 1996; Charles Taylor: Modern Social Imaginaries, Durham, NC 2004; id.: A Secular Age, Cambridge, MA 2007; John R. Searle: The Construction of Social Reality, New York 1997 or Claudia Strauss: The Imaginary, in: Anthropological Theory 6.3, 2006, pp. 322–344.

71 Cf. Mohr: Männer, p. 210. The German original reads: "'Helden' haben teil an der Konstituierung und Formierung der symbolischen Ordnungen gesellschaftlichen Zusammenlebens."

72 Habermas: Facts and Norms, p. 22.

the evoking and constant re-evoking of certain values in the context of the vocabulary of the heroic in *CJ*, a heroic imaginary emerges as an agreed-upon notion of extraordinarily exemplary behaviour. The following analyses will show how the moral implications of the heroic and its function for the collective are at the centre of this imaginary.

Three dominant properties of the heroic come up in a large number of texts and seem to point to continuities, transformations, and functions of the heroic. Courage reflects a major change from physical to moral heroism, while selflessness and perseverance mirror a general change in Victorian society and highlight the identificatory function which heroism performs in its use in *CJ*.

Courage

In the context of the heroic in *CJ*, courage is always a relational and social category rather than referring to boldness or pluck. The latter is even discouraged, as can be seen in the article "A Remarkable Rogue" which states about its protagonist at the outset: "It is [the story] of a remarkable man whose acquaintance I made many years ago, one whose abilities and talents, had they been directed aright, might have placed him in a very different position from that in which I met him" (A Remarkable Rogue, *CJ*, 8 Jan 1881, 30). The narrator is referring to a man who makes a living by mere boldness. He feigns having fits when expensive carriages come by or on streets frequented by wealthy men and women. His acting is so convincing that he succeeds in obtaining money or shelter from passers-by each and every time. The text describes the following incident as his most bold act: he had heard of a woman and her children whose husband had deserted them and – "whether at his own expense or not, is not material" (ibid., 31) – had gone to Australia years ago. Knowing that the woman was reasonably well off, he approached her and pretended to be her returned husband. When the woman, who knew it could not be her husband from the mere physicality of the man with his crippled arm and weak posture, accused him of fraud, he "bore all this in silence" (ibid.). He then went on to tell a fantastical story of misery and accidents in Australia and further gave her examples of their previous life together, so that the woman by the end was convinced that he was her lost husband. Though the narrator – as the assessment above shows – has sympathies for the man, his talents are shown as being wasted for one crucial reason: they are selfish. His fearless behaviour is merely for his own benefit and therefore lacks a social or communal function, which denies the man of many "abilities and talents" (ibid., 30) the possibility to be a "hero" (ibid., 31). However, "had he chosen a different walk in life, he might have risen to eminence and honour" (ibid., 32).

Similarly, physical courage is also revalued as a tool which can only become heroic through a moral component. This becomes apparent in a poem on "Chivalry" published in 1862. Over thirteen stanzas of iambs, the poem narrates the actions of a medieval knight who is evoked as a positive example for the present-day reader. The poem opens with a knight who "came at evening-time/Unto a lonely ford" (Chivalry, *CJ*, 9 Aug 1862, 69) where he discovers two impoverished children. In direct speech they ask him for charity "'for Jesus' sake our Lord.' / 'Good sir,' they cried, 'for him who died, / carry us o'er the flood'" (ibid.). The knight himself has no voice in the poem, but the pleas of the children spark his action: reminiscent of Saint Christopher, he lifts them on his horse and carries them through woods and stream, endangering his own life for the sake of the children ("The water lapped against his feet, / And o'er his saddle-bow; / He rode until his charger's mane / Was washing to and fro", ibid.). On the whole, the knight is described as a man of impressive physical strength. The rhyme scheme interestingly does not link the knight's violent actions with each other but links the man's physical and martial elements to other traits:

> His chest was like a mountain bull's
>   And he was strong of arm;
> Upon his face, though seamed and scarred,
>   There was a Sabbath calm;
> He rode a stately destriere,
>   All dappled with the gray;
> And splashed into the shallowing ford,
>   At the closing of the day
>
> A golden statue shone the knight,
>   Wrapped in his golden mail;
> His banner, of the crimson sheen,
>   Blew flapping like a sail. (ibid.)

The very first rhyme ("strong of arm" / "sabbath calm") links the knight's physical strength and his religious belief which – echoing the children's cry for help "'For Jesus' sake our Lord'" – seems to be the motivation for helping the children. Apart from physical courage, he also possesses moral courage and charges into the ford at nightfall without hesitation. The connection between his "golden mail" and the banner "like a sail" further shows that the armoured knight does not act primarily as a destroyer, but as a protector.[73]

After the encounter with the children, which is told over eight stanzas, the following three stanzas inform the reader about the knight's other deeds. Most of them are physical, even violent acts, but all of them are motivated by charity and altruism:

---

[73] Symbolically, the sail turns him into the children's 'ship' which, in line with Christian symbolism, makes him their protector against the stormy waves of evil. His status as a protector is enhanced by the fact that, after bringing them to safety, he does not abandon them but guards "them from wolf and boar / Until the break of day; / And at the dawn he gave them alms, / And sped them on their way." Chivalry, *CJ*, 9 Aug 1862, 69.

He slew the wild thief in his den;
  He freed the ravaged town;
He helped the poor man at the plough,
  And struck his tyrant down.
In at the widow's broken pane,
  He flung the welcome gold;
He sacked the cruel baron's tower,
  And burned the robber's hold.
He never knelt except to God;
  To good men he was meek:
But to the bad, his voice it seemed
  As when the thunders speak. (ibid.)

Apart from the plain fact that he is fighting for the weak against the strong, his actions are reinforced by his Christian motivation. The reference to the knight's voice is especially interesting given that he does not himself speak in the poem. The readers are implicitly linked to the "good men" because the knight's thunderous voice cannot be heard – he is "meek" on a very concrete verbal level.

The last two stanzas of the poem strengthen the knight's association with Christ:

How did he die ! – with back to tree,
  His death-wound in his breast,
With shivered sword still raised to strike,
  And broken lance in rest.
And now he lies upon his tomb,
  Rapt in eternal prayer;
And round him windows jewel-like
  Shine with a radiance fair. (ibid.)

Though the knight is not crucified, the image of crucifixion is evoked in the description: the knight dies standing up, resting on wood, his deadly wound in his breast, the same as the wound with which Christ's death was finally determined. Importantly, the knight does not die hopeless or in surrender, but with raised sword, fighting to the last. The chivalric knight, a traditionally martial military figure, is turned into a Christian martyr in this poem, a notion which is emphasised through the symbolism of light in the last stanza, which not only places him within a church but also surrounds him with a halo-like, bejewelled crown of light.

Although the poem, which stands at the end of this particular issue of *CJ*, tells a story of a distant past, the emphasis on the values behind the knight's action make the narrative relatable. The knight's physical courage is, however, less important than his moral (Christian) motivation for his actions, which the readers could have identified with and aspired to.

As will become apparent in the discussion of the different domains of the heroic in *CJ*, courage is an integral part of the heroic. However, as the example clearly shows, it needs to be aimed towards a higher goal that not only benefits the courageous person.[74] In that respect, the boldness of the imposter is amoral and hence, in the context of *CJ*'s didactic agenda, not worthy of emulation. With a strong focus on morality, courage is in the majority of cases presented as a "heroic [...] presence of mind" (Presence of Mind, *CJ*, 30 Apr 1870, 273). This will become especially pertinent in the representation of acts of lifesaving, which always stressed the courageous readiness to come to the help of another person in distress without regard to the hero's own safety. Similarly, courage in military contexts was considered a self-denying category. The soldiers who are fearlessly going into battle do so for the good of their country and the benefit of the whole population – not because they are daring or adventure-hungry. Consequently, heroic courage in *CJ* may better be described as the fearlessness in action for a communal good. As a result, the virtue of selflessness can be seen as the trait of the heroic which encompasses and exceeds heroic courage.

Selflessness

The centrality of the word selflessness (and other related terms such as self-denial or self-sacrifice) in representations of the heroic in *CJ* can be seen as both a reflection on the social changes in nineteenth-century Britain and a result of the general rationale of the periodical: whereas courage implicates a strong degree of activity and agency (such as saving a life or fighting for one's country in battle), selflessness can be applied to non-practical and everyday actions as well. It is hence a property which can be found in and applied to a greater number of situations and a greater social range of people. In relation to the heroic, a focus on the trait of selflessness in contrast to or complementing courage would have increased the personnel that could be represented on the pages of the magazine and would have brought the realm of heroic conduct closer to *CJ*'s readership. Thus, the identificatory function of the heroic for the intended readership of the journal becomes obvious in the use of selflessness as a heroic attribute.

In this vein, selflessness is presented as an innate human quality in many articles, which can be fostered and cultivated, but is not linked to professional training or social status. Significantly, children feature prominently in these representations and advice is frequently given to parents to encourage selfless behaviour in their children. An essay published in 1851 puts forth the belief that

[74] This is often referred to as "higher courage" or "moral courage" in contrast to a form of courage which centres on the danger of the physical integrity of the courageous person. Cf. for example An Umbrella Eclogue, *CJ*, 7 Nov 1863, 294–296, A Seaside Story, *CJ*, 27 Feb 1858, 129–132, Domestic Help and Hindrances, *CJ*, 9 Dec 1899, 17–21, Moral Without Physical Courage, *CJ*, 24 Feb 1849, 128, The Clyffards of Clyffe, *CJ*, 19 Aug 1865, 516–519, The Proudest Moment of My Life, *CJ*, 4 Jan 1862, 9–12, or True Chivalry, *CJ*, 15 Sep 1866, 416.

human character is innate, and "[c]ircumstances are powerful, but theirs is only a secondary influence in human life: they yield to the internal pressure of the soul" (The Prophetic Thought, *CJ*, 6 Sep 1851, 145). Different from later representations, the author of this piece seems to be convinced that both a positive as well as a negative "prophecy" (ibid.) can be embedded into human character from birth onwards, which will fulfil itself throughout the individual's life. This idea, which might have seemed grim to some readers, is softened slightly through the introduction of a metaphorical 'prophet' in the form of each individual's personal environment which can support or hamper their development. Using examples from classical antiquity, the author states that "[a]ccordingly [according to a child's 'prophecy'] they made the infant Hercules strangle a serpent while yet in his cradle, and tell how bees gave sweetness to the infant lips of Plato" (ibid.); thereby, although limited, a degree of influence on the development of a child's character is assigned to its environment. Transferred to the present day of the reader this would mean that an infant's parents could – once they had recognised the 'prophecy' of their child's future – support or moderate the tendencies they observed (and, for example, cultivate its strength like Hercules or its qualities of persuasion and rhetoric). Hence, the author gives parents a responsibility to observe their children closely and (counter)act according to the character traits they see in them:

> If in our birth we are all big with our future selves, parents at the earliest day should study, learn, and watch the prophetic thought of each of their children. [...] This child is forgiving, that child is vindictive. See what an affectionate nature shines forth in the eyes and looks of that little girl! That boy has the soul of a braggadocio, and that other possesses the self-denial and generosity of a hero. Do not all these qualities require cultivation? Some may be encouraged, others must be restrained; and others again must be counteracted, overcome – nay, eradicated. (ibid., 146)

Strikingly, it is not the children that are supposed to "study, learn", but the parents. They are responsible for recognising the innate tendencies of their children and are also given the duty of dealing with these characteristics accordingly. In binary opposites ("forgiven" – "vindictive", "braggadocio" – "self-denial"), suggestions are given to parents on what to look out for – and what to support and what to suppress, "nay, eradicat[e]".

This responsibility, however, can also be interpreted as an attempt to account for the periodical's intended readership. As the editors intended their publications for an audience ranging from the middle classes to the "poorest labourer in the country" (Editor's Address, *CJ*, 4 Feb 1932, 1), large parts of this anticipated audience would not have possessed a formal education or domestic employees to take care of the education of their children. Although the article's initial claim that a person's innate 'prophecy' will likely be fulfilled can seem rather pessimistic, it also can be read as a positive prediction, especially for the lower ranks of society: if a child shows positive characteristics, the author implicitly ensures its parents that an institutional education might not be necessary for it to get on well in life. The essay asking parents to look for their children's 'prophecy' can thus be read as mirroring the audience's life, in which formal education was an exception and a parent's influence was often the only means of educating a child.

Regarding the heroic, the brief mention of the "self-denial and generosity of a hero" in the essay on "The Prophetic Thought" substantiates two tendencies already observed above. Firstly, the opposition with "braggadocio" (The Prophetic Thought, *CJ*, 6 Sep 1851, 146) takes up the call of the programmatic "What is Heroism" and many other articles in *CJ* for a type of heroism which does not ask for a stage or an audience. Unlike the Spenserian 'Braggadocchio', true heroes are not boastful and do not brag about their achievements. "Self-denial" is at the core of their being a hero, since it is this very quality which prevents them from seeking public recognition. Therefore, the selflessness of heroes ensures the *moral* motivation of their actions and prevents them from being driven by individual craving for recognition and personal gains. Secondly, the excerpt shows the tendency to promote heroism as a means of personal appreciation available to all parts of society. No great deeds are mentioned, but only "self-denial and generosity", resources available to each and every one if they are willing (and "cultivat[e]" and "encourag[e]" those qualities). Heroism is not limited or restricted by financial, professional or social status. Although the specific denotation refers to a boy, the surrounding examples of "forgiving" child and the girl with an "affectionate nature" additionally open the realm of the heroic to boys and girls alike, which stresses the fact that moral heroism is not a male quality but can be ascribed to members of both sexes.[75] The shift of focus towards a moral heroism allows (at least theoretically) for both men and women of all social classes to be similarly heroic. Thus, properties like selflessness allow heroism to transcend the boundaries of gender and class and thereby contribute to the growing tendency of democratisation regarding the heroic.

"The Prophetic Thought" foregrounded the prospects of talented children without formal education. However, as the century progressed, various articles can be found in *CJ* which include heroic selflessness *and* the importance of children's education – both formal and familial. These grow in frequency in the 1880s and can be linked to the Elementary Education Act which – at least theoretically – had made schooling from the age of five to ten compulsory and was

[75] This does, of course, not mean that male and female heroism are equally represented both in frequency and in quality. As the analyses in subsequent chapters will show, moral heroism nevertheless remains distinctly gendered. Although properties such as selflessness or endurance allowed identification by women as well, the majority of heroic figures represented in *CJ* are men.

intended to provide school education regardless of social status and income.[76] For example, "The Art of Fireside Story-Telling" stresses the importance of filling the "intellectual pockets" (The Art of Fireside Story-Telling, *CJ*, 19 Feb 1881, 120) of children as a preparation for their future. As a means of doing so, the author proposes story-telling. The lesson a child can learn through the moral of a story is "far more successful than the direct teaching [...]. Boys will see for themselves the honour and moral courage of their school-boy hero; the girls will be won to imitate the self-sacrifice or constancy of their heroine, when these qualities are hardly named" (ibid., 122–123).[77] In this case, the heroes of narratives act as role models for their audience and the values which they are intended to mediate are "honour", "moral courage", "self-sacrifice" and "constancy". Significantly, these virtues are gendered. Whereas boys should be equipped with "honour" and "courage" which can imply public actions, the more silent and private "self-sacrifice" and "constancy" are assigned to girls. However, selflessness can be seen as a property which connects both boys and girls, since "moral courage" seems to be very close to selflessness. If one takes courage to be the ability to face a situation with no regard to possible dangers and one's personal safety[78], and selflessness as facing a situation with no regards to one's personal safety or gain,[79] courage transferred on a *moral* level and abstracted from practical activities is essentially included within selflessness. Thus, selflessness as a property of the heroic can again be identified as a gender-integrating factor. The difference which remains, however, is that of ascribing public, practical actions to male heroes, whereas female heroics are, even through the allocation of virtues and values, located in a more private sphere with a greater degree of passivity.[80]

---

76 Although school education itself is not commented upon or demanded in the articles, the very fact that articles reflecting on children's education in general become more frequent in the 1880s can be seen as a result of the Education Act.

77 For educational use, a "true story" is considered more effective than "an untrue story". The Art of Fireside Story-Telling, *CJ*, 19 Feb 1881, 121.

78 The *OED* defines "courage" as "that quality of mind which shows itself in facing danger without fear". Courage, in: OED Online, Oxford University Press 2015, www.oed.com/view/Entry/43146?rskey=aDwFNN&result=1#eid, 22 January 2020.

79 The *OED* defines "selfless" as "Having no regard for or thought of self". Selfless, in: OED Online, Oxford University Press, 2015, www.oed.com/view/Entry/175323?redirectedFrom=selfless#eid, 9 April 2015.

80 One exception to this can be seen in the poem "True Chivalry" (*CJ*, 15 Sep 1866, 592) which depicts a young woman performing "hero-deeds" (ibid.) in the public space of a hospital during a cholera epidemic. In her selfless voluntary contribution, she is active, yet her agency is diminished through a stress on passive virtues often marked as female. She is described as "tender, steadfast, meek, and calm", possessing "Pity's priceless balm" and "Sympathy's divinest grace" (ibid.). Furthermore, her achievement is not shown as that of an individual, but rather as that of specific type cast after the prominent example of Florence Nightingale. As a topos, the female nurse – often also in a military context – represented an accepted form of female activity in the form of caretaking (on the representation of nurses in nineteenth century literature see also Brian Abel-Smith: History of the Nursing Profession, London 1960; Tracey Alison Baker: The Figure of the Nurse. Struggles for

"Filling Little Pitchers", an essay on education published in August 1881, takes a similar stance as "The Prophecy of Thought" in that it proposes that all children are born with a certain set of abilities. However, thirty years after the publication of the earlier text, the author of "Filling Little Pitchers" argues for the importance of education (with the children as metaphorical pitchers that need to be filled through schooling) and the impact of heroic models for children to emulate. Here again the target audience of the magazine is reflected strongly in the essay's argumentation and an attempt to valorise manual labour and the working classes can be observed:

> Our little pitchers [...] have diversity of powers, and the great aim must be their perfect, solid preparation for the kind of life for which they are destined. [...] Education is "a building up." It is the discovery and training of the child's gifts, the development of what is good, the casting out of what is evil. And we take it that the labourer's child, who is taught our five *Rs* – Reading, Writing, Arithmetic, Respect, and above all Reverence, and who is also taught the work he is to do, has received as serviceable an education as the heir to a baronetcy who wins the honours of a university career. (Filling Little Pitchers, *CJ*, 20 Aug 1881, 534)

The schooling of the working classes and the instruction in a manual trade ("the work he is to do") is put on a level with the higher education of the upper classes. Importantly, however, the moral education ("Respect", "Reverence" and "the development of what is good") is regarded as even more important than elementary learning. In stark contrast to the 1851 article, the author seems to take for granted that even a "labourer's child" learns "Reading, Writing, Arithmetic"; schooling of the working classes by now seems an accepted fact. However, the performance in these subjects is considered of lesser significance than the moral instruction which a child receives:

> See that girl, who promises to make some day the angel of home, a woman full of kindly helpfulness and sweetness, and capable of the heroism of self-sacrifice – the commonplace girl who tried Latin three times and could not get past the declensions; and whose chief musical qualifications find an outlet in humming her baby-brother to sleep. (ibid.)

Wholeness in the Novels of Jane Austen, Anne, Charlotte, Emily Bronte, and George Eliot, in: Dissertation Abstracts International 46.2, 1985, pp. 427a–428a; Edward H. Cohen: Henley Among the Nightingales, in: Nineteenth-Century Studies 8, 1994, pp. 23–43; Kevin J. Hayes: Maggie in the Hospital, in: Notes and Queries 61.259, 2014, pp. 582–583; Catherine Anne Judd: Hygienic Aesthetics. Sick Nursing and Social Reform in the Victorian Novel 1845–1880, in: Dissertation Abstracts International 53.10, 1993, pp. 3537a–3537a; Bronwyn Rivers: Reforming the Angel. Morality, Language and Mid-Victorian Nursing Heroines, Australasian Victorian Studies Journal 8, 2002, pp. 60–76; Keaghan Kane Turner: In Perfect Sympathy. Representations of Nursing in New Woman Fiction, in: Dissertation Abstracts International, 68.4, 2007, pp. 1472a–1472a or Arlene Young: "Entirely a Woman's Question". Class, Gender, and the Victorian Nurse, in: Journal of Victorian Culture 13.1, 2008, pp. 18–41.

Although the girl's school education is not doubted or regarded as unnecessary, the focus lies on the development of her moral qualities and those character traits regarded desirable for Victorian women: kindness, helpfulness and sweetness. Interestingly, it is these qualities which in her future will make her eligible for "heroism of self-sacrifice" as a validation for her domestic life. Additionally, the example of the girl who is heading for a life as a mother and wife in the private realm of the household shows how selflessness, as a property of the heroic, makes heroism applicable to many members of society who did not stand in the limelight of heroic concepts due to their lack of public visibility.

Progressing from the education and moral heroism of children[81] to the selflessness of adults, those articles in *CJ* which assign selflessness a central position in the heroic imaginary also show the range of applicability of selflessness and self-sacrifice to a broad spectrum of situations, contexts and players. Professional, public as well as private acts of heroism are presented to the reader and considered equally heroic. Through the foregrounding of the different properties of heroic conduct, all professions (and non-professions) are potentially included in the heroic sphere.[82] This includes acts of life-saving, in which selflessness is again used as a term which includes and even exceeds the term courage. This can be seen in the article "A Hospital Hero", in which a surgeon, though sick and weak himself, goes out onto a hospital's slippery roof to help a patient suffering from mental illness who climbed out there (cf. A Hospital Hero, *CJ*, 25 Jun 1859, 144–145). The "hero" (ibid., 144) is contrasted to two other doctors who only witness the scene. While watching the rescue, they discuss the fact that they would not have gone out on the roof to help the patient because they could have been held accountable if something had happened to the patient in their presence on the roof. Thus, the surgeon's selflessness is emphasised through the selfishness of the other doctors. More importantly, the narrative points to the fact that any act of selflessness is always performed in relation to another self. In order to do something regardless of one's own benefit, it is necessarily done for the benefit of another. The courage of the surgeon in that light does not consist in his going out on the roof and facing the danger of a fall, but in putting the patient's safety before his own, in acting according to another rather than to himself.

---

81 The articles discussed above are a sample of a whole range of articles which show children as heroic due to their high morality. I have selected them due to their foregrounding of education; other examples, in which children are regarded heroic because of their moral integrity and/or deeds they performed because of their selflessness include: The Fairy Queen, *CJ*, 11 Jan 1851, 19–22, Eliza Warick, *CJ*, 12 Dec 1874, 785–787, Little Heroes, *CJ*, 12 Dec 1882, 806–807, Won – not Wooed, *CJ*, 11 Feb 1871, 82–87 and 18 Feb 1871, 102–107, or Heroes of Peace, *CJ*, 6 Jun 1885, 353–355.

82 As will be shown in Chapter 4.6, a strong focus on certain professions can be observed with regard to the working classes. Especially the communal aspect of men loyally working together, for example in mines, is stressed.

This 'other' is especially foregrounded in texts which label female acts of selflessness heroic. In most cases, these articles are set in the domestic sphere and describe women who devote their life to their husband, children and home. An 1884 article explores the question "What are heroines after all?" (Heroines, *CJ*, 2 Aug 1884, 492) and comes to the conclusion that modern heroines are the self-sacrificing housewives who lead a seemingly "uneventful life" (ibid., 494): "if it be objected that the heroic means something greatly above the ordinary level, we would answer, that their whole life is above the level; that the essence of heroism – sacrifice – has become to them an unconsciously acting second nature, and that all that is life-long, surely is great" (ibid., 494). Mirroring the contemporary unease regarding women in public, this kind of domestic heroism, which is described as "homely, easy, and attainable for all" (ibid., 493), is depicted as (the only acceptable) possibility for both female activity and female heroics. Throughout the article, the heroism of the housewife is contrasted with other professional fields and occupations such as politics, intellectual life, literature and charity,[83] all of which are deemed unfitting for a true heroine because they are both too visible and imply the possibility of public attention and recognition, which can too easily lead to a lust for fame. By putting the everyday life of domesticity at the centre and presenting selflessness as its key characteristic, an attempt is made to validate the lifestyle of the average woman through the semantics of heroism.

This ideal of the silent, domestic life of the female members of society is also implied in the texts cited about children's education and is – in combination with the vocabulary of the heroic – perpetuated in several other articles in *CJ*.[84] By giving the ordinary, uneventful life a more adventurous and appealing sound, being a housewife is depicted as the only possible and most rewarding profession for girls and women. Significantly, this is done at a time at which the women's rights movement was already active[85] and therefore this danger to societal stabil-

---

83 Remarkably, even charity is seen as too public by the text. This will be explored in more detail in relation to the heroisation of female domesticity in chapter 4.6.

84 Other examples are The Professor's Wife, *CJ*, 26 May 1860, 326–330, Female Heroism, *CJ*, 12 Aug 1848, 108–110 or A Heroine at the Diggings, *CJ*, 29 Aug 1874, 560.

85 Especially noteworthy in this context is the Langham Place Group which operated as early as 1859 and, with members such as Helen Blackburn, Maria Rye or Emily Davies, was very public in voicing their opinion (in events as well as in their own print organs such as the *English Woman's Journal* (1858–1864)). For detailed information on the early Women's Rights Movement see for example Barbara Caine: English Feminism 1780–1980, Oxford 1997; Susan Kingsley Kent: Sex and Suffrage in Britain 1860–1914, Princeton 1987 or Melanie Phillips: The Ascent of Woman. A History of the Suffragette Movement and the Ideas Behind It, London 2004. For the Langham Place Group and its publications see Sheila Herstein: The Langham Place Circle and Feminist Periodicals of the 1860s, in: Victorian Periodicals Review 26.1, 1993, pp. 24–27; Jane Rendall: Langham Place Group, in: Lawrence Goldman (ed.): Oxford Dictionary of National Biography, 2015, DOI: 10.1093/ref:odnb/93708 or Solveig C. Robinson: "Amazed at Our Success". The Langham Place

ity will have been perceived as the implied counter image in the text by contemporary readers.

In general, selflessness as part of the heroic imaginary seems to be most frequently applied to those members of society who are left out by other concepts of heroism, which, for example, foreground physical courage rather than the more abstract moral selflessness. Thus, male self-denial is often related to acts of lifesaving and thus rooted in the discourse of everyday heroism often attributed to members of the working classes. However, as the broad range of applicability has shown, almost all areas of social interaction (in which a 'self' can stand back for or act for the benefit of an 'other') can be included in the heroic realm by stressing the property of selflessness – domestic life, education, children's play, the professional lives of doctors, teachers or miners. Even sport is given as a playing field for heroic selflessness in one article: a "heroic little" boy – within the narrative the "scapegrace" of the family – casts himself between the ball and an opposing player to save the game (The Family Scapegrace, *CJ*, 12 Jan 1861, 25). This example not only shows the scope to which the broad usage of the heroic imaginary exemplified through selflessness can be applied. Through the double terming of the boy as both the family's "scapegrace" and a hero, it also emphasises that selfless behaviour offers an entrance into the heroic realm to exactly those members of society who might be marginalised in the public perception – children, women, uneducated people of the lower classes.

The centrality of selflessness for the heroic imaginary points to the moral function of heroism. Heroes, as implied in the texts discussed above, are persons (male, female, adult or child) with a cultivated and educated morality, who do not look for their own benefit but act according to their moral codex without regarding their own safety or looking for the best possible outcome for themselves. In that way, selflessness anticipates and includes the virtue of courage and allows for heroism in all kinds of situations and environments, both public and private, active and passive. As a heroic attribute, it allows for heroism to transcend class and gender boundaries. Despite this broad applicability, the selfless hero always needs an external reference point which is regarded higher than one's own interests in a given circumstance. This might be valuing another's safety higher than one's own in a moment of danger or motherly devotion to husband and children. In the medium of the magazine, narratives of selflessness perform a didactic function and are used to create role models for the readers, heroic figures which they can emulate and also easily identify with. Even if the examples given do not exactly resemble the life of the readers, the virtue of selflessness, which is always presented as non-class specific, gives every reader the opportunity to partake in the heroic realm. This does, however, also have a so-

Editors and the Emergence of a Feminist Critical Tradition, Victorian Periodicals Review 29.2, 1996, pp. 159–172.

cially problematic side: although the narratives of heroic selflessness depict a heroism independent of gender and class and most importantly regardless of public visibility, the promotion of these invisible selfless acts as acts of heroism aim at maintaining the existing societal status of invisibility of specific groups and members of society. This is especially pertinent with regard to gender roles, since, for example, selfless women devoting their lives heroically to their husband and children are represented in this form of heroism in the public space of the periodical – while the individual women it addresses remain invisible, though.

Perseverance

The third property which surfaces in a great number of articles in the context of the heroic is perseverance. Similar to selflessness, it is primarily utilised in didactic contexts and is strongly linked to the contemporary movement of self-improvement and individual progress. However, perseverance as a heroic trait in *CJ* is always used with a social function in mind and for either the common good or the benefit of a specific group. As in the examples given in Samuel Smiles's *Self-Help*, which promoted personal improvement through untiring perseverance in order to contribute to the progress of society as a whole, perseverance in articles in *CJ* is often described as the individual – heroic – work for a greater good.

Accordingly, many articles which foreground perseverance are stories of progress and improvement in the vein of Smiles, and often this dedication and endurance is deemed heroic. The essay "Scrambles Up the Hill of Life" traces several such – fictitious – stories of improvement and shows examples of those men who "snapped the chains which in early life held them in poverty or obscurity, and by sheer perseverance have borne down opposing agencies, reaching in course of time the coveted goal of competency and distinction" (Scrambles Up the Hill of Life, *CJ*, 23 Apr 1881, 267). In a description reminiscent of the articles on children's education, the author explains that each "hero" whose example he gives has reached their position "by the force of his native character" (ibid., 268). Strikingly, these two short quotes also support two points made in relation to selflessness: firstly, that it is the cultivation of the men's innate abilities which allows them to progress in a way which is considered heroic, and secondly, the "early life [...] in poverty and obscurity" points to the tension between heroism and visibility and illustrates how social status and public recognition are linked. In its effort to redefine the heroic as a moral mind-set, *CJ* exhibits an effort to validate those members of society who – in other media – are kept in "obscurity" by including them into the realm of heroism.[86] Unlike the examples given above, "Scrambles Up the Hill of Life" presents the reader with men (women are not mentioned in the article) that have left the invisibility of their early social condition and have moved up "the hill of life" (ibid.). What is deemed heroic, however, is not that later social recognition, of – for example – one man later being "ranked with the sober, industrious, and useful inhabitants of a flourishing seaport town" (ibid.), but the way in which he came into that position. Perseverance is a property which often entails a heroic transformation. Unlike chivalry or selflessness, the persevering heroes need a goal towards which they are working, and it is not the accomplishment which makes them heroic, but the journey that took them there and the sufferings it caused them.[87]

Keeping in mind the observations regarding human progress and the heroic by Samuel Smiles, it is not surprising that a review of his *Industrial Biography* in 1864 emphasises the importance of perseverance. Though most of the review concerns itself with the hard subject matter of British iron works in general, it also turns to the biographies of some of the "industrial magnates" (The Age of Iron, *CJ*, 20 Aug 1864, 536). Significantly, the text presents those men who had to work hard for their privileged position, such as "Mr Nasmyth [...] [who] began his industrial career in an attic, with an income of ten shillings a week" (ibid.) or William Fairbairn who started out as a "lad, penniless, hungry" (ibid.). Yet the men have made something of themselves, have grown in "true heroic proportions" (ibid.) because they did not give up and pursued their goals with determination and untiring energy.

Similarly, a short report which quotes a lecture on temperance and the working classes praises "those heroic peasants" who have – through hard persevering work – risen from their humble circumstances and climbed the social ladder. Hereby, the importance of education and especially the *desire* to educate oneself is stressed: "many individuals of the working-classes [...] [have] by self-education, attained not merely a large amount of knowledge, but a high degree of mental cultivation and refinement" (Cultivation of Mind Amongst Artizans, *CJ*, 25 Jan 1851, 64). The act of self-education among the working classes is thus not a mere acquisition of knowledge, but more importantly a *moral* education as

86 As has been commented upon, this method reflects the social circumstances and might also criticise them occasionally; in the long run, its heroisation strategy however rather stabilises than changes the described system.

87 Another example of this is the "Story of a Dramatist" which narrates the social ascent and descent of an impoverished playwright said to be the son of Louis Quinze and "the young orphan daughter of the Count d'Archambaud". Story of a Dramatist, *CJ*, 26 Jul 1851, 63. The narration finds its hero in a young general who used to work as his servant in the playwright's better days. His moral heroism is twofold: on the one hand, he is praised for having worked his way up the social ladder by perseverance and determination, on the other hand for loyally concerning himself with the fate of his former master. Contrasted by the descent of the dramatist from his upper-class background, the former servant's ascent through perseverance is highlighted.

well. Due to the fact that the educational effort of the "artizans" necessarily has to happen in the few hours of leisure time they possess, the act is in itself presented as an example of perseverance in the face of adverse conditions.

Furthermore, perseverance is often mentioned in the context of worker's lives and their untiring, physically exhausting labour.[88] But it can as easily be applied to the actress Sarah Siddons, who is reported as heroically making the persevering attempt at improving her acting skills for the pleasure of her audience (cf. The Kembles, *CJ*, 11 Nov 1871, 717–720). Significantly, both of the examples show the ultimate goal of the act of perseverance to be a social one; Sarah Siddons wants to increase the pleasure of her audience, and the workers' contribution to the industrial economy "affect[s] the lives of the people [more] than all the acts of statesmen from Magna Charta to the present day" (Lamp Oils, *CJ*, 10 Jun 1891, 389). Thus the contribution to some form of collective benefit is essential to the conception of persevering heroes. With these prerequisites – hard work towards a goal which not only benefits oneself – perseverance as part of the heroic imaginary can be ascribed to all parts of society, to the publicly prominent such as Siddons, as well as to less visible figures.

This can be seen in the article entitled "The Ugly Duckling Theory": the author instructs the reader to "[n]ever when rubbing shoulders with the unprosperous, to forget that success may await them in the future, is a golden rule" (The Ugly Duckling Theory, CJ, 15 Jan 1881, 46). Framed by the narrative of a school reunion, the author gives different examples of successful men whom he and his fellow class mates used to bully as boys, because they were poor ("he was of low birth", ibid., 47), not clever enough ("he had no virtues that we knew of", ibid.) or of non-Christian faith ("he was a Jew", ibid., 48). All of these characters, marginal by class or religion, are then shown at the reunion as having worked hard and come into respectable positions with a social implication: one of them has become a teacher, thus exerting his influence on the next generation and another – after being rejected thrice – joined the army to fight for his country. The three-time rejection of the later military man then again points to the fact that perseverance as depicted in *CJ* entails hardship and possible frustration.

Whereas male examples of perseverance often show this property in the realm of professional life and are praised for having worked hard on their career and bettering their personal situation and that of their families, perseverance is in some instances also applied to women. Once again, their untiring efforts are restricted to the private realm in *CJ* and the goals towards which they are working perseveringly are usually the happiness of the family and the maintenance of domestic integrity. These goals are, interestingly, not ones which can be reached so that female endurance, as for example in the constant efforts of women to exert

[88] Some further examples include What to Do in the Meantime, *CJ*, 6 Dec 1851, Lamp Oils *CJ*, 10 Jun 1891, 389–391 or Livingstonia Mission and Central Africa, *CJ*, 6 Jan 1900, 90–93.

the best possible influence on husband and children, is a continuous process with no definite ending.[89] Fittingly, perseverance is without exception paired with selflessness in the representation of women in the heroic imaginary.

Perseverance as a property of the heroic imaginary, similar to selflessness, can primarily be seen as a property which performs a social function. With its necessity of a clear goal – be it the improvement of one's professional life, the contribution to industrial progress or the securing of domestic happiness – it combines an individual progress with a collective one. In its broad applicability it also includes marginalised groups into the heroic sphere and the texts can – like Samuel Smiles' instructional biographies – be read as motivational texts for the intended readership.

The examination of the heroic imaginary through three of its most prominent properties – courage, selflessness and perseverance – has advocated the shift from a more physical, action-bound heroism of an unspecified past towards a heroisation of moral character traits. This trend, which could also be observed in the articles which explicitly dealt with and defined heroism and hero worship, on a functional level allows for a greater applicability of the heroic to a larger group of members of society. By foregrounding properties which are either considered desirable or are part of the everyday life of many people, each and every reader regardless of his or her age, gender or social position can become part of the heroic imaginary in the public sphere of *CJ*. Accordingly, the 'heroic personnel' of the material analysed belongs in large parts to the middle and working classes and therefore represents the intended audience of the magazine. By emphasising traits which are not necessarily linked to public and/or physical and practical action, members of different generations and both men and women are represented as heroic. In stressing the social function of the heroic, especially through the traits of selflessness and perseverance, the heroic is not only used as a motivational and educational means for the intended audience, but as a reminder of each individual's responsibility for others and obligation within the social collective. The tension between public recognition of the heroic and a call for the modesty of the hero, between publicity and invisibility remains present and unresolved in regard to the heroic imaginary. The fact that articles evoking the heroic imaginary almost exclusively deal with fictional stories and anecdotes can be read as an attempt of *CJ* not to itself become part of the machinery which produces fame and glory, which it considered amoral. Even within essays, the examples used for conduct deemed heroic and worthy of imitation are never historical examples but fictitious ones.

---

[89] This is only different in cases in which women show physical endurance (for example in the narrative A Homely Heroine, *CJ*, 31 Jan 1874, 65–68 or The True Amazon, *CJ*, 25 Jun 1859, 416); in these cases, however, the effort is nevertheless motivated by social factors and the desire for domestic integrity.

The material in *CJ* which I have subsumed under the idea of a heroic imaginary shows, after a closer examination, a strong tendency towards the idea of exemplary heroism as understood by Cubitt. By presenting examples of lives with which the readers can identify, the contributors, in the public sphere of the periodical, evoked a set of values which were shared by the consumers and thereby created a common identity. In presenting mostly community-oriented ideals such as selflessness and perseverance, *CJ*'s heroic imaginary acts chiefly as an archive or reservoir for the preservation of socially acceptable behaviour and the promotion of individual progress in order to maintain the status quo rather than to utilise its potential for social transformation.

4.4 Military Heroism

Although technological innovations, urbanisation, political reform, class conflicts and religious insecurities and the transformations these entailed are – and rightly so – at the centre of many interpretations of the Victorian age, militarism and public attitudes towards it also underwent crucial changes over the course of the nineteenth century. Militarism and war were topics under critical examination throughout the decades and, especially in the context of the British Empire, changing attitudes in British society can be perceived. Further, it is not surprising that the discussion of militarism in the media often resorts to the vocabulary of the heroic.

When Queen Victoria ascended the throne, the Battle of Waterloo was more than twenty years in the past. Nevertheless, the Napoleonic Wars' length, human and financial expenditure had left a strong imprint on British memory for the time to come. Despite the stronger domestic focus that shaped politics throughout the period, militarism and the memory of the war against France were a fascination for many people. The experience of the war was kept alive in a great number of biographies, histories, literary works and lectures[90] and monuments such as the Nelson Column, which was erected in Trafalgar Square in 1843, were public reminders of the war and Britain's successful role in it. After the Duke of Wellington's death, almost a quarter of a million people came to pay their respects in front of the coffin and more than a million people lined the streets on his funeral day.[91] After 1815, Britain saw almost forty years of peace in Europe and conducted wars predominantly in colonial context.

---

90 In this context, texts like Carlyle's *On Heroes* and his use of Napoleon as an example for heroic conduct can be seen as a commemoration of the Napoleonic Wars as well.

91 Train schedules had been altered and additional trains added to bring people from all over the country to London for the funeral and even ships "due to sail to Australia that week, would 'In consequence of the request of many of the passenger … not leave the East India Docks until after the day of the funeral of the Duke of Wellington'". Judith Flanders: The Victorian City. Everyday Life in Dickens' London, London 2012, p. 338. Flanders argues

Though the mid-century revival of chivalry can be seen as an attraction to militarism,[92] peace movements were on the rise and the Peace Society, founded in 1816 as a distributor of moral tracts, turned into "a political pressure group"[93] by the 1830s. As Spiers argues, the movement's leaders acted on "the assumption that only the ruling classes wanted war, and that 'the people' would rally in support of peace."[94] However, as Martin Ceadel shows in his study *The Origins of War Prevention*, "peace thinking faced four setbacks from the autumn of 1851 onwards, caused by both domestic and international factors".[95] He identifies the Kossuth's tour of Britain in 1851, Louis Napoleon's *coup d'état* and his taking on the title of Emperor Napoleon III, and finally the Eastern Question and its culmination in the Crimean War as crucial events.

The Crimean War, Britain's first major war effort after the Napoleonic Wars "absorbed the attention of the newspaper-reading public"[96] and contradicted the assumption that the common people would not support a war. Generally considered as the first media-war in British history, the public was able to follow the war action almost in real-time. For the first time, war correspondents were working close to the front in large numbers and the technological advances made it possible for their accounts to travel to the British public very quickly. However, this near real-time depiction of the war actions not only sparked enthusiasm, but also resulted in a concern for the welfare of the troops, as the reports from the front, especially the famous reports of William Howard Russell for *The Times*, provided a realistic account of the battlefield and the poor conditions under which the ordinary soldiers had to live. This brought attention to the file-and-rank soldiers and, rather than to a criticism of war in general, led to a solidarisation and support of the troops.[97] For the first time, as Olive Anderson argues, the "troops were hailed as 'the people's army', and idealized notions of

convincingly that, though the funeral was an "extravaganza" (ibid., p. 339), most of the visitors were not primarily concerned with the spectacle but wanted to mourn and remember "the man himself." Ibid., p. 345.

92 Significantly, the popularity of chivalrous ideals does not necessarily contradict the growing struggle to morally justify war: with its centrality of gentlemanliness, chivalrous militarism was, as Mark Girouard has argued, a humane form of war which "softened its potential barbarity by putting it into the hands of men committed to high standards of behaviour". Girouard: Chivalry, p. 16.

93 Edward Spiers: War, in: Francis O'Gorman (ed.): The Cambridge Companion to Victorian Culture, Cambridge 2010, p. 85.

94 Ibid.

95 Martin Ceadel: The Origins of War Prevention. The British Peace Movement and International Relations 1730–1854, Oxford 1996, p. 470.

96 Spiers: War, p. 86.

97 As John Reed notes, "the war was immensely popular with the greater part of the population, being regarded as a just war, Tennyson's allusion to the Crimean War in *Maud* (1855) as a redemptive action morally contrasting with the degrading commercialism prevalent in Britain, and by implication, western culture generally, was characteristic of public sentiment. This public support soon turned to outrage, however, when stories about conditions

what they were fighting for, together with unparalleled public identification with their hardships before Sebastopol, combined to give them an immense emotional appeal".[98]

This shift of focus onto the suffering of the soldiers for their country in combination with the intensified colonial aspirations of the British finally led to the newly formed idea of a 'Christian soldier'. Not only was he – in the context of the Empire – seen as a soldier who defended Christianity, but he also epitomised altruism and kindness, much in the way that the classical ideal of the chivalrous knight, fighting for the good of the people, did.[99] As the century progressed, this idea resulted in a large-scale support of the many 'little wars', as the wars for British control over their imperial territories were commonly described. Many of them lasted only a short time, such as the Anglo-Zulu War in 1879 with less than six months, or the three-month Anglo-Boer conflict in 1880/81, which resulted in a British defeat that increased public anxiety and support of the second Anglo-Boer War in 1899–1902. These wars, significantly, were not only perceived as conflicts threatening Britain's economic supremacy, but also its religious and cultural superiority as a colonial power.[100] As MacKenzie has argued, the colonial wars "fitted perfectly a number of cultural and literary traditions of the period – the enthusiasm for knightly virtues, the adventure tradition of heightened

at the front began to circulate." John R. Reed: The Army and Navy in 19th-Century British Literature, New York 2011, p. 312. J. B. Conacher shows that political action was taken with a close eye on public opinion about the war. Especially Secretary of Foreign Affairs Clarendon "was always concerned about it". James B. Conacher: Britain and the Crimea 1855–56. Problems of War and Peace, Basingstoke 1987, p. 175. He further notes that "Claredon's apprehensions about English public opinion were not without some foundation. *The Times* correspondent in Paris reporting on 16 December [1855] on the rumours of peace overtures being made through Vienna, commented: 'It is well known at St. Petersburg as it is at Vienna what the feelings of the English people are on the war. It is no secret ... that England is determined to make no imperfect peace ... And it is known at Vienna quite as well at it is in Paris and London, that to-morrow Lord Palmerston would have much more chance of being supported by the English Parliament in his demand for men and money to carry on the war than he would when laying on the table the propositions for peace.'" Ibid., p. 163.

98 Olive Anderson: The Growth of Christian Militarism in Mid-Victorian Britain, in: The English Historical Review 86.338, 1971, p. 46.

99 For many contemporaries, General Gordon epitomised the ideals of a Christian military man; Spiers argues that as "[a] deeply religious man, he [Gordon] earned accolades as a Christian soldier after confronting the Taiping rebellion in China and the slavers in the Sudan." Spiers: War, p. 92. For a more detailed account of the emergence of the Christian soldier see Anderson: Christian Militarism, who traces the origins of the type from the 1850s onwards. In the imperial context, J. A. Mangan also relates the idea of a 'muscular Christianity' to the importance of athleticism in upper- and middle-class Britain which, he argues, contributed to the construction of "inspirational stereotypes embodying self-sacrificing service, personifying national nobility, justifying the grandeur of imperialism". J. A. Mangan: "Muscular, militaristic and manly". The British Middle-Class Hero as Moral Messenger, in: The International Journal of the History of Sport 13.1, 1996, p. 44.

100 Cf. Anderson: Christian Militarism, p. 72.

moral absolutes, a fascination with individual heroic action in the service of the state".[101]

The Second Anglo-Boer War "was much closer in nature to the all-embracing total wars that occurred in the twentieth century. Thus, the second Boer war pulled the civilian population into the conflict through the employment of tactics such as scorched earth and concentration camps." [102] Also, this "last great [...] imperial war"[103] was the first to employ propaganda on a large scale to direct public opinion.[104] This was deemed necessary as the new way of fighting a war, and especially the descriptions of concentration camps caused an increasingly negative attitude towards the war amongst the public as the years went by. As Pakenham summarises, the second Boer War "proved to be the longest (two and three-quarter years), the costliest (over £200 million), the bloodiest (at least twenty-two thousand British, twenty-five thousand Boer and twelve thousand African lives) and the most humiliating war for Britain between 1815 and 1914".[105] This last war of the era then truly marks the transition to the twentieth century: as Patricia Morton argues, it can be seen as the last British war, in which "Victorian faith that military success was ultimately assured by the traditional moral virtues of heroism and 'character'"[106] could still be seen, a faith which "died [...] in the trenches of World War I".[107] However, with its enormous effect on domestic and European politics (it damaged the Unionist Government and fuelled the growing Anglo-German opposition) and, as a milestone in the growth of anti-imperialism, it marks the crisis of the Empire as the Victorian age ended.

As a topic of national consequence, which was often emotionally charged in public opinion, it is not surprising that war and the military were a recurring topic in *CJ* and also discussed in the vocabulary of the heroic. The following section will examine the depiction of military heroism in the specific context of war and peace and how changing public attitudes towards militarism were reflected in the pages of the publication. Given its moral didactic orientation, *CJ* in general professed a peace-oriented attitude; however, as the following will show, the publication needed to negotiate this orientation in times of war. The political context of publication acted as a regulatory measure on the depiction of military heroism in the periodical.

---

101 John M. MacKenzie: Popular Imperialism and the Military 1850–1950, Manchester 1992, p. 3.

102 David Smurthwaite: The Boer War 1899–1902, London 1999, p. 9.

103 Thomas Pakenham: The Boer War, London 1980, p. xv.

104 Cf. Nicholas John Cull et al. (eds.): Propaganda and Mass Persuasion. A Historical Encyclopedia 1500 to the Present, Santa Barbara 2003, p. 12–13.

105 Pakenham: Boer War, p. xv.

106 Patricia Morton: Wars and Military Engagements, in: Sally Mitchell (ed.): Victorian Britain. An Encyclopedia, New York 1988, p. 845.

107 Ibid.

"She Is Waiting the Return of Her Hero" – Representation of Military Heroism During War Time

When examining the representation of military heroism in *CJ*, significant variations in the evaluation of military acts become apparent. The military profession and heroisation of soldierly actions in *CJ* are fundamentally different in times of war as compared to periods of peace. This becomes obvious when looking at material shortly before the Crimean War and during the British involvement in the campaign.

In February 1854, an article entitled "The Ideal and Real, Afloat and Ashore" tries to de-mystify the profession of navy sailors and starts by stating that:

> Long before we had ever seen the ocean, we had an exceedingly vivid ideal of the men who battle with its stormy waves; and this ideal is, we more than suspect, cherished not merely by school-boys, but by a large majority of all individuals whose avocations are not such as to bring them in frequent personal contact with sailors ashore and afloat. (The Ideal and Real, Afloat and Ashore, *CJ*, 18 Feb 1854, 103)

The text attempts to deconstruct this romanticised image of the navy, so closely linked to British national identity for centuries. The sailors are, in this very first description, not depicted as battling an enemy on sea, but nature, the "stormy waves" (ibid.). This gives them a self-defending rather than nation-saving or empire-enlarging function and immediately diminishes their value for the common good and contradicts the beliefs of "a large majority of individuals" (ibid.) who admire those venturing out on the sea.[108] The popular image of the sailors is subsequently only described in terms of outward appearance and evaluated as overly romanticised:

> We could hardly sufficiently admire this ship-shape rig-out; and the sailor himself, with his bold, bronzed hairy face, his reckless air, his rolling gait – so pleasantly suggestive of a ship at sea – and his tar-stained paws, with their fish-hooks of fingers, was to us the very beau-ideal of all that is manly and romantic. We knew not that this was his holiday, go-ashore attire, and thought he always dressed precisely the same, and looked the same daring hero. (ibid.)

The sailor ashore is described only in terms of outward effect, in terms of what the man's appearance inspires in the imagination of the onlooker. His hairstyle and walk suggest an adventurer and his hands are imagined to be used in daring acts. His clothes – "trousers of Russian duck", a "tarpauling hat" and a "red silk real Indian bandana" (ibid.) – speak of his travels and evoke exotic locations and enterprises. The fact that the general public is only presented with the "go-ashore attire", and thereby a beautified version of the common sailor, contributes to a

---

108 The comment that most of those who "cheris[h]" (The Ideal and Real, Afloat and Ashore, *CJ*, 18 Feb 1854, 103) the idea of men at sea have not come into contact with sailors stresses the previously made assumption that specific forms of heroism and hero-worship are only possible with distance between the adored object and the adoring subject.

romanticised image of sailors at sea who are imagined in the same exotic attire during their work on the ships. The description shows how the profession of sailor exists as a cultural imagination and escapist longing for many who "in those happy days, talked of how we should like to be sailors, and how we secretly vowed that we would be sailors, and not stupid, plodding prosaic tradesmen, or merchants, or lawyers, or doctors, as our parents and guardians so absurdly and cruelly intended" (ibid.). The sailor is depicted as existing as an adventurous counter-image to traditional middle-class professions: "Jack afloat has the easiest, jolliest, happiest, and most enviable life that can be conceived. When there is a fair wind and all sails set, he has nothing in the world to do but [...] enjoy the picturesque and romantic scenes around, or muse on the sublimity of the ocean over which he is sailing" (ibid., 104).

Through the focus on the outward impression, the central role of imagination in the perception of sailors and the necessity of distance between the image of the sailor and the imagining subjects, the public perception of sailors as represented in the text resembles the instances of precarious heroicity. Against this imagined adventurous image of the "daring hero" (ibid., 103), the "ideal sailor", the text then sets the description of "the other side of the medal" (ibid., 104).

First, the image of the sailor's outward appearance is corrected; he is not wearing fine garments from exotic locations, but "rough tarry jackets [...] and coarse canvas trousers, in most instances made by himself" (ibid.). In the navy, "cloth and canvas are served out to them at prime cost, to make their own jackets and trousers. [...] They also wash their own linen, &c., and these prosaic duties they have to perform as they may" (ibid.). The first duties of a sailor that the text describes are domestic ones, which directly undermine the afore-described images of "tar-stained paws" and "fish-hooks of fingers". The sailorly duties aboard the ship are not then described in the same detail and the portrayal focuses on presenting the work on the ship as 'just another profession' which is no more interesting than the "stupid, plodding prosaic" (ibid., 103) professional lives of the middle class. The sailors are described "as brave and daring", yet only in specific contexts, "when there is any necessity in the case [...]: but the hard reality of his daily lot generally deadens or destroys everything tending to a feeling of enthusiasm for his profession, which he probably would gladly quit for an easier berth ashore, were it in his power" (ibid., 104). Bravery and daring are thus situational and part of the job description, they do not correlate with a specific individual configuration.

Although these descriptions are applied to sailors "both in the merchant service and in the royal navy" (ibid.), the navy sailors are further devalued by stating – in the form of a dialogue "between a tar of the old school, and one of the modern school" (ibid., 105) – that the current generation of military sailors would not be as capable of actions in battle as former generations:

"Well; but, Bill, d'ye mean to say that the present race o' seamen are not just as good as before Trafflygar?"

"I does. I means to say they haven't the mind as they had; they doesn't think the same way (That is, they thinks too much); and more, they're not by one-half as active aloft as we were in the war. Chaps now reefin' topsails crawl out by the foot-ropes, and you now never see a weather-earin'-man fling himself out by the to'-gallant-studdin'sail halliards!" (ibid.)

The dialogue – both in content and style – points towards young sailors being more educated ("they thinks too much"), and also towards an inferior evaluation of the more pragmatic, task-oriented execution of the job as described in the rest of the text.[109] The old man's description creates the same opposition: the reality of a sailor's life is one which is no different from any other job in that it is executed in a pragmatic way, whereas in the self-conception of the old man the sailors of "the old school" were created along the lines of the "romantic and heroic" (ibid., 104) image of the sailor.

On the whole, the text can be read as a deconstruction of a heroic image of seamen and the creation of a more sober and pragmatic counter-image. Especially navy sailors are de-romanticised and depicted as men executing rather prosaic, even domestic, tasks who do not care for heroic actions. Accordingly, their heroism is only ever situational, only performed "when there is any necessity". The sailor as constructed in the text is not one fighting for the nation or contributing to the continuation of Britain's empire, but an individual carrying out their job like any of the readers. This is especially striking in light of the fact that only weeks later, on 27/28 March, Britain entered the Crimean War. Where the text had situated its evaluation of the sailors' lives in "these times of peace" (ibid., 105), a similar evaluation would not have been possible only weeks later, when the outcome of the war depended on those men that the text described as unenthusiastic and unheroic. The representation of sailors and the navy changed during the subsequent years of war and the image of a heroic fighting sailor reemerges. However, by transferring active heroic agency predominantly to British military men of the past and to the allies in the present war and not praising the involvement of Britain in the Crimea directly, *CJ* tried to acknowledge the concern of contemporary readers with the war effort while still maintaining and mediating their middle-class values.

Less than two months later, "The British Navy. From Coracle to the Line-of-Battle" traces the history of the British navy from its origins and comes to a different conclusion. The text describes in detail both the different types of ships

109 Furthermore, the "tar of the old school" (ibid., 105) dismisses the young generation of navy sailors because they are non-belligerent, and because they seem to go about their daily work with a different attitude. Whereas the first criticism is a circumstantial one – if there is no fight to be fought, the navy sailors cannot prove themselves in battle –the reproach that they are "not by one-half as active" (ibid.) is a general one which devaluated the navy sailors regardless of their opportunity to take part in a war-effort.

and their armaments, as well as the skill of the fighting men.[110] The "Duke of Wellington", the ship which led the Baltic campaign in 1854 under the command of Charles Napier, is then described in greatest detail. The exact measurements are noted as well as its weight, draught of water, the number and strength of engines and men on board. The account closes with a list of its total of 137 guns, including measurements and weight (cf. The British Navy, *CJ*, 8 Apr 1854, 218). The ship is presented as part of a long lineage of navy ships, as one step within an evolution, with possibly even better ships to come. As the only ship described in such detail, it is nevertheless clearly shown as one of the most modern war ships of the time and the focus on its strength and the power of its armament can, in the context of the Crimean War in which the ship was already being used, be read as a reassurance to the readers of *CJ* that the British navy was operating the best possible machinery and weaponry in its fight against the Russians.

However, not only the ships are presented as part of a tradition of British naval supremacy, the commanders and sailors are shown in a lineage of "great navigators" (ibid.) as well. Despite the detailed account of the ships and their materiality, it is the men of the royal navy who "from the time of Blake to that of Nelson" are said to have ensured the prosperity and global supremacy of Great Britain. The "naval heroes" (ibid.) are described as fulfilling a decidedly national function and thereby become workers for the common good, which gives their actions not only a military but also a social and communal component. It is not only their "adventure-spirit" (ibid., 217), but also the love for their "mother-country" (ibid., 218) which motivates their actions and – as the examples of Blake and Nelson evoke – makes them successful. The navy's success is strongly attributed to these "noble specimens of British men-of-war" (ibid.), rather than to the modern ships only.[111] The description attributes two central values of *CJ*'s

110 Interestingly, the natives of Britain are described as not having been drawn to the sea and only having been inspired "with a portion of [that] adventure-spirit" by the "Danish invaders, an essentially maritime people". The British Navy, *CJ*, 8 Apr 1854, 217. The text then follows the development of the English fleet through the reigns of Edward III, Henry VII and Henry VIII until the time of Elizabeth, which is praised as "the solid and enduring foundation of [...] naval superiority on a broad basis." (ibid.) As a decisive moment, the text naturally evokes the defeat of the Spanish Armada which "was perhaps less important in its immediate deliverance of the nation from the danger of foreign invasion, than in the spirit of naval skill and prowess it evoked, and the future of brilliant triumphs it inaugurated" (ibid.). The text goes on to describe the different types of ships the navy used throughout the ages, which kinds of materials they were built from, how much metal was used, etc.

111 It is worth noting that this passage refers to a period with a start and end point ("from the time of Blake to that of Nelson", ibid., 218) and thus implicitly states that the time of conquering new territories is past, whereas the important contemporary function of the navy is the preservation and defence of the British Empire. This change in focus shows that, though an integral part of British identity as an island nation, the military import-

heroic imaginary to the "naval heroes" (ibid.): they are described as persevering and courageous.[112]

The combination of both the "truly magnificent" (ibid.) ships – especially the "Duke of Wellington" currently leading the war effort in the Crimea – and the heroic actions of British navy men throughout history can be seen as a propagation of security and confidence in the British navy and their actions in the current war. Through the historical examples, the Baltic Campaign is placed in a line not only of military actions in defence of the British Empire, but more importantly in a line of successful battles, thereby implicitly evoking an inevitable military victory.

Like "The British Navy", various articles throughout the first months of the British war effort against Russia stress the supremacy of the Royal Navy throughout history. All of them describe the importance of British naval power, but especially stress the skill and heroic disposition of the men working on the ships. "Remarkable Naval Duels", published in September 1854, emphasises the "[m]any acts of great individual heroism" (Remarkable Naval Duels, *CJ*, 2 Sep 1854, 155) which are decisive for the victory in battle. Again, the heroism is related to the seamen's extraordinary "desperate valour" (ibid., 156),[113] but also to their skills and vigorous training:

> [I]n a properly disciplined ship, everything is done without confusion, and in a space of time amazingly short. Every man and boy capable of duty is at his post; and when an action is imminent, British tars on the doctor's list have frequently been known to drag their languid limbs from the sick-bay, to give what help they are able to fight Old England's battle. (ibid., 153)

---

ance of the navy diminished over the course of the nineteenth century: "In the case of the Crimean War (1854–1856), the value but also limitations of the naval power emerged. Britain could take the war to Russia but needed to use forces on land to defeat her, and the latter outcome required both allies and a propitious international situation." Jeremy Black: The Victorian Maritime Empire in its Global Context, in: Miles Taylor (ed.): The Victorian Empire and Britain's Maritime World, 1837–1901, Basingstoke 2013, p. 170. As the century progressed, the importance of commercial ships rose and, as Miles Taylor shows, "by the end of the nineteenth century commercial steam shipping dominated the seas to the extent that when Britain needed to mobilise for war as in South Africa in 1899–1902 and at the outbreak of the First World War in 1914, it turned not to the navy but to private passenger lines for sending out troops." Miles Taylor (ed.): The Victorian Empire and Britain's Maritime World 1837–1901. The Sea and Global History, Basingstoke 2013, pp. 1–2. In the context of the Empire, the navy had become more of an "agent of cultural imperialism" (ibid., p. 2) than a military institution.

112 The "naval victories [we owed] solely to the skill and indomitable valour of our seamen, who conquered in spite of the inferiority of their vessels to those of the enemy." The British Navy. From Coracle to the Line-of-Battle, *CJ*, 8 Apr 1854, 218.

113 The additional qualifying of the valour as "desperate" again shows that the "acts of great individual heroism" (Remarkable Naval Duels, *CJ*, 2 Sep 1854, 155) were performed in situations which might objectively have been hopeless. It's the seamen's distinction that they acted upon their duty *nevertheless*.

The text displays an interesting conjunction of both heroic enthusiasm – the author's description wants to make the readers join in "the wild hurra of your country" (ibid.) – and a professionalisation of the naval vocation. Both can be seen as an attempt to appeal to the readers' feelings "during the present war" (ibid.). Whereas the description of the organised and smoothly running procedures on the ship might enhance the feeling of security and trust in the navy, the allusion to "individual acts of great heroism" (ibid., 155) and the image of historical wounded "British tars" giving their last for their country, might aim at a more emotional involvement of the reader. With the text's call to join in the "hurra" (ibid., 153), it emotionally includes the readers in this endeavour of national importance.[114]

Another strand of representations of military heroism inspired by the Crimean War dealt with Britain's allies. Since the military institutions of countries such as France or Sardinia could be seen as defending Britain's as well as their own interests, members of their political and military ranks are compared to British heroic figures and presented as heroes. On the one hand, this could already be observed in texts such as "Remarkable Naval Duels" which reinterpreted previous campaigns against France and attributed heroic properties, such as courage, perseverance or gallantry, to the then-enemies as well. A further example of this heroisation of the allies' military is "Our New Ally", an essay which appeared in two parts in the summer of 1855. The Kingdom of Sardinia had joined the forces opposing Russia in the winter of 1854/55 and by July, when the articles appeared, had already been involved in the Siege of Sevastopol. The two-part essay then describes the Savoy dynasty throughout history and takes a special interest in its military prowess. After giving some general information about Sardinia and the current war – e.g. who their current king is and that they have given "18,000 of her choicest troops" (Our New Ally, *CJ*, 21 Jul 1855, 40) – the text emphasises the common Russian enemy's "bigoted Absolutism" (ibid.) before returning to the description of Sardinian military excellence. This excellence is established through comparison to ideals of British strength and excellence.[115] So are the people of Piedmont described as "these Highlanders of Italy" (ibid.,

114 In the context of the Crimean War, it is worth noting that the examples of "Remarkable Naval Duels" given in the text refer to battles against the French; given the changed political situation in which France and Britain were fighting on the same side, the text then stresses that "valour [was] displayed on *both* sides" (ibid.). Thus, in this specific historical context, the heroisation of one's allies is used to contribute to a feeling of superiority against the common enemy. This can also be seen in a number of texts about the history of Sardinia, which I will discuss later in this section.

115 Throughout the text, previous points of contact with Britain are highlighted. It is, for example, mentioned that "[t]he duke [in the war of Spanish succession in the eighteenth century] sided with the imperial party, which England also supported" (Our New Ally, *CJ*, 28 Jul 1855, 55) or stressed that Count Cavour, "the head of cabinet in Turin" shows "a strong leaning towards the institutions and political economy of England". Ibid.

42) in their strength or their "heroes['] [...] daring and achievements" are called worthy of depiction by the "genius of a Scott" (ibid., 41).

The second part of the essay then focuses on two military men involved in the current military struggle: Alfonso La Marmora, who is shown as having "qualified him[self] for his present position of commander-in-chief to the Sardinian forces in the East" through his "zeal [...] on the king's behalf" (Our New Ally, *CJ*, 28 Jul 1855, 53–54) and the prime minister Count Cavour. Both are presented as loyal to their country and courageous. Cavour, who "by study and personal observation [had] made himself thoroughly acquainted" with Britain (ibid., 54), is the main focus of attention of the second part. He is ascribed the same heroic properties as the British navy men above, is additionally praised for his intelligence and strategic thinking and described as a visionary

> gifted with *enlarged views*, and a *keen perception* of the requirements of the age, yet capable of concentrating his faculties on the minutest details of finance, and indefatigable in the labours of his office; *invulnerable* to the shafts of satire and invective by which he is perpetually assailed; equally impassable amid the thunders of the Vatican, or the abuse of the Red Republicans; denounced as sacrilegious and levelling by one party; as still truckling to the pretensions of the priesthood and the prejudices of caste by the other – the extremes of antagonistic opinion only uniting in their opposition to Cavour – he, nevertheless, *maintains his ground*." (ibid., emphases mine)

Just as the sailors on their warships, Cavour is described as persevering, organised, concentrated and unfearful when under attack – only on the political rather than the military field.

Even more than for their military prowess or extraordinary leadership, the Sardinian army and their leaders are praised for joining the war, as Sardinia's "present interests were not so closely involved as to render such a proceeding indispensable" (ibid.). By nevertheless participating in the campaign for a greater good of Western Europe against the "Absolutism" (ibid., 40) of Russia,[116] they are morally elevated. It is thus their superior moral character which makes them heroic, rather than previous victories:

> [I]n shewing themselves cheerful, and unquestioningly obedient, the military – representing, be it remembered, every grade of society, through the working of the conscription – [...] [they] furni[sh] the best commentary on the history of the House of Savoy, an heir-loom more important in its results than the annexation of territories or the most far-sighted political combination. (ibid.)

It is important to note here that the text, having up to that point only mentioned high-ranking officials of Sardinian military and government, turns to "every grade of society" (ibid.) when emphasising the moral extraordinariness of

---

[116] It is remarkable in this context that Sardinia-Piedmont was portrayed as joining the allied forces without any own interests. This was, of course, not the case and Cavour had made the strategic political decision to participate in the war effort in order to gain France's support on the issue of Italian unification.

the people. It is said that their excelling "nationality, [...] patriotism, [and] war-like traditions [are] deep sunk in every heart, familiar to the lips of every child" (ibid.). In addition to their military strength depicted in the first part of the essay, it is the people's "faith", their "hardihood and endurance" and their "spirit [...] on the battlefields" (ibid., 54–55) – in short, the moral motivation of their physical, military power which turns them into heroes worth portraying by great authors.

A text such as this performs a dual function: by depicting the Sardinians as a people of military prowess whose seemingly selfless decision enhances the strength of the allied forces, the superiority of the alliance is stressed and the hope of a victory among the readers encouraged without explicitly praising the British troops. By connecting Sardinian figures and their political aspirations to British heroes and politics, the qualities praised in the Sardinians can, however, also be reciprocally referred back to the British people. Especially the description of the selfless behaviour of the common people can then be read as an appeal to the readers to behave in a similar way and act loyally towards their country. The essay, in the context of the Crimean War, thus describes Britain in its relationship to Sardinia both as a patron who can act as a role model for Italian politicians and military leaders in political matters, and as an equal partner in war and the moral attitude towards the fight against Russia.

In February 1856, only a few weeks after the fighting in the Crimea ended, the magazine acknowledges the sacrifice of military men. This is notably expressed in an article on "Mr Thackeray's Ballads" in which the eminent writer is criticised for his scepticism towards the military profession. The text quotes Thackeray's "The Chronicles of the Drum", a ballad that Thackeray had written in Paris in 1841 at the time of Napoleon's second funeral. The "moral of the whole" (ibid.) is explained as "strongly incentive to peace; [...] being, that historians neglect to relate the progress of the people whilst engaged upon nothing but war" (The Chronicles of the Drum, *CJ*, 2 Feb 1856, 73). This is illustrated with a passage from the ballad:

> Your orthodox historian puts
> In foremost rank the soldier thus,
> The red-coat bully in his boots,
> That hides the march of men from us.
> He put him there in foremost rank:
> You wonder at his cap of hair;
> You hear his sabre's cursed clank;
> His spurs are jingling everywhere.
> Go to! I hate him and his trade:
> Who bade us so to cringe and bend,
> And all God's peaceful people made
> To such as him subservient?
> Tell me what find we to admire

In epaulets and scarlet coats;
In men, because they load and fire,
And know the art of cutting throats? (quoted ibid.).

Thackeray's own critique is aimed in two directions; on the one hand, it criticises historians in their effort to heroise war actions, but on the other hand, the poet also strongly devalues the soldiers themselves. The poem describes the military men as murderers with no higher motives or specific skills apart from killing and operating war machinery. In the context of the Crimean War, however, the contributor disagrees with the ballad. The reader is informed that "[t]he subject, no doubt has its other side; and at a time when military men have done and suffered too much, we think Pierre [the speaker of the ballad][117] might have added a gracious postscript" (ibid., 74). With this comment, the text adds a moral component to Thackeray's description of military men as they have not only inflicted suffering, but they have suffered themselves. The idea of doing and suffering "too much" (ibid.), rather than doing just what it takes, implies that the actions of soldiers and sailors were not motivated by individual objectives but for a national good. Thereby, the focus is – like in the other texts discussed – shifted to the moral and national motivation of military actions away from the descriptions of actual battle scenes or violence.[118]

After the end of the war, *CJ* returns to a more critical stance towards military conflict and also criticises the public climate during the Crimean Campaign in retrospect. A striking example, which shows both *CJ*'s attitude as well as reactions of other segments of the popular print market, can be found in "Street Ballads of the War". The Crimean War had officially ended with the Treaty of Paris on 30 March 1856, the article was published in May and already shows a move back towards a rather critical evaluation of war and military actions. In its opening sentences, the text already clearly situates the war in the past when it ironically hands over the critical discussion of the events to the prolific historiographer Macaulay:

> It will be for Mr Macaulay, in the hundredth volume of his History, to set forth the more prominent results of the war with Russia; to tell us, or our descendants, how the balance of power in Europe was affected thereby, and how the prosperity of England was not affected at all by the addition of Ten millions to the national debt. But there are certain minor results which do not properly belong to the province of the historian, yet are worth recording for the benefit of the philosophical and inquiring minds of a future generation. (Street Ballads of the War, *CJ*, 17 May 1856, 305)

[117] It is worth noting that it is not Thackeray as the author who is criticised for his anti-soldierly opinions here but the fictitious speaker of the ballad.

[118] Interestingly, the text only refers to the context of the ballad in regard to Napoleon's funeral, but does not, like other texts from the same time, mention the fundamentally different relation to France during the present and the past war.

Unlike during the years of active conflict, *CJ* now criticises the war effort for its enormous costs and the damage this may cause Britain in the future.[119] At the same time, a scepticism towards the traditional forms of history writing is expressed, the trustworthiness of which is doubted and the accounts of which are expected to be window-dressed for the audience. The "minor results" of the war, which the text wants to record "for the benefit of [...] a future generation", then consist of a presumed enlarged knowledge among the British public regarding Eastern Europe. The popular print market is described as "a Popular Educator" (ibid.). In comparison to the "Ten millions" of national debt, the increased information which people now possess regarding the geography, people and culture of the Crimea seems ridiculous. Apart from this form of dubious popular education, the text ironically thanks the war for the "gush of songs we owe to the same cause" (ibid.):

> Our poets, one and all, from Tennyson to Tupper, have had their trumpet-stops out, and have discoursed most eloquent martial music. For the first time these forty years, there has been a brisk demand for warlike rhymes; and transactions in "brave – grave," "field – yield," "foe – no!" "fly – die," "Old England's banner – fare thee well, Anna," have gone off freely. [...] But it is in our street-ballads, the lowest notes in our scale of harmony, that martial enthusiasm may be had in any quantity. (ibid.)

These sentences already show the unease the text expresses towards the popular songs and ballads about the war and especially towards the glorification of violence.[120] Giving examples such as "Here's to the Allied Powers, / My boys, with three times three / That beat the cowardly Russians / Then gain'd a victory; / Tho' the Russians fought us two to 1 / With fire sword and ball / To Frenchmen and Britannia's sons / They was no use at all" (ibid., 306). Although this is probably not one of the best examples of the "martial enthusiasm" criticised above – examples of this are only criticised, but not given to the reader – a clear difference to the reaction to the Crimean War in *CJ* described above can be seen. Whereas *CJ* had omitted descriptions of battle-scenes and had mostly referred to battles of the past or more abstract concepts – such as the Russian's Absolutism or British, French or Sardinian loyalty and gallantry – the sample song shows more concrete scenes. The Russian enemies are depicted as cowardly and the British and French as superior fighters – though outnumbered and seemingly using inferior equipment. Their victory is not shown as one of moral superiority,

119 As Conacher puts it: "The Crimean War was over except for the bills to be paid, the wounded pensioners to be cared for and the long drawn out task of implementing the Treaty." Conacher: Crimea, p. 219.

120 It is worth noting that the text does not seem to differentiate between the "martial music" (Street Ballads of the War, *CJ*, 17 May 1856, 305) brought forth by Tennyson's "The Charge of the Light Brigade" (1854), ballads like Martin Tupper's "Never Give Up" (written in 1851 already, but said to have been sung by the soldiers on the Crimean battlefields) and the "warlike rhymes" sensationalising the violence of war. All of them are portrayed as worth denouncing for their open support of war.

as *CJ* might have preferred it. On the whole, examples such as this are condemned as too keen on displaying violence and idolising the martial. No wonder then that the text also attributes a part of the responsibility for the fact that "[f]rom first to last, the voice of the masses has been steadily for war" (ibid.) to the circulation of popular war-songs.

It is striking how, only two months after the end of the war, the journal returns to the war-critical position it had articulated before the Crimean Campaign. The text ends by stating: "Of the peace, esto perpetua would be a vain and impolitic wish; but we will say, and with all possible respect and affection to the writers, may it be long before we are enabled to make up such another bundle of war-ballads as that which now lies beside us" (ibid., 309). Interestingly, *CJ* had throughout the two years of war only ever heroised the soldiers and sailors fighting for a common cause and mostly focused on historically removed actors and Britain's allies. Through these strategies the periodical had never openly supported the war effort and Britain's involvement in general. The periodical thereby negotiated the middle-class value of peacefulness it wanted to convey to its readers and the fact that a large number of readers and their families would have actually been affected by the war against Russia. Thus, a generally supportive attitude towards the individuals engaged in the fight for Britain as a national community was created, while still latently preserving their peace-oriented approach, which is taken up overtly again immediately after the peace treaty has been signed.

Times of war, such as in 1854–56, clearly acted as a regulation on *CJ*. While on other occasions calling soldierly heroism an easily attainable form of heroics, in times of war *CJ* validated and encouraged individual acts of military conduct in its texts, yet seemed to differentiate between its attitude towards the individuals and the war as whole.[121] On the one hand, this can be seen as an attempt to set their readers' minds at ease, since they might have been related to someone actually fighting in the war, and give them a sense of security. On the other hand, the individual acts of heroism described in the texts are presented in a way that emphasises the values and morals behind the violent acts. The texts focus on the loyalty of the soldiers and sailors, their courage, perseverance and their selflessness. Thereby, the heroisation of soldierly action can be related to the larger didactic agenda of *CJ*, as part of their effort to relate modest middle-class values to the lower classes.

---

121 This can for example also be seen in the fact that the journal publishes a note which criticises the lack of appreciation of "the blighted hopes, the desolate hearths, the crushed fortunes, and countless domestic miseries which war occasions" (The Expense of War, *CJ*, 20 Sep 1856, 192) and further criticises in September 1856 that too few English 'common' soldiers and sailors were given medals and awards for their "individual acts of heroism". English Heroes and French Honours, *CJ*, 6 Sep 1856, 155. This is then contrasted with French military awards which are said to be more inclusive.

While military disputes in the Indian colonies such as the Indian Rebellion or the Bhutan War did not cause *CJ* to adopt a more positive attitude towards military men, the two Boer Wars from 1879–1880 and 1899–1902 again resulted in an increase in the heroisation of soldiers and their actions. However, most of these texts do not directly refer to the Boer War and sometimes not even to the British military, but deal with past battles and even other nations. One can thus argue that *CJ* used these examples to acknowledge the effort and suffering of British soldiers in South Africa, to strengthen morale among the people and encourage virtuous behaviour, yet did not openly want to support the specific war effort in order to remain loyal to its self-defined identity.

The 1879 text "German Heroes" is a good example for the kind of text which does not situate military heroism in the British society of the current war, but nevertheless can be read as a piece which mediates clear values for identification to the readership. This potential for identification is already enunciated in the first sentences, when the text criticises that

> [w]henever two nations have been at war, the fame of the most striking acts of heroism on either side spreads all over the civilised world; newspapers mention the names of generals and commanders, history takes possession of their career, which future generations admire, and point to as examples of heroic bravery. Whilst according all due praise to their commanders, perhaps a few instances of daring on the part of the subordinates may not be out of place. (German Heroes, *CJ*, 15 Feb 1879, 111)

Much like the intended readership of *CJ*, the text aims at a depiction of those members of society who do not have a leadership position, but constitute the workforce and accordingly also execute most of the uncomfortable tasks. The text validates the work of the common soldiers and – again – especially emphasises the virtues which motivate their actions. So can, for example, the description of a severely wounded soldier be found, who, "always full of regard for others" (ibid.), persuades the surgeons not to put his name on the list of severely wounded "so that his wife and children might not be alarmed" (ibid.). After his duty for Britain is fulfilled, the soldier turns into a husband and father and tries to act in protection of his family, now that his protective measures for his country have come to their natural end. With such anecdotes, the importance of self-sacrifice and of both duty and the interest of the group, rather than the individual, during war-time is stressed.

The closing paragraph of the text can then almost be read as a programmatic guide to the texts which *CJ* itself publishes during war time, when it states that:

> In every regiment, similar acts of heroism have been performed by men, who in consequence are looked upon by their comrades with envy and admiration. At night, when the brave soldiers gathered round the watch-fires […] thousands of noble deeds were narrated by those who had witnessed them. Those tales went from mouth to mouth, and served to cheer the drooping spirits and to double the courage of the hearers, and inspired them with the desire of imitating examples, such as that of the brave gunner

who stuck to his cannon though a fragment of a shell had carried off one of his legs. (ibid., 112)

The function of heroism in war-time is made obvious: through narration and subsequent dissemination, tales of the heroic act as motivation and inspiration which is finally intended to lead to imitation. This can, in the case of *CJ*, also be transferred to the readership at the home front. Texts such as "German Heroes" strongly emphasise the values underlying heroism such as selflessness or a sense of duty towards one's country[122] and peer-group, so that the non-combatant readers can be inspired and motivated as well. Thus, an imitation of the propagated values and the soothing and inspiring effect of the tales of heroism are not limited to the front, but can occur in British everyday life just as well.

Loyalty, determination and selflessness – especially the ability to suffer – are the most common themes of the anecdotes published at the time of the Anglo-Zulu War. Many of the texts are, for example, set during the Indian Rebellion or the American Civil war and show a "cheery encouragement" (An Incident of War, *CJ*, 6 Mar 1880, 158) of "young heroic boy[s]" (ibid.). They feature stories (e.g. The Bells of Yarrick, *CJ*, 3, 10 and 17 Apr 1880) which do not only describe soldiers' excellent conduct in the field, but depict their recruitment and even their happy return. This can be read as a reflection of the period between the Anglo-Zulu and the first Boer War when another war was looming, yet, after the victory against the South African troops in 1879, another military engagement in South Africa was met with a certain confidence.

The stories of previous wars not only emphasise a moral attitude deemed desirable for the readers, but also attempt to create a calm and confident mood, when stories of previous victories are told with the comment that history and the "heroic stories [...] of British bravery and pluck [...] repeats itself" (Recollections of an Anglo-Indian Chaplain, *CJ*, 19 Jun 1880, 290). The confidence mediated through the texts, however, was destabilised in the reality of the First Boer War, a war in which the good equipment and military strength of the Boer opponents had come as a surprise to the British. The effect of the defeat in 1880 can then be seen in *CJ* at the turn of the century, when the British forces were facing Boer troops again.

During the Second Boer War, *CJ*'s stance towards the war effort is most pronounced. If the articles discussed above were rather subtle in their support of war in general and focused on the strength and extraordinary capabilities of the soldiers, their position becomes increasingly more pro-war at the turn of the century. After the last effort in South Africa had been unsuccessful, the journal now

---

122 A direct appeal to the reader to remember their duty towards their country can, for example, also be found in the text "A Few Words About the Guides" which closes with the words: "Our readers need scarcely be reminded that absence without leave, especially in troublous times, is a very serious offence in her majesty's service." A Few Words About the Guides, *CJ*, 3 Jan 1880, 11.

supported the British military more obviously and – often in fictional texts – implicitly encouraged their readers to join the campaign. In November 1899, only few weeks after the war broke out, the tale "The Heroine of Lydenberg. An Episode in the Transvaal War of 1880 –81" evoked the experience of the *First* Boer War. With its focus on a female protagonist, the wife of the British Lieutenant Walter Long, the narrative could both be read as an appeal to men to imitate the husband's behaviour, as well as an encouragement for women to adopt the selfless attitude of the woman portrayed.

In its opening sentences, the text reflects upon the scarce representation of female heroics when it states that the story to follow "is forgotten by all except the surviving actors" yet "such a signal instance of British pluck should not be allowed to die" (The Heroine of Lydenberg, *CJ*, 18 Nov 1899, 801). The tale then tells the historical story of the Siege of Lydenberg and of Walter Long, the "junior subaltern" who had been left "in sole command of the troops left behind [in Lydenberg after a regiment had left for Pretoria] – a responsible position of a youngster of barely two-and-twenty" (ibid.). Mrs Long, the title-giving heroine, is introduced as a naïve young middle-class woman, as the lieutenant's "pretty young wife" (ibid.).

However, this changes when she "without a moment's hesitation decided to leave her comfortable home and take up her quarters with her husband" (ibid.) and his soldiers outside of town. As the reason for this, "the brave little woman said that her place was beside her husband" (ibid.). Admired by the soldiers for "her pluck" (ibid.), she moves into a hut with her husband and becomes a member of the male group. She helps the soldiers to build defence works around the camp and works "as hard as any of them" so that the camp in the end is called "Fort May, in honour of Mrs. Long" (ibid., 802). Even after the Boer forces come into sight, the woman refuses to leave the camp and continues to work with the soldiers and "even when the Boers brought a couple of cannon to bear on the fort, [...] she frequently slept right through the cannonade" (ibid.). When the camp has only a few weapons left, she even thinks of re-purposing an old pump as a gun and thereby contributes to the fighting. Her being a woman makes her especially exceptional in the given environment and also acts as a motivation for the soldiers: "What wonder that the men fought like heroes with this daintily-bred English lady sharing all their dangers and setting them an example of patience and courage and cheerfulness" (ibid.). Although having established heroic strength – both physical and moral – of the "heroine of Lydenberg", the reader is also constantly reminded that Mrs Long is "woman-like" (ibid.) and flawed; so she, for example, goes back to her hut to try and rescue her bonnet, cups, saucers and crockery when the camp is under attack.[123] After the "humiliating" (ibid., 803) surrender of the British, the remaining men and Mrs Long are described as physically marked by their experience of intense suffering during the siege.

The text has a different quality than those discussed before in that it not only shows the actions of brave soldiers in battle, but also depicts a woman supporting her husband in his military actions. In this respect, the last sentences of the text are significant: "Lieutenant Long and his men were publicly complimented in a General Order 'for their successful and heroic defence.' But I am disposed to think that the largest share of the praise was due to the brave woman who set them so noble an example" (ibid.). Not only does this show that public honouring of heroic acts was reserved for men, but calling Mrs Long the "noble example" of the men makes her role accessible to the female readers of the periodical. The narrative offers an identificatory potential for both men and women reading the journal. The men can relate to the soldiers who defend their nation and – foregrounded through the strongly emphasised relation of Mrs Long to the whole of the group – their wives and families in a situation of war. Since the text clearly establishes Mrs Long's private and domestic motivation for her extraordinary actions – her main goal is for her marriage to remain intact – female readers in Britain would be able to take up this effort in their own environment. The text thus establishes a heroic potential for women and depicts the suffering for the integrity of the family as worthwhile. Although the active physical actions Mrs Long is depicted performing cannot compare to the acts of women on the home front, they are united in suffering and waiting (Mrs Long during the siege, the women in Britain for their husbands/fathers to return and the war to end). Further, Mrs Long's encouragement not to surrender could act as a motivator for other women to encourage their husbands and the narrative thus offered role models to the readers of *CJ* in times of war.

The tale "Patriot and Traitor" by Alan Oscar encourages joining the forces even more openly. In the narrative, which appeared in March 1900, the protagonist Lily Trevor, a young woman with "no great depth of character" (Patriot and Traitor, *CJ*, 31 Mar 1900, 283), is in a dilemma: both young Leverson, partner at "Leverson, Shafskop, & Company" as well as Fred Selby, whose profession is not specified, are wooing her. The young woman, who is obviously wealthy and whose life is full of receptions and charity functions, is naturally drawn to the lifestyle of Leverson, who accompanies her to the "War Fund Concert" and whose financial means would allow her to retain her standards of living when choosing him. Fred Selby, on the other hand, does not take Lily out and on the

[123] Furthermore, she is depicted performing tasks in the camp typically associated with women at the time, for example she tends to the "sick and wounded". The Heroine of Lydenberg, *CJ*, 18 Nov 1899, 802. When the camp is besieged, Mrs Long nurses her wounded husband and encourages him to "hold out to the last" and not give in to the Boer troops.

whole, lacks courage: "[he] followed somewhat at a distance, a 'devout lover.' He worshipped her; but she had hitherto somewhat ignored him. Yet his devotion touched her. Once or twice she had caught herself wishing he had more ardour for the attack" (ibid.).

For the first time, a narration is set in the present day of the readers. The ongoing war not only shows in the mentioned "War Fund Concert", but the contemporary political situation also becomes ironically apparent in the cancellation of a ball which "showed even the young women [like Lily Trevor] that war had its serious side" (ibid.). In this situation of war, Yeomanry groups began to join the British forces – both in the text's represented world as well as in the living environment of readers in 1900. The decision whether or not to join the forces then shows which of the two suitors is the eponymous patriot and who is the traitor. As Leverson's business partnership with the German company of Shafskop already suggests, it is not he who joins the volunteers. On the contrary, he even uses the heightened demand to sell ammunition to the Dutch. When asked about his non-participation by Lily, Leverson argues that he cannot leave his business alone and mocks his opponent. He calls Selby, who has not hesitated to join the volunteers for South Africa, a "cub" (ibid., 284) and thus ridicules him as inexperienced and thoughtless. This is when Lily develops a greater "depth of character" (ibid., 283) and she defends the young recruit, deeming him a "brave man" (ibid., 284). Leverson then slips up with a comment that "those Dutchmen pay well" (ibid.) and reveals his relationship to the Dutch enemy; Lily leaves the house immediately – only to meet Fred Selby in the street, since "the militia were to march through the town to-day [...]. It was a supreme moment for both. For him a moment of passionate love; for her – she could hardly have said. In such moments an emotional woman loses the mastery over herself" (ibid., 283–284). From that moment, Lily is decided; she chooses Fred Selby who risks his life for Queen and country. The "ardour for attack" he had lacked in his private life is compensated for by his decision to join the military forces in the Boer War, his participation in an actual military operation. A short epilogue informs the reader that Selby was wounded at Jagersfontein. The text then ends in the present tense, thereby connecting the narrative to the present day of the readers: "He is recovering. She is waiting the return of her hero" (ibid., 284).

"Patriot and Traitor" clearly positions itself in support of the ongoing military efforts in South Africa. With its setting so close to the actual reality of the readers, it presents an obvious national agenda and shows the exceptional circumstances of war as calling for the individual's commitment for the group on different levels. On the one hand, the text implicitly asks for British men to actively support the troops. On the other hand, it asks the female members of society to adapt to the situation in their own way. Although depicting a very traditional form of gender roles and portraying the young woman as superficial in the beginning, the experience of war (albeit on the home front) not only results in lifestyle changes, but also is a moral education for the young woman. However, the text displays an additional, decidedly national component and patriotism acts as the central motivation for Fred Selby, while any non-participation in the war effort is questioned. With its romantic plot, the narrative was probably directed mostly at a female readership and can thus be read as an implicit appeal to test one's own social relations against the categories given above – national loyalty, courage, selflessness. Through the interpersonal relationship at the centre of the narrative, a high potential for identification from both youth and adult readers can be presumed.

An interpersonal relationship also stands at the centre of the tale "An Escape". Its protagonist, Reverend Bryce-Ritson, does not quite feel comfortable in his profession for he possesses too much "energy" (An Escape, *CJ*, 6 Oct 1900, 719). It is with longing, therefore, that he watches the other young men joining the forces and leaving for the front in South Africa. Not only were they popular (in public perception in general and with young ladies in particular), he remarks, but they were performing a duty towards their country:

> Suppose matters politic got worse. Suppose America should interfere and the Continent take advantage! Suppose England fighting for her very existence! Who would care for the clergy and their work then? If it came to conscription his cloth would protect him; he would be sneered at as one sitting snug at home, and the soldier would – even more than at present – be the popular hero. (ibid.)

The motivation for wanting to join the army expressed in this text is twofold. On the one hand, a patriotic impulse is obvious, a want to do good for one's country and countrymen. On the other hand, the excerpt also shows the importance of public perception and reputation. The growth in popularity of the young men joining the forces, such as "young Turner" who, nothing more than an average youth before, was transformed in the eyes of the onlookers: "To-day young Turner was a volunteer, was going out to fight for the Empire, was a hero in the eyes of every girl in the town" (ibid.). The reverend especially notices the admiring looks which Lily Hardinge casts Turner and has to admit his envy. Only days later, after having read a note in the newspaper that the Bishop of Stamford encouraged curates to volunteer, Reverend Bryce-Ritson joins the army.

The war that had only been seen through the imagination of the reverend and discussed in abstract terms before is then presented to the reader in a very concrete way: The text describes a "frightful day" of fighting in "the fierce heat" with "the wounded lying where they fell; many of them were now dead with thirst and horror" (ibid.). Reverend Bryce-Ritson has become "Trooper Ritson" (ibid., 720) and is called towards a wounded comrade: young Turner of his former parish. He is fatally wounded and takes a torn image from his breast-pocket showing Lily Hardinge. Ritson's spontaneous gesture towards his own pocket reveals that he is carrying the very same picture. Turner then elucidates the meaning of the text's title "An Escape" when he says that "'If it hadn't been for that thing I might have escaped; it deflected the bullet and sent it through my chest. Been a Bible it would have been all right, I suppose – eh?'" (ibid.). The escape of the title is thus a failed one which is frustrated by shallow reasons for joining the army – the desire for popularity and the intention to impress a woman. The mentioning of the bible and its more fortunate effect in the same situation further stresses the duality of the reverend/trooper. It reveals that joining the army for reputation and popularity with women is not the right approach, but that a moral motivation, a want to fight for the greater good of the country, should drive the soldiers.[124] This selfishness is exemplified by Ritson's reaction to Turner's death: after a brief moment of shock, "he triumphed. 'The road is clear; I'll win her yet'" (ibid.). Although he casts this thought away immediately, calling himself a "brute to think such a thing" (ibid.), the reader is once again reminded that a war is a collective effort which one should join with sound morals and not for one's own (in this case private) profit.

In the end, Ritson realises that he should not have pursued Lily Hardinge and tried to impress her by joining the army.[125] Through the depiction of this shallow inter-personal relationship and the vanity of the two soldiers' lust for reputation, the text stresses the importance of morale in the ongoing fight in South Africa and calls for individuals' dedication towards the collective rather than to their own benefit.

Reputational gain through an individual's involvement in the war effort is brought up in several texts. The article "In Kimberley During the Siege", published in March 1900, also depicts events of the ongoing war in South Africa. Written "by a Hospital Nurse" (In Kimberley During the Siege, *CJ*, 19 Mar 1900, 385), it tells the story of the mining town which had been besieged from October 1899 until February 1900, a siege which, unlike that in "The Heroine of Lydenberg", resulted in a British victory. Only one month after the historical events, the nurse narrator speaks of the siege as "one of the most notable episodes in the exciting and eventful history of the South Africa campaign" (ibid.).

124 It is worth noting that this claim cannot be generalised for the depiction of war-efforts and interpersonal relationships in *CJ*. I would argue that in this case, it is not so much the inter-personal relationship as such which is criticised as a motivation to join the forces but the fact that this relationship is not an established one yet. Therefore, the two men who both long for Lily Hardinge want to impress the girl through their soldierly actions in order to win her over. Thus, the act of joining is shown as a selfish one for the purpose of the men's own profit. In other cases, such as the aforementioned "Patriot and Traitor", an inter-personal relationship can enhance the moral credibility of a man's decision to join the war, when he is doing so for the 'greater good' of their future and – importantly – in combination with a patriotic impulse.

125 Interestingly, he only does so after he reads her wedding announcement with a wealthy Jew in the paper. The fact that the young woman married a Jewish man who did not fight in the Boer War then implicitly elevates both Turner and Ritson again, because they, in contrast to Lily's husband, contributed to the maintenance of the British Empire – albeit for shallow reasons.

A similar enthusiastic description is given of the hospital at which the nurse was employed and which "is recognised far and wide as one of the best institutions of its kind [...] and appointments on its nursing staff are eagerly sought after by those who have adopted the tending of the sick and wounded as their career in life" (ibid.). Accordingly, the nurse "cannot but plead guilty to a certain feeling of pride and self-satisfaction at having been afforded an opportunity of aiding to assuage the sufferings of the patients" (ibid.). Although the text then elaborates upon the cruelty of the siege, the I-narrator cannot disguise her pride in having contributed to the British war effort and having witnessed the siege. By depicting the siege as an "exciting" part of the war and the hospital as a prestigious one before situating herself in that very scene, she elevates herself before the eyes of the reader and shows her own desire for reputation connected to the war effort.[126]

However, it is not her own work then which is called heroic, and not that of "the brave men fighting for Queen and country" (ibid.), but that of the besieged city's inhabitants. It is stated that had it not been for "the fortitude and heroism which animated the inhabitants [...] a humiliating surrender instead of a gallant and successful resistance might have had to be recorded" (ibid., 388). In attributing the heroic acts in the siege to the 'common' inhabitants, the text gives the reader a possibility to identify with the represented heroes. The properties of this kind of heroism can be identified as inner strength, perseverance and the ability to suffer both physically, since the food and water supplies were getting sparse, and mentally through the mere situation of being besieged and unable to move freely. The identificatory potential, especially for the lower ranks of society, of this situation and the necessary virtues to deal with them would have been high. Even without the war in South Africa, the difficulty to provide enough food for one's family was a reality for many lower class families. Furthermore, the war effort itself also had an effect on the British motherland. A large number of families had to deal with everyday life without their husbands or fathers, and news of casualties was continuously arriving in Britain. Additionally, the war proved to be a financial strain for both individuals and the British economy as a whole and thus the population could, on a smaller scale, be compared to the inhabitants of Kimberley. In this context, the text and its validation of the "heroism" (ibid.) of the inhabitants of the South African town can be read as an encouragement for Britain's inhabitants to keep up their form of suffering so as not to experience a "humiliating surrender" (ibid.).

On the whole, the depiction of the Second Boer War shows two fundamental differences from the treatment of the Crimean War and the First Boer War in *CJ*. The descriptions became more direct and more positive. Whereas the texts about

126 The rather negative impression of the narrating nurse is further reinforced by the fact that she expresses a hysterical panic whenever there is a bombardment.

the British military at war-time in the 1850s and 1880s had been more indirect, the texts during the second South African Campaign became more pronounced. The war was not only no longer described as a necessary evil, but several texts also speak of the thrill of the war, call it "exciting" (ibid., 385) and discuss the prestige and popularity which participation in the war effort (of both military men and civilians like the nurse in the Kimberley Siege) can bring to individuals. Furthermore, tales like "Patriot and Traitor" or "An Escape" – though in different ways – implicitly called upon the readers' own voluntary participation in the war or, in the case of the short romantic tale, ask the female readers to check their own interpersonal relations for 'patriots' and 'traitors' as represented in the text. Around the turn of the century, the magazine took a clearer stance in favour of the war effort and emphasised patriotism and loyalty more strongly than before.

The second major difference lies in the setting of the texts. The texts published during the Crimean and first South African Campaign had mostly been set in a distant past or in a different country; in contrast, the texts on military heroism published during the Second Boer War were set in the present or in a past which was still part of the living memory of many readers. By placing various texts during the *First* Boer War, they also evoke the memory of a British defeat. This memory of a weakened British power and the shifting global politics at the turn of the century can also serve as an explanation for the heightened interest of the journal in the success of the campaign. Furthermore, the texts became more personal. Rather than matter-of-fact essays, the military actions were represented in tales and mediated through first person narrators who could draw the reader closer to the subject than the more sober reports observed before. This more personalised style of narration and the fact that inter-personal relationships featured more frequently in the texts enlarged their identificatory potential. On the whole, an attempt can be perceived to involve the readers emotionally and to appeal to their own experience. The values which were mediated in this different form remain the same – selflessness, courage, ability to suffer, placing the fate of the collective before one's own – yet the more engaging presentation contributes to a closer tie between reader, text and mediated message and thus also between public morale and war effort.[127]

---

127 *CJ* is only digitised up until the end of 1900. A cursory analysis of the periodical's issues from 1901 and 1902 held at the National Library of Scotland has shown that the Boer War remained present in the periodical in those years. On the one hand, texts directly relating to the military conflict can be found (e.g. Looting a Boer Camp, *CJ*, 5 Jan 1901; Leniency: Why and How it Failed in South Africa, *CJ*, 9 Mar 1901; Military Prisoners, *CJ*, 13 April 1901; The Fight with Lotters, *CJ*, 22 Mar 1902; A Vaal River Adventure, *CJ*, 23 Nov 1901; or My Midnight Visitor. A South African Story, *CJ*, 21 and 28 Jun 1902. "My Midnight Visitor", a tale published in two parts, can, though published one month after the end of the Boer War, be considered a wartime story, since it was written and most certainly also put into print when the war was still going on, since issues were set and printed weeks in advance, also several articles commemorating past wars, such as "Some Episodes of the Afghan War of 1880" which is introduced with regards to present day as a

With the shifting power dynamics in global politics at the close of the nineteenth century, additional players entered the field of heroism. At the time of the Second Boer War, a new form of non-belligerent national heroism can be found in the pages of *CJ*. Embodied in the figure of the diplomat and spy, a representative of heroism emerged who was a special case due to the invisibility and seclusion of the profession to the public eye. In late 1899 and early 1900, this area of politics was the centre of the serial novel "Of Royal Blood. A Story of the Secret Service".

The novel was written by William Le Queux, who had done diplomatic work in San Marino himself[128] and had travelled widely in Europe, the Balkans and Africa. His most popular works were invasion fantasies which propagated 'preparedness' against foreign invasion.[129] Most popular among them were *The Great War in England in 1897* (published in 1894), which imagined a Russian invasion in Britain, and *The Invasion of 1910* (published in 1906), which told the story of a fictitious German invasion.[130] "Of Royal Blood", though not representing a scenario as drastic as the two novels,[131] is related in its themes and propagates patriotic loyalty towards Britain. With its combination of romance, politics and sensationalism, Smith and White argue in *Cloak and Dagger Fiction*, it "made excellent propaganda".[132] At a time when Britain was still fighting a war on the African

"time, when military affairs occupy the minds of the whole community" (Some Episodes of the Afghan War of 1880, *CJ*, 19 Jan 1901, 113), Sedan, *CJ*, 2 Feb 1901, or The Bravest Briton at Waterloo, *CJ*, 25 May 1901. On the whole, the texts emphasise the individual contribution and sacrifices of the British soldiers, yet become more and more critical as the war goes on (one of the points most texts make is that the British troops were not trained for the guerrilla-style fighting they had to face).

128 In a letter to Charles Chambers, Le Queux describes his qualification for working in San Marino as follows: "I happened to have explored the place + knew the officials etc." and sums it up as follows: "Curious work for a novelist – eh?" William Le Queux: Letter to Charles Chambers, 1900, Dep 341/143: No 36, National Library of Scotland, Edinburgh.

129 During the First World War, the Library Fund that collected novels for military camps lists Le Queux as one of its most popular authors. Cf. George Robb: British Culture and the First World War, Basingstoke 2002, p. 183.

130 The case of *The Invasion of 1910* shows an interesting mechanism of the popular print market. Le Queux had been commissioned to write the novel by the *Daily Mail* and had been asked to include specific towns in the novel, which subsequently resulted in an enormous increase in sales in those regions. Cf. Cecil D. Eby: The Road to Armageddon. The Martial Spirit in English Popular Literature 1870–1914, Durham, NC 1987, p. 33.

131 As can be presumed from the correspondence left in Chambers's archive material in the National Library of Scotland, this less drastic depiction was also due to suggestions made by Charles Chambers. He had asked for parts of the plot to be rewritten and had deemed some scenes too violent. Subsequently, Le Queux agreed to "tone that down". William Le Queux: Letter to Charles Chambers, 1899, Dep 341/143: No 37, National Library of Scotland, Edinburgh.

132 Myron J. Smith / Terry White: Cloak and Dagger Fiction. An Annotated Guide to Spy Thrillers, Westport 1995, p. 26. Smith and White do not specifically refer to "Of Royal Blood", which does not feature in their bibliography (of the around 100 works of Le Queux, they have recorded and annotated 26), but to his "early tales" (ibid.) in general.

continent, the novel draws attention to the shifting power dynamics in Europe and – different from other novels of Le Queux's, but in line with *CJ*'s overall agenda – propagates a non-militant form of competition amongst the leading countries of Europe.

The novel centres on Crawford, an experienced diplomat in the British secret service, who is sent on a mission to Brussels by the Foreign Secretary. There, he meets a young woman, who turns out to be a Hapsburg princess and whose fate seems to be bound to a secret. A number of sub-plots are developed in the narrative's 26 chapters; in the following, I will only discuss those two themes which are relevant to the representation of heroism and its properties in this specific context. The first strand is related to the profession of the protagonist – the secret service and its duties towards Britain. The second one is concerned with the relationship between Crawford and Mélanie of Hapsburg and it is the tension between those two strands which puts the protagonist's heroic attributes to the test.

On the whole, the novel evokes an atmosphere of looming danger in Europe and of changing power dynamics threatening Britain. It opens with a conversation between the protagonist Crawford and his superior, Foreign Secretary Marquess of Macclesfield, in which the former is briefed for his new assignment in Brussels.[133] The foreign secretary opens his conversation with a description of the current situation in Europe and the importance of diplomacy:

> "It is imperative that active steps must be taken to preserve England's supremacy, and at the same time frustrate the aggressive policy towards us, which is undoubtedly growing. I need not tell you that the outlook is far from reassuring. As a diplomatist you know that as well as I do. [...] You quite follow me?" "I have always striven to do my utmost towards that end," I answered. (Le Queux: Of Royal Blood, *CJ*, 2 Dec 1899, 1)

The text from the outset establishes the British Empire as endangered and in need of protection to "preserve" its "supremacy" (ibid.). The "aggressive policy" towards the country evokes a possible European military struggle.[134] With France, Russia and Germany, countries are named as possible threats which were also big political players in the present-day political environment of the readers. Thereby, the text takes up existing political fears of the time and additionally creates the fear of a looming war: "War is always within the bounds of possibility"

[133] Crawford's actual task in Brussels is never specified. He mingles with other diplomats and traces a stolen despatch box, his main occupation remains secret.

[134] The "[p]owers who were striving to undermine England's prestige" (Le Queux: Of Royal Blood, *CJ*, 2 Dec 1899, 2) are identified in the next instalment: "'France, Russia, and Germany are all three our possible enemies; and with such Powers against her, England would have to strain every effort to preserve her own. [...] [One should consider] whether to conciliate is better than to provoke a costly and bloody war.'" Ibid., 16 Dec 1899, 36.

(ibid., 20 Jan 1900, 116), says the first-person narrator Crawford at one point.[135] However, the text at the same time presents the reader with a solution to this dooming military conflict in Europe: diplomacy and espionage. "[I]t is only by careful and diligent diplomacy that the colossal armies and navies of Europe are prevented from coming into collision" (ibid.).

The work of the foreign ministry and the secret service is presented as the only possible way to evade war with one or several of the powers of the European mainland. The general public is not only described as ignorant of the dangerous situation – "English men and women at home little realise this, and are too fond of relying for their safety upon their insular impregnability" (ibid.) – but are also shown as uninformed about the importance of men such as Crawford. For example, chapter VIII begins with the statement that the British public is "strangely ignorant of the work of our embassies and the legations beyond the seas" (ibid., 20 Jan 1900, 115). Since the invisibility of their actions to the public is a prerequisite of their profession, the men of the Secret Service fit the ideal of a silent, unmediated hero so frequently propagated by *CJ*. When one of Crawford's colleagues has been murdered in a conspiracy, the foreign secretary says: "'[H]e has died, having done his duty honourably. He is one of the many *silent heroes*, and will always be remembered by me as a man who, knowing the risks he ran and the danger that surrounded him, acted with manful courage and saved England a war'" (ibid., 13 Jan 1900, 101–102, emphasis mine). The heroic and honourable actions of the men of the secret service are only ever known among their peers and cannot be mediated to the public or praised and admired by them (unless in fictional stories such as the one to hand).

Though the diplomats and the soldiers discussed above share the goal of defending the British people and its prestige, their actions are very different, in some respects even contrasting. This also becomes apparent in the first conversation between the foreign secretary and Crawford in which the former describes the latter: "'I have sufficient confidence in your diplomatic instinct to know that you will *never act rashly*, nor display any *ill-advised zeal*. The secret of England's greatness is her *smart diplomacy*; and in this affair you have, Crawford, every chance of distinction'" (ibid., 2 Dec 1899, 1, emphases mine). The properties of Crawford which are praised here are the opposite of what would be desirable in a soldier. In battle, it is exactly the ability to act fast and show zeal which is necessary. In Crawford's form of international encounter (often as hostile in intention as a battle in war), those qualities become disadvantages. Contrary to the more traditional forms of patriotic heroism, rationality and calm intellect are the crucial characteristics for the defence of Britain. This form of defence is always

135 This impending fate of Britain is evoked over and over again throughout the whole narrative in phrases such as "'As you well know, there's a conspiracy to isolate England'" (ibid., 20 Jan 1900, 117) or "[t]here was no disguising the fact that the British Empire, the pride of the world, was in deadly peril". Ibid., 27 Jan 1900, 131.

shown as a peace-oriented effort as well and the actions of the diplomats are presented as war-prevention: "Upon the Marquess of Macclesfield's tact and far-sightedness depended the prosperity of England, the lives of her millions, and the peace of Europe. A single stroke of the pen, a hasty or ill-advised action, and a war might result which would cost our Empire millions in money and millions in valuable lives" (ibid., 2).

Diplomacy is thereby depicted as a possible alternative, as a solution to prevent those sufferings which are lamented in the texts about military heroism. The emphasis on the British Empire in the text, rather than just on Britain, also shows the growingly contested status of British supremacy in the world – something which the readers themselves perceived in their everyday life through the Second Boer War.

Apart from the differences in action, the values shown as motivating the diplomats are then quite similar to the soldierly virtues: first and foremost, it is "patriotism" (ibid.) which motivates them, their "duty is towards [...] country and Queen" (ibid., 13 Jan 1900, 102). Much like the military acts, their profession requires "acts of courage" (ibid.), though they are played out on a battlefield invisible to the public.[136] Equally, selflessness is a natural part of the diplomat's self-conception; on more than one occasion, the narrator remarks that he "had saved the honour of England at the cost of [his] own" (ibid., 16 Dec 1899, 37). Similar to the depiction of heroic figures in other domains in *CJ*, the novel focuses not on a high-level diplomat, but on a lower-ranking employee and the work which is called heroic is distinctly not that done by "figurehead[s], but it is men such as you [Crawford] who man the ship" (ibid.).

The first plot-strand of the text thus revolves around Britain and its fate in the future. The diplomats and agents of the secret service are established as unmediated heroic figures that remain invisible if they perform their duty correctly. Led by the same ideals as the military heroes discussed above, their operations aim at establishing peace, rather than seeking military conflict. One of the core characteristics, the adherence to duty, is however put to the test in the novel through the second important plot-strand, Crawford's infatuation and later developing relationship with the Hapsburg princess.

Crawford, who first meets Princess Mélanie in disguise– which she puts on to be able to ride her bicycle in a park in Brussels – and only later finds out that she is of the title-giving "royal blood", emphasises at various points throughout the novel that she is like an "ordinary woman". Thereby, he implicitly creates an

136 Although most of the diplomatic manoeuvres are non-violent ones (though several murders happen throughout the narrative), they are often described in the vocabulary of violent conflict, when it is, for example, said that: "our dignity and prestige must be preserved (but at all cost). [...] Our enemies must be outwitted and crushed, or this will indeed be a sorry day in the history of our government and our country." Ibid., 6 Jan 1900, 90.

ideal of what an "ordinary woman" – like the female readers of the magazine – should be like, when he for example says:

> Cautious lest she should commit an error of etiquette, and give offence to her proud family, she was nevertheless *plain, honest,* outspoken, and *charming, modest,* and *unassuming,* like any ordinary woman; and fond of throwing off the constant exclusiveness with which every member of a royal family must of necessity be enveloped. (ibid., 3 Feb 1900, 152, emphases mine)

After some time, Crawford and Mélanie grow closer, they go on regular cycling-trips together and the princess then takes up this ideal of a 'normal' woman of the lower-middle classes and presents it as a lifestyle which she longs for:

> "[...] Indeed – but perhaps you would not believe it – when driving out on Sundays I have often envied the young shop-girl contentedly walking with hand on her lover's arm; for she is free to love or to hate, and can enjoy the pleasures of life untrammelled, with no fear of scandal or of the idle, envenomed gossip of jealous women; the world is hers, and she enjoys it to the full, though she works for her bread and her happiness may not be unmixed with tears." (ibid., 3 Mar 1900, 216)

From the perspective of the aristocratic Mélanie, the lives of "ordinary women" similar to the readers of *CJ* are valorised. What lies at the centre of the princess's jealousy is something else, though: it is the privateness of the "ordinary" women's lives which is something that money and status cannot buy. Through the above two descriptions, the novel thereby implicitly achieves an idealisation of the kind of life which its readers lead and propagates the ideal of a humble, private woman. When compared to previously discussed depictions of women, a development in the conception of a womanly ideal can be perceived though: the privateness so envied by Mélanie is not to be used synonymously with domesticity anymore and the referral to "outspokenness" (ibid., 3 Feb 1900, 152) and the freedom "to love or to hate" (ibid., 3 Mar 1900, 216) show the effects the women's rights movement had on society by the turn of the century.

Quite predictably, Crawford falls in love with Mélanie – though he prizes himself on having done so before he knew that she was aristocratic. His feelings for her lead him into a deep inner conflict. She not only stands above him in the social order and Crawford "well seasoned by ten years of Court life" knows that "such a thing was utterly ridiculous" (ibid., 3 Feb 1900, 152). He is nevertheless "overrode" by love and has to admit that he is "irretrievably her slave" (ibid.). However, the conflict is not only a societal one, but later also a conflict of interest regarding his professional life and the duty towards his country. Not only is Mélanie associated with the threatening German power and later marries a Hohenzollern prince, but she is also entrapped in an extortion which Crawford vows to help her out of. This effort, however, tests his loyalty and he is torn between his duty towards Queen and country and the private desire to help the Hapsburg princess in distress. This ambiguity becomes especially pronounced in one passage of the novel when Crawford vows: "I was compelled to remain silent in order to avoid compromising her, for she was princess of an imperial house, while I was a humble member of Her Majesty's Diplomatic Service. I had promised to remain loyal to her" (ibid., 24 Feb 1900, 198). However, this vow is highly ambiguous; since he had professed loyalty to both the Queen and Mélanie, the reference of loyalty "to her" (ibid.) remains unclear and makes the inner conflict obvious. For several chapters of the novel it then seems as if Crawford has decided in favour of the princess. Nevertheless, all affirmations of loyalty towards her address the conflict with his professional and patriotic duty.[137] Over the course of the novel, though, Crawford realises that he

> had, by loving Mélanie, departed from the first tenets of my religion as a diplomatist, besides having neglected a great degree the special duty of which I had been nominated to Brussels. Had not the great Marquess of Macclesfield, the greatest diplomatist of his age, told me plainly the folly of allowing myself to be drawn into any serious affair of the heart? The more I reflected, the more impossible seemed happiness. (ibid., 14 April 1900, 308)

The unfulfilled romance between the protagonist and the princess reveals another property of the silent heroes of diplomacy and espionage. As part of their selflessness, their duty requires them to sacrifice their private lives in order to achieve peace for the rest of the nation. The diplomats, as represented in "Of Royal Blood", need to give up on their own happiness for that of the collective.[138] Regarding romance, Crawford concludes: "To be a successful diplomatist a man must needs steel his heart against all feminine blandishments" (ibid., 28 April 1900, 340).

The new type of the heroic secret agent shows both similarities as well as differences to the type of the soldierly hero. On the one hand, both share the motivation for their actions: patriotism and a feeling of duty towards one's country and community. Both need to act courageously, yet where the soldier needs to act rashly, spontaneously, physically and violently, the secret agent needs to be far-sighted, tactical, calm and uses his intellect and words rather than violent means. Also, the circumstances which activate the respective heroic acts are very different: while the military man is called into action to defend his country when a violent conflict has already broken out, the man of the secret service uses his means to prevent such conflicts from escalating in the first place. Though

137 This for example becomes apparent in the following conversation: "'Well, my oath to my Queen entails the combating of the machinations of unscrupulous enemies; […]. Towards you, however, I assure you that if ever I can render you a service you have only to command me.'" Ibid., 24 Feb 1900, 199.

138 The impossibility of a fulfilled private life in the secret service is also emphasised by another plot-line which features the only married agent of the narrative. Gordon Clunes, a friend of Crawford's, is newlywed and subsequently murdered by his wife who turns out to be a German agent.

clearly situated in the lived-in world of the readers[139] – and thus the time of the British war-effort in South Africa – the text shows *CJ*'s overall antipathy towards military action. By avoiding the situation in Africa and focusing on the powers of the European continent, the novel in its popular form[140] can put forth this opinion without undermining the journal's support for the specific war effort against the Boers.

On the whole, the usage of the vocabulary of heroism in relation to military actions clearly increases during times of British involvement in major war efforts. As the example of texts published during the Crimean War and the two Boer Wars have shown, *CJ*, though in general opposing violent military conflicts, adapted their texts to the political situation around them. The publication context thus acted as a regulatory means, which made the periodical negotiate its self-defined didactic and humanist identity with the societal reality of the day. In focusing on common sailors and soldiers, the magazine offered a means of identification to their readership. Through the depiction of successful historical battles of the past, an attempt to assure the readership of the British troops' strength in order to keep up the morale can be detected. On the whole, descriptions of the front are avoided and the representation of soldierly heroism omits rather than describes the physicality and brutality of war actions. Instead, the texts focus on the motivating forces behind the soldierly acts and heroise their courage, selflessness, patriotism and willingness to sacrifice themselves for the greater good of the collective. In emphasising these underlying values, the magazine again creates an opportunity for the readers to identify with the depicted heroes and emulate their behaviour in their own everyday life, since the values depicted can also be transferred to the lives at the home front.[141]

---

139 The text is clearly placed in the last years of the nineteenth century through various cultural, technological and political references: The foreign secretary's office sports a "life-size portrait of Her Majesty" (ibid., 2 Dec 1899, 1), Crawford seems to be used to "telephonic" communication (ibid., 13 Jan 1900, 101). Furthermore, the "Fashoda incident" of 1898 (ibid., 20 Jan 1900, 116), and "the recent International Exhibition" (ibid., 17 Feb 1900, 180) in Brussels which had taken place in 1897 clearly place the text in temporal proximity to the readers' lives.

140 Both Charles Chambers and Le Queux seemed pleased with the readers' response to the novel. Le Queux remarks: "My novel [...] is, I hear, going splendidly" (William Le Queux: Letter to Charles Chambers, 1900, Dep 341/143: No 36, National Library of Scotland, Edinburgh) and Chambers confirms: "our readers tell me they like [the novel] very much". Charles Chambers: Letter to William Le Queux, 1900, Dep 341/167: No 355, National Library of Scotland, Edinburgh.

141 Furthermore, occasional heroisation of the sacrifices made at the home front can be found in *CJ* as well. Significantly, the function of heroic acts on the home front are often directly connected to the heroic agency of the soldiers on the battle field, both of which are shown as acting for the stabilisation of a community in a situation of existential danger. While a soldier acts for the defence of the national community, those left at the home front have to protect their familial community.

However, as the examination of the Second Boer War after the British defeat in the 1880s has shown, the journal reacted to the changing global power dynamics. In its more pronounced support of the war in South Africa, it acknowledges the growing instability of the British Empire and the importance of winning the second campaign. Though still generally opposed to war – as the narrative "Of Royal Blood" has indicated – the magazine's politics of heroisation indicates the shifting political dynamics in Europe.

Heroism and the Military in Times of Peace

In times of peace, *CJ* featured narratives or essays dealing with military men as heroic figures less frequently and, in those cases which can be found, the attitude towards military heroism is quite different from the texts discussed above. In general, the periodical shows a critical attitude towards the heroic potential of the military profession, which had surfaced in the idea of situational heroism, and – in line with their general agenda to morally elevate their readers – propagated a peace-oriented attitude. Therefore, most of the texts which will be discussed in the following present a rather dubious and vain form of military heroism or assign heroism in situations of war and battle to non-military players.

In a number of texts, soldierly heroism is not only described as "easy" (True Chivalry, *CJ*, 15 Sep 1866, 592) because the given situation 'forces' the soldiers to act heroically, but also as a form of heroics which is often performed by uneducated, unintelligent or immature characters. The ballad "The Twin Brothers" exemplifies this by contrasting two brothers:

Time passed – one was a wilting boy
  Robust of health, of stature tall;
The other wore a forehead high,
  Of weakly frame, of stature small; (The Twin Brothers, *CJ*, 3 Jan 1851: 16)

The two brothers not only differ greatly in physical appearance and strength but also in their intellectual capacities. While the "weakly" one is very intelligent, his "robust" brother struggles in school, is described as "a fool" (ibid.). Having to depend on his physical abilities for his livelihood, the poem presents the battlefield as the only possible realm for him:

That strong-thewed brother, where is he? –
  On the van amid the brave;
A freeman 'mong the dauntless free,
  He found a hero's glorious grave;
[...]
  The hero fought, the hero died. (ibid.)

And though the "strong-thewed brother" is called a hero, fighting a hero's fight and dying a hero's death, the context of his previous characterisation establishes military heroism as a purely physical form of heroics which requires neither intellectual nor moral skills.[142]

Similarly, the historical narrative "Blanchette: A Fairy Tale" also establishes the want for military heroics as something which comes rather to the uneducated, immature mind than to the more intelligent and educated. The tale is set in fifteenth-century France and shows the infant Dauphin Charles (later to be Charles VIII of France). He is depicted as an unhappy child who lives under his "old tyrant" father (Blanchette, *CJ*, 4 Feb 1854, 77) and is in a general state of neglect: "Without employment for his mind, he lived nearly as solitary and secluded as his father's prisoners" (ibid.). This lack of education and familial attention then leads to the following pastime:

> Therefore, after notching his sword for a long time against the wall, and spelling the large characters, red and blue, of his Rosary of Wars and Holy Bible, this dreamy youth would pass his time leaning on the window-sill, and gazing for hours upon the beautiful sky of Touraine and imagining the changing forms of the clouds armies and battles. (ibid.)

The boy's only confidante in the story is Blanchette, "a little white mouse" (ibid.). It is to her the boy talks daily and she communicates with him as well. By pointing her paws to a passage in the opened bible – "*To visit the prisoners!*" (ibid.) – she leads him into the dungeons and directs him to the cell of the Duke of Nemours. The young man of seventeen who is "a guest of that frightful dwelling-place" (ibid., 78) is then established as the "hero" (ibid.) of the narrative. Having led him to the young Duke, Charles inquires whether he knows Blanchette and their first encounter mostly consists of a fight over who has the prior claim over Blanchette. Befitting the Dauphin's preoccupation with wars and battles, the sequence satirises territorial conflict by staging the fight as one about the supremacy over Blanchette. After having agreed upon a joint 'ownership' of the mouse, the Dauphin and the Duke become friends and the "hero" (ibid.) performs the role of an educator for Charles. The boy's secluded life, his boredom and limited education become apparent in their conversations in which his unreflected want for military exploits frequently comes up. When Nemours asks him to imagine his own future kingship, the boy answers with deliberation: "'A Fine question! I will make war'" (ibid.). When Nemours sighs "sadly" (ibid.) and asks him to elaborate upon this plan, the conversation continues:

> "Yes," continued the dauphin, tapping his forehead with his forefinger, "I have had the design for a long time. First, I will go and conquer Italy – Italy, you see, Nemours, is a marvellous country: there the streets are filled with music, the bushes laden with oranges and there are as many churches as houses. I will keep Italy for myself – then I will

142 On the whole, the poem calls for a balance between physical and intellectual powers, since the twin brother, whose skills are merely intellectual and who is physically challenged, does not turn out to be successful either.

go and take Constantinople in passing, for my friend Andrew Palaeologus; and afterwards, with the aid of Heaven, I reckon upon delivering the Holy Sepulchre."
"And after that?" inquired the young duke with a leer.
"Ah! After that – after that" – repeated the ignorant dauphin, somewhat embarrassed – "afterwards – I shall still have time to conquer other countries, if there be any." (ibid.)

The reason for the boy's lust for military conquest is quite obvious: his familial neglect, his boredom and his ignorance. He dreams of war and battle because it seems an exciting alternative to his dreary life and an opportunity to find the recognition and appreciation which he presently seems to lack. This is further emphasised by the fact that he judges the countries for imagined conquest by their entertainment value rather than for reasons of politics or power. The Duke lives in forced seclusion and boredom as well, yet his age and greater maturity seem to prevent such fantasies. He questions the Dauphin's ideas and exposes them as vain, motivated by an "anxiety for glory" which makes the Dauphin only think of himself rather than of his "people" (ibid.).[143] The conversations with Nemours seem to impress the boy, yet his demeanour only changes later, in a very symbolic act. After Charles' father, Louis XI of France, has died, the thirteen-year-old boy enters the dungeons and releases Nemours.[144] Only through this symbolic freeing, the anti-form of his imagined wars and a sort of counter-conquest, the boy's character seems to change, he is "no longer timid, constrained, dejected [...] but calm, grave" (ibid., 79). Through his 'education' by Nemours and the practical application of newly found morals, the boy has matured and emancipated himself from his unreflected war lust.[145]

The contrast between the "hero" Nemours who perseveres in a cage for several years and the young Dauphin in his immature want for attention can also be read as an advice to the reader. Nemours is shown as being mentally and emotionally unscarred by his imprisonment and, apart from their dispute over Blanchette, he does not utter any negative feelings towards the Dauphin upon their first meeting, although he is the son of his captor. The usage of the vocabulary of the heroic in relation to Nemours thus draws attention to the virtues of perseverance, selflessness and altruism in spite of a hopeless situation. More importantly, though, the contrasting depiction of the young Dauphin can be read as an educational advice; by showing the boy's excitement about war as a result

143 Once again, this passage creates a direct opposition between heroism which seeks glory and reputation and heroic acts which are performed for the wellbeing of a larger group.

144 This is where the fairy-tale like quality of the narrative plays out, because Nemours' cage cannot be opened, even after the Dauphin's father has died and Charles (now Charles VIII) wants to free him. They need the help of Blanchette, who turns out to be a fairy, in destroying the cage and freeing Nemours.

145 Interestingly, the story ends with the freeing of Nemours and does not comment upon the Dauphin's future attitude towards war or give facts about the historical Charles VIII. This could for one be due to the fact that, though being called "the Affable", Charles was involved in several conquests and actually acted out the dream formulated in the narrative to conquer Italy.

of his intellectual and emotional neglect, the text stresses the importance of the bond between parent and child. Furthermore, it emphasises the necessity of education; the Dauphin obviously has some form of formal education, he can read and write and possesses knowledge of geography and culture (which he utilises in his dreams of conquest), however, he lacks a moral compass which, if one follows the logic of the story, cannot be taught by books and not even by the bible. Thereby, the text not only criticises military endeavours motivated by an uneducated, unmoral want for attention and glory, but also stresses the importance of parental moral instruction.

A mockery of the intellectual capacity of military men can even be found in relation to the navy and their major hero Nelson: the narrator of the satirical text "The Great Teaboard School", a city man who recently moved to the seaside with his family, shares his assessment of the navy and its men with the reader:

> There is something in the sea-air which is opposed to intellectual vitality. I hope I am too much of an Englishman to say one word in depreciation of the naval profession, whose heroism, whose simplicity, and whose freedom from sea-sickness have always extorted my admiration; but I think it may be stated, without offence, that sailors are dull folks. The saline particles that stick to the hair [...] affect in time the brain itself. Nelson was a noble hero, and we are all grateful to his memory; but the saline particles certainly affected him. (The Great Teaboard School, *CJ*, 16 Jul 1870, 462)

In place of the sailorly virtues depicted in war-time such as courage and selflessness, the text shows them as foolish men whose best characteristics are their "simplicity" and "freedom from sea-sickness" (ibid.). The narrator depicts the profession of the sailor as one which requires no specific skills – neither physically nor intellectually – and thus caricatures the established type of the British naval hero exemplified by Nelson.[146] The text then goes on to criticise the moral integrity of the profession and calls the navy men hard-hearted: "while the brain softens the heart hardens" (ibid.). Though the text is clearly a satire and not to be taken as an opinion piece, it nevertheless stands in striking contrast to those texts about the army published in times of war. It can be seen as a representation of the magazine's general distrust of the military and their peace-oriented rationale.

Severe and direct criticism of violent military acts and war-lust, however, only seems possible when dealing with other nations. This becomes especially apparent in "Modern Spartans"; the text about contemporary Greece aims at showing how close military heroism and brutality are linked. If motivated by war-lust, the text argues, heroics turn into barbarism and it is this tendency which is shown in relation to the Greek region of the Maniots. The text already identifies the doubtful liking for war in the cultivation of the landscape: "It is impossible to pass through the country without remarking the number of defensive works [...].

[146] The description of the sailors' set of skills and its exemplification through Nelson is in itself a satire, since it was well known that Nelson throughout his career remained prone to seasickness. Cf. e.g. John Sugden: Nelson. A Dream of Glory, London 2005, p. 56.

The highest rocks, the entrances to the defiles, the inaccessible precipices, are alike covered with fortifications" (Modern Spartans, *CJ*, 29 Apr 1871, 257). This constant presence of war, the text argues further, is also part of the inhabitants' character: "They wander around these old fortresses like soldiers weighed down by inaction. Each man professes a religious worship for his arms, and his pride is to adorn them with the richest ornaments. [...] Every castle has its legend of heroic or barbarous deeds" (ibid.). The decision between heroism or barbarism seems to be only a matter of perspective and the text suggests to the reader that the actions of the "modern Spartans", who seem to long for war as part of their innate identity, are "barbarous" (ibid.).[147]

In an archetypical description of the local male, it is said that: "At twelve he handles his gun and joins the men: to fire with a certain aim; never to count the numbers of the enemy; to defend himself to the death behind the towers or entrenchments – such are the tactics he is taught" (ibid., 258).[148] As an adult, the typical male gives "himself up to his savage temper. He began by killing his wife, whom he accused of infidelity; and a short time after, in consequence of an unimportant quarrel, relieved himself in the same way of an unhappy foreigner" (ibid.). All this is attributed to the local "military honour" (ibid.) which is based on "primitive formulas" (ibid.) of morale. The text shows a brutality which is drastic for *CJ* in its depiction and uses the region of the Maniots as a stage to discuss the connection between brutality and military endeavours. The negative counter image and their perception of their own acts as "heroism" (ibid.) and "heroic deeds" (ibid., 258) not only criticises violence for its own sake, but also stresses the fact that heroism is always dependent on a specific perspective and often already implicitly contains its opposite. By emphasising that it is the modern Spartans' lack of "morals" (ibid.) which makes them cling to their violent ideals, the text also creates a counter image of a collective which is bound by higher ideals and does not lust for war, but for peace. Only in the transferral of the subject matter to a distant country and a culture which is described as fundamentally different from the common readers' does this depiction of misdirected military ambition and open propagation of pacifism seem to be possible.[149]

---

147 Furthermore, it is worth noting that in this negative form of military conduct, the contested idea of worship is evoked again. Not only does this bring up the general unease the periodical had with the concept, but the idea of religious worship in relation to the armaments establishes violence and barbarism as a form of religious belief of the Greek.

148 Significantly, similar descriptions of tactics taught to British soldiers cannot be found in the magazine.

149 Another strategy of criticizing violence yet attributing heroism to deeds in the context of war was to depict actors alongside the battlefield. There are for example a number of texts devoted to medical staff, such as a "Non-Combatant Hero" in 1862. These "healers and preservers" (A Non-Combatant Hero, *CJ*, 8 Mar 1862, 158) are described utilising the main characteristics of *CJ*'s heroic imaginary as selfless, courageous and responsible – even more so than the soldiers themselves since the medical staff is not armed. The heroic doctor is thus established as a non-violent counter-figure to the military hero.

The periodical also displays explicit remarks against war and its consequences. This becomes apparent in texts which deal with army veterans and their lives after the war. The essay "Up and Down Regent Street", which on the whole is a critical evaluation of West-London society, depicts

> a guard of honour proper to the establishment itself, in the shape of a Crimean hero, medalled, bi-medalled, or tri-medalled, and perhaps lacking a limb or two in addition – realising the reward of valour and patriotism, won at the cannon's mouth, in the honourable vocation of circulating puffs for the Messrs Goose and Goldeneggs. (Up and Down Regent Street, *CJ*, 16 Jun 1860, 369)

This drastically shows the results of a war and the worth of being a "Crimean hero" (ibid.) after the campaign has ended. Although having been publicly honoured, "medalled, bi-medalled", and having sacrificed his health in a patriotic and courageous effort, the former soldier now has to work as a street monger to earn his living. The repeated usage of "honour" for both the area around Regent Street and the former military man's task of "circulating puffs" emphasises the absurdity of the situation and the emptiness of the honours bestowed on veterans. The status as a war hero in this context does not inspire admiration in the passers-by and the man possibly only displays his medals and shows his disabilities in order to inspire pity and increase sales. Thereby, the situation depicted offers a glimpse at the effects of war once the fighting is over and the 'heroes' return into civilian life. Whereas class seemed to be less of an issue in the field and even common soldiers were publicly honoured for their war effort, the social rank becomes an existential concern again back at home. Sacrifices of war, such as serious injury which in the context of the battle could have made a man a hero and put him among the most highly regarded men of the country, back in civilian life become a risk for the social decline of whole families.[150]

A similar situation is depicted in "Portland Prison"; the text describes the prison on Portland Island and its efforts to educate inmates. However, the text also notes that "[c]omplaints have been made that the convicts live too well" (Portland Prison, *CJ*, 23 Mar 1861, 191) and that their lives are too comfortable compared to free working men like their guards. These guards, which the text shows as being disadvantaged in contrast to the criminals in Portland Prison, are then identified as "mostly Crimean heroes, now half-policemen, half-soldiers" (ibid., 190). Although not as drastically, this text also shows how the soldiers returning from a major war effort for their country struggle to find a place in society. The guards, though fortunate enough to have found a job, do not seem to have a

---

150 These depictions of returning file-and-rank soldiers affirm John Reed's argument that "[a]lthough the Crimean War marked a new respect for the common soldier, that did not necessarily translate into a widespread embracing of the ranker at home. As Kipling's work at the end of the century suggests, the general public was still inclined to dismiss the common soldier as a morally inferior being, given to drinking and brawling and unwelcome in good company." Reed: Army, pp. 312–313.

clear-cut identity after the end of the war and in their new profession as "half-policemen, half-soldiers" (ibid.) seem to be stuck between life as a soldier and a civilian, though in their new employment only the weapons – "cutlass and rifle" (ibid.) – seem to be reminiscent of their life as soldiers. Being regarded as "Crimean heroes" is again of no practical worth and does not result in social improvement for the men, who are surpassed in quality of life by the prisoners they guard.

The depiction of military men after their return to life in Britain clearly shows how dependant the worth of a heroic reputation is on class. While common soldiers from the lower ranks struggle to find their way back into civilian life and have to realise that their military honours do not result in social security, *CJ* also shows instances of military men of higher social rank after the war. These, however, are often shown as pompous and boastful, like an elderly seaman who prides himself on having "fought with 'our Nelly' – as he familiarly termed the hero of Trafalgar" – and who takes this fact as the reason that "gave him right to grapple everybody" (Meliboeus Has a Fish-Dinner At Greenwich, *CJ*, 5 Oct 1861, 220). A further class difference can be seen in the self-conception of the represented men: whereas the 'common soldiers' represented in *CJ* had to find a way back into civilian life and can rarely profit from the social capital of their military heroism, those of the upper classes can safely remain in their identity as a "military man" (The Wild Huntress, *CJ*, 21 July 1860, 41) and live off "the right" (Meliboeus Has a Fish-Dinner At Greenwich, *CJ*, 5 Oct 1861, 220) which this status gives them.

Military Heroism and Hierarchy

The above analysis of the representation of military heroism in *CJ* has shown that the periodical rarely depicted great historical leaders of army and navy. On the contrary, most accounts focused on soldiers and sailors of lower ranks and often showed fictitious men, the representation of whom was strongly focused on their motivation, suffering and moral fibre rather than their violent actions in battle. This tendency to heroise the common and unknown soldier is in line with the journal's attempt at publicly validating the lives of silent heroes of the lower classes, while attempting at the same time not to encourage a lust for fame and public recognition in individuals. However, heroism– despite the attempts of privatisation and functionalisation of exemplarity – always depicts something which is 'better than' and necessarily needs a frame of reference; therefore, culturally agreed upon military heroes feature in the magazine in various articles – yet always only as an established reference for military excellence which is not elaborated upon.

The reference figure used most frequently is Horatio Nelson. Nelson comes up in references such as "the hero of Trafalgar" (ibid.) or "the Portsmouth naval hero" (The Glove, *CJ*, 22 Dec 1860, 340), but is, however, only used as a frame of reference for other – unknown – military men. On the one hand, this shows that the story of Nelson's heroism did not need to be told, because it was well known to the audience and brought to mind a specific set of characteristics; on the other hand, the specific example of Nelson also activated a second narrative, one of fame and morals, and it is no wonder then that reference to the naval commander is also used in articles which criticise military actions. It was known that Nelson had been a vain man who liked attention, and was a skilled self-promoter.[151] Many Victorians, in a self-conception as modest, respectable and faithful, took offence at Nelson's open extramarital relationship with Emma Hamilton. This part of Nelson's life was commonly considered as diminishing his status as a representative of national greatness and is shown as belittling his heroic reputation in *CJ* as well. A historical account of court life at the beginning of the nineteenth century calls Nelson's private life a "vulgarity and absurdity [...] beyond belief" (Continental Courts Sixty Years Ago, *CJ*, 24 Aug 1861, 124). Although the text nevertheless calls Nelson "the hero" (ibid.) in relation to his naval achievements, it closes with a strong de-heroisation: "This is certainly a disenchanting recital. [...] After all, much of human greatness is a matter of accident. Some are exalted by the accident of birth; some by the possession of special gifts. Unless there be also a natural dignity and purity, these kinds of greatness, of course must shew ill behind the scenes" (ibid., 125). This last paragraph, though affirming Nelson as a great man of cultural importance who possessed "special gifts", stresses once again that true heroism in *CJ*'s definition can only be achieved with a sound moral character, "natural dignity and purity".[152]

A reference to Nelson also implicitly included a link to fame and dubious morals. His military success ("greatness") and its importance for Britain being undisputed though, *CJ* then uses Nelson in some instances as reference for victory rather than heroic behaviour and attributes the heroic status to the men who "fought under Nelson" (The Fortune of Bertram Oakley, *CJ*, 23 Apr 1881, 261) or "the brave seamen who served under [...] Horatio Viscount Nelson" (The British Navy, As it Was, *CJ*, 17 Mar 1877, 162). Thereby, figures such as Nel-

[151] He had, for example, changed his name from Horace to Horatio at the age of eighteen because he thought it sounded more impressive, had cleverly networked throughout his career and been careful to make all his smaller and larger achievements publicly known, "for no man wanted more to be a hero. He exhibited his trophies, stage managed public appearances and manipulated the press to shape the desired image". John Sugden: Nelson. The Sword of Albion, London 2012, p. 2. For example, the "Nelson touch", his specific strategy of boarding enemy ships, became known under that name because Nelson himself propagated the term. Cf. ibid., p. 773.

[152] Placing this at the very end of the text, the remark can be read as an appeal to the reader to cultivate these morals.

son, or the occasionally referenced Wellington,[153] can be seen as an implication of national importance and British supremacy rather than examples of the form of moral heroism so often mediated in *CJ*. This kind of moral motivation for heroic actions is, in the pages of the magazine, more often than not attributed to the lower ranks of society and/or those people who do not stand at the centre of public attention.

Despite the periodical's often-repeated aim not to contribute to the fame of established figures, but to tell the stories of 'unsung' heroes and their values, which their readers could identify with, there is one well-known military man whom *CJ* presents frequently, especially around 1860, the year of the so-called Expedition of the Thousand: Guiseppe Garibaldi. Between 1859 and 1900, almost a hundred articles were devoted to Garibaldi, many of which call the Italian general a hero and praise his actions and character. The articles about Garibaldi could have been appealing to the audience for two reasons: since Garibaldi was still an active part of European politics, the texts on the one hand touched on contemporary developments and current political and military topics; on the other hand, their entertainment value was high: all articles which dealt with Garibaldi contained at least one adventurous anecdote of his earlier years as a sailor,[154] and the vast majority of them was travel writing. Thus, the texts not only depicted Garibaldi's military actions and his virtues worthy of emulation, but also described landscapes and local customs.

In this appealing format, the texts always label Garibaldi a hero and strategically depict him as a common man, thereby utilising him as a possible role model for the readers. One contribution takes the publication of the English-language version of Garibaldi's memoirs as an occasion to comment upon "the Best soldier of his time" (The Story of a Hero, *CJ*, 15 Oct 1859, 243).[155] The article's title, "The Story of a Hero", already affirms Garibaldi's status as a hero. The text then uses the same strategies in the depiction of Garibaldi that could be observed in the depiction of rank-and-file military heroes above: it focuses on his morals and virtues rather than on the specific actions he performed. The text traces his development from childhood onwards, presents his character traits as

153 Interestingly, *CJ* did not report on Wellington's funeral in 1852, but only referenced it in "Things Talked of in London" in November 1852: "Apart from the striking and absorbing ceremony of the funeral of the Duke of Wellington, affairs have taken their usual course [...]." Things Talked of in London, *CJ*, 27 Nov 1852, 350. Other periodicals, such as *Leisure Hour*, devoted more than one article to the description of the funeral itself and furthermore portrayed Wellington as a hero in these texts.

154 In "The Story of a Hero" he is, for example, described as a "modern Ulysses" (The Story of a Hero, *CJ*, 15 Oct 1859, 244) in his early years on sea.

155 The phrase "his time" (ibid., 243) seems odd in this context, since the time referred to is the present of author and reader and therefore could just as easily have been called "our time" or "this time".

exemplary and worth emulating and especially foregrounds his actions and responsibility towards the group of soldiers entrusted to him.

In his characterisation, the text shows Garibaldi as a man of the lower classes rather than a man of high military rank:

> His fights throughout life have all been fought *up-hill.* Now the *servant* of this republic and now of that, he has been contending, almost from boyhood, against despots, dictators, and all sorts of powers of darkness in both the New and the Old Worlds [...]; and yet this Soldier of Misfortune, [...] roamed the world like a *faithful Knight-errant*, wearing the favour of his mistress, *Liberty*, at all times in his helm. (ibid., emphases mine)

This first description of Garibaldi in the text distinctly shows him not as a general or as a commander, but as a man who has dedicated his life to a greater cause. By calling him a "servant" and a "faithful Knight-errant" in the name of "Liberty", the image of a foot-soldier rather than a leader is painted. The initial remark on his battles being "fought up-hill" further stresses his perseverance[156] and struggle towards success.

For the remainder of the text, anecdotes from Garibaldi's memoirs are quoted and thereby given the authenticity of being "related by his own lips" (ibid.). The comments upon these anecdotes then strongly focus on Garibaldi's compassionate character and his high morals which the text already identifies in his early youth: he is described as "a good son to both his parents" with a "tenderness of disposition" (ibid.). His "good deeds" are explained by "nothing less" than his "great and modest mind" (ibid.). These characteristics seen in the child Garibaldi are also foregrounded as his motivation in the fight for a united Italy. Above all, it is the selfless "affection for his fellow-countrymen" (ibid., 245) which is praised and the "noble ideas" (ibid.) which motivated even his military decisions. Special attention is drawn to Garibaldi's dislike of violence and he is quoted:

> "I wish for myself and for every other person who has not forgotten to be a man, to be exempt from the necessity of witnessing the sack of a town. A long and minute description would not be sufficient to give a just idea of the baseness and wickedness of such a deed! May God save me from such a spectacle hereafter! I never spent a day in such wretchedness and in such lamentation. I was filled with horror; and the fatigue I endured in restraining personal violence was excessive." (ibid.)

Garibaldi describes this encounter as highly inhumane and immediately distances himself from his peers. Unlike them, he shows himself as not having "forgotten to be a man" and, while they sack the town, he sees it as his task to stop

---

156 His determined and persevering nature is also mentioned in relation to his naval skills; the texts states that he "perfected his seamanship" on "many voyages" (ibid.). His skills are thereby not shown as innate talent, but as acquired through diligence and perseverance. In this respect, Garibaldi is made equal to the intended audience of the periodical, who were (as could be seen in the discussion of *CJ*'s heroic imaginary) given the opportunity to achieve hero-status through persevering self-improvement. This idea is not contradicted by the later assertion that Garibaldi was special from childhood onwards, since the talents presented as innate concern his moral disposition and not a genial skill-set.

their "personal violence" (ibid.). Although revered as a military hero,[157] Garibaldi is presented as different from other military men and as essentially opposed to personal violence, that is violence not necessary in the fight for the good of "his fellow countrymen" (ibid.).[158]

In the case of Garibaldi, who as a celebrity-like figure does not fit all the requirements which *CJ* so often asks for in relation to true heroism, the relationship and closeness to the Italian people and his subordinates are key to his heroic reputation in the periodical. Despite the repeated claim not to want to encourage a lust for public attention, *CJ* also depicts the enthusiastic reaction of the Italian people towards Garibaldi and describes how people crowded the streets, displayed flags and chanted Garibaldi's name when he came to their town (cf. All the World Over, *CJ*, 11 May 1861, 298–299). However, these displays of admiration seem to be acceptable since Garibaldi so strongly resembles his subordinates and has the interest of those men and women who cheer at him in mind in his military actions. Through the links between Garibaldi, his soldiers and the population at large, the "hero", despite his public status, offers an identificatory potential for a large number of people and is established as a role model.

Significantly, all of the articles in *CJ* which praise Garibaldi as a common hero of the people were published before his visits to Britain in 1862 and 1864; his reception in 1864 was as enthusiastic as the reaction of his Italian supporters disseminated through the periodical. Garibaldi drew a lot of attention, 25,000 supporters attended his speech at the Crystal Palace, and he drew people from all ranks of society.[159] Riall notes that the "welcome given to him was unique, or at least unprecedented in the history of London".[160] In his speech, Garibaldi famously called Britain admirable in their "splendid institutions and their [...] liberty".[161] With his claims, he found support in the growing democratic move-

157 Garibaldi himself in his memoir draws upon this reputation as a military man, the title of the book being *The Life of* General *Garibaldi. Written by Himself* (emphasis mine).

158 Garibaldi's heroic humility and his disliking for violence is stressed in a number of other texts as well, cf. Over the Var, *CJ*, 29 Sep 1860; All the World Over, *CJ*, 11 May 1861; or On the Rock with Garibaldi, *CJ*, 29 Jun 1861.

159 Cf. Lucy Riall: Garibaldi. Invention of a Hero, New Haven 2008, p. 3 and pp. 330–346; Alfonso Scirocco: Garibaldi. Citizen of the World, Princeton 2007, pp. 331–342; Derek Beales: Garibaldi in England. The Politics of Italian Enthusiasm, in: John A. Davis / Paul Ginsborg (eds.): Society and Politics in the Age of the Risorgimento. Essays in Honour of Denis Mack Smith, Cambridge 2002, pp. 184–216. For Garibaldi's visit in Britain and the political implications and instrumentalisations, see Beales: Garibaldi in England; Nick Carter: Britain, Ireland and the Italian Risorgimento, Basingstoke 2015; Margot C. Finn: After Chartism. Class and Nation in English Radical Politics 1848–1874, Cambridge 1993; Ed Podesta / Pam Canning: Enquiring History. Italian Unification 1815–1871, London 2015; Riall: Garibaldi; E. D. Steele: Palmerston and Liberalism 1855–1865, Cambridge 1991 or Marcella Pellegrino Sutcliffe: Garibaldi in London, in: History Today 64.4, 2014, pp. 42–49.

160 Riall: Garibaldi, p. 336.

161 Quoted in Steele: Liberalism, p. 231.

ment,[162] in Protestantism, which supported his anti-Papal ideas, but also the political radicals, who were aiming for political equality across class boundaries. Garibaldi had contact with trade unions, was associated with the fight for freedom and democracy and the support he gained threatened political conservatives as well as the aristocracy.[163] Although *CJ* claimed political neutrality and support for the lower classes, their functionalisation of heroism can also be seen in the context of social stability. The periodical aimed to disseminate knowledge and improve living conditions, but did not propagate a radical re-structuring of society. *CJ*'s heroic imaginary in its focus on humble virtues such as selflessness and perseverance and the call for unmediated heroism can thereby be seen as a tool to stabilise those societal norms which some of Garibaldi's supporters in Britain questioned. It is thus unsurprising that the heroisation of Garibaldi as a humble common man working for the common good does not continue once he is openly associated with radical political ideas and becomes unattractive in the identity-forming agenda that heroism performed in the periodical.

It has become apparent that *CJ*, though using the military success of established national figures such as Nelson or Wellington as a frame of reference, tried to break down the hierarchical structures of army and navy in their depiction of military heroism – albeit without openly criticising the existence of hierarchies. Instead of reiterating the triumphs of the well-known 'great men', they focused on those men who constituted the largest part of the military in war time: middle-class and working-class men. In heroising these men, the contributors acknowledged their intended readership and their class-membership and – in their didactic agenda – focused on the values of courage, selflessness and the ability to suffer as virtues which they wanted their readership to admire and to emulate. In referring to military men of the past and resorting predominantly to fictional representations of military heroes located in the present day, the periodical on the one hand acknowledged the violent reality of war, and on the other hand did not contribute to an active worship of actual military figures. Guiseppe Garibaldi, the only major deviation from this pattern, is described as a common man with a focus on the same virtues and character traits and thus, though an exception because of his fame, is presented as a model for imitation as well.

John Reed argues that the British did not only "view themselves against a variety of othernesses that helped to define the way they might define their own character" in their military endeavours, but had to deal with a more complicated threat than the "external other": "Class differences in the home country were

[162] Riall argues that Garibaldi's visit in 1864 contributed to the mobilisation in support of "domestic reform and, in particular, an extension of the franchise which was to culminate in the Second Reform Act of 1867". Riall: Garibaldi, p. 339.

[163] Queen Victoria is quoted to have written to her daughter "Garibaldi – thank God! – is gone!" (quoted ibid.) after his departure from Britain.

also an issue. What was manhood as it related to class?"[164] This can easily be related to the representation of military heroism in *CJ*. The focus on rank-and-file soldiers and (to a lesser extent) sailors mirrors the changing dynamics within the military system and the intended readership of the periodical; furthermore, the fact that, as Reed notes, manliness becomes contested as the military becomes less elite-centred shows in *CJ* as well.[165] The concentration on moral actions rather than on descriptions of physicality and pomp shows a movement away from traditional warrior-like manhood and offers a broader spectrum of identification, which not only included other male self-conceptions but could even cross gender boundaries. In emphasising the moral and communal motivation of soldierly actions, these underlying values, constituting in this context a decidedly national identity, could appeal to men as well as women amongst the readers. The focus on the communal function of the heroic can thus be seen as the one major constant in the depiction of military heroism in the periodical through times of war and peace. It has also become clear, how *CJ* had to adapt its peace-oriented approach to the societal realities around its publication and regulate its depiction of military actions accordingly.

4.5 Heroes of Civilisation

While the contested nature of military heroism played an important role in the representation of heroism in *CJ*, the periodical also presented civil forms of heroism. The Victorian era as a whole, and the second half of the nineteenth century in particular, was an age of progress. Industrialisation impacted all aspects of life, changed the industrial workplace, and transformed people's experience of time and space. Sparked by the rapid developments in technology and invention, progress came to be a defining idea of the age, in scientific terms as well as in relation to people's personal (educational) development.[166] The idea of advancement was, as a civilisatory project, often defined against a negative other,

---

164 Reed: Army, p. 311.

165 However, as the examples of the lower class soldiers after their return have shown, the treatment of military men within Britain in times of peace was complicated by class issues. Whereas class and elite become, so Reed, less important within the military at war time (cf. ibid.), social status remains an issue for an individual soldier's or sailor's reputation and recognition within Britain.

166 For more detailed information on the industrial and scientific development and its effects on Victorian culture see Sally Alexander: St. Giles's Fair, 1830–1914. Popular Culture and the Industrial Revolution in the 19th Century, Oxford 1970; Asa Briggs: Iron Bridge to Crystal Palace. Impact and Images of the Industrial Revolution, London 1979; David Edgerton: Science, Technology and the British Industrial "Decline" 1870– 1970, Cambridge 1996; Lawrence Goldman: Science, Reform, and Politics in Victorian Britain. The Social Science Association 1857–1886, Cambridge 2007; MacLeod: Invention; Morgan: Industrial Britain; Robert Nisbet: History of the Idea of Progress, New York 1980; John W. Osborne: The Silent Revolution. The Industrial Revolution in England as a Source of

and also connected to Britain's imperial actions. The idea of individual participation in the advancement of civilisation, which had so strongly been propagated by Samuel Smiles in his idea of self-help, also featured in *CJ*. The following section will examine instances of heroism in *CJ*, which are shown as contributing to that progress. Played out on the diverse fields of science, medicine, and education, all examples are united by the idea of an individual contribution to the advancement of society as a whole.

Science

Science was a rapidly growing field in Victorian Britain and the findings of men such as T. H. Huxley, John Tyndall, Michael Faraday and Charles Darwin were revolutionising the way in which people perceived the world and themselves, and aroused many heated responses – both positive and negative. Especially to religious institutions and believers, the new insights into the history and evolution of mankind posed a serious threat, which could be perceived in many popular publications of the time. *CJ*, with its decided claim *not* to orient itself towards any religious denomination and its devotion to the mediation of popular science, rarely portrays scientists as heroes. Though scientists and inventors who, as MacLeod observes, "toiled in an anonymous workshop, far from the glorious field of battle, or the terrors of the ice floes, the desert or the jungle"[167] would have fitted the heroic imaginary of *CJ* with its focus on peacefulness and its closeness to the ideas of Samuel Smiles, almost no heroisation of members of these professions can be found.[168] When MacLeod states that "in a century remarkable for its celebration of heroes, the inventor too had his pedestal and his laurel wreath"[169] this decidedly does *not* hold true for the portrayal in *CJ*.

Different to other publications (such as, for example, *Leisure Hour*, as will become apparent in upcoming chapters), there are only a small number of texts in *CJ* which call scientific research or scientists heroic. Though science and techno-

Cultural Change, New York 1970; James Paradis: Victorian Science and Victorian Values. Literary Perspective, New Brunswick 1985; L. D. Smith: Carpet Weavers and Carpet Masters. The Handloom Carpet Industry of Kidderminster 1780–1850, Kidderminster 1986; Frank M. Turner: Between Science and Religion. The Reaction to Scientific Naturalism in Late Victorian England, New Haven 1974; Edwin G. West: Education and the Industrial Revolution, London 1975 or Martin Wiener: English Culture and the Decline of the Industrial Spirit 1850–1980, Cambridge/New York 2004.

167 MacLeod: Invention, p. 1.

168 A further investigation into specific scientists, inventors or engineers have shown that a number of them (such as Darwin, Lyell, Newton or Stephenson) were introduced to the readers in biographical articles, yet none of them is described in the vocabulary of the heroic (cf. for example Lyell's Second Visit to the United States, *CJ*, 21 Jul 1849, 38–40 and 28 Jul 1849, 53–55; Newton, *CJ*, 13 Sept 1856, 168–170 and 20 Sept 1856, 179–182; George Stephenson, *CJ*, 22 Aug 1857, 125–128; or Darwin, *CJ*, 28 Jan 1888, 49–52).

169 MacLeod: Invention, p. 1.

logy as fields of inquiry played a significant role in *CJ*, technological and scientific advances and their personnel – scientists, inventors, engineers – were only seldom heroised. This points to two things. For one, it shows that the representation of science and technology in *CJ* was strongly focused on the mediation of knowledge. Articles about new inventions were often highly theoretical and described processes and machines in great detail in order to convey as much information as possible.[170] Secondly, the scarce usage of the vocabulary of heroism also highlights that the heroic was not used to convey knowledge, but was utilised on a different level. Whereas personal identification did not seem necessary in the reception of new factual information, the heroic and its identificatory potential was utilised as a vehicle for more abstract social instruction and (group) identity formation. It is not surprising then that the few examples of heroic scientists in the periodical focus on the personal investment and moral behaviour of specific individuals in their work for the collective rather than on the conveyance of facts, which dominate the general treatment of science in *CJ*.

It is through this sense of personal investment and duty that a number of texts connect the scientific field with the realm of heroism. Using the example of Galileo Galilei, "The Crown of Life" in 1876 establishes a relation between scientific work – more explicitly unappreciated scientific work – and values often connected to the heroic in *CJ*: "conscientiousness, self-sacrifice, love of right […] – all of which virtues are gathered together in that one word, Duty" (The Crown of Life, *CJ*, 24 Jun 1876, 401). Galileo is presented as an example of a "race of heroes" (ibid., 402) who act upon a sense of duty "irrespective of personal reward here or hereafter; duty apart from the praise of men, and without the hope of gain" (ibid., 401). It is not the scientific effort as such which is heroised in the text, but the continuation of scientific work even when it meets public rejection, ignorance or, as the case of Galileo implies, leads to prosecution and personal suffering.

Another instance of unappreciated scientific work can be found in Grant Allen's serial novel *Dumaresq's Daughter*, which appeared weekly in *CJ* between January and October 1891. One of the novel's protagonists, Haviland Du-

170 For example, numerous articles on paper and print technology in the 1830, 1840s, and 1850s that gave detailed information about technological processes and step-by-step descriptions of the different jobs performed in a print shop and entailed in paper making. Thereby, the readers were included into a realm of quasi-professionality through the mediation of knowledge on the pages of the periodical (cf. for example Mechanisms of Chambers's Journal, *CJ*, 6 Jun 1835, 149–151; The Printing-Office – A Visit to Clowes's Establishment, *CJ*, 11 April 1840, 94–95; Soiree to Working People by Their Employers, *CJ*, 7 August 1841, 231–232; Printing By Magic, *CJ*, 4 Feb 1854, 68–70; or Old Inventions of New Discoveries, 17 Nov 1860, 306–309). The fact that such information gave readers practical knowledge is substantiated by letters from readers who, after the article "Printing By Magic" in 1854, had tried their hand at paper-making and sent in sheets of self-made paper to the journal. Cf. Paper Sent in by Readers, 1854, Dept 341/131: unnumbered, National Library of Scotland, Edinburgh.

maresq, is frequently characterised as heroic in his pursuit of scientific excellence for the benefit of mankind at large. Significantly, the fictional character Dumaresq is not a natural scientist but a philosopher. Thus, he represents a scientific field which, given the transformations in Victorian society at large, was not of pressing societal relevancy, but could be important in the *reflection* of the effects of science and technology on society. As a representative of this very abstract scientific profession with a less tangible output than, for example, the natural sciences, the philosopher symbolises intellectual progress. Similar to the first example, Dumaresq is described as lacking public appreciation and being poorly compensated for his work throughout the novel. As a consequence, his heroism is as constituted by the core values of *CJ*'s heroic imaginary, selflessness and perseverance, which motivate him to keep up his efforts for the benefit of society as a whole. Characterised as a genius, Dumaresq also embodies different contemporary concepts of the heroic at the same time.

The plot of the novel connects different spheres of life and fields of work and displays indicative tensions where they intersect. The main protagonists of the narrative are Charles Austen Linnell, a young painter, Haviland Dumaresq and his daughter Psyche.[171] On a retreat to the countryside, Linnell meets Dumaresq, whom he is said to have admired for many years and whose *Encyclopaedic Philosophy* is a constant companion of his – "I never went anywhere that I didn't take it" (Grant Allen: Dumaresq's Daughter, *CJ*, 3 Jan 1891, 3). As the title already suggests, the overarching plot focuses on Dumaresq's daughter and the painter, who fall for each other but whose love has to overcome many obstacles, face societal preconceptions, paternal protectiveness and the cruelties of war when Linnell joins Gordon of Karthoum in his fight against the Madhi. Only after more than a year of trials, separation and illness are the lovers finally united in the last chapter of the novel.

At the outset of the novel, Linnell has taken up his summer residence in Petherton, Somerset, where Haviland Dumaresq lives in a humble small cottage. Dumaresq is set up as a heroic figure, yet in a way which is very different from the characterisations of heroic figures discussed in previous chapters. The philosopher is constructed as an otherworldly genius, described as "the philosopher who transcends space and time – the profoundest thinker of our age and nation – the greatest mathematician and deepest metaphysician in all Europe" (ibid.), "the deepest thinker of our age and race" (ibid., 5), and "nothing short of heroic" (ibid., 54). Over the first half of the novel, the philosopher is constructed as a prophet-like figure from the point of view of Linnell who calls him "noble" and "pure" (ibid., 19), even "majestic" (ibid., 10 Jan 1891, 20) with a "vivid apostolic energy" (ibid., 24 Jan 1891, 54). This implies Dumaresq possesses knowledge into

171 The choice of name for the philosopher's daughter is already foreshadowing the young woman's fate of suffering and enduring before she and Linnell are happily united.

which a large number of others do *not* have insight and thus links him to the strand of thinking about the heroic which constructs heroes as leader figures and supposes distance between a hero and the group of followers.

The characterisation of Dumaresq and his work differs strongly depending on who is speaking. For Linnell he is, in a quite Carlylean sense, "a prophet born" (ibid., 14 Mar 1891, 163) who sacrifices his life for science and is "'[...] wholly absorbed and swallowed up in his work. [...] He lives for nothing on earth, I do believe, but two things now – Philosophy and Psyche'" (ibid., 17 Jan 1891, 37). For other members of the society of Petherton, he is an oddity: "'Yes, he's wasted his life on writing books'" (ibid.) it is remarked, and Mrs Maitland, who fulfils the role of the shallow gossip in the novel, points out clearly that she considers Dumaresq inappropriate company:

> "Oh yes, Mr Dumaresq's very clever, I believe," Mrs. Maitland answered [...]. "He's very clever, I've always understood, though hardly the sort of person, of course, one quite cares to mix with in society. He wears such extremely curious hats, and expresses himself so very oddly sometimes. But he's very clever in his own way, extremely clever, so people tell me, and full of information about all the ologies." (ibid., 36–37)

Mrs Maitland stands for all those members of society who lack the understanding of Dumaresq's work due to their own intellectual inability. Her assessment of his capacities is based on what "people" have told her and while her reference to "all the ologies" may show that she knows of Dumaresq's talents in various fields, it also exhibits her own incomprehension. For one, she judges Dumaresq by his compatibility to social etiquette, his outer appearance, talents of conversation, and class membership. The fact that "'he was once a gentleman'" (ibid., 37) whose social progress has been a descent strengthens her aversion. Though commenting upon the same virtues – Dumaresq's perseverance, his devotion and selflessness – Linnell and the other inhabitants of Petherton come to a fundamentally different evaluation. While the former has nothing but admiration for the philosopher and his work, those not interested in philosophy cannot sympathise with the old man and paint him as a hopeless, quixotic figure.[172] Dumaresq himself frequently expresses the high standards he sets for himself and emphasises his attempt to contribute to "'the advancement of thought'" (ibid., 24 Jan 1891, 55) and "'the good of the race'" (ibid., 7 Mar 1891, 148).

Though an eccentric figure, Dumaresq is established as an extraordinary thinker and man of high moral standards with the ability to suffer for a greater good. This is mostly achieved through the characterisations by Linnell, the narrator, and the contrast to the other summer guests, many of whom are shown as

---

172 Interestingly, the narrator at one point calls Dumaresq "quixotic" (Dumaresq's Daughter, *CJ*, 7 Feb 1891, 86) but does not stress the hopelessness of the Quixotean cause, but the idealistic motivation behind it and the fact that Dumaresq does not give up though he is discouraged by his surroundings.

unintelligent and shallow.[173] What enhances Dumaresq's heroic suffering is the fact that, despite his renown in the scientific community and intellectual world, his untiring work does not give him financial freedom.[174] The very fact that his symbolic capital[175] seems to be more important to him than economic capital and the resulting struggle to get by seems to constitute his heroism. Stressing the fact that Dumaresq does not work for his own gain, but locates himself in a larger frame of reference, contributes to his idealistic reputation and also puts him in a line of scientists who were only appreciated after their death. The narrator compares Dumaresq to Newton, whose "gravitation was disbelieved for half a century" and Lamarck who "went blind and poor to his grave without finding one adherent for his evolutionary theories" (ibid., 31 Jan 1891, 69).

The novel recalls two fundamentally different concepts of heroism in its depiction of Dumaresq. On the one hand, the philosopher is described as a prophet figure reminiscent of Thomas Carlyle's ideal of heroism. The philosopher's intellectual capacities exceed those of his fellows and he possesses a superior insight into the nature of things. On the other hand, the values of perseverance and suffering and the fact that his work is not universally acknowledged is reminiscent of the depiction of scientists and engineers in the biographical sketches published by Samuel Smiles. Smiles had especially stressed these two virtues and encouraged his readers to perceive their work in the grander framework of human progress.[176] Though depicting a subject matter which is, especially through its limited applicability in everyday life when compared to other scientific advancements, removed from the lives of the prospective readers, the text nevertheless offers an identificatory potential through the emphasis on the core values of Dumaresq and his moral integrity. This potential is even stronger in Psyche, who is at various points in the text said to have characteristics similar to her father's, yet is – especially through her love for Linnell – more easily accessible for social identification.

---

173 Among those belittling Dumaresq is also a vicar, whose rejection of Dumaresq is of a religious motivation, since the philosophical theories also take up theories of evolution which threaten religious power. Cf. ibid.

174 This is also due to the contemporary situation on the print market, as Psyche remarks, since "'[t]he Americans, of course, who read it so much, read it all in pirated editions'" (ibid., 31 Jan 1891, 69). Additionally Dumaresq, under financial pressure, has sold his copyright to the publishers and thus Linnell's efforts to indirectly financially support his "hero" (ibid., 24 Jan 1891, 53) by buying hundreds of copies of the *Encyclopaedic Philosophy* fails.

175 The fact that Dumaresq is renowned is not only stressed by his admirer Linnell, but affirmed in a different plot strand in which a group of young wealthy Americans in a conversation with Psyche – not knowing they are speaking to Dumaresq's daughter – praise the philosopher and the impact his thought has had on them.

176 Cf. for example: "All experience of life indeed serves to prove that the impediments thrown in the way of human advancement, may for the most part be overcome by steady good conduct, honest zeal, activity, perseverance, and above all by the determined resolution to surmount difficulties, and stand up manfully against misfortune" (*SH*, 277).

On the whole, however, the depiction of Dumaresq as a morally excellent scientist is an exception in *CJ*. Over the course of the second half of the nineteenth century, the periodical discusses many new scientific developments on its pages and, for example, gives information about the latest inventions and scientific findings in the series "The Month" which appeared from 1854 onwards. However, scientists are rarely attributed heroic status or their scientific endeavours called heroism, as in the case of Dumaresq. The texts are predominantly written in a matter-of-fact style, introducing a new invention or discovery, its merits and area of applicability and giving the names of the scientists and inventors involved. If those are then discussed at all, it is mostly in regard to their extraordinary intellectual capacities, which for the contributors seem to rather call for the term genius than that of the hero. The scientific genius, as a cursory consideration of articles about scientific progress has shown, seemed to be considered only for its intellectual qualities, whereas those men and women labelled heroes in *CJ* seem to have a moral disposition which makes them relatable to the audience. The potential for identification and subsequent emulation hence emerges again as a main prerequisite for heroic figures in the periodical and emphasises its didactic intention. The domain of science shows clearly how extraordinary figures removed from the readers' lives and praised for their ingenuity and outstanding brilliance cannot perform the function of role models. Since genius is something which one cannot aspire to, the focus on the moral disposition of scientists in face of public disregard[177] of their work opens an avenue for the consumers to relate.

It is no surprise then that those few instances in which scientists are heroised stress their likeness to the 'common man'. For example, a text about "Peter Mackenzie the Naturalist" elaborates upon his scientific devotion to botany in a two-page article. It is not, however, his specific findings in horticulture which are called heroic but his attitude, the fact that he was, though "from the humblest rank of society" (Peter Mackenzie the Naturalist, *CJ*, 11 May 1850, 299), committed to better his life and educate himself. His life story, the text proclaims, is "one likely to prove interesting, as showing, [...] that the labourer, after his hard day's work is done, may calmly sit down by the fireside, and spend his evenings in the prosecution of scientific study, without any sacrifice of domestic enjoyment" (ibid.). This remark in the first paragraph immediately establishes a bond between Mackenzie and the readers implicitly addressed as "the labourer". Beginning from Mackenzie's childhood "in a very humble station" (ibid.), the text then traces his education and thirst for knowledge. Among his personal "heroes" are not military men "from the Duke of Wellington downwards" (ibid.) but "such eminent horticulturists as Mr Ingram, gardener to her Majesty, and Mr

177 In this respect, the unappreciated scientific hero complies with the call of *CJ* for silent heroism without public recognition elaborated upon in chapter 4.2.

Towers, now overseer to his Royal Highness Prince Albert at Osborne" (ibid.). Through the progression of Mackenzie's career, the text stresses his perseverance and dedication, the fact that he was always "[a]nxious to improve himself as much as possible" (ibid.). He is shown teaching himself Latin because one of the important works of botany is only accessible to him in this language and studies daily "when the labours of the day were over" (ibid., 300). In presenting Mackenzie as one of the "heroes" (ibid., 299) of horticulture, the magazine does not aim at a validation of the specific field of scientific research but praises the attitude with which Mackenzie went about his studies, his perseverance, determination and the fact that he was "unambitious of fame" (ibid., 300). Through his humble family background and the comparison with the "labourer" in the first paragraph, the text offers Mackenzie as a role model for the readers to identify with and can be read as an invitation to the readers to educate themselves further, even if they have a full-time job.[178] In this emphasis on perseverance and hard work, MacKenzie is distinctly differentiated from the figure of the genius and constructed as a more relatable character.

The rarity of the usage of the vocabulary of the heroic in relation to scientists and scientific research[179] is remarkable. The fact that *CJ* agreed with the theories of leading scientists such as Darwin[180] and did not object to the new ideas for religious reasons,[181] might not have made the topics potentially destabilising enough for scientific figures to be heroised (or de-heroised), but may have resulted in a more matter-of-fact mediation of new scientific findings. Rather, the scientists are shown as performing a duty and – since the scientific community itself was not part of the intended readership and scientists at large were of no great identificatory potential for the audience – a heroisation of their work would not necessarily have furthered the journal's didactic agenda to give the readers role models within the realistic scope of their emulation. In this context,

---

178 It is worth noting that the text also refers to Mackenzie's contributions to various popular horticultural magazines. The connection between the praising of the scientist and the popular print market is a clever marketing tool to establish periodicals – and thus implicitly also *CJ* – as a reliable source of educational material for "the labourer". Peter Mackenzie the Naturalist, *CJ*, 11 May 1850, 299.

179 The heroisation of men of industry and invention is similarly scarce in *CJ*.

180 The editor Robert Chambers's *Vestiges of the Natural History of Creation* in 1844 proposed a theory of natural history independent from religious thought and a model of transmutation of species. The book, which was published anonymously at the time, created a public sensation and Chambers is often considered one of the most important precursors of Darwin. Cf. Peter J. Bowler: Evolution. The History of an Idea, Berkeley 1989; Edward Larson: Evolution. The Remarkable History of a Scientific Theory, New York 2006 or James A. Secord: Victorian Sensation. The Extraordinary Publication, Reception, and Secret Authorship of Vestiges of the Natural History of Creation, Chicago 2003.

181 The above-discussed text "The Crown of Life" shows that *CJ* takes a diametrically opposed stance: the text identifies "narrowness and illiberality" (The Crown of Life, *CJ*, 24 Jun 1876, 403) in many religious institutions throughout history which interferes with the "free action" (ibid.) necessary for the proper development of human ideas.

the exceptions constituted by "Dumaresq's Daughter" and "Mackenzie the Naturalist" can be explained as well, since the two scientific men discussed in the texts are both closer to the readership, through birth or financial status, than many other eminent scientists.

While scientists seemed to be too far removed from readers' lives, another profession concerned with the progress of society was described more frequently with the vocabulary of the heroic: the medical profession.

Medicine

The medical profession, with its fundamental social function of preserving life and helping others, fits well into *CJ*'s heroic imaginary and it is not surprising that men and women caring for the health of others are frequently called heroic in the journal. In the context of selflessness, the story of the "Hospital Hero" has already served as an example of the self-denying actions of a doctor saving a mentally ill patient thereby risking his own life, and this pattern of medical professionals endangering their own safety to secure the well-being of their patients re-emerges in various other contributions. Furthermore, medicine acts as a marker of civilisatory standards, which *CJ* for example established using the contrasting example of Russia. Thereby it implies that the status and professionalism of medicine also sheds light on the more general standard of a civilisation.

Representatives of medical professions considered heroic can, for example, be found in "Men of the Time". The article is a review of a book of *Biographical Sketches of Eminent Living Characters* published by Bogue's in 1856. The text starts with a critical examination of the book, which according to the reviewer needs "numerous amendments" (Men of the Time, *CJ*, 22 Mar 1856, 183) and most importantly needs a "withdrawal of the critical opinions of the editor" (ibid.). Further, the reviewer emphasises that important men and women, particularly ones from the medical profession such as James Clark and William Ferguson, have been omitted from the volume. Interestingly, a further criticism is that artists feature so prominently in the book whereas those texts which are deemed worthy as "encouragement" (ibid., 184) for the readers are too few in number. Not only do these statements show that the author values the medical profession higher in its societal influence than that of the artist, but they also clearly point out that the function of such a collection of biographies is to give the readers examples to aspire to. Accordingly, the article only renarrates examples of men such as Elihu Burritt, Richard Cobden or William Cubitt, who made their way to public recognition from a humble background presumed to be similar to that of the intended readers.

In its second part, the review compliments the book's section on "distinguished females" and expresses the "hope to see this department fuller in another edition" (ibid., 184). Elizabeth Blackwood is identified as the prime example of "female heroism" (ibid.) in the book and is one of the only biographies which the review sketches in greater detail. The American "lady-physician" (ibid.) is depicted as being motivated by "sound and reasonable motives" (ibid., 185) to enter "her calling" (ibid.) – medicine:

> She was influenced in this determination [to pursue the study of medicine], not by a personal taste for and curiosity about its mysteries [...] but first by a desire to open a new field for the exercise of feminine talent and energy, hitherto restricted within limits wholly inadequate to their requirements. (ibid.)

Apart from the will to do good, which is implied in the medical profession as such, Blackwood is described as being not only motivated by personal interests (such as "taste" or "curiosity", ibid.)[182] but by an interest to improve society for women at large. The text subsequently describes her struggle to gain access to the necessary education and emphasises her dedication and perseverance. Once she has finally found an institution willing to teach her, she is shown working hard in the more 'womanly' profession of teaching music and languages in order to be able to earn the money she needs to be able to attend the lectures. She works and learns in an untiring effort "where most men would have rested from their labours, she started anew" (ibid.). The "female heroism" of Blackwood is on the one hand one of individual achievement through relentless persevering work and determination. On the other hand, the herorization of the doctor stresses the social aspect of the profession and her being a female further emphasises the contribution of her effort to the possibilities for women on a larger scale. The fact that her profession directly results in an enhanced wellbeing of a larger group of people then seems to make her transgression from the ideal of the domestic woman and the pursuit of her individual educational goal acceptable.

Furthermore, the status of the medical profession is used as an indicator for the more general status of civilisation. In 1881, the essay "Popular Medicine in Russia" examines the situation in Russian hospitals and paints a bleak picture. Drawing on information from the publication *Old and New Russia* written by a Russian national, the text depicts the Russian medical system as belonging to a different stage of civilisation, full of "gross superstitions and almost barbaric customs" (Popular Medicine in Russia, *CJ*, Mar 5 1881, 159). In many more remote villages, access to medical help is scarce:

> we know that of the regularly qualified doctors who take up their abode in small provincial towns, there are but few who will consent to travel for many miles on bad roads to visit a patient from whom they can in most cases expect no larger remuneration than a loaf of new bread or half-a-dozen eggs. If the patient is not too ill to be moved, and can be brought either to the doctor's house or the hospital, something will be done for him,

[182] In this respect the medical hero is clearly differentiated from the scientific hero, whose endeavours, though possibly directed at the advancement of knowledge for humankind at large, are per se driven by curiosity.

and he may recover; but if he cannot leave his village, it is his own look-out, not the doctor's. (ibid.)

The Russian doctors are depicted as selfish and unwilling to sacrifice their own comfort for the sake of the patients – even if that endangers their lives and they have to resort to the "village quack" (ibid.) for dubious help which makes them "rather suffer" (ibid.) than recover. These quacks, or "witches" and "wizard" (ibid., 160) as the text calls them, are then presented in an even worse light as they spread superstition. Therefore the Russian common folk, so the text, views the "prevalent diseases" (ibid., 159), for example fevers like malaria or ague, anthropomorphised as invisible women who "go from village to village and from house to house in search of some human being, in whom they may conveniently take up their abode" (ibid., 160). The "quacks" then seemingly provide the knowledge of cures for the fevers: "Each of the twelve Sisters [i.e. the different kinds of fever] is supposed to have a great dislike to some special mode of treatment, and will at once leave the patient if it should be resorted to" (ibid.). However, what is so casually called a "treatment" (ibid.) is in some cases a rather dubious means to cure fever. One "sister" (ibid.) is supposed to be "afraid of cutting-instruments" (ibid.) so that the villagers are advised to "surround the patient's bed with knives, axes, scythes, spades, saws, &c., which must be laid with their sharp edges turned towards the door" (ibid.). Other kinds of fever are said to respond to even more absurd forms of treatment, such as taking the sick person outside close to an ash-tree of similar height as the patient, cleaving the tree in two and letting the patient climb naked through the cleft trunk (cf. ibid.). Other cures even turn to violent measures, for example one illness is "attributed to the sprouting of wings, in that particular region [of the chest]" (ibid.). The healer then 'removes' these invisible wings in a painful operation by pinching "the skin of the back, beginning at the shoulder-blades" (ibid.) with a sharp object.

Against this backdrop of selfishness on the side of the medical professionals and brutality and irrationality on the side of the "quack[s]" (ibid., 159), the text then shows "exceptions" (ibid.) from this Russian rule: "examples of heroic self-sacrifice on the part of medical men during the late epidemics of diphtheria and typhoid fever" (ibid.). Although the article leaves it at that short mention and does not give actual "examples" (ibid.) of these men, the sober statement, which is in stark contrast to the quasi-fantastical descriptions of the treatments against the "twelve Sisters", emphasises the value of these "exceptions". The medical men are shown as embodiments of selflessness because they – unlike the doctors mentioned before – are willing to compromise their own comfort for the health of their patients. Additionally, the "heroic" men are representatives and agents of rationality and civilisation against the barbarism and irrational superstitions spread and perpetuated by the presumed village healers.

In a different context, a note in the series "The Month: Science and the Arts" in July 1900 shows two doctors who compromise their own safety for the sake of curing others: under the heading "A Daring Experiment" (The Month, *CJ*, 28 Jul 1900, 557) the reader is presented with the story of two English doctors who are reported to be on their way to the Roman Campagna. The region is said to be a "fever-stricken district" (ibid.) of Italy and the two men embark on a self-experiment to prove that malaria is transmitted through mosquitoes. For six months, so the text, they will be "mixing freely with the populace during the day, but [will be] shut up in a mosquito-proof house at night. [...] If the inmates escape malaria – living as they will [...] – it may be considered a certainty that the disease is spread by the mosquitoes" (ibid.). In the second part of the experiment, the doctors will then expose themselves to "thirty or forty" mosquitoes to prove the matter "beyond doubt" (ibid.). The actions of the two men, the note concludes, are to be celebrated as "heroism [...] [which] requires something more than a Victoria Cross for due recognition" (ibid.). Their heroism is of social value on the largest possible scale since the benefit of their medical experiment could possibly benefit the global population. Significantly, this last phrase not only heroises the two men, but – as has been seen in other cases – values their act of self-endangerment[183] for the sake of humanity at large *higher* than military heroics rewarded with the Victoria Cross.

The heroisation of the medical profession in *CJ* can be seen in the general context of the periodical's social agenda. Just as the publication itself wanted to contribute to the well-being of society at large – though on an intellectual level – the medical professionals represented as heroic are contributing to the stability of society by devoting their strength and energy to the preservation of individual lives or the safety of humanity at large through the research of entire diseases. In doing so, the medical professionals are often shown compromising or even endangering their own lives for the sake of the patient in an act of communal loyalty and devotion.

Education

As was already discussed in relation to selflessness, the education of children was regarded as the crucial part of their journey to becoming a being of high moral standard and virtues. Whether through the telling of stories or within the formal education system, the acquisition of knowledge was seen as essential in the furthering of good character. In this context, mothers are frequently valued as the first educators of children. The idea that children's raw potential needed to be

[183] Another instance of the selfless risk-taking of a medical man can for example be seen in "Quarantine", in which a doctor volunteers to enter a ship on which cholera has broken out and all the Englishmen have died already. Only the Indian coolies are still alive, yet severely sick. The surgeon enters the ship and manages to save "the lives of half the Indians" (Quarantine, *CJ*, 16 Nov 1889, 732) in an act of "heroism" (ibid.) that could have cost him his own life.

cultivated and tamed makes a mother's influence a civilising one. It is unsurprising then that women feature prominently in the articles which show the effort to educate and elevate children as a form of heroism. Strikingly, almost all articles which are devoted to the female involvement in formal *public* education efforts are placed in the British colonies, whereas the female influence on children in a domestic British setting is largely restricted to the familial household. Thus, the foreign setting seemed to have allowed more liberty regarding the positive depiction of women's professional life, while the same might have proven more difficult for women engaged in the fight for education within Britain.

The article "Female Heroism" illustrates very pointedly how female work[184] in education is heroised in *CJ*. The woman performing the "female heroism" of the title is Mary Ann Wilson who had come to Calcutta in 1821 and devoted the rest of her life to the education of native women. From the outset of the text, Wilson is described in terms of the heroic imaginary, her "chivalry" (Female Heroism, *CJ*, 12 Aug 1848, 108) is praised and the fact that she "voluntarily devoted herself to this difficult task" (ibid.) is stressed. She is shown as selfless in her efforts and persevering though having to face many obstacles. The main hindrance, so the text, was the attitude towards female education in Calcutta. Though the population is described as eagerly engaging in the British educational programmes for boys ("these attempts [...] met with no opposition on the part of the natives; on the contrary, they warmly seconded them, and the schools were crowded with boys", ibid.), "the prejudices against educating females were not to be easily overcome" (ibid.). Indian women, so the depiction in the text, were only allowed to learn domestic skills ("making a curry or a pillau", ibid.) and were nothing but a "plaything of the family" (ibid.) until the time to marry and perform the "domestic duties of the wife" (ibid.) came upon the young women. "[I]ntellectual acquirements" (ibid.), however, were not deemed fitting for women and were highly discouraged. Interestingly, this situation is described as cruel and overly restrictive, the housewife's life is called "intolerable", her condition a "confinement" (ibid.). The women living as such are described as "depressed" and "whithered" (ibid.); this is highly interesting in the light of *CJ*'s later depiction of female education and employment in Britain. For example, "Filling Little Pitchers" in 1881 showed girls less capable of intellectual capacities than boys and saw their destiny in one day making "the angel of home, a woman full of kindly helpfulness and sweetness, and capable of the heroism of self-sacrifice" (Filling Little Pitchers, *CJ*, 20 Aug 1881, 534). Essays like "Heroines" propagated the domestic realm and deemed activities just like the ones denigrated with regard to the Indian women as being worthy of the highest admiration (cf. Heroines, *CJ*, 2 Aug 1884, 492–494). The present text, however, rejects an

184 In this and the following cases, work always refers to public education efforts, not to the private work of educating one's children. The latter is usually not termed education but often subsumed under the term influence, which a mother should exert on her children.

uneducated life confined to the domestic sphere for the native women of Calcutta and then describes Mary Wilson's efforts to overcome these resentments:

> The *task was difficult*; [...] Animated with a *determination* to spare no *personal exertion*, she had herself trained to the business of general instruction, and *did not fear* the effects of an Indian climate. Physically, morally, and intellectually, she was fitted for her task. Her health was excellent, her spirits elastic; her temper even; her mind clear, quick and shrewd. Her manners most engaging, though dignified; and her *will indomitable*. (Female Heroism, *CJ*, 12 Aug 1848, 108, emphases mine)

Apart from attributes which show general good education and character, Mrs Wilson is presented as possessing various character traits which are associated with the heroic in many texts in *CJ*: she is determined, "her will indomitable" (ibid.), fearless regarding possible physical discomfort, does not falter in the face of certain difficulty sure to come but perseveres. Furthermore, her actions are self-denying, she does not shy away from "personal exertion" (ibid.) if it aids bettering the situation of women in Calcutta. At first, her efforts are described as unsuccessful, yet she is shown to have "hoped, trusted, and [was] determined to remedy what appeared remediable" (ibid.). In time, she resorts to paying poor women to come to her school and, after some time, her class room fills. However, the eventual success of her school is not enough for her and she becomes determined to find a way to educate children "from their very infancy, uncontaminated by the evil examples of a native home" (ibid.).[185] Finally, she opens an orphanage where she is not only shown to successfully educate children, but also gives refuge to families after natural catastrophes and "a home to all who would take it" (ibid., 110). In conclusion, it is emphasised again that it was not for her own benefit that Wilson worked but "to elevate the native woman; not merely to teach reading, writing, arithmetic, the use of the needle, &c., but to purify the mind, to subdue the temper, to raise her in the scale of being, to render her the companion and helpmate of her husband, instead of his slave and drudge" (ibid.). The process of "female heroism" conducted by Wilson is depicted as an evolution from a helpless slave to a more self-determined woman[186] rather than a mere acquisition of knowledge and the heroism as represented in the text can thus literally be seen as a civilising act. Nevertheless, the emphasis on Wilson giving "a home" to others frames her places in a domestic setting and counterbalances her otherwise progressive role as a professional woman.

A biographical sketch of Caroline Chisholm in 1852 shows similar strategies of herorization. Right from the outset of the text, which was placed on the cover of the issue, she is established as a "heroic Englishwoman" (Mrs. Chisholm, *CJ*,

---

[185] This agenda, which is praised by the text, shows clearly the British resentments towards the natives of India – and their other colonies – in terms of their capabilities.

[186] The initial state of the Indian women is further stressed by the fact that the article published after "Female Heroism" in *CJ* is concerned with helpless "babes in the woods" of Shetland. The Babes in the Woods, *CJ*, 12 Aug 1848, 110–111.

25 Sep 1852, 193) with the following characteristics: "her enthusiastic and ceaseless endeavours to do good, the discretion and intelligence with which she pursues her aims, and her remarkable self-sacrifices in the cause of humanity" (ibid.). The virtues are listed in ascending order with the "remarkable self-sacrifices in the cause of humanity" being the climax. Her philanthropic efforts – which would have been known to the contemporary reader prior to reading the article – are embedded in a larger framework of her devotion towards mankind at large. The text then focuses on Chisholm's time in Australia and her work with British, and especially female, emigrants. Like Wilson, she is thus dealing with a group of people which is not regarded highly in public opinion, since many emigrations to Australia at the time were caused by debt and would still have been associated with the penal transportations of convicts. She also has to overcome obstacles and at first fails to find funding for her educational projects ("much jealousy and prejudice, however, required to be overcome. Bigotry was even brought into play", ibid.). Nevertheless, Chisholm "persevered" (ibid.) until she had sufficient funds to equip a home for female emigrants who entered the country without companions or funds. The text then also gives voice to Chisholm herself, whose recently published memoir is quoted. After several anecdotes about her life with the women, the text then especially praises the goal set in the following excerpt from the memoir: "'It is my intention to return to Australia in the early part of the next year, and there endeavour to still further promote the reunion of families [...].'" Through her efforts, so her words, she wants to contribute to "'a new element of peace, order, and civilisation, more powerful than soldiers – to a golden chain of domestic feeling [...]'" (ibid.). Chisholm's self-professed civilising aim is one of education, but ultimately a domestic goal. Since it is reported that Chisholm is always in want of funds, the text's final sentence "Every one may well concur in paying honour to Caroline Chisholm!" (ibid.) can thus be seen in a double sense: on the one hand, the paying of honour to the "heroic Englishwoman" in an idealistic sense emphasises her heroism, on the other hand, it clearly calls for concrete financial contributions.

Similar depictions of female heroism on civilising missions can also be found in later decades, for example in the 1878 text "The Jubilee Singers" which reports of American "movement ladies" who "extend[ed] the blessings of elementary education to hordes of negroes" (The Jubilee Singers, *CJ*, 12 Jan 1878, 18). In a selfless act despite "the confusion and rankling animosities that prevailed in the south [in the time directly after the Civil War], the efforts to uplift the negro by means of schools were heroic, often dangerous, and always attended with difficulty" (ibid.). Again – the "heroic" (ibid.) educational project of the women is described as the act of civilising an inferior group of people – as an action for the good of others rather than oneself.

The texts discussed offer an interesting image of female heroism, one in which the women possess a strong agency never attributed to women in texts set in Britain. The foreign setting seems to be a distant realm and different enough for women to be allowed to act more freely. All of the above cases are strong examples for contemporary readers because they claim to be authentic and would – especially in the case of Caroline Chisholm – have been well-known already. Therefore, the female hero as represented in the colonial context transgresses her traditional realm in a second way, in that she is 'allowed' to be publicly praised for her heroic actions and is even encouraged to continue them. This stands in stark contrast to the silent heroism so often propagated for both men and women in *CJ*. Nevertheless though, the humility of the heroines is emphasised, of which the last sentences of "Eliza Warick. A Heroine in Humble Life"[187] are representative: "The facts of this history are strictly true; the incidents are not imaginary, but real. The circumstances were known to many who benefited by this meek heroine's kindness" (Eliza Warick, *CJ*, 12 Dec 1874, 787). The identificatory potential of the text for female readers is not as clear as for different types of heroic behaviour in *CJ*. The exotic setting, which seemed to have enabled this active and public form of female heroics, can also be seen as distancing and alienating for the contemporary reader. On the other hand, the abstract virtues established as heroic in all of the texts and their caring devotion to others who are less fortunate than they are, could be transferred to the life of the readers as well. On a higher level, the texts also stress the importance of education and strongly propagate domestic stability, which readers could have aspired to themselves.

On the whole, the texts depicting heroes of civilisation play to the core values of *CJ*'s heroic imaginary: selflessness and perseverance. All the examples discussed from the fields of science, medicine and education are thereby an identificatory offer for the readers, the heroes are role models worth aspiring to. However, gender acts as a complicating factor in this context. It has become obvious that the heroism of the professional female educators is only possible when removed to a setting shown as uncivilised. A similar depiction of female heroic agency in a public environment was, however, not possible within Britain. Though exemplifying similar virtues, female heroism within mainland Britain was strictly limited to an everyday domestic setting. The fact that selflessness and perseverance were the basis of such different types of female heroism in terms of individual agency also emphasises the broad accessibility of this form of moral heroism. It is this very fact which *CJ* utilised in their didactic application of the heroic.

[187] This article presents another example of a female civilisation effort in Calcutta in the eighteenth century and – before Eliza Warick's venture into the educational profession – is also a tale of adventure at sea.

4.6 Everyday Heroism

Another major domain of heroism in *CJ* is everyday life. Under that term, I subsume two larger categories. The first depicts heroic acts of lifesaving which make a person transgress from the normality of their everyday life in order to come to the help of another. John Price defines this form of everyday heroism as "acts of life-risking bravery, undertaken by otherwise ordinary individuals, largely in the course of their daily lives, and within quotidian surroundings".[188] Stories of the saving of others while risking one's own life were popular in the Victorian era and real-life instances of lifesaving, especially those performed by "otherwise ordinary individuals" (as opposed to professional lifesavers such as lifeboat men or firemen), were honoured in popular media and institutionally through medals such as those given by the Royal Humane Society.[189] The term everyday applies to these acts in so far as most of the cases which I will discuss in the following are spontaneous acts in the everyday life of those later heroised in *CJ*.

The second type of everyday heroism is a distinctly class-bound one. Here, examples can be found of the heroisation of everyday work life as well as the representation of a gender-integrative heroism of working class private life. It is not an extraordinary act that transgresses the normal routines of everyday which is heroised, but that very routine, the successful handling of everyday life *itself*, which is called heroic. Both categories, even more strongly the second one, emphasise the social position of the heroes, which makes the everyday hero in *CJ* a distinctly working class and lower-middle class representative. While the acts of lifesaving once again propagate the values of *CJ*'s heroic imaginary, the latter form of everyday heroism is most distinctly used as a means of validation of the intended consumers' lives. Since existing social structures are heroised rather than a utopia of a future society is developed, the represented heroism constitutes a tool to stabilise existing norms and discourage social change.

Saving Lives Abroad

During the 1850s and 1860s, the articles on heroic acts of lifesaving are largely set outside the British Isles and often placed in colonial settings. The texts, a number of which I will discuss in the following, read like adventure tales and are mostly fictional accounts. Though the exotic setting allowed for more colourful and spectacular stories, the lifesavers' moral mindset and selfless motivation is

188 Price: Everyday Heroism, p. 2.

189 For a detailed analysis of acts of lifesaving in Victorian everyday life and their valorisation see John Price's study *Everyday Heroism. Victorian Constructions of the Heroic Civilian.* It gives a comprehensive description of institutionalised rewards such as the Albert Medal or the awards of the Royal Humane Society and the Carnegie Hero Fund Trust and further analyses public commemoration of everyday heroism such as monuments.

stressed, which – despite the more sensational form – integrates the heroes into *CJ*'s heroic imaginary. Furthermore, the fact that the heroic protagonists are exclusively British in a colonial setting constructs and emphasises Britain's supremacy in a global context.

"A Swim for Life" is set in the Caribbean Sea outside of Antigua. It tells the story of a number of English sailors, who – on a whim and despite the suspicious weather conditions – take their ship's pinnace for a sail. Outside of the harbour, their boat is soon caught up in the high waves and capsized. With a fast-rising sea and a hurricane forming, "[t]he prospect of affairs was certainly not inspiriting [...]. They were clinging to the wreck of a small boat, their ship was hidden from sight by clouds of rain – for the storm had now come on in all its fury – and the land was invisible from the same cause" (A Swim for Life, *CJ*, 26 Mar 1859, 207). In this hopeless situation, the young men are "determined upon a plan, which nothing but the desperate emergency of the case could have suggested" (ibid., 208). This phrase clearly shows that the act of heroism to come is a situational one: heroism which is activated by a specific circumstance rather than premeditation. The two strongest swimmers of the group decide to try and swim ashore, "the place swarmed with sharks" (ibid.) and looming death in the shape of the "horrid monsters" (ibid.) constantly surrounds the two men. Despite their own fear of being attacked by the shark or drowned in the storm, the men go on because "the thought of their comrades clinging to that upturned boat roused them to fresh exertions" (ibid.). The "heroes" (ibid.) are then shown finally reaching the shore, only to be attacked by "a number of negroes" (ibid.) who do not recognise them as Englishmen. Only after they communicate to them that they are Britons can the men go and send help to their comrades. While the men on the capsized pinnace are then brought to safety, the selfless act of the two swimmers has left its mark on them. Not only are they "nearly dead from exhaustion" (ibid.) when they have fulfilled their task, but both fall "victim to [their] heroism" (ibid.), which is constituted by their sacrifice for the rest of the group: one of the men dies while the other "was seriously injured, and his powers of mind affected by all that he had gone through" (ibid.). The title "Swim for Life" can thus primarily be read from the perspectives of those who remained on the wrecked boat: their lives were saved while the two "heroes" themselves did not swim towards their own safety but accepted death and injury for the well-being of their comrades.

Another example of saving lives at sea in the Caribbean can be found in "A Long Swim". It tells the tale of a group of Englishmen embarking on a leisurely sail in the Caribbean Sea before Antigua. On the open sea, a wind gets hold of the ship which falls on the "beams-end" (A Long Swim, *CJ*, 17 Nov 1866, 721). Because a rather unskilled member of the party is holding the wheel at that time, the whole of the group finds itself in the water. As several of the group are not able to swim and their fear of sharks grows by the minute, two men take charge of the situation, help the others onto the pinnace's keel and set out to swim to the harbour for the sake of the whole group: "'If we were forced to remain in this desperately uncomfortable situation all night, there was every probability that some one, overcome by sleep, would be slipping off his unpleasant perch into the sea [...]'" (ibid., 722). The "two heroes" (ibid.) leave the group behind and steadily swim towards the coast. After some time, though, one of them grows weaker and weaker and finally demands to be left behind by the other. However, the other refuses to "desert a friend in difficulty" (ibid., 723) and resumes his journey with the friend on his back. Having to fight several sharks, he finally reaches the shore, with the "half-dead" man in tow; his "heroic conduct in taking that perilous swim in the dark" (ibid., 724) then results in the rescue of the entire party.

The tale, which above all is an entertaining story of adventure at sea,[190] still has a didactic message that the narrator expresses explicitly:

> People talk a good deal about our national degeneracy now a days; it doesn't look much like national degeneracy, I imagine, when, out of ten men – some of whom, as not being able to swim at all, must be left out for the account – two could be found to go in for such a very forlorn-hope as this. (ibid., 722)

Despite the fact that the text places a strong emphasis on the adventure-elements and even shows some comic moments, this narratorial comment connects the adventure in the exotic setting of the Caribbean with the reality of the reader. It takes up the public debate on the moral state of society and rejects the assumption brought forth by many members of the elite that contemporary society was one without remarkable figures. With the counter-example of the fearless swimmer, the text sets up courageous behaviour and brave actions for the sake of a collective as a desirable national standard and thus establishes values which the readers can identify with.

Both of the stories set in the Caribbean Sea depict acts of lifesaving which were caused by members of the respective groups themselves. In the first story, the sailors could have known better than to leave the port in that kind of weather; in the second story, the fact that an inexperienced man was in charge of the wheel leads to the situation which makes a rescue necessary in the first place. The stories can thus not only be seen as adventure tales in exotic climes, but can also be read as an appeal for responsible action at sea. Furthermore, in a context of global politics, the representations of British heroism in colonial settings emphasise British supremacy. Through depicting moments of struggle and un-

190 A scene which adds to this entertaining quality shows the "hero" directly after reaching the shore where he realises that he is naked. He worries that he will not be taken for sane and no help will be sent to the party still clinging to the pinnace. When he meets a native on the shore, he bargains with him for his clothes and only succeeds so after knocking him "down". A Long Swim, *CJ*, 17 Nov 1866, 724. This scene not only acts as a comic instance, but stresses the perceived British supremacy over the colonial natives.

friendly encounters with natives, the British men prove their moral and physical dominance.

Saving Lives in British Waters

The tendency to place acts of lifesaving at sea in colonial settings ends after the 1860s and more and more stories of heroic acts in British waters can be found in *CJ*. This increase is not surprising, since the institution of the Albert Medal in 1866 had drawn much public attention to acts of lifesaving at sea – a dynamic on the consumer market that *CJ* identified and answered. The fact that the medal was only awarded for acts of lifesaving at sea can also account for the fact why stories about heroic acts on the water can be found much more frequently in *CJ* than similar acts on land.[191]

One example of a heroic act on the British coast can be found in the serial novel "Won – Not Wooed". Within the larger frame of the narrative, set in a British coastal town, one chapter shows an incident of distress at sea.[192] A party of summer guests is visiting a lighthouse and want to take a walk towards some rocks that are only accessible during low tide. The group reaches their destination in good spirits and, in their fascination with the flora and fauna of the rock, fail to notice the returning water. Within minutes the "rock had become an island, separated by a great waste of water from the shore" (Won – Not Wooed, *CJ*, 11 Jan 1871, 84). While the tide is rising around them, the group discusses whom to leave on the rock and whom to save; only two of the men know how to swim and only the younger one feels confident to try and take someone with him on his swim. The two women argue that they should be left behind,[193] yet no decision is made. In growing despair the group finally succeeds in catching the attention of a young man on shore, who, as their "hero of the day" (ibid., 18 Jan 1871, 102), attempts – and finally succeeds – to rescue them. Since the tide has not yet reached the shore, the young man has to push and carry a boat big enough to hold the whole of the party until he reaches waters deep enough for it to float. The group watches his struggle and constructs his everyday heroism in

191 This changed after the medal was extended to acts of lifesaving on land in 1877, as will be shown in a subsequent part of this chapter.

192 For the purpose of this study, the larger frame of the narrative is not relevant; therefore, I will only refer to the pertinent sequence.

193 Taking responsibility, the young woman demands the men "'to leave us, and look to your own safety. It was my wish that brought you all to this place: do not let my last moments be embittered by the thought that you have lost your lives, twice over, through my means'." Won – Not Wooed, *CJ*, 11 Jan 1871, 85. Thereby, she herself proposes a selfless act which might be considered heroic, and which mirrors common contemporary conceptions of female virtues such as willingness to sacrifice and regard for others. The construction of a distinctly female form of heroism around these virtues will be discussed in greater detail later on.

line with established communal heroic figures: "'He must have the strength of Hercules. That is the very feat which Bruce performed in Scotland, and Garibaldi in South America – the taking one's ships over dry land'" (ibid., 11 Jan 1871, 86). After a part of the way, the young man has to carry the boat and "Hercules had become Atlas, and was carrying, not the world, indeed, but their own hope of rejoining the world, upon his shoulders. He staggered under the enormous burden, but he staggered *on*" (ibid., 87). The task performed by the "young hero" (ibid., 18 Jan 1871, 104) is primarily due to his physicality, his being "'strong and well built'" (ibid., 11 Jan 1871, 83) and his perseverance, the fact that he "stagger[s] on" despite his own physical exhaustion. Thus, the young man saving the group is not only established as a "hero" of considerable physical strength, but of moral fibre as well.

"Lambert, the 'Hero and Martyr'", an article published in 1876, gives the "true account of a frail and blind old man in Glasgow, named James Lambert, who is noted for having saved numerous persons from drowning" (Lambert, the "Hero and Martyr", *CJ*, 26 Aug 1876, 545).[194] The Scotsman, who is said to have held the European record of lives saved from drowning, "had nothing but his own active body, his rare power of suspending the breath, and his lion heart" (ibid.). His heroism is one of strong physique as well as of moral disposition – of "body" and "heart" alike. The text in several anecdotes establishes Lambert as a selfless man who regards the lives of others higher than his own. On one occasion, so the report, he saved a man who had broken into the ice on the frozen Clyde: "James Lambert dived under the ice, and groped for the man till he was nearly breathless, and dragged him back to the hole, and all but died in saving him. Here the chances were nine to one against his ever finding that small aperture again and coming out alive" (ibid.). His "heroism" (ibid.) is thus not only constituted by his physical abilities, but especially by his self-denying qualities, "his goodness" (ibid.) of not regarding the risk for himself, but thinking of the life to be saved. Having lost his eyesight in one of these acts, Lambert's blindness functions as a physical manifestation of his selflessness. The article closes with an appeal for the "hero" (ibid.) related to his class-membership. Unlike others – the text gives the example of a "Frenchman" (ibid., 546) who had saved several lives from drowning as well and had received a lot of public and financial attention – the Glaswegian "lives unhappily [...] in an almshouse" (ibid.). The text closes with a request by the editor William Chambers himself to financially

194 The occasion for the recollection of the story, though not relating to the representation of the heroic, is still interesting in the context of nineteenth-century print culture: a narrative about Lambert had appeared in the *Pall Mall Gazette* (1865–1923), yet the author had retained his copyright. Subsequently, a Glasgow paper had copied and published the text, which had led to a trial and fine of £90 for the Glasgow publishers. *CJ* explains the legal situation as follows: "Floating news may be freely copied by one newspaper from another, but not a story or narrative *valuable in a literary point of view.*" Lambert, the "Hero and Martyr", *CJ*, 26 Aug 1876, 545, emphasis mine.

support Lambert and give the "greatest man in that city" (ibid.) a life deserving of his contribution to society. With this ending, the text again draws attention to the relation between a heroic figure and the public and makes clear that public attention is not necessarily linked to wealth and a comfortable life.[195] Like the philosopher Dumaresq who was discussed in relation to the herorization of scientists, Lambert is shown as a figure who has a place in the public realm and whose actions are praised in the media, yet his personal contribution to society does not result in a sufficient return.[196]

A similar appeal for public financial contributions can be found only two months later. The article "Storm Warriors" deals with the "life-boat movement" and tells the history of the National Life-Boat Institution from the late eighteenth century onwards. In short anecdotes, the danger of the task performed by the volunteer boatmen is illustrated. Unlike the previous examples, their physicality, however, plays a subordinate role and it is their motivation and selflessness which is praised. One of the men remarks that "'I had my inward feelings, as a man naturally must have when he is face to face with danger. [...] but [...] I determined to do it'" (Storm Warriors, *CJ*, 28 Oct 1876, 690). The text comments upon this utterance by stating that "[i]n this spirit these men often perform deeds of individual heroism, which have been equalled but never surpassed in the annals of self-sacrifice" (ibid.).[197] The anecdotes then stress this determination and selflessness further, when stating how the men "make a great many attempts to reach a wreck" (ibid., 691). Though referring to acts of individual heroism, the institution as a collective is heroised. The text states that "the mission of our Storm Warriors is to save" (ibid., 692) and emphasises the restorative quality of the men's heroism. Though not in a religious framework, the reference to their work being a "mission" clearly gives it a communal aspect directed at the welfare of a larger group. In its closing, the text includes the readers "who live at home at ease" with a "warm hearth" and "their luxurious sense of comfort enhanced by the angry storm which is raging at our doors" (ibid., 691). This contrasting description makes the situation of the lifeboat men even more starkly apparent and introduces an appeal to "aid in the good cause" (ibid., 692) with a

---

195 The fact that Lambert is still alive, though, is remarkable in relation to the article's headline. Introduced there as a "Hero and Martyr", Lambert can, as a living person, not be considered a martyr. Furthermore, his motivation as presented in the text is not a religious one. Thus, it can be presumed that the addition of "Martyr" was used to heighten the praise of Lambert and his actions and possibly point out clearly how close to death he had frequently been for the sake of others.

196 Additionally, this line of argument also implicitly includes its opposite – the case of men and women who draw financial gains from public attention though not having contributed to society in such a way as Lambert.

197 The reference to the "annals of self-sacrifice" (Storm Warriors, *CJ*, 28 Oct 1876, 690) also associates this form of everyday heroism with other established domains of the heroic. Through the focus on the communal aspect of their voluntary work and the reference to the men as "warriors" against nature, the text implicitly evokes military heroics.

financial contribution. Though at home around the "warm hearth", the final sentence – the emphatic exclamation "Speed the life-boat!" (ibid.) – includes the readers symbolically into the heroic realm of the "Storm Warriors" and asks for their active participation. Though the participation the text calls for is restricted to a donation, the exclamation gives the donating reader a feeling of being part of the group through the financial contribution.

Though not strictly depicting a rescue at sea but merely at the seaside, the tale "A Leap for Life" emphasises the willingness of self-sacrifice in a familial context. The text is narrated by "an elderly gentleman" who "commemorates a rare instance of combined pluck, presence of mind, and heroic self-sacrifice" (A Leap for Life, *CJ*, 30 Jun 1883, 406). The story, which the narrator takes from his own youth, is set at the Welsh coast where a group of boys and men go on a geological excursion and climb the rocks to see special formations. During the expedition, though "all experienced climbers" (ibid., 407), the narrator's younger self slips and finds himself suspended over a sharp rock formation, only holding onto his uncle's hand. Under the eyes of their "powerless [...] horrified friends", the narrator's uncle is shown undertaking an "awful risk" (ibid.): "'Tom, there is but one way for it. I'll save you, or we will both perish together [...]'" (ibid.). In a spectacular jump, he succeeds in circumnavigating the rocks and directing himself and the boy into the sea. Since the steep cliffs give no possibility to get back on land, the youth and his uncle have to remain swimming until they are eventually picked up by a fisherman who takes them back to his cabin and – though of very humble means – feeds and clothes them and lets them rest. The tale thus shows two "heroic" (ibid., 406) and selfless men – the uncle who risked his life to save his nephew as well as the fisherman and his wife who sacrificed their scarce belongings for the two endangered men. The narrator stresses that his uncle later not only expressed his deepest gratitude towards the fisher and his wife, but "rewarded" (ibid., 408) them for their selfless conduct. Thereby, the text raises the question of selfless acts and their repayment. Additionally, the text also draws attention to the function of texts such as this and the above: "Few people are ever likely to be placed in a similar position; should, however, such an occasion arise, let us hope they may not be found wanting in ability to follow so admirable an example" (ibid., 406). While it is unlikely that the readers of *CJ* would find themselves in a similar situation, the text nevertheless wants to encourage an imitation of the represented behaviour and an incorporation of the selfless attitude into their self-conception.

The didactic function of the stories about heroic acts of lifesaving – and life-risking – is even more pronounced in the poem "'This Ought Ye to Have Done'". It shows not only an incident of heroism at sea, but also points to the function of narratives such as these and contextualises everyday heroism with heroic acts of other domains. The occurrences are stated to the reader in an introductory paragraph. A fishing boat in Scotland had come into stormy water and the boat, which "was manned by a father and his four sons" (This Ought Ye to Have Done, *CJ*, 11 Aug 1900, 592), sunk, taking three of the sons with it. The father and the last son hold on to a remaining oar, which can however only support one of them. Surprisingly, it is the son then who lets go of the oar and in a "depth of kingly resignation and true feeling" (ibid.) leaves the father to be saved. The following poem then contrasts the "genuine heroism" (ibid.) of the young man to the heroics of the military and criticises the attention the latter receives: "We filled the leisure of the day, / When from the north the wintry rain / Was driv'n against the window pane, / With tales that told our soldiers' praise" (ibid.). These practices of commemoration for military heroism are then compared to the attention that the fisherman – as a representative for a different kind of less visible heroism – receives: "The lad who, with the sea at strife, / Let go his hold on life and youth / [...] Was soon forgotten by the few / Who chanced to read the scanty note / Which told the sinking of the boat" (ibid.). And although the speaker acknowledges the "soldier's honest faith" (ibid.), he closes with the assessment: "But spare a kindly thought for one – / That Scottish fisher-lad – who gave / His own another's life to save, / For braver deed was never done" (ibid.).

The poem clearly values the actions of the young fisherman who sacrificed his life over the bravery of the military. Though both are situational forms of heroism – the soldier is forced to be brave in a situation of combat and the fisherman needs to make a decision in the unexpected situation of a shipwreck – they perform different functions. Whereas the soldier shows courage and risks his life to defend *himself* and his country, the fisherman sacrifices his own life in order to save that of his father. In contrasting soldier and fisherman, the poem implies that the soldier risking his life still includes regard for his own safety, while the fisherman's self-denial is existential and uncompromising.

Furthermore, the title of the poem "This Ought Ye to Have Done" clearly states the identificatory function the poem wants to fulfil. As a direct address to the reader of the poem – and thus of the journal – the sentence creates a relation between the audience and the mediated story. Under this header, the behaviour of the young man towards his father can be read as a guideline for desired action. The son and his motivation become a role model for self-denial and self-sacrifice.

Bravery in Mining Accidents

While the depictions of heroic acts of lifesaving at sea showed representatives of different professions and classes, another set of texts in *CJ* depict a form of heroic lifesaving which was more strongly class-bound. While referring to the same core values, acts of lifesaving on land, especially those in mines, represented a distinctly working-class form of heroism and often reported real-life accidents.

As one of the key industries of the time, which many of the innovative technologies relied upon,[198] the coal industry was also a symbol of working-class Britain. The article "Fighting for Life. A Story of a Welsh Coal-Mine" presents the reader with the story of "the brave deed [...] accomplished in the Welsh coal-pit at Troedyrhiw" (Fighting for Life, *CJ*, 18 Aug 1877, 526).[199] The conduct of the miners during an accident is marked as "a splendid victory gained for humanity" (ibid.), a conduct worthy of "national pride" (ibid.). Furthermore, this text draws a connection between a collective national virtue and the heroic acts as shown in the incident: "The whole story is one more splendid instance of the noble qualities which are innate in the breasts of those who form the sinew and the backbone of Britain" (ibid.). The "noble qualities" as represented by the Welsh miners are – from the outset of the article – offered as a means of identification to the reader and the text stresses the particular importance of the working classes and the working man by calling the miners the "sinew and backbone of Britain" (ibid.). This is further highlighted by an anecdote which is narrated before dealing with the incident in Wales. Sharing the experience of a personal visit to a coal-pit, the author describes the fear and unease while "descending the shaft [...] [as] almost indescribable; and [it] is only equalled by the exquisite feeling of relief which pervades the mind once again returning to the surface" (ibid., 527). Having through this expression of intense fear emphasised that the pitmen risk their lives daily to supply the country with coal, the text turns to the incident in April 1877. Water had broken through an abandoned worksite and flooded the pit while some workers were still under ground. The text stresses how "[i]n an instance and without the slightest hesitation" (ibid., 527) all other miners volunteered to rescue the fourteen men and boys left behind. After a first group of men could be brought to safety, a second group of men is detected, the rescue of which spanned over ten days. The brave act of going back for their colleagues at that point turns into an act of endurance on both sides of the tunnel: "it thus became a question of patient endurance on the one hand and of unceasing labour and noble efforts on the other. And never did men work more nobly than did those who were thus doing all that lay in the power of man to save the lives of their devoted comrades" (ibid.). On the eighth day after the accident, the miners find a way towards the men trapped in the pit, yet the situation has become a danger for all involved and the determination of those above ground to nevertheless try and rescue their mates is emphasised: "Gloomy indeed was the prospect at this critical moment, for it had now become a question of life and

198 As fuel for the 'Age of Steam', the coal mining industry was integral to the industrial revolution of nineteenth-century Britain.

199 The accident referred to is the one which led Queen Victoria to extend the Albert Medal to acts of valour on land. Though it was – compared to other mining accidents which often claimed a great number of lives – a rather small incident, the story had featured prominently in the press, for which the present article serves as an example.

death to either party; but were the men who had been rescued thus far to be left after all to the death which seemed to hunger for them?" (ibid., 528). After this rhetorical question, the text describes how the men enter the shaft on ropes and without lamps (since bringing gas lamps into the pit could have caused another explosion), supply their fellow-workers with food, and finally bring them to the surface.

Significantly, it is not only the men of the rescue party who are called heroic for their actions, but "*the* pitman" (ibid., emphasis mine) in general. In its usage of the vocabulary of the heroic, the text attributes equal status to the suffering, fear and exhaustion of the men entrapped in the mine as to the bravery, endurance and selflessness of the miners above ground. Furthermore, the text can be seen as a heroisation of the mining profession as a whole, and even of the working classes as such. The text propagates a sense of community and loyalty among working men which is valued higher than that of other domains of the heroic: "It was a greater deed than the capture of an enemy's colours on the battle-field" (ibid.). The military realm once again functions as a contrasting form of heroism against which the selflessness and loyalty shown by the miners on both sides of the shaft is set as superior.

Other articles similarly heroise the actions of miners and often stress their endurance and unhesitating behaviour in face of danger. So, for example, two men entering a destroyed salt mine in "The Subsidence of Land in the Salt Districts of Cheshire" are described as "daring and experienced" and praised for continuing on their way through the "breast-high" water (The Subsidence of Land in the Salt Districts of Cheshire, *CJ*, 22 Jan 1881, 61), although having extinguished one of their candles. Similarly, a text which describes a visit to a coal mine partially destroyed in an explosion, praises the daring of the "heroic searchers" (After An Explosion, *CJ*, 7 Aug 1886, 511) trying to rescue their fellow-workers. Further, stress is put on the fact that the "gallant band of rescuers" (ibid.) are "always ready to risk their lives in helping others" (ibid.) and nevertheless remain humble: "most mining heroes [...] [are] modest and rarely mentio[n their deeds]" (The Subsidence of Land in the Salt Districts of Cheshire, *CJ*, 22 Jan 1881, 61). The loyalty described in the rescuers in "After an Explosion" persists beyond death so that they "bore out also the bodies of the dead; and not till then, yielded to the numbing, stifling influence of the poisonous vapours, which left them aching and ill for days" (After an Explosion, *CJ*, 7 Aug 1886, 511).

The heroism as represented by the miners is distinctly a working-class heroism and one which is linked to the miners' specific profession. The act of going underground every day is in itself already considered brave and this bravery is then depicted as being even more heightened in situations of danger. The men shown in the texts are moral exemplars; they show a high degree of loyalty towards their peers, do not hesitate to come to their aid – and do so voluntarily – and above all regard the lives of their fellow-workers higher than their own. Selflessness and an orientation towards the common good are at the heart of the heroic miner as represented in *CJ* and the communal tendencies of the heroes within their community offer a means of identification to the audience.

Prize-Winning Heroic Acts

As has been observed, an increase in texts which present acts of lifesaving as heroism occurs after the institution of the Albert Medal and the awards given by the Royal Humane Society. It is not surprising then that there are also a number of articles which explicitly deal with those awards and their winners. The text "Little Heroes" in 1882 focuses especially on children's acts of lifesaving since "[t]he heroism of men and women is often chronicled and rewarded" (Little Heroes, *CJ*, 16 Dec 1882, 806), yet that of children is not mediated to the public as often. With the account of young medal winners of the Royal Humane Society, the text wants to rectify this situation.[200] In short anecdotes, it retells the "many examples of youthful heroism" (ibid., 807) in saving other children from drowning. The accounts emphasise the "little heroes"' unhesitant behaviour, their readiness of action, "presence of mind" (ibid.), the risk they took regarding their own safety, and stress the fact that self-denying acts of bravery are bound to neither age nor class. The children represented come from different classes, one girl saves her governess which clearly indicates that she comes from a comfortable middle-class background, other "act[s] of courage and devotedness" (ibid.) show children playing in the rather shabby environment of a canal (cf. ibid., 806).

"Heroes of Peace", another text which gives accounts of incidents honoured by the Royal Humane Society, sets the acts described in a broader context. Taking up the discussion about the moral state of British society, the text rejects the diagnosis that "as a race we are deteriorating, and that the Englishmen of today are not equal to those of former ages in spirit and daring" (Heroes of Peace, *CJ*, 6 Jun 1885, 353),[201] as the recipients of The Royal Humane Society are evidence to the contrary: "the claimants for these rewards are more numerous, and the deeds for which these rewards are asked are not inferior, in self-devotion and heroism on the part of the rescuers, to any of the past ages, be they ever so noble" (ibid.). The reference to the growing number of these acts of "self-devotion and heroism" (ibid.) is interestingly a positive one and the heroism of the "claimants"

200 In this specific case, as well as regarding other articles which retell factual contemporary events of lifesaving, this argumentation is slightly askew since it represents actions which have already been publicly honoured through the awarding of the medal and/or other forms of public attention.

201 In connection with the headline – which implicitly includes its counter-image of the 'heroes of war' – the article reflects the more traditionalist and past-oriented side of the ongoing debate about heroics, which not only favoured leader figures but also clung more to an ideal of a battling hero.

(ibid.) seems not to be belittled by the fact that they are not singular examples of this form of heroism. On the contrary, the high number of awards given is seen as a proof of the heroic potential of society at large: "Never before has the number of rewards in a single year been so great. These figures in themselves, one would think, are a sufficiently potent answer to the criticism to which we have alluded" (ibid.). The article then gives examples of awardees and their deeds, ordered by the different ranks of awards, starting with the highest. The winner of the "Stanhope Gold Medal, which is awarded every year to the hero of the most meritorious case" (ibid.), is a man who, after another passenger on a steamship had gone overboard, jumped right after the non-swimmer and "for forty minutes supported him in the water" (ibid.). With considerable admiration, the text states: "Such a deed as this needs no extolling. Its singular daring is patent" (ibid.).[202] Daring, bravery and gallantry are then the three characteristics attributed to all of the examples. The mentioning of gallantry as a core feature of this form of heroism can be related to the phrasing of the Stanhope Medal award, which rewarded the "most gallant rescue".[203] Many of the cases rewarded concern distress at sea, and the heroism of professionals at sea, such as navy men, and civilian passengers, like the Stanhope Medal winner, are regarded as equally heroic.

What is emphasised is the "ready manner in which help" (Heroes of Peace, *CJ*, 6 Jun 1885, 354) was given, the fact that their actions were voluntary (cf. ibid.)[204] and, most importantly, the fact that their attempts "exposed [them] to the same risk" (ibid.) as those they wanted to help. The heroes of the Royal Humane Society in the representation in *CJ* are thus not chiefly praised for their bravery and daring alone, but, evoking *CJ*'s heroic imaginary, most importantly for the fact that they acted selflessly and regarded the lives of others higher than their own without hesitation.

Remarkably, the text only refers generally to the "ten women and girls and sixteen quite young persons" (ibid., 355) who received the medal in 1885, and then gives only one example of an instance of "female heroism" (ibid.), that of Alice Ayres, a servant-girl who saved several children from a burning house, but lost her own life in the process. Where bravery and daring had been the words used to describe the heroism of the men at sea, Ayres is portrayed in terms of sacri-

---

202 The contradiction between the singularity of the deeds and large number of these seeming singular actions is not reflected in the text. This brings up the general difficulty in *CJ* to integrate exceptionality in its idea of heroism, which most of the time clearly utilised heroes as role models.

203 Quoted in W. H. Fevyer / Craig P. Barclay: Acts of Gallantry, vol. 3, Luton 2013, p. 3.

204 In my opinion, the act of volunteering to help is what connects the navy men and the civilians, since both of them are not professionally obliged to help someone in distress. The military men might be bound more strongly by a military codex which includes loyalty towards their comrades, but unlike, for example, coastguards, it is not their job description to save others.

fice. The focus is put even more strongly on the self-denying quality of the attempt to save another's life than on the courage it takes. Ayres is called a "noble" woman who "sacrificed" (ibid.) herself for the wellbeing of others. She is described as repeatedly going into the burning house to rescue the children of her employers[205] although she "herself nearly suffocated by smoke" (ibid.) in the process. Despite her own physical weakness, she does not stop "until she had rescued all the children […] through her own life" (ibid.). After finally having secured the lives of the children, she jumps from a window but misses the mattresses which had been laid out for her safety. The emphasis on her selflessness is repeated in the last lines of the text, which also speaks to the dissemination of stories about everyday acts of heroic lifesaving: the

> […] disregard of her own safety, as shown by Alice Ayres, was even greater than that exhibited by the light-keeper's daughter. Granted that Alice was but a poor servant-girl in a squalid part of the town; but if one has been celebrated in verse and received a well-earned renown, it should surely not be sufficient for the other to dismiss her, perhaps to a pauper's grave, with only a line in the daily papers to record her death. (ibid.)

These lines, which *CJ* took from the up-market weekly *The Queen,* do not only show that the article itself is behind on the occurrences after Ayre's death,[206] but also display a criticism of a growing celebrity cult, even regarding the representation of common heroes. Through the comparison of Alice Ayres' actions and those of Grace Darling,[207] the famous "light-keeper's daughter" (ibid.), the text on the one hand criticises the massive medial presence of Grace Darling, but on

---

205 The relationship between Ayres and the family is described as a professional one although, in fact, she helped in the household of her sister and the children were her nieces and nephews. This is remarkable given the fact that the fire on Union Street and Ayre's death had been a very public affair, as had been the funeral and a memorial service held on 10 May 1885. As John Price argues, the attendants of both events can be presumed to have mostly come from the working classes. cf. Price: Everyday Heroism, pp. 22–23. Thus, at least *CJ*'s London audience, through the coverage in other papers (e.g. in *The Queen* from which the present article says to have taken their information, or the *Illustrated London New* [1842–2003] which printed an illustration of Ayres which was reproduced widely), but also a wider audience, would have already been familiar with the particulars of the event.

206 By the time the article had appeared in *CJ*, Ayres had been praised in many a "verse" (Heroes of Peace, *CJ*, 6 Jun 1885, 355) and had *not* been buried in a pauper's grave but had been given a funeral at Isleworth Cemetery which was attended by 10,000 mourners and received a lot of public attention. Interestingly, Ayre's sister, brother-in-law and the two children whom she could not rescue were buried in a different and less prestigious cemetery. Cf. Price: Everyday Heroism, pp. 58–59.

207 Grace Darling, daughter of a lighthouse keeper on one of the Outer Farne Islands off the Northumbrian coast, had, together with her father, saved nine members of the paddle steamer "Forfarshire"'s crew in September 1838 by rowing out to their wrecked ship in harsh weather. Interestingly, the *Oxford Dictionary of National Biography* until today gives "heroine" as Darling's decisive trait, where the dictionary would normally note a person's profession. Cf. H. C. G. Matthew: Darling, Grace Horsley (1815–1842), in: Lawrence Goldman (ed.): Oxford Dictionary of National Biography, 2010, DOI: 10.1093/ref:odnb/7155.

the other hand also seems to perceive a different public treatment according to a hero's class.[208] Ayres, the "poor servant-girl" is suspected to receive a different public treatment than Darling, who is regarded as higher up the social ladder. The prediction that the heroic girl might not enter the public memory also implies there are other heroic acts of members of the lower classes which never come to the attention of society at large.

Though being clearly mistaken in the prediction of Ayres ending in a "pauper's grave" (ibid.) and not being publicly recognised, the text about the Humane Society and its awardees clearly puts forth the claim that members of all social classes are capable of heroic acts and that these should be publicly rewarded. However, selfless behaviour is still at the centre of this form of heroism, which is constituted by acts of self-denying courage in which the heroes risk their own life for that of another. Further stress is put on the fact that the acts of heroism thus represented are *peaceful* acts, in opposition to the military heroism which is more frequently acknowledged through awards and medals.[209] As spontaneous acts representing the individual's virtuous character, they cannot be planned and therefore can never be deliberately seeking attention or fame. This might act as an explanation for the fact why *CJ*, which on the whole so often emphasises that a hero should *not* seek public recognition, argues *for* rewards and public attention for this specific form of heroism.[210]

On the whole, all texts about heroic acts of lifesaving particularly stress the selflessness of their protagonists. They show a social form of courage in their acts, in that the men and women do not hesitate to risk their own lives in order to save another's. Using examples of the middle and predominantly of the working classes, this form of heroism is established as a distinctly working-class type of heroics.[211] This would have allowed the readers of *CJ* to identify with the

---

208 Not only was she celebrated in poems by Swineburn and Wordsworth, but frequently painted; her autograph could be bought and she had received a large number of financial donations – even £50 from Queen Victoria. Cf. Hugh Cunningham: Grace Darling. Victorian Heroine, London 2007, p. 174.

209 Apart from the examples cited above, "Medals and Medal-Collecting" in 1892 explicitly states that "But as in our time these rewards are given, for instance, by the Royal Humane Society to celebrate individual heroism in the saving of life, so in former days they were sometimes, though rarely, given as an *incentive to peace* as well as by way of reward in war." Medals and Medal-Collecting, *CJ*, 20 Feb 1892, 125, emphasis mine.

210 In the specific comparison of public attention for Grace Darling and Alice Ayres it is further noteworthy that the text criticises the public celebration of Darling, who was still alive when the public furore around her person began, while the dead Ayres could have no selfish advantages from public attention.

211 Furthermore, both the acts of lifesaving at sea and in the mines are situated in realms removed from civilisation. The sea, a space with a history of heroic tales, as a representation of the supremacy of nature acts as a catalyst for daring, physical individual heroic acts. The environment of a mine, however, though removed from the civilisation above ground stands for the progress of society and is clearly centred on a working-class collective rather than on individuals.

protagonists – with the exception of the earlier adventure-tales of saving lives in exotic climes – and imagine themselves in similar kinds of situations. In that respect, the texts can be seen as guidelines for appropriate behaviour in exceptional circumstances and propagated both group loyalty (again in specifically *working-class* form) as well as loyalty towards strangers. Though presenting similar core-values to those discussed in the context of different domains of heroism, the heroics of lifesaving as shown in *CJ* are fundamentally different in one aspect: the periodical *encourages* acts such as these to be disseminated and publicly recognised. The highly situational and often singular character of the acts might provide a possible explanation for this. On the other hand, everyday heroism such as that shown above might have been considered a domain of the heroic with greater access to members of the working classes. Thereby, public acts of appreciation in this context could have been seen as acts of validation for the working classes as such. Nevertheless, the various calls for public acknowledgement of acts of lifesaving seems anachronistic in the context of the journal's general propagation of more *silent* forms of heroism.[212]

Heroic Work

The social effects of urbanisation were apparent in all parts of Victorian society. A growing anxiety regarding the emerging working classes could be perceived among the propertied classes. The fear of a revolutionary class of labourers which would be able to destabilise the wealth and status of the established middle and upper classes grew steadily over the course of the century. Although attempts such as those of the Chartists did not prove successful in the long run,[213] social anxiety regarding the working classes and their potential for upward mobility remained.[214] Though not in a revolutionary manner, the working classes[215] still saw their potential power within the economy and thus the nineteenth century saw

212 Especially in light of the fact that lifesavers such as Grace Darling did receive the kind of attention and glorification that *CJ* criticised so often.

213 For a detailed discussion of Chartism and its consequences see for example Chase 2008, Finn 1993, Royle 2006 [1996] or Shaw 1995.

214 This anxiety, as Lara Baker Whelan argues, became especially apparent in the suburban space, which came to be occupied by members of both the middle and the working classes. Frequently, this environment could be seen "as a site of terror as middle-class anxiety about the lack of social homogeneity in the suburbs grew". Lara Baker Whelan: Class, Culture and Suburban Anxieties in the Victorian Era, London 2010, p. 11.

215 Though the term working classes often evokes a homogenous notion, the plural already indicates that it covered a broad spectrum, not only professionally, but socially as well. Charles Booth in his *Life and Labour of the People in London*, a survey which he began to conduct in the 1880s and which led to the impressive *Maps of London Poverty* in 1889, differentiates six main categories of the working classes: "high-paid labour", "regular standard earnings", "small regular earnings", "intermittent earnings", "casual earnings" and the "lowest class" Cf. Charles Booth: Labour and Life of the People, London 1902 [1889].

the establishment of trade unions and utilisation of strikes.[216] In the context of this middle-class fear regarding the loss of supremacy, the distinctly positive depiction of the working classes in *CJ* – which in terms of its editors and contributors was clearly an upper-middle-class paper – is striking. It reaffirms the didactic motives of the periodical, but could however, in its validation of existing structures rather than a promotion of radical social change, also be read as an attempt to stabilise existing societal norms.

Over the course of the period under examination, a growing number of articles which heroise the manual labour of the working classes can be found in *CJ*. These articles show a tension: on the one hand, the texts call the work life, and especially the work ethos, of working-class men heroic and thereby mark the labourers as ranking on the topmost end of a moral scale. On the other hand, though, the texts always also show a didactic agenda and depict the men as – despite their moral excellence – still needing further education. The workmen are represented as heroic *despite* the fact that they could still improve themselves.

The text "Working-Men", which reviews the 1867 book *Some Habits and Customs of the Working-Classes*,[217] exhibits this tension. The article praises the book for its authenticity, since it was "written by one of themselves" (Working-Men, *CJ*, 18 May 1867, 317) and the author has gone about the book in a "fair trustworthy, modest" (ibid.) way. By marking the author as a member of the group of "[m]echanic" (ibid.) working men, the virtues attributed to him in the opening passage already act as a description of the whole class of working men. Quoting from the book, they are described as follows: "'Working-men, as a body […] have many virtues: they are honest, industrious, and provident, and none but themselves can know with what fortitude they face the hardship incidental to their sphere of life, or how they are to each other in the hour of need […]'" (ibid., 318). Affirming this evaluation, the reviewer then calls the working men described as such "heroic" (ibid.). The heroism of the workers as depicted in this contribution is therefore clearly a moral one and despite dealing with manual labourers, their heroism is an abstract one. It is not the usage of their hands as such that is praised, but the way they go about the work and their relation with their co-workers. While the virtues of honesty, industry and providence refer to the men's work ethos, which manifests itself in specific "traditions and customs" (ibid., 319) of individual workplaces, the fact that they help each other "in the

216 The trade unions are noteworthy in the context of this study since they not only campaigned for appropriate wages and work-place safety, but were often dedicated to the idea of self-help and often were linked to Friendly Societies which gave workers the opportunity to educate themselves.

217 The book referred to is: Thomas Wright: *Some Habits and Customs of the Working Classes*, London 1867. The first edition of the book calls the author "A Journeyman Engineer" in set print and only gives his name in a printed signature, the last name of which is hard to read and probably the reason why the article in *CJ* falsely refers to the author as "Mr Bright". Working-Men, *CJ*, 18 May 1867, 317–320.

hour of need" (ibid., 318) stresses the relational character of their collective heroism. What is "deemed heroic" (ibid.) about the workers is, on a more abstract level, their work for a larger group, the fact that they "endure" (ibid.) exhausting manual labour for their fellow-workers and for their "wi[ves] and children" (ibid.). What further contributes to the workers' heroism is their humility, the fact that "none but themselves" know about their moral "fortitude" (ibid.). Their exemplary morals are not on display, which makes their heroism conform with *CJ*'s heroic imaginary. By referencing the communal aspect not only to their fellow workers but to the men's families as well, their heroism also gains a domestic facet and benefits the integrity of intact familial structures.

Despite this moral excellence identified in the workers by both the reviewed book and the reviewer, the latter criticises the "lack of education" (ibid.) among members of the working class. The text attributes this to two factors. On the one hand, it is shown as a political and institutional problem caused by the fact that access to education was still limited among the working classes.[218] Furthermore, the existing educational institutions accessible to the lower classes are criticised for not teaching the children properly and only letting them memorise knowledge which "evaporates in the first six months after leaving" (ibid.) the school. On the other hand, the text also identifies the likelihood of working men to be prone to vices and spending their time with "brutal and brutalising sports" (ibid.) rather than engaging in measures of self-education in their leisure hours. The text justified its own didactic cause by juxtaposing the validation of the whole group of working men in the heroisation of their selfless work morale with the educative effort still to be made. Since these very men and their women and children were part of the target audience and the societal group which the publication wanted to educate further, the text both states the necessity of their own didactic endeavour but at the same time – by means of herorization – encourages the workers that they have already accomplished something which they can now build on. Interestingly, the heroism of the represented workers is closely linked to their work life and a sort of moral professional codex they adhere to. The heroism as represented of the working man is therefore a *collective* and *communal* form of heroism. Though *CJ* continuously defines its idea of heroism in contrast to the military hero, this concept of class heroism in its adherence to duty for a larger group clearly draws on a model of military heroics.[219]

218 The Elementary Education Act which encouraged schooling for children between the ages of five and thirteen was only to be passed three years after the article appeared in *CJ*, and schooling was not made compulsory until 1880. Even after that, the fees which needed to be paid and the fact that financial state support for education was not established until the 1890s, meant that many working-class children still did not receive a formal education.

219 Similar to the military hero, the motivation for the heroic professional conduct can still be a private and individual one, such as wanting to provide for one's family. Cf. Working-Men, *CJ*, 18 May 1867, 318.

The collective form of heroism which adheres to and exemplifies a specific professional codex is also put forth in various articles dealing with individual professions, of which I will present a selection in the following. One example can be found in an article from 1874 dealing with "The Street News-Boys of London" which – again collectively – calls the actions of the news-boys "heroism" (The Street News-Boys of London, *CJ*, 21 Feb 1874, 114). Although the boys and young men are described as mostly taking up their profession out of necessity – "because they have been brought up to no trade, and but little capital is needed [for the selling of newspapers]" (ibid., 113) – they still feel a "duty" (ibid.) towards the larger group of news-boys. The trade is subsequently described as one with clear principles regarding where which kinds of publications are to be sold, a clear hierarchy, but also a strong bond between the workers and a moral code they adhere to (cf. ibid., 113–114). The latter is illustrated by an anecdote about a man "at the *Swiss Goat's Horns*, who sells papers to the bus passengers in the morning, but he never has sufficient number; no boy would, however, be found to come and compete with him" (ibid., 114). The boys' behaviour exemplifies a collective moral codex which forbids them to take advantage of weaker parts of their community for the sake of any possible individual interest. However, the text still – like the more abstract article on working men – bemoans the lack of education that often brings the boys into the profession in the first place.

The heroic morality of working in a community is also shown in "Pitmen, Past and Present". The pitmen working together – in this specific case in a village entirely made up of miners and therefore a community which is also bound together in private life through their profession – are shown as "exhibits of true heroism" (Pitmen, Past and Present, *CJ*, 30 Oct 1886, 699). In contrast to the articles heroising miners' extraordinary work in accidents, this text praises the ordinary everyday working life and the men's work ethos, the way they behave "amongst them" (ibid.). The specific setting in an all-miners' village is interesting in so far as its description allows an assessment of the text's opinion on miners "in general" (ibid.). In the description of the community, the aspects of loyalty and decency are striking; the text even compliments the village's school, which can – again an emphasis on the strong bond within the community – only be kept up because "all the workers, whether married or single, agreed to pay a weekly sum" (ibid). Furthermore, the absence of crime in the village is stressed and the fact that the leisure activities – which in the view of many observers at the time constituted a possible danger for the working classes – are ones designed to benefit the "physical, intellectual, moral, and spiritual well-being of the populace" (ibid.).

Nevertheless, the situation of the heroic workers is depicted as being worthy of improvement. In the case of the miners, the often poor working conditions are criticised as well as the fact that their hard work and long hours affect the domestic life of families: many children "did not know their fathers, as the children were asleep all the time the father was at home" (ibid., 697). Yet even this criticism is related to a communal aspect, since the fathers take on the strenuous work for the benefit of their families.

The examples of heroic workers stress the relational and communal function of heroism in *CJ*. The heroic everyday life of the workers is governed by a concern for the well-being of a larger group and motivated by a professional codex. Though depicting different professions, the texts all stress the importance of loyalty and solidarity towards the larger group. None of the texts show individual heroes, but heroise the workers as a collective. In that, the texts can serve as role models for the readers and a connection of the heroism in the text to all members of the working classes easily be drawn, while still calling for further measures to improve the situation of the working class. As the text about the news-boys concludes: the heroic acts could have been intended to show the readers that, through dutiful and loyal behaviour, they themselves could be part of the heroic "character of England" (The Street News-Boys of London, *CJ*, 21 Feb 1874, 115).

Domestic Heroism – The Everyday Life of Women

> *It is true.* Such heroism as this, such utter forgetfulness of self, for the sake of some dearer self in husband or child, is not a rare thing among women. We rejoice to know of this sublime strength of love put forth in many a character deemed commonplace, and in circumstances that may and do happen every day [...]. (The Professor's Wife, *CJ*, 26 May 1860, 329)

Although many of the abstract values motivating the heroic, which are so often stressed in *CJ*, are open for identification to men and women alike, a number of texts construct a specific kind of female heroism which is linked to the domestic sphere. This form of heroism is not necessarily a passive one or limited to the private sphere – although the ideal of women at home can be found in many texts in *CJ* – but one which is in all cases *motivated* by a longing for domestic stability and integrity. Especially in fictional texts, various examples can be found in which the determination to preserve domestic bliss enables the female characters to perform acts which transgress the contemporary gender norms. Nevertheless, this form of heroism can be described as fundamentally domestic, since the domestic sphere is its starting point, motivation and final goal.

This is exemplified in a tale under the telling title "A Homely Heroine". The fictional story appeared on the cover page of *CJ* in January 1874 and centres around the young Scottish girl Kristie who, from girlhood, is extraordinary compared to others of her age and gender. She is an orphan, "remarkably tall", has "masses of thick soft brown hair", a "large mouth" and "arms, which were rather long" (A Homely Heroine, *CJ*, 31 Jan 1874, 65). Also, she has "a difficulty of utterance", but is pious, her religion "truly [being] a part of herself and of her daily life" (ibid.). She grows up with Archie, a "delicate, puny boy" who is – in contrast to Kristie, whose "heart is infinitely greater than her intellect" (ibid.) – described as very intelligent. The two lose track of one another in their youth yet meet again by chance working for the same farmer. The farmer, being fond of the two, gives them a shepherd's cottage to start their own living. They marry and go on to live in the solitude of the Scottish wilderness. Whenever they return to a more densely populated area, however, they are the cause of ridicule because of the odd impression which the couple leaves. Not only is Kristie her husband's opposite in intellect, but they also contrast each other in terms of physicality. What she has in strength, he is lacking, being "two or three inches" smaller than his wife, "little and slight" and having "a fair boyish face, which made him look younger than Kristie" (ibid.). The couple, which seems to transgress gender norms, settles for more traditional roles once they have a child. Archie herds the sheep on his own, while Kristie's "occupation" (ibid.) is to stay in the cottage with their child.

Having been established as a loving, yet somewhat unusual family, the story turns to the act of "homely" (ibid.) heroism by Kristie alluded to in the title. The scene is set on New Year's Eve and the landscape around the cottage already foreshadows the looming danger:

> The sun was low in the west, enveloped in a strange reddish haze; behind the hills to the north, great masses of heavy clouds were rolling up, piled on above another; a bitter icy wind whistled down the valley, bearing on its wings an occasional snow-flake; while to the south the great range of hills rose up, clear and distinct in the slight mantle of snow, against the purplish sky. (ibid., 67)

Kristie is waiting for her husband to return and eventually, after night has fallen, she leaves the cottage and her child to search for him. The way is icy and dangerous and Kristie is frightened by the remembrance of several deaths which have occurred in the area due to bad weather conditions. She hesitates, "but there was no other way; it was life or death and she must hasten on: […] but her foot slipped, and she narrowly escaped falling. […] [S]he had to trust more to memory for the path than actual sight" (ibid., 66). Rather than trusting in god, the young woman, previously described as pious, trusts in her own abilities and courageously goes on until she finds Archie lying motionless on the ground. He regains consciousness and says goodbye to his wife, since he is sure that no help could come in time to save him. Kristie then replies: "Mony a time, Archie, have I wondered why the Lord gied me my great strength and my lang arms, but I see it now, and if it be His will, I will save you this nicht" (ibid.). In her heroic action, her physical nonconformity seems to find its godly legitimisation. She carries her husband homewards,

> she felt as if she could overcome everything, and soon was within a few yards of their own door. Then her strength utterly failed; she struggled with beating heart and labouring breath against her weakness as if it were some physical obstacle; and she did manage,

> though how she never know, to reach the house, enter the door, place Archie on the long settle by the fireside, and then fell on the floor perfectly unconscious. (ibid., 68)

It is significant how her strength only diminishes once she comes close to her own domestic realm again, in which her role is that of a housewife. It is worth examining more closely what constitutes the young woman's act of heroism. On the one hand, it is characterised by her extraordinary strength, made possible through her rather unwomanly physique and her courage to face the dangerous weather, despite the fact that a number of people have already died in similar conditions. The features which, on a practical level, enable her to perform her act of heroism are the very characteristics which had been used at the outset of the text to other her, which make her not conform to the norms of the time. She is an orphan, of no remarkable intellectual capacity, yet possesses physical strength which she cannot utilise in her daily life described as consisting of knitting and rocking the cradle. However, it is this abnormality which makes it possible for her to save her husband: she is strong enough to carry him and her faith in god gives her the trust that nothing will happen to her infant child alone at home (cf. ibid., 66). Thus, Kristie's unwomanly physicality is at the core of her heroic self. However, there is a second component to Kristie's heroism, which is already spelled out in the tale's title: although Kristie sets out into wild nature, her heroism is a homely one and she essentially is a domestic hero. An ideal of domestic bliss is both the motivation and the effect of her heroic act. She is going out to save her husband, who is an integral part of her domestic life and its maintenance. She is utilising her unwomanly qualities in order to secure her status as a homely woman, as a wife. The fact that her transgression of gender norms is motivated by an existential necessity for the restoration of domestic unity is further emphasised by the fact that she loses this stamina when she returns home.[220] Having returned into the domestic realm *with* her husband, it is no longer necessary for her to act out her physical abilities, but she can instead fulfil the cliché of the Victorian woman – faint.

Similar acts of female physical heroism can be found throughout the 1870s, 1880s and 1890s, yet not earlier.[221] "Some Brave Women" in September 1880 makes the domestic frame of the heroic act even more obvious; the collection of

---

220 Additionally, Kristie is presented as a humble person who does not understand "why people called her a 'heroine'". A Homely Heroine, *CJ*, 31 Jan 1874, 68. This further emphasises her actions as being motivated by private, domestic interests.

221 Other examples include "A Heroine at the Diggings" (*CJ*, 29 Aug 1874, 560) in which a woman accompanies her brother to Australia and works at his side as a gold digger (in male disguise) to secure more money for the family. In closing, the article however feels the need to assure the reader that the young woman has stopped her masquerade by now and is happily married. Or "Eliza Warick. A Heroine in Ordinary Life" (*CJ*, 12 Dec 1874, 785–787) whose adventures in the story are anything but ordinary. Similar to the aforementioned examples, the longing for an ordinary family life is the *motivation* for her heroic acts on a Portuguese pirate ship. Furthermore, the story about the "Heroine of Lydenberg" set in the Transvaal War shows similar tendencies.

anecdotes of "brave women" are mostly set on the American continent and show them utilising their physical strength in the fight against an 'other' (be it the considered less civilised native population or wild animals) and the introduction states that:

> When the lives of those she [a generalised type of 'the woman' as such] loves are at stake, then, if ever, a woman will prove valiant; but even then, it is odd that she breaks down as soon as the danger is past. Lady Cochrane readily put her life to the hazard for her husband's sake, to shame his faltering crew into sticking to their guns; but although it is not so recorded, it would have been nothing surprising if she had indulged in a good cry when the end was accomplished and the victory achieved. (Some Brave Women, *CJ*, 18 Sep 1880, 606)

Although the stories which follow are ones of daring and physical strength, the introductory sentences clearly put the act of female heroism in a domestic frame by stating that the strength is only motivated by the endangerment of those "she loves" (ibid.) and the breakdown of such extraordinary behaviour after order is restored. This is even further stressed by the speculative retelling of the reaction of Lady Cochrane after "the victory" (ibid.). Unlike the examples discussed in chapter 4.5, the foreign setting of the heroic acts does not direct their heroism at the advancement of civilisation or society as a whole. The women shown in the examples are not transgressing gender norms in an attempt to further civilisation, but in most of the cases for the protection of domestic integrity.

The physical acts in some cases even include violence, yet the heroism remains domestic in its intention, as the example of "British Amazons" shows. The article features the story of an Irishwoman, whose husband – under the influence of drink – joins the "Lord Orrery's Regiment of Foot" (British Amazons, *CJ*, 13 May 1893, 299). After not having heard from him for twelve months, she decides to search for him. Having "provided for the welfare of her children" (ibid.), she disguises herself as a man, joins the regiment herself and leaves for the battlefield in Flanders. There, she actively participates in the Nine Year's War, is wounded yet still performs her duty in combat – all the while looking out for her husband. Despite the odds, she finally meets her husband again only for him to be killed in battle shortly afterwards. In her quest for domestic integrity, she continues to – literally – fight until she eventually meets a man who is to become her future husband and replaces the father of her children in the domestic sphere. After their return to Ireland, they lead a life with traditional gender roles, the "amazon" (ibid.) taking her place as a wife and mother again.[222]

The previous articles showed women transgressing gender norms in terms of their physical abilities with a domestic motivation. Their heroism thus results in domestic norm-conformity. However, a number of texts raise this domestic in-

[222] The last paragraph of the narrative even describes her nursing her husband after he has fallen sick, which stands in stark contrast to her violent heroic deeds in battle. This shows how her transgressive agency is lost after domestic integrity is regained.

tegrity itself into the realm of heroism. This becomes most obvious in the article "Heroines": The text, which discusses the possibility or impossibility of female heroism, concludes that the domestic sphere is the only desirable realm for female heroics. It is interesting, though, why other fields are denied to women. Firstly, the intellectual life is said not to be suited for female heroism, due to women's "unreasoning nature" (Heroines, *CJ*, 2 Aug 1884, 493). "[I]ntellectual culture belongs to the few" (ibid.) and, as the text argues, women are not, by nature, suited for that kind of profession. On the contrary, "too much" knowledge (ibid.) is depicted as being dangerous for women who – with growing knowledge – are claimed to turn into "passionless creatures", a "third sex" (ibid.).[223] As a second field of activity, philanthropy is considered; though this area may prove more suitable for women, as it requires "loving compassion" for "the common good" (ibid.), charitable work is still not deemed the appropriate place for female heroics because most of it is conducted in public, by "'women with a mission'" (ibid.), and "the woman with a mission flaunts it before the world, and gets more or less in everybody's way" (ibid.). Only if they had a "desire to remain unknown" (ibid.) could they be considered heroines, yet – so the assessment of the text – most women doing charitable work decidedly do not want to remain unknown. Finally then, the text finds the ideal place for womanly heroics in the private sphere and female dedication to husband, children and domestic integrity. These heroines "of commonplace life" possess, so the text, a "greatness [that] does not need striking incidents. Their worth makes precious those trivial atoms of which life is composed" (ibid., 494). The question of the recognition of heroic acts, which frequently creates a tension in *CJ*, is mentioned in the text as well and a seemingly easy solution is presented: the heroic mother and wife's efforts are not only recognised, but become eternal, since their "immortal influence" (ibid.) lives on in the generations to come.

Their heroism is one of "sacrifice" (ibid.) and its characteristics are: "tenderness, gentleness, self-forgetfulness, suffering. The last may not be universal, like the rest. But the highest love can only exist where suffering has touched the object loved" (ibid.). The prototypical heroine designed in the article is thus clearly modelled after an interesting combination of both working- and middle-class women. In showing suffering as the characteristic which crowns the heroic love for one's family, the text clearly refers to more precarious households of the working classes which struggle to make ends meet and keep their family fed and healthy. On the other hand, the heroine whose scope is restricted to the domestic sphere clearly mirrors an ideal of middle-class femininity in which women were not required to work in order to contribute to the family's finances. In its heroisation of the domestic woman, the text wants to mediate a middle-class

223 On a – from today's perspective humorous – side note, the text argues further that women should have a limited education so that they can still be impressed by the knowledge of men "to tell her about". Heroines, *CJ*, 2 Aug 1884, 493.

ideal, yet also reveals that it wants to appeal to and offer a means of identification to a lower social rank. In this creation of a heroism which wants "to remain unknown", the text is in line with the other meta-heroic reflections in *CJ*, all of which struggle with the public nature of heroism, necessarily created through its mediality. "Heroines" thus again tries to imagine a form of heroism which is unmediated. In its focus on female heroes, the text further takes up the contemporary discussion of women and their role in a public environment,[224] and clearly takes the side of those who locate women exclusively in the domestic sphere.

The influence a heroic woman is said to have over her family is also emphasised in the essay "Good Form". The text states that a "hero" (Good Form, *CJ*, 3 Jan 1891, 9) can only be someone who follows the "social rules [...] needed to preserve the harmony and decorum in daily life" (ibid., 7). The hero of everyday life in this case is a stabiliser, an enabler of harmony and peaceful community. This virtue of "Good Form" is put on the same level with values that have already appeared regarding the heroic: "Patriotism, Virtue, Honour, and even Love" (ibid.). Form, which the text decidedly distinguished from "Etiquette" (ibid.), a related, yet more superficial form, needs to be mediated to children from birth onwards. Though "flexible" (ibid.) and hard to define, form is defined as a codex for appropriate behaviour. Among the characteristics mentioned are politeness, courteousness, chivalry, negative examples are "self-indulgence and luxuriousness" as well as "elbo[wing]" (ibid.) one's way to one's goals. In short, "Good Form" can be seen as behaviour guided by "morality" (ibid.) and strongly mirrors the virtues of private heroism seen above. In the context of the articles on heroic women, domestic integrity and education, one could see this as an appeal to educate one's children to become 'heroes' themselves.

A celebration of female ordinariness, yet from a male perspective, can be found in the poem "My Heroine". In the vein of Shakespeare's Sonnet 130, the male speaker praises the 'plainness' of his wife. As the object of comparison, the speaker criticises contemporary ideals of fashion and beauty. He states that

224 For scholarship on the idea of separate spheres and the 'woman question' see for instance Lynn Abrams: Ideals of Womanhood in Victorian Britain, in: BBC History 9, 2001, pp. 1–9; Cynthia Curran: Private Women, Public Needs. Middle-Class Widows in Victorian England, in: Albion. A Quarterly Journal Concerned with British Studies 25.2, 1993, pp. 217–236; Leonore Davidoff: Gender and the "Great Divide". Public and Private in British Gender History, in: Journal of Women's History 15.1, 2003, pp. 11–27; Eleanor Gordon / Gwyneth Nair: Public Lives. Women, Family, and Society in Victorian Britain, New Haven 2003; Patricia Hollis: Women in Public 1850–1900. Documents of the Victorian Women's Movement, London 2013; Linda K. Kerber: Separate Spheres, Female Worlds, Woman's Place. The Rhetoric of Women's History, in: The Journal of American History 75.1, 1988, pp. 9–39; Robert B. Shoemaker: Gender in English Society 1650–1850. The Emergence of Separate Spheres, London 2014; John Tosh: A Man's Place. Masculinity and the Middle-Cass Home in Victorian England, New Haven 2007 or Amanda Vickery: Golden Age to Separate Spheres? A Review of the Categories and Chronology of English Women's History, in: The Historical Journal 36.2, 1993, pp. 383–414.

"She's not accomplished – no, indeed, poor dear. / I dare assert / She does not know the latest slang – I fear / She's not a flirt" (My Heroine, *CJ*, 29 Nov 1879, 768). About her looks he says that "Perhaps she has not Mrs L – y's eyes, / Or rose-leaf skin, / But still so sweet a face to criticise / Were downright sin" (ibid.). The speaker thus established his "girl I know" (ibid.) – it is only later revealed that she is his wife – as an honest and sweet woman, in contrast to the fashionable "flirt[s]" with beautiful eyes, who go out at night to "bet" and to smoke "A cigarette" (ibid.). She is not only described as faithful, but above all shows domestic skills: while other women lust for entertainment, she works around the rural home (indicated by the mentioning of a "five-barred gate", ibid.) and her "*cakes* / Are just divine" (ibid.). Her attire is rather practical than of the latest fashion and she decorates the house with flowers from her garden. Her hair of "modest brown" (ibid.) is not artfully made every day, but worn "in a simple knot behind" (ibid.), so as not to be in the way during the hours of work at home. On the whole, the speaker constructs his "Heroine" (ibid.) as a devoted housewife, who – as her practical outfit and her chores imply – does not have any servants but carries out all household work herself and seems rather plain in comparison to the women about town, who lust for entertainment whereas the woman described seeks domestic happiness in baking cakes. It is this plainness which the speaker seems to cherish about his wife, which turns her into his "heroine".

The final two stanzas give the poem a surprising twist with the woman herself speaking: instead of being delighted by her husband's praise, she tells him off for making her "the subject of your stupid rhymes" (ibid.). Her agitation makes clear that she herself would rather be fashionable than a devoted wife confined to the domestic sphere and even threatens him with "Domestic strife" if he ever were to write more of what she considers "nasty, spiteful things" (ibid.) about her. The two speakers of the poem represent two different perspectives on women in the domestic sphere. The woman's addition at the end of the poem shows that women's confinement to the private sphere and the question of which recreational activities would be appropriate for them was already a topic being widely discussed in British society in the late 1870s. On the other hand, the husband speaks for the majority of the time (six of eight stanzas), the poem's title is written from his perspective, and by the time she speaks herself, he has already established his wife's intellectual plainness. Therefore, the theme of the praiseworthy domestic, unassuming heroine still dominates the piece.

The values propagated in the articles about heroic women are similar to those exhibited in other domains of the heroic: the women are shown as devoted, persevering,[225] humble and above all selflessly working for the greater good of their

225 Interestingly, none of the texts about female domestic heroism include the idea of social ascent or bettering oneself so often connected with perseverance in other contexts.

family. Although these private moral virtues occur in many different contexts in *CJ*, for example in relation to soldiers, medical professionals or men working in the colonies, they are only used in regard to women in a distinctly domestic frame. Although a number of texts show women physically transgressing contemporary gender norms, all of the narratives are embedded in a domestic framework through the women's motivation and their longing for a family and its stability.[226]

The article "Common-Place People" discusses the heroism of private life on a more general level and links up with the initial considerations of "What is Heroism" in chapter 4.2. "What is Heroism" had called for an unmediated form of private heroism and revealed a fundamental tension between the appeal of public recognition as a hero and the utilisation of heroism to stabilise existing societal norms. "Common-Place People", a fictitious dispute between a husband and a wife, illustrates the difficulty of judging the legitimacy of publicly renowned heroism in comparison with a more private kind of heroics. The husband, narrator of the article, poses the "knotty question" (Common-Place People, *CJ*, 10 Jan 1857, 18) of "common-place people", their talents and contributions to society. He himself is undecided in this respect and ponders the significance of "the vast body of mankind [...] who are neither detestably bad nor admirably good" (ibid.). On the one hand, he believes that those 'average' people take themselves too seriously in the present age, since "[n]o one is insignificant to himself; and the most common-place being in the world would assuredly be the last person to suspect the small degree of his own value in the social scale" (ibid.). He diagnoses a want for "*prestige*" (ibid.) in the whole of the population despite their class or talents and criticises the focus on "deceitful" (ibid.) appearance: "Let a man quote from one or two abstruse books, interlaid his conversation with Latin and Greek, comb his hair but seldom, and shave still less frequently, and he will find a sufficient number of persons ready to admire him as the wisest, most erudite of men" (ibid.). These statements identify a problem regarding the individual in the public sphere: on the side of the individual, the narrator criticises a growing want for public attention (depending on the particular individual this 'public' would certainly be of a different scope); this tendency is both caused by, as well as reinforces, a contorted perception of oneself and one's significance within society.

The perspective *on* the individual, however, is identified as distorted as well, with criteria to judge a person's talents lacking and outward factors being the main gauge for judgement. This dynamic reinforces itself: If society is looking for outward clues for the societal worth of an individual and individuals within

226 One could argue that some cases discussed in the context of military heroism strive for domestic integrity as well, yet it is important to note that the regard for the family in all examples only comes up when a soldier has been severely wounded and knows that his duty towards his country is fulfilled, never before that.

society are seeking public recognition for themselves, no 'actual' proof of social benefit caused by the individual is necessary. The individuals who regard themselves as significant and know how to perform this role through their appearance will be perceived as such without society being any the better for it. The "knotty question" (ibid., 18) for the narrator is whether "common-place people" can ever be 'true' "heroes" (ibid., 17) or are only ever perceived so by putting on a façade.[227] With the opinion of the narrator's wife, the discussion takes a different turn. Rather than looking at a "set of people [who] are overrated" (ibid., 18) while average beneath the surface, she interprets "common-place people" as those who do not get any public attention *despite* being of service to their social environment or being exceptionally moral and virtuous. These men and women are seldom called heroes, since society – in this case referring to the public sphere focused on appearances – "seeks its heroes from among its peers" (ibid.) and therefore cannot recognise those heroic figures who do not conform to their outward criteria of social profit. Reflecting the discussion of gender and the public and private sphere, it is significant that it is the woman who takes the side of the private "common-place people" whereas her husband doubts that heroism without public appreciation can occur.

The narrator's wife believes that that "commonplaceism *per se* does not exist" (ibid.) because every individual is of significance to a number of others, is "admire[d]" (ibid.) and contributes to their wellbeing. The "heroes" (ibid.) she is talking about are men and women who act selflessly and according to a high moral standard for mere idealistic reasons and without an agenda for public recognition. Thus, she considers these "heroes" superior to those who are rewarded with the attention of a larger group. She gives two examples for this kind of 'commonplace heroism'. The first example is a man who was too poor to marry the girl he loved and worked hard so that, "middle-aged", he could finally marry her. The second anecdote depicts a young woman, a "merchant's daughter" who was neglected by her family for her sisters were both "more accomplished" and "more handsome". Yet she did not complain and when the family fell into misfortune, it was her who supported the whole of the family despite being treated badly before.

The examples stress the importance of domestic stability and the acts performed by the 'heroes' are directed at the benefit of the whole of the family at the – at least temporary – expense of the individual performing them. The text, like many others discussed before, foregrounds the underlying values such as "constancy [...], quiet energy" (ibid.) and above all the ability to suffer for the sake of others. Though the narrator leaves the reader to be the "[j]udge" of the "knotty question" (ibid.), the stark contrast between the different kinds of "com-

[227] This links up with the considerations on false heroism in chapter 4.2 which showed a close connection between those heroes considered of no advantage to society at large but rather a personal fancy based on outward appearance and the adorer's imagination.

mon-place" people and the emphatic description of the 'silent' and 'unsung' form of heroism brought forth by the woman leave no question as to which form is more desirable. The statement that "the world's common-place people are *my* heroes" (ibid.) seems to finally settle the matter in favour of the unassuming, private individual seeking domestic peace and the happiness of the whole of its family, as opposed to their own personal – and possibly public – reward.

More generally, the text can be seen as embodying the fundamental tension of heroism as represented in *CJ*. On the one hand, it shows the attractiveness of public recognition and admiration perceived by many; on the other hand, the text propagates a veneration of the normality of life and constructs a kind of extraordinary mediocracy. In this way the text links up nicely with the initial ideas put forth in the programmatic text "What is Heroism" and presents a solution to put heroism "within the reach [...] of the private citizen" (What is Heroism, *CJ*, 9 May 1857, 298): heroic normality.

4.7 Different Heroes for Different Readers?

Chambers's publishing portfolio was broad and included a variety of products from instructional tracts to educational courses, school books, collections of entertaining stories for leisure time, biography collections and school quizzes. Many of these products targeted different audiences and were intended for a range of different environments. Therefore, it is productive to take a cursory look at the usage of the vocabulary of the heroic in other Chambers publications in the second half of the nineteenth century to establish whether the usage of the semantic field as analysed above is specific to *CJ* and its target audience or can be found in other publications aimed at different readers as well.

Popular Instruction for Private Consumption

A range of material can be found which utilises the vocabulary of the heroic similarly to *CJ*. In this material, the heroic is used to denote (morally) desirable exemplary behaviour and encourage emulation on the part of the reader. This can especially be found in works of popular instruction intended for private consumption and self-study. Robert Cochrane's collection *Lives of Good and Great Women*, published with Chambers in 1888, provides role models for the contemporary female reader. In its preface, it professes that

> [n]ew books of biographies are, on the face of things, an absolute necessity. We need not forget our old heroes, our ancient ideals, and yet we may well feel that to learn something about the trials and struggles, the methods of work, and the ultimate triumph

of those who have but recently passed away, or who are still among us, may be more helpful to us in our own place.[228]

The contents include biographical sketches of women such as Queen Victoria, Florence Nightingale, Mary Somerville, Angela Burdett-Coutts or Octavia Hill, almost all of whom are called heroic within the individual texts. In doing this, the book created a form of moral heroism which propagated behaviour that could be imitated by the readers and was distinctly different from the "old heroes". In this didactic approach, aimed at individual private readers, the work complied with the use of the heroic as identified in *CJ*.[229]

Another parallel to the journal can be found in the depiction of science and technology for the lower middle class. Similarly to the findings in chapter 4.5, books such as *Great Thinkers and Workers* (1888, edited by Robert Cochrane), William Chambers's *Chambers's Social Science Tracts* (1860), or *Chambers's British Science-Biographies* (1886, edited by Alleyne Nicholson) all focused on the productivity and industry of the scientists and intellectuals, yet none of them are portrayed in the vocabulary of the heroic or shown as role models.

Biography Collections

Chambers published a wide variety of popular biography collections. Books such as *Entertaining Biography* (1855), *Exemplary and Instructive Biography* (1846), *Famous Men* (1886), *Biographical Dictionary of Eminent Scotsmen* (1857) or *Chambers's Biographical Dictionary* (1897) served a number of purposes. Works such as *Exemplary and Instructive Biography* fell in the category of popular education. Thus, its preface states that

> the study of Biography is profitable in two ways. Its least, though most obvious use, is to convey historical information in a pleasing manner. Its more important utility has a reference to the great Educational principle of imitation, which, though inferior to training and exercise, has a decided advantage over precept, the advantages of which it may be said, indeed, to combine with those more properly its own.[230]

By showing the readers other examples of "successful contendings with depressing circumstances", a manifestation of "similar virtues"[231] was intended.

The biographical dictionaries contained descriptions of the lives of historical and contemporary persons[232] and were intended as reference books. Though written in a matter-of-fact style, the short paragraphs also occasionally contained

---

228 Robert Cochrane: Lives of Good and Great Women, Edinburgh 1888, p. 1.

229 Although none of the collections I have encountered contained reprints from *CJ*.

230 Robert Chambers / William Chambers (eds.): Exemplary and Instructive Biography, Edinburgh 1846, n.p.

231 Ibid.

232 The preface of an 1897 edition notes that it shows "the world's Upper Ten Thousand [...]; still, the lower, even the lowest, have not been wholly neglected." David Patrick /

criticism and thus gave a hint at the values the contributors and editors wanted to convey.[233] The entries varied from short notes[234] to text which was up to two columns long.[235] Both the reference works and the instructional biographies only infrequently employ the language of the heroic. In the former, this may primarily be due to the traditionally unemotional and rarely narrative style of the dictionary. Also, in their aim of instructing and educating their readers, the instructive biographies in particular were located in the same market segment as *CJ* and a lack of herorization of historical actors complies with the attempt not to create celebrities, but to praise silent, unsung heroes.

However, a different strategy can be observed in those biography collections which from the outset do not propose an educating, but an entertaining intention. For example, books such as *Famous Men*, a collection from 1886, did not contain any paratextual matter such as a preface or advertisements. In publications intended for private instruction, this material would have hinted at the author's or publisher's intentions, might have given the readers a guideline for how to deal with the text and what to take away from it. Such paratexts would also have provided them with a list of other material for further education through the adverts in the back. By not providing any of these guiding paratexts, the entertaining biographies left the text to the interpretation of the reader and thus did not object to mere enjoyment as a reason for reading the books. Interestingly, these biographies are full of language of the heroic: Lord Dundonald's biography introduces him as a "heroic seaman" in its first sentence[236] ("Lord Dundonald", 1); the "hero" George Stephenson is praised ("George Stephenson", 2)[237] and "such a hero" as Oberlin venerated ("Life of Oberlin", 31). Although the collection includes philanthropists such as John Howard, and social reformers like John Frederick Oberlin are commemorated, the collection also constructs historical figures as heroes who were not called such in *CJ*. Most notably, inventors such as Stephenson or Watt, who were never called heroic in the periodical, are heroised in the collection, and military and navy men such as Dundonald, Washington, Nelson, and Napoleon are at the centre of attention in the

Francis Hindes Groome: Chambers's Biographical Dictionary. The Great of All Times and Nations, London/Edinburgh 1897, n.p.

233 For example, the entry on the composer Mozart noted that "[h]is carelessness, improvidence, and senseless generosity overwhelmed him with endless embarrassments." Ibid., p. 678.

234 Such as the entry on Moctezuma, which reads "Mexican emperor, ascended the throne about 1437, annexed Chalco, crushed the Tlascalans, and died in 1471". Ibid., p. 670.

235 The longer texts are mostly concerned with English worthies (e.g. Milton, Shakespeare, Nelson) and/or figures from recent history (e.g. Peel, Garibaldi, Dickens, Cardinal Newman or Napoleon to whom one of the longest entries is devoted).

236 William Chambers (ed.): Famous Men. Being Biographical Sketches from Chambers's Miscellany, Edinburgh 1886.

237 Every one of the biographies has their own page numbering, which suggests that the texts were used for individual publication as well.

work. Furthermore, details from the private lives of the men biographed are included in the texts, a practice which had been criticised in the periodical. Entertaining biographies, such as *Famous Men*, appealed to a different market than that which the publishers imagined for their periodical: in a style which focused less on moral instruction and more on entertainment and adventure, the heroic personnel did not have to act as role models and be within the realm of experience of the prospective readers, but were predominantly used as representatives of exciting and thrilling lives.

Educational Publications

Many of Chambers's publications were intended for the instruction of pupils in schools or other institutional educational contexts. Apart from subject-bound factual matter such as maths or spelling books, the company also published reading material on history or story readers in a more narrative style. Interestingly, none of the latter – which could easily have employed the vocabulary of the heroic to indicate what behaviour of historical actors or protagonists of stories was considered worth emulating or deemed unfit – utilise these semantics. For example, *Chambers's National Reading-Books* of 1873, intended for use in schools, contained stories and poems about the seasons, about landscapes and animals, as well as texts about literary men such as Marlowe or Milton and well-known figures such as Robin Hood, written in a very sober style. Similarly, *Chambers's Graduate Readers* published in 1884, sold at 7d per volume, contained stories and verse about farm life, pets or weekend vacations and stories of countryside life and interaction with animals. It is obvious that such story books were written with the practice of reading skills in mind, which explains the simple and sober style.[238] The subject matter and setting, which unless portraying a historical person was almost exclusively rural Britain, also suggests that the texts were intended to increase young readers' knowledge (e.g. about the seasons, animals or farming), yet the texts did not aim at the moral education of their readers or provide role models for them. The 1872 *Chambers's Supplementary Reader* (1872) was priced at 8d, contained illustrated "interesting and instructive reading" and was intended for the usage of "teachers and school managers".[239] Similar to the texts discussed above, the tracts about Columbus, William Tell or Lord Dundonald did not utilise the vocabulary of the heroic and focused on the mediation of facts rather than the more "entertaining" potential that a more narrative account

---

238 Each story opened with a list of the most complex words, which were also listed in the back of each volume as "The More Difficult Words of Three Syllables in Common Use" (cf. e.g. Chambers / Chambers: National Reading-Books, vol. 3, p. 157) with indication of stresses and syllables.

239 Robert Chambers / William Chambers (eds.): Chambers's Supplementary Reader, Edinburgh 1872, n.p.

could have offered. Other historical readers, such as *Chambers's Summary of English History*, presented the content to their readers as a list. For example, the chapter on "Waterloo – And Afterwards" reads as follows:

> 1. As soon as all the allies had withdrawn from Paris, Napoleon escaped from Elba, and once more became Emperor of the French. The great powers of Europe declared war against France.
> 2. The British under Wellington, and the Prussians under Blücher, were the first to muster near the French frontier.
> 3. Napoleon defeated the Prussians at Ligny; Ney attacked Wellington at Quatre Bras, but was repulsed.
> […]
> 11. In 1829, George III. died. For nearly ten years, owing to insanity, he had taken no part in the government. During these years his eldest son, afterwards George IV., acted as regent.[240]

Similarly, *Leading Events in English History: Adapted to the Requirements of the Educational Code* in 1880 was written in a very matter-of-fact tone, listing information and omitting narrative style. Given the didactic agenda that the publishing house pursued in the use of the vocabulary of the heroic in their journal, this omission of the semantics in educational texts, especially in story books and history readers which in their display of 'great men' would have lent themselves well for the creation of role models for the young readers, is astonishing. The extraction of morals from historical events and the lives of well-known figures seems to have been missing in a type of material which was at its core didactic. Nevertheless, Chambers's tendency for moral improvement through role models is still present in the educational texts. This, however, only becomes apparent when considering the different environments in which *CJ* and the educational works would be consumed. While the journal was intended for solitary consumption at home or reading within the family, the educational texts were to be read in the institutional context of schools or other educational institutions implying a mediator (a teacher, a lecturer, …). It is this mediator, then, who fulfils the function of a role model in moral terms in the context of the educational publications. This is expressed strongly in Eliza Greenup's *Friendly Advice to Pupil-Teachers*, which was published with Chambers in 1877. The slim 31-page volume reminded teachers that it was not merely the factual instruction that lay within their responsibility – the facts would be supplied in books such as those mentioned above – but in particular the moral education which was in their hands. "[I]n order that the education of our country be effectually carried out, it becomes necessary that those who assume the office of educator or teacher be morally, intellectually and physically equal. *Morally* because a teacher must be an *example*."[241] In its conclu-

240 Robert Chambers / William Chambers (eds.): Chambers's Summary of English History, Edinburgh 1904, pp. 53–54.
241 Eliza Greenup: Friendly Advice to Pupil-Teachers, Edinburgh 1877, pp. 7–8.

sion, the text ends with a poem by Henry Wadsworth Longfellow and demands: "Set a high value upon your character; and if you wish to become truly great, endeavour first to become truly good. 'Lives of great men all remind us / We can make *our* lives sublime, / And departing, leave behind us / Footprints on the sands of time.'"[242]

In the institutional educational context, not Robin Hood or Wellington, Milton or Marlowe are the 'great men' whom the pupils should emulate, but the teachers who are standing before them in the flesh. It is their lives which, in the ideal sense of education and influence as shown above, become great and leave an impression on the moral advancement of the children they educate.

It has become clear that the use of the vocabulary of the heroic in *CJ* was quite specific to the publication, its didactic aim, and its intended readership. As the comparison with other publication formats has shown, words from the semantic field of the heroic were chiefly used in order to morally instruct readers outside of formal education within a setting of private consumption. Thus, the periodical regulated the personnel to whom it attributed heroic status according to this primary goal and this restriction did not apply to publications for other segments of the market, which were intended to chiefly amuse and entertain, such as the biographies. Within *CJ*'s didactic agenda the heroic was a central tool to mark and promote morally desirable behaviour.

4.8 Heroism in Chambers's Journal *– Forms and Functions*

As the examination of the dominant domains of the heroic in *CJ* – military heroism, heroism of civilisation and everyday heroism – has shown, the concept of heroism played an important role in the periodical's didactic agenda. In combination with those texts that explicitly define and reflect upon heroism, a distinct set of values of heroism have emerged, which form a heroic imaginary that the periodical evoked whenever the semantics of heroism were employed. Courage, selflessness and perseverance have been established as central properties of this heroic imaginary. All of these were utilised didactically to create a form of heroism that strongly emphasised communal aspects and was intended to inspire identification and imitation in the readers.

In opposition to traditional notions of heroism, which often centred on exceptional, genial leader figures to guide the masses, the periodical focused on a personnel which was like their intended readership. In the attribution of hero-status to rank-and-file soldiers, working men, and women exerting influence in the domestic sphere, the periodical tried to make the values which heroism embodied attractive and worthy of emulation for even the "poorest labourer" appealed to in the editor's address of *CJ*'s very first issue in 1832 (Editor's Address,

[242] Ibid., p. 31.

CJ, Feb 4 1832, 1). On the whole, the texts representing heroic acts – such as the bravery of miners or the efforts of medical men – or a state of heroism – such as the heroic normality of everyday life analysed in the last section – try to establish a relation between the presented heroes and the consumers. This relation is in most cases based on the likeness and proximity between the two, whereas attempts at herorization which involve a greater distance are shown as precarious.

However, this is complicated by the factors of class and gender in particular, which the periodical struggles to seamlessly integrate into its imaginary. Especially the herorization of women, which the periodical attempted at various points throughout the second half of the nineteenth century, proves difficult. At a time in which women were still predominantly seen in the private sphere and women's rights activists were still fighting to be heard, the periodical takes a conservative stance and paints the picture of a heroic woman as a domestic housewife with no profession or role within the public sphere. This pattern is only transgressed in colonial contexts. The spatial removal and the idea of British supremacy over a less civilised culture which needed guidance allowed women to display a more active heroism with a stronger individual agency in some cases. However, the domestic framework is nevertheless alluded to even in these instances and the educational efforts of women in colonial contexts can be related to the idea of women exerting influence over those who are still unformed and uneducated, with the colonial students taking the place of a woman's own children in a British domestic setting. Within Britain, however, female heroic agency as displayed in *CJ* seems to have been limited to the private realm. The privatisation of heroism which occurred through the continuous evoking of moral ideals and the insistence that private honour was the ultimate reward for a heroic moral disposition, however, also challenged the idea of masculinity. The shift of attention from the heroic act to a moral heroism which found its manifestation in a person's disposition and attitude rather than in active behaviour, thus also led to a change in perception of male agency, in line with middle-class emphasis on the importance of the private sphere for both men *and* women.[243] As John Tosh notes, "to an unprecedented degree, the Victorians also insisted that the home was the proper sphere of the husband, as the spouse who was more exposed to the moral degradation of the world of work, and therefore more in need of refuge and refreshment".[244]

In the mediation of predominantly middle-class ideals directed at a presumed readership of the lower ranks, class plays a crucial role in the depiction of heroism in *CJ*. Within their didactic agenda, rooted in the Scottish Presbyterian idea of equal access to education regardless of social status, the periodical wanted to

243 Cf. Leonore Davidoff / Catherine Hall (eds.): Family Fortunes. Men and Women of the English Middle Class 1780–1850, London 2002.

244 John Tosh: Home and Away. The Flight from Domesticity in Late-Nineteenth-Century England Re-Visited, in: Gender and History 27.3, 2015, p. 561.

symbolically empower the lower classes and thus created examples of heroes from the lower ranks. Interestingly, this was mostly achieved in fictional texts, since reports of non-fictional established heroic figures would less frequently have been located within the identificatory reach of the readership. This further shows how the heroic and its functionalisations coincide with specific genres. Examples of 'real-life' heroes were mostly presented in the non-fictional reports and essays; these, however, in most cases referred to either established hero figures (for example in the case of military heroism, which referenced military men such as Nelson of Wellington), members of the upper middle classes (such as the medical men), or heroes who had already been acknowledged in some other public form, such as the awardees of the Albert Medal or the Royal Humane Society. Thus, heroes represented in non-fiction genres were sometimes less adaptable as attainable role models for the readers. In cases of non-fictional representation of everyday and/or working-class heroism, the represented heroes, however, sometimes clashed with the periodical's proclaimed aim not to further the glorification and public adulation of individuals. In re-telling the stories, which had already been attracting public attention through the award of a prize or media attention, the contradiction of exceptionality and exemplarity becomes apparent. For example, the public attention given to Grace Darling is explicitly criticised in *CJ*, while the periodical was part of the same machinery of hero-production in their portrayal of award-winning lifesavers. This inconsistency between, on the one hand, demanding "unsung heroes" which exist without a medium and at the same time metaphorically singing their praise, is a tension which remains unresolved throughout the decades and is not reflected upon.

However, the fact that most of the texts which create and mediate heroic figures and heroic properties are fictional texts can be read as a way of dealing with this tension, since the heroisation of a fictional character could not contribute to the actual public fame of a person and to their public honour which the periodical criticised. In the fictional texts, mostly tales and only occasionally serial novels, heroism could be designed and played out in such a way that readers could identify with the represented heroes. Thereby, the periodical produced hero-figures as didactic tools to guide their readership in their processes of identity formation and moral education. Interestingly then, though on the whole opposed to the traditional idea of a single exceptional leader figure for the masses and the power dynamics involved, the periodical utilised the same dynamics. Using heroism as a marker for desirable and norm-conform behaviour, the narratives were themselves intended as guides for the readers. Thus, the power dynamics often criticised in the paradigm of the hero as a leader figure were not abandoned in the more inclusive idea of heroism, but they were only canalised differently in the didactic application of the concept. The represented heroes were seldom transgressive (with the exception of the depicted instances of lifesaving which often included a temporary transgression of a person's physical abilities) and cannot be seen as performing boundary work in a strict sense. However, the fact that heroism was so closely defined in moral terms creates a boundary without heroic infringement. Thus, the clear definition of the desirable norm embodied by heroes results in a distinct notion of accepted social behaviour and a delineation of a social group united by middle-class values.

Throughout the period under examination, the representation of heroism in *CJ* is frequently linked to larger societal issues. Heroism, in many cases, is strongly connected to questions of national identity. This is shown, for one, in the depiction of military heroics, which – highly criticised in times of peace – was adapted for the greater concern of national integrity during times of war. Furthermore, the depiction of lifesaving in exotic settings or women's efforts of education in the colonies can also be read as stories of British supremacy in a global context.[245] Similarly, the heroisation of miners and their work ethos as the backbone of the British industry can be read as a display of the country's superiority in the industrial sector. Additionally, the heroisation of the workforce can be seen as a sign of the growing importance of the manual labourers for the functioning society and the growing democratisation, as well as a validation to counterbalance possible tendencies for unrest. This points to another major functionalisation of the vocabulary of heroism in *CJ*. Although genuinely involved in the cause of universal education and improving living conditions for the lower ranks of society, the periodical shows no interest in fundamentally changing the societal order. The attribution of heroic status to the disadvantaged in their selfless work for others can thus also be seen as a means of stabilisation of that part of society, which it was feared would become a threat to the existing order. The heroisation of the domestic woman up until the turn of the century, a time at which the women's rights movement had already gathered considerable public attention, can be read along the same lines. In a phase when societal boundaries were becoming increasingly blurred and existing structures were threatened with overthrowal, the heroisation and thus validation of the current status quo can be seen as an attempt to stabilise endangered norms. Through the establishment of attainable role models – the importance of which for individual development from childhood onwards *CJ* had stressed in many texts – and the semantic attribution of hero-status, the periodical tried to make the current situation more appealing in a larger framework of heroic selflessness for the community.[246] Much like the example of the news-boys, the periodical did not con-

245 It is also noteworthy in this context that heroes in *CJ* are exclusively white (though not exclusively British) and no representation of the heroism of colonial natives can be found, which again stresses the idea of Western supremacy over the colonised countries.

246 The heroic was thus clearly utilised to make norm-conforming behaviour more attractive and give it a more glamorous appeal. This, however, again points to the fundamental tension between exemplarity and exceptionality; the heroic was attractive for many for the very fact that it was commonly associated with exceptional and singular things, rather than with the mass-phenomenon which publications like *CJ* turned it into.

struct the ideal of a society of equals, but that of a society which is led by specific morals while still maintaining a fundamentally hierarchical structure.

Unlike thinkers such as Carlyle, *CJ* in its didactic mission did not perceive a lack of heroism in the present day. In imbuing heroism with a very distinct notion of selfless, community-oriented behaviour, the editors and contributors to the periodical adapted the idea of the heroic potential of a society to the contemporary age; in a growing mass society, they propagated the idea of not one person being beyond all standards, but a mass of people who heroically embody the norm.

Part 3:
Leader or Role Model? – A Comparative Analysis of Heroism in *Leisure Hour* and *Fraser's Magazine*

5. Comparative Analysis of *Leisure Hour* and *Fraser's Magazine*

It has become clear that *CJ* associated the idea of the heroic with a specific set of values and utilised the idea of an attainable moral heroism as a tool for their intended readership. As a central vehicle for its didactic message, the vocabulary of heroism was prominent in the periodical. In order to establish whether this centrality of heroism in the mediation of a joint identity was a common means in the periodical press of the day, the following section is going to examine the representation of heroism in *Leisure Hour* [1] and *Fraser's Magazine*.[2] Thereby, a clearer picture will emerge as to how the target audience, specific orientation and institutional background of a periodical publication could have influenced the way in which the heroic is – or is not – employed.

The two periodicals had very distinct publishing identities and wanted to cater to specific audiences. While *LH* aimed at a working and lower-middle class readership with a moral and didactic goal grounded in religious faith, *FM* was designed as a political organ for an intellectual readership. These different goals are also mirrored in the publications' representation of the heroic. *FM* displays a very specific concept of heroism modelled after the ideas of Thomas Carlyle – a writer who had been engaged in the periodical in its early decades and with whom it had been infatuated after the phase of his active involvement. In *FM*, heroism, and especially heroic leader figures, can predominantly be observed in the domain of politics and in relation to a glorified past. In *LH*, on the other hand, vocabulary of the heroic is not used in an equally consistent and conceptualised way. Complicated by the religious affiliation of the periodical, its representation of heroism shifts between an unreflected use in relation to established military figures, a utilisation of the identificatory potential of heroes for the readers and open criticism of hero-worship as blasphemous.

5.1 Leisure Hour

Established in 1852, the publication can be seen as part of the second generation of family magazines which not only wanted to provide information, but also entertaining, often illustrated reading matter. *LH* was a publication of the Religious Tract Society[3], a society founded in 1799 to publish Christian reading matter for Sunday schools, which offered a broad range of products from tracts to book ser-

---

1 In the following referred to as *LH*.
2 In the following abbreviated as *FM*.
3 In the following referred to as RTS.

ies and periodicals by the mid-nineteenth century.[4] With the rapid growth of affordable family magazines around the mid-century, the RTS sought to enter that market and, with a didactic goal in mind, reach a working-class audience with *LH*. Periodicals which published entertainment, especially serialised fiction, were most popular among the readers the RTS wanted to reach with *LH*. The form of the periodical was designed accordingly, which meant that it "adopted a serious Christian tone but avoided overt religiosity".[5] As Doris Lechner notes, the magazine operated "at the boundary between secular and religious reading matter".[6]

Prior to *LH*, the RTS had already published periodicals; generally more appealing to a broader readership in its less specifically religious tone, the periodicals were intended as an addition to the Society's tract publications. In 1824, the RTS had launched the *Child's Companion* and the *Tract Magazine*, which were aimed at children and parents from the working classes. In 1833, the time of the first generation of penny weeklies such as *CJ* or *Penny Magazine*, the *Visitor* entered the market and would finally merge into *LH*. Those early periodicals, as well as *LH* later, were published in an attempt to provide suitable reading matter for the working classes, who were seen as being endangered by the sensational press and its effects. With this distinct institutional evangelical identity,[7] *LH* entered the market place of popular family magazines – a tension which it needed to negotiate. On the one hand, it wanted to appeal to the working classes with a popular format and entertaining genres; on the other hand, it wanted to mediate its religious beliefs to the readers in order to shape their ways of thinking and their identities. As Aileen Fyfe notes, the periodical had to "balance between the requirement for Christian content and the equally strong need to avoid scaring

---

4 For more information on the RTS's general publishing programme see especially Aileen Fyfe: Commerce and Philanthropy. The Religious Tract Society and the Business of Publishing, in: Journal of Victorian Culture 9.2, 2004, pp. 164–188; ead.: Periodicals and Book Series. Complementary Aspects of a Publisher's Mission, in: Louise Henson (ed.): Culture and Science in the Nineteenth-Century Media, Aldershot 2004, pp. 71–82; ead.: Science and Salvation. Evangelical Popular Science Publishing in Victorian Britain, Chicago 2004 and Dennis Butts / Pat Garrett (eds.): From the Dairyman's Daughter to Worrals of the WAAF. The Religious Tract Society, Cambridge 2006.

5 Geoffrey Cantor et al. (eds.): Introduction, in: Louise Henson (ed.): Culture and Science in the Nineteenth-Century Media, Aldershot 2004, p. xxi.

6 Doris Lechner: Histories for the Many. The Victorian Family Magazine and Popular Representations of the Past, Bielefeld 2017, p. 28.

7 The institutional background of the publication also meant that decision processes were very different from those of traditional publishing houses. Aileen Fyfe notes that in "contemporary commercial publishing houses, the chain of command terminated in a very small number of individuals, usually one or two, who were both the owners and managers of the firm. [...] The RTS, however, had a rather different organisation at the executive level, and was more similar to the limited liability company, with its shareholders, annual meetings, and board of directors." Fyfe: Commerce, p. 168.

off potential readers".[8] Loyd and Law observe that *LH* was often even printed without the RTS's imprint, so that readers would not associate the periodical with religious tracts.[9]

From the beginning, *LH* included fiction. A serialised narrative, together with an illustration, always appeared on its cover page, a practice that was established from the very first issue in January 1852. Apart from that, *LH* consisted of articles, on average one to six pages long, "on popular science, history, biography, and poetry of uplifting character. Later, there were columns devoted to domestic and moral advice for housewives or servants, and prize competitions in composition or needlework".[10] The weekly was sold for 1d and with its quarto size, the periodical was clearly intended for domestic consumption, which the editor's address in the first issue also emphasised.

The editor's address stressed the relationship in which the editor and his periodical wanted to engage with the readers. Repeatedly, the text declares the desire to win the "reader's friendship" (A Word with Our Readers, *LH*, 1 Jan 1852, 8) and to have "the honour of being introduced to the amenities of his fireside; of talking to him with the easy confidence of a friend, and of being presented, with the advantage of his good opinion, to all who may enjoy the happiness of his friendship" (ibid.). Both the idea of being introduced to the "fireside" and the word "Leisure" in the periodical's title point out clearly that the publication was intended for domestic consumption. The text then actively discusses the idea of leisure and work, clearly differentiating it from idleness.[11] In the praise of improved working hours – which made the consumption of the journal for certain readers possible – the journal distinctly identifies its intended readers as belonging to the working classes, though still remaining inclusive: "we dedicate our pen to the thoughtful of every class. [...] From the highest to the lowest, there is no circle from which we desire to exclude ourselves" (ibid., 9). Different from other periodicals such as *CJ* or *FM*, *LH* from the outset presents itself as a publication with a large writing staff. Whereas *CJ* was for many years not only run but also largely written by Robert and William Chambers, and *FM* fashioned itself as being run by a close-knit group of writers, *LH* markets their number of writers as an asset in expertise: "guided by the botanist, we shall break our way through the thick tresses of grass and bramble [...]. The entomologists will explain to us the habits of insect life; [...] the miner will take us into the labyrinths of labour under ground. [...] the manufacturer will conduct us to the loom [...]" (ibid.).

8 Fyfe: Commerce, p. 105.

9 Graham Law / Amy Loyd: The Leisure Hour, in: Laurel Brake / Marysa Demoor (eds.): Dictionary of Nineteenth Century Journalism, Ghent/London 2009, p. 357.

10 Ibid.

11 "[P]ublic opinion very wisely holds idlers in contempt, and we have no wish to mitigate in the least the retributive ills of their condition. Business is a sacred thing." A Word with Our Readers, *LH*, 1 Jan 1852, 8.

In line with the goal of disseminating the religious message in a more popular package, the periodical's "self-chosen mission" (ibid.) is voiced in a secular tone:

> It will be our aim to bring out from obscurity forgotten truths; to clear away the mists which obscure those views of human life and conduct, which to be recognised require only to be beheld; to point out with a friendly hand the obstacles to social advancement which lie in the bosoms of the people; and stimulate them to the attainment of every virtue which ought to elevate and gladden our English home. (ibid., 8–9)

Thus framing their aims as more widely educational, didactic and philanthropic, the address to the readers tones down the RTS's Christian programme in order to reach a wider audience. However, the working class audience implied in large parts of the text was not the only social segment that consumed the publication. Similar to *CJ*, which was aimed at working class readers and the editors of which had voiced their disappointment in having a large middle-class audience, *LH* was also consumed by the middle classes. Thus, the periodical had to cater to a dual readership: on the one hand, the working class reader who could, as Fyfe argues, have been discouraged by the religious institutional background, and a middle class audience which could have read the publication for that very reason.[12] Thus, the periodical's content will in the following be seen in the context of negotiating two different audiences – the working-class reader who was meant to be evangelised and the already religious middle-class reader whose identity was to be stabilised in the publication.

5.2 Fraser's Magazine

Quite different from *LH*, *FM* was established at a time at which popular periodical entertainment was still in its early stages. The periodical, which was begun in 1830, situated itself in a different segment of the print market and targeted a specific intellectual upper class audience.

Walter Houghton narrates the story of the foundation of *FM* almost like a legend.[13] In 1830, William Maginn, the Irish writer who was to become a leader for the 'Fraserians' of the first years, had long been writing for *Blackwood's*. However, his articles had been rejected more and more often for their candour and boldness so that Maginn was forced to look for other sources of income and an-

---

12 One way of catering to the different readerships can be seen in the dual publication format of the periodical, which could be both purchased weekly and in a monthly format. Lechner notes that "[b]ecause of their cheap price, weekly numbers were likely to reach readers with a small income, while monthly publications had a higher reputation" (Lechner: Histories, p. 61) and due to the higher price for a single purchase would thus have been more likely consumed by the middle classes. Cf. also Fyfe: Commerce, p. 178. In 1881, the periodical switched the whole production to monthly publication. Cf. Law / Loyd: Leisure Hour.

13 Walter Houghton: The Wellesley Index to Victorian Periodicals 1824–1900, vol. 2, Toronto 1972, p. 304.

other way to make his voice heard. Thus, he wanted to create a periodical similar to *Blackwood's*, which would give him the opportunity to print his provocative articles and in the best scenario put *Blackwood's* out of business or at least make them lose as many readers as possible. In pursuit of a business partner, and

> [with] a roll of manuscript under his arm, Maginn and his friend Hugh Fraser, possessor of the required cash, were walking down Regent Street, so the story goes, when they came to the shop of James Fraser the publisher, and Maginn exclaimed "Fraser! Here's a namesake of yours. Let's try him." By great luck the publisher was just then thinking of trying a monthly magazine that would be both popular and scholarly. Since Maginn could promise both requisites, a bargain was soon struck, and a periodical named after Hugh Fraser began publication in February 1830. (ibid.)

Thus, *FM* was intended by Maginn to become "a successful intruder into what was once thought a peculiar preserve [of] *Blackwood*" (A Wind-up for our Seventh Volume, Literary, Political and Anti-Peelish, *FM*, Jun 1833, 750). In the magazine's first phase, from 1830 to 1842, Maginn was the dominant force behind the publication and made it known chiefly for its variety of material. It included "scholarly articles on Homer or Egyptian antiquities, Scottish and Irish stories, ecclesiastical warfare, political tracts, foreign travels, translations from Persian and Hebrew, satiric sketches of contemporaries, essays on German transcendentalism, and literary spoofs".[14] The tone of the magazine under Maginn's leadership was provocative and bold, so that it became the prime "organ [...] of progressive thought"[15] of the day and was "at the forefront of monthly miscellanies in the nineteenth century."[16] The magazine's main emphasis, according to the *Wellesley Index*, lay in "politics, religion, and social conditions, in contrast to journals like the *Cornhill* or *Temple Bar*, so largely devoted to literature and literary criticism".[17]

The first issue of the magazine was opened by a "Confession of Faith", in which Maginn characterises the magazine and from the start indirectly states what kind of audience he is looking for: "our political tendencies will be sufficiently apparent to the intelligent from what we have said already; – to the non-intelligent it would be useless to address ourselves" (Our Confession of Faith, *FM*, Feb 1830, 4). The "confession" then goes on to address several topics such as religion, foreign policy, domestic policy and other current fields of interest, but remains quite abstract. Thus, from the very first issue, Maginn wants to en-

---

14 Ibid., p. 305.

15 Ibid., p. 303.

16 Mark W. Turner: Fraser's Magazine, in: Laurel Brake / Marysa Demoor (eds.): Dictionary of Nineteenth Century Journalism, Ghent/London 2009, p. 230.

17 Houghton: Wellesley Index, p. 303. This does, however, not hold true completely, since *FM* printed a large number of reviews and also literary works (for example novels by Thackeray or Carlyle) and one of its most successful series in the early years was "The Gallery of Illustrious Literary Characters" which portrayed contemporary figures of the literary field, yet sometimes in a very sarcastic fashion.

courage his readers to think for themselves. Taking a bold stance, the editor calls his journal "fearless and fair" (ibid., 7) and states that "no pains shall be spared to make our Magazine equal, in the ordinary sources of information, to its contemporaries" (ibid.). Yet, he does not simply place it among those "ordinary sources", but claims to also present "extraordinary sources [that will] speak for themselves" (ibid.).

Especially in its early years, what made the magazine "extraordinary" was on the one hand the indeed fearless way in which it dealt with current issues and the people involved and on the other hand the competences expected from the readership. Throughout its runtime, the articles, which were mostly non-fictional essays, were seldom shorter than fifteen pages, frequently from twenty-five to thirty pages long, and thus required the readers to be fully literate, intelligent, well-informed on current topics and able to reflect on them, in order to handle the frequent sarcasm with which topics were treated. The targeting of the magazine at an educated, conservative, intellectual middle and upper class is further emphasized by the fact that, unlike many other magazines, *FM* did not normally include illustrations, but focused solely on text.[18] The intended audience is also reflected in the magazine's price, which, at 2s6d, ranked among the more expensive periodicals. Although the periodical's quarto size meant that it would not fit into a pocket, this does not, as in the case of *CJ* or *LH*, suggest that *FM* was intended for private and domestic consumption only. Given the intended readership, the periodical could have been consumed in the private atmosphere of one's study just as well as in an office or a gentlemen's club.

In the first decade of the magazine, the group that called themselves the 'Fraserians' marketed themselves as a close-knit circle who worked together collaboratively. Thrall argues that many of the articles in the first ten years were written collaboratively, making it impossible to identify one definite author. However, Patrick Leary, in his article "*Fraser's Magazine* and the Literary Life, 1830–1847", points out that half of the staff writing for *FM* had no close bond to the magazine and did not support themselves by writing for *FM*, simply making it one of many magazines they sold their articles to.[19] In their self-fashioning as a group, the periodical established a distinct identity for themselves that would have appealed to a specific male upper-class readership. *FM* soon became known for publishing frank comments on political and literary activities[20] and many of the frequent contributors joined *FM* not primarily out of economic necessity, but out of curiosity and interest. Thus, the magazine attracted many young aspir-

18 The very rare exceptions were occasional portraits accompanying biographical sketches.

19 Cf. Patrick Leary: Fraser's Magazine and the Literary Life 1830–1847, in: Victorian Periodicals Review 27.2, 1994, pp. 113–114.

20 Cf. ibid., p. 105.

ing writers who started their career in *FM*, of whom Carlyle and Thackeray are only the most prominent figures.[21]

In 1847 the magazine was acquired by John William Parker, whose son became its editor. It did, however, take two years until an editorial address, similar to the "Confession of Faith", was published by Parker. In his "A Happy New Year", which opened the first issue of the year 1849, he "say[s] a few words concerning ourselves" (Parker: A Happy New Year, *FM*, Jan 1849, 1) and points out what the new leadership stands for. First of all, he stresses the continuity and refers back to Maginn's "Confession":

> It will be seen from that document [the "Confession of Faith"], that we undertook to bolster up no faction; to pin our faith on no man, nor any set of men; […] Our leanings have been Conservative throughout, we freely allow, they are Conservative still; and we intend that they shall continue so. (ibid., 2)

Parker emphasises their outspokenness and independence in political matters and even credits the magazine with helping "to write [Wellington] out of office" (ibid.).[22] However, Parker also wants to distinguish himself from the magazine's heritage when he states that the "practice of calling hard names and imputing unworthy motives" (ibid., 3) was now dismissed and would not return again under his editorship. The climate of polemics and attempts at active involvement turned into a more "open-minded and tolerant"[23] spirit at the magazine and Parker aimed at enabling "the most free discussion, when the representatives of two different schools of opinion had the fullest opportunity of expressing themselves".[24] Though the main political focus remained conservative along the lines of Carlyle and Disraeli, who had also been contributors to *FM* in the early years, the magazine became more tolerant and a "liberty of opinion, which is the life of knowledge" was adopted.[25] Turner notes that under Parker's editorship, "*Fraser's* relied less on brilliant wit and more on distinguished liberal thinking, with writers such as G.H. Lewes, Charles Kingsley and J.A. Froude",[26] the latter

---

21 For a more detailed account of the early years of the magazine, see Miriam M. H. Thrall: Rebellious Fraser's. Nol Yorke's Magazine in the Days of Maginn, Thackeray, and Carlyle, New York 1934, who provides the only monograph in existence on the topic of *FM*. However, her work is only partially useful for this study, since Thrall concentrates on the years of the magazine's foundation and its early work and her description, though giving much information on the contributors and the socio-cultural context of the 1830s and 1840s, is often tainted by an admiration of Maginn and the group surrounding him.

22 Parker here refers to the fall of the Tory government in November 1830. As a result of his vehement opposition to parliamentary reform, Wellington resigned as prime minister and was succeeded by Earl Grey and a Whig government. The reform plan in question was the Reform Act of 1832, which was the first reform act to enlarge franchise through a reformation of the property qualification and the creation of additional constituencies.

23 Houghton: Wellesley Index, p. 311.

24 Froude on Parker's editorship; quoted ibid.

25 Quoted ibid., p. 312.

26 Turner: Fraser's Magazine, p. 230.

taking over the editorship in 1860. However, the periodical's conservative opinions were clashing more and more with the political and societal developments of the era and the circulation of *FM* continually decreased. It had dropped from approximately 10,000 during the 1830s to 1870s to 500 in 1880, and the October issue of 1882 was to be the last of *FM*.[27]

As the editors' addresses show, the periodical was intended for consumption by conservative intellectual men from the upper and upper-middle classes whom the contributors would have assumed to be able to follow and reflect upon the ideas discussed. The fact that the articles were mostly of essay-length and would have demanded a high degree of concentration confirms that the periodical was aimed at a readership which had enough time to read articles of more than fifteen pages length and had an income which would allow them to spend 2s6d per month on reading material. Given the fact that the circulation had always been low in comparison to other, often cheaper, periodicals and the specific political stance of the journal, one can argue that *FM* sold a very distinct political, cultural and also class identity to its consumers, which did not aim at the most widespread distribution possible but more at the production and stabilisation of a distinct worldview shared by the magazine and readers.

As the short overview of the two periodicals' production background and political and religious orientation has shown, both *LH* and *FM* had specific publication identities and wanted to cater to a specific target audience. While *LH* took a religiously oriented didactic approach to supply information and moral education to families of the working and lower-middle classes, *FM* aimed at a male, conservative, intellectual upper-class readership. These different target audiences and publication backgrounds are also reflected in the usage of the vocabulary of the heroic. In the following sections, the domains established in the analysis of *CJ* – military heroism, heroism of civilisation and everyday heroism – will also be examined in *LH* and *FM*. From this basis, a final comparison between the three periodicals will be drawn, which will allow for broader conclusions about the functionalisation of heroism in the periodical market place of nineteenth-century Britain and the status of heroism within Victorian society.

27 *Longman's Magazine*, which succeeded *FM* directly under the same proprietor, Charles Longman, radically differed from its predecessor in orientation. It catered to the established family magazine market. With a price of 6d per monthly issue, it was significantly cheaper and "unlike *Fraser's*, was dedicated to a non-partisan political stance and studiously avoided controversy, favouring light, entertaining fiction and informative articles". Marie Alexis Easley: Longman's Magazine, in: Laurel Brake / Marysa Demoor (eds.): Dictionary of Nineteenth Century Journalism, Ghent/London 2009, pp. 378–379. With circulation of 74,000 for its initial issue, the periodical clearly mirrors the demands of the popular print market which *FM* had not met.

5.3 Military Heroism

Christian Pacifism and the Rhetoric of Heroism in Leisure Hour

As a publication firmly rooted in evangelical Christianity, *LH* struggled with the idea of military conflict. Nevertheless, its semantic use of the heroic seems to be deeply rooted in traditional patterns of military achievements. Significantly, the journal does not try to re-interpret this idea of heroism nor build associations with values it deems worth mediating – as could be seen in *CJ* – but heavily relies on established notions of heroism. Thus, while frequently employing the vocabulary of heroism in relation to established historical personnel such as Nelson, Wellington or the mythical King Arthur, the magazine nevertheless renounces war in general. Consequently, almost no positive depictions of *contemporary* military prowess can be found in the periodical (for example during the Crimean Campaign).

Opposition to Wars

In many texts *LH* openly expresses its opposition to war. In 1852, for example, a biographical article on Johann Gottfried Seume, which largely centres on the writer's turbulent and tragic years of being enforcedly drafted to fight in North America and later for the Prussian Army, declares:

> Among the many tales of suffering, more or less intimately connected with the American War of Independence, few are better calculated to inspire the reader with a *horror of war in general*, and more particularly of that *military despotism* which then existed on the continent of Europe, than the history of the subject of our present memoir. (The Adventures of Johann Gottfried Seume, *LH*, 7 Oct 1852, 650, emphases mine)

The narration then follows Seume's desperation during the American Revolutionary War and later in the Prussian army and stresses how much the man who "possessed a mind well stored with the treasures of ancient and modern literature, and exquisitely sensitive feelings that revolted at the very name of injustice" (ibid.) had to suffer under the horror and despotism of violent combat.

Similarly, but given the political context even more strongly, "The Deadly Art of War" in August 1854 proclaims a firm anti-war stance. Though the article describes and depicts ancient artillery machines (such as arches, rams or catapults) and their use, it wants the reader to understand these remarks as mere historical information, not as a political statement for military action. The opening of the article thus reads:

> In presenting to our readers the following notices of the deadly art of war, we venture to express a hope to the effect that our tendencies and principles are so well known, that there is no necessity for us to assure our readers by many protestations of our aversion to war. We lament its existence; we abhor its horrors. (The Deadly Art of War, *LH*, 10 Aug 1854, 503)

In a very matter-of-fact tone, the article and the other parts in the series published throughout the month of August[28] chronologically describe the building and workings of weapons from ancient times up until the nineteenth century. The last part on 31 August concludes with the description of rockets and their deadly effect. While, as the title of the series suggests, the intellectual effort going into the construction of these works of military "art" are admired, their effect is denounced and the last paragraph of the series then connects to the introductory sentences, stating that

> [n]o humane mind can wish the modern Moloch to have his hecatombs of human sacrifices offered up to him, attended by the wails of the widow and the orphan. But alas, the cure of the evil is difficult to suggest, and he is the best patriot who fervently solicits God to remove the scourge of war from our land. (The Deadly Art of War, *LH*, 31 Aug 1854, 557)

By directing its hope for an end of war – which at this point in time could both be understood in a general way as well as more specifically in relation to the war in the Crimea – to god, the text avoids political opinion regarding the present war and responsibility for concrete action, while still clearly positioning itself against military action in general, detached from the current situation.[29]

Thus, *LH* acknowledged the political situation in the Balkans as "possess[ing] a special interest" (Woolwich Arsenal, *LH*, 3 Aug 1854, 490), yet only alluded to the actual conflict in passing[30] and avoided political opinion. Similar to *CJ*, *LH* resorts to texts about history in order to acknowledge the present situation. Thus,

---

28 Doris Lechner has identified the article "Woolwich Arsenal" published on 3 August as one associated with the series as well. Though having appeared under a different title, its final paragraph, which tells the reader that "[i]n some future number of our journal we shall resume this subject more fully" (Woolwich Arsenal, *LH*, 3 Aug 1854, 490), clearly connects it to "The Deadly Art of War" appearing in the following issues. For a more detailed analysis of the texts as a series see Lechner: Histories, p. 173–175.

29 Interestingly, the articles appeared throughout August 1854, a point in the war at which peace – at least politically – was within reach. At the end of July, Russia had withdrawn from the Danubian Principalities and thus withdrawn the immediate cause for war. However, the public in both France and Britain was already sworn in on war by large parts of the popular media, and politicians saw themselves unable to propose peace. Cf. Orlando Figes: Crimea. The Last Crusade, London 2010, p. 192.

30 This was on the one hand due to the tax on news, which periodicals still had to pay. However, as the example of *FM* will show later, this problem could be avoided by resorting to genres such as travel writing or analysing battle action in hindsight, when it was not current 'news' anymore. On the other hand, the war seemed to have sparked a general interest in Russia and the Baltic region; as Barbara Korte notes, a general rise in reporting on the cultures involved can be observed during the Crimean War and the Indian Mutiny. Cf.

various articles on the culture and history of Russia and the Crimea can be found during the war.[31] Unlike the depiction in *CJ*, the texts do not, however, create an implicit image of military heroism which the readers could have related to.

When dealing with war theoretically and without the topicality of a specific current (or historical) situation, *LH* states a clear opposition to war throughout its runtime, which is often shown as rooted in Christianity. In 1870, for example, a poem by "Bishop Porteous" not only calls war "the foulest stain and scandal of our nature" (Varieties, *LH*, 24 Sep 1870, 624) but also strongly criticises the hero worship of soldiers: "One murder makes a villain, / Millions a hero!" (ibid.). The poem calls for a return to Christian interests and to the "Great God" who has, so the speaker, not created mankind to rage war against each other but to "knit their souls together / In one soft bond of amity and love" (ibid.). Embedded in a Christian worldview, military acts are thus seen as mere violence, even murder, as directly contradicting the Christian ideals of altruism and mercy and thus not worthy of praise. Although strongly critical, the magazine did nevertheless use the rhetoric of heroism frequently – and unreflectedly – in relation to military figures of the past.

The "Hero of the Peninsula" – Established Military Heroes in Leisure Hour

Texts such as the above, while acknowledging the political reality of the day, took a generally critical stance towards war and rarely employed the vocabulary of the heroic. Nevertheless, many articles can be found in different contexts in which established military figures are called heroic. However, the texts exclusively use

---

Barbara Korte: Krimkrieg und „Indian Mutiny" als Anlass zum Kulturvergleich in viktorianischen Publikumszeitschriften, in: Angelika Epple / Walter Erhart: Die Welt beobachten. Praktiken des Vergleichens, Frankfurt am Main 2016.

31 Examples of this are A Glance at Sebastopol, *LH*, 16 Feb 1854, 104–106; The Baltic, and the Russian Towns on its Coasts, *LH*, 18 May 1854, 311–314; An Anecdote of the Russian Police, *LH*, 18 May 1854, 318; Russian Campaigns in Turkey 1828 and 1829, *LH*, 20 Jun 1854, 455–458; A Russian Aesop, *LH*, 28 Sep 1854, 619–620; Russia under Peter the Great, *LH*, 12 Oct 1854, 650–653; Russia Under Catherine II and Paul, *LH*, 18 Oct 1854, 660–663; Russia under Alexander and Nicholas, *LH*, 26 Oct 1854, 676–679, The Mother of the Czar, *LH*, 21 Dec 1854, 811–813; Prince Michael Woronzoff, *LH*, 28 Dec 1854, 820–823; Early English Intercourse with Russia, *LH*, 18 Jan 1855, 45–46; Visit of Peter the Great to the Prussian Court, *LH*, 8 Feb 1855, 93–95; The Perkin Warbeck of Russian History, *LH*, 22 Mar 1855, 182–183; Sketches of the Crimea, *LH*, Mar–May 1855; A Visit of Sebastopol in the Time of Peace, *LH*, 31 May 1855, 350–351; The Fortress of St. Petersburg, *LH*, 27 Sep 1855, 616–168; or Russia as I Saw it Forty Years Ago, *LH*, 15 Nov 1855, 726–728. Of these texts, which are all set in the past, only "Russia under Catherine II and Paul" and "Russia under Peter the Great" employ the vocabulary of the heroic. Both employ the word hero in its traditional military use as a man who faces an enemy and both times it is used without reflection upon the concept or a closer description of what constitutes their heroism, apart from the military context.

this kind of language in an unreflected manner. Heroism is thus not used as a concept to convey specific values or encourage certain behaviours, but rather as a title awarded to certain publicly (and nationally) agreed upon personalities. In the belief that "Clio constructs the royal youth in history, and tells him of the deeds that have been achieved by great kings and heroes" (Footprints of Frederick the Great, *LH*, 11 Mar 1858, 151), the 'heroes' are almost exclusively military men of the *past*. The two most frequent examples are Wellington and Nelson. After the death of Wellington, a number of articles concerned themselves with "the hero" (The Eighteenth of November, *LH*, 1 Jan 1853, 16). He is described as being one of the "greatest martial heroes" (The Duke's Funeral, *LH*, 9 Dec 1852, 789).[32] By calling him the "hero of the peninsula" (e.g. ibid., 788) or the "hero of a hundred fights" (The Duke of Wellington, *LH*, 4 Nov 1852, 713), the memory of his military achievements and especially his actions in the Napoleonic Wars is evoked. Similarly, Nelson is referred to as a "hero" (e.g. The Funeral of Lord Nelson, *LH*, 25 Nov 1852, 754) who distinguished himself by "his brilliant deeds of arms" (ibid., 753).[33]

While these texts[34] dealing with established national military hero figures[35] do not reflect upon the violent nature of the deeds that earned the men their hero-status, some of them re-interpret their military actions in Christian terms. For example, Wellington is called "the instrument of divine Providence" (The Duke's Funeral, *LH*, 9 Dec 1852, 788) through whom god saved "our beloved country from the evils which then ravaged the continent" (ibid.) or the "apostolic spirit and peculiar call which the Lord alone can give" (One of Nelson's Captains, *LH*, Oct 1899, 59). Another text concludes:

---

32 *LH* published a detailed report on both Nelson's and Wellington's funeral processions. Interestingly, the article on Nelson's funeral appeared upon the death of Wellington in late 1852. Thus, the two military men were directly connected and the description of Nelson's funeral can be seen as both a preparation as well as a standard for comparison of the subsequent commemoration of Wellington.

33 Similarly, a description of Napoleon's funeral can be found which describes his final resting place as the "shelter of heroes". Three Visits to the Hotel des Invalides, 1705, 1806, 1840, *LH*, 2 Aug 1854, 484.

34 Other articles referring to Nelson as a hero include A Few Days in Copenhagen, LH, 30 Jan 1864, 70–74; Books of Remembrance, *LH*, Sep 1884, 553–557; On Board Nelson's Ship, *LH*, Feb 1887, 135–137; or A Parcel of Anecdotes, *LH*, Jul 1899, 595–598. Further articles depicting Wellington as a hero are The Duke of Wellington, *LH*, 4 Nov 1852, 713–718; A Visit to Walmer Castle in November, 1852, *LH*, 10 Feb 1853, 105–107; Thirty Years of the Reign of Victoria, *LH*, 27 Jul 1872, 471–472; Naval Crests and Badges, *LH*, 10 Mar 1877, 152–154; London in the Streets, *LH*, 17 Nov 1877, 725–728; On Autographs, *LH*, Feb 1882, 93–99; Some of the Men of the Great Reform Bill, *LH*, Sep 1883, 554–559 and Nov 1883, 663–668; or The Iron Duke, *LH*, Mar 1900, 405–414.

35 Other examples of these kinds of texts are Sir Henry Havelock, *LH*, 31 May 1860, 250–252; Arthur and the Round Table, *LH*, 13 Dec 1860, 790–794; A Hundred Years Ago, *LH*, 16 Dec 1865, 795–796; American National Songs, *LH*, 5 Feb 1876, 90–92; The Battle of Waterloo, *LH*, Jun 1890, 531–541; or A Day in Ancient Athens, B.C., 470, *LH*, July 1890, 615–618.

> True patriots and true heroes are often his [god's] instruments in bringing this [the defeat of despots and tyrants] about. Such an instrument in the hand of God we have been in the habit of regarding the Duke of Wellington. [...] As such an instrument we would award him the meed of honour which is his due. (The Duke of Wellington, *LH*, 4 Nov 1852, 718)

Thereby, the violent acts, which the peace-oriented *LH* would generally not have encouraged, are re-interpreted as religiously motivated and thus justified as god-given acts of providence.[36]

In a similar Christian vein, the fight of minorities against superior powers is repeatedly portrayed as heroic. Reminiscent of the biblical story of David and Goliath, the journal shows the fight of small, oppressed groups in a positive light, which does not fit their overall claim of pacifism, but suits its self-conception as a religious publication. Significantly, these minorities depicted fighting for their freedom are never shown as professional fighters, but as ordinary people standing up for their own identity. Associated with general developments in British society in favour of ideas such as liberalism and democracy, men such as Garibaldi were celebrated as fighting for freedom and independence.[37] The most prominent example of such a positive depiction of the violent struggle of a small group can be seen in "Andreas Hofer", a biographical text written by the contributor R. Heath upon the occasion of the unveiling of a Hofer monument in Innsbruck in 1894. The "hero both in victory and death" (Heath: Andreas Hofer, *LH*, Feb 1894, 225) is depicted in a lineage of ancient and mythical heroes. He has a "mystical look" about him, the "limbs of a Hercules" and "ate and drank like one of the heroes in the Valhalla" (ibid.). Thus physically equipped, he is shown as a strong leader to the Tyrolese in their "heroic effort" against the Bavarian troops. The "heroic peasants" (ibid.) of Tyrol are established as an independent group who get caught up in the power struggle of other European nations and are forced to fight a battle which is not their own, but that of Austria, and take up arms because their own independence is on the line. Significantly, it is not this political motivation which is stressed and praised in the text, but a religious and class component is emphasised and offered to the reader of *LH* as a possibility for identification. Much like the intended readership of the journal, the courageous acts were "done by the poorer classes; the rich approved, but took no part" (ibid., 226). Thus, not only political, but social injustice is estab-

---

[36] A similar strategy is employed to justify the rare representations of female violent acts. A text about Joan of Arc, for example, reads "simple faith, sublime trust" (Jeanne D'Arc, *LH*, Mar 1893, 343) in her actions and stresses her "martyrdom" (cf. ibid.) rather than her own violent actions. By integrating it into a religious framework, her agency is subdued and explained as coming from "the heart of a woman from her tenderness and her tears" (ibid.). The text favours Joan of Arc's religious affiliation over her nationality. Taking a clear side, the text explains the English to have acted from a place of "hatred and fear" (ibid., 344) sparked by the religious power Joan of Arc displayed.

[37] Cf. also the depiction of Garibaldi in *CJ* in chapter 4.4.

lished as a justification for the Tyrolese violence. Most importantly, however, faith is stressed as the source of the Tyrolese strength. The text shows "priests, who, crucifix in hand, aroused their faith and their courage" (ibid.) and stresses that they "fought alike for God, the Emperor, and our country" (ibid.) with god, significantly, standing at the top of the list.[38] Even the enemy is reported as seeing divine intervention behind the peasants' power: "'That long Beard has an angel near him!'" (ibid.). Although the text describes the fight between the Tyrolese and the Bavarian troops, these violent measures are shown as a disruption to their general nature and, once the fight is over, the group is shown as merciful and just, in line with the emerging idea of a kind and merciful Christian soldier: "The prisoners taken, their lives were held sacred by the Tyrolese. 'Tear them to pieces,' cried Hofer, 'as long as they resist, but the moment they are on their knees, show mercy'" (ibid.). Similarly, the text says that Hofer "would not allow the slightest thing to be taken from the enemy, and had every house in Innsbruck searched to see if anything was there which belonged to the Bavarians" (ibid., 229). Thus, the violent actions of the Tyrolese are depicted as a mere necessity, a disruption to their peaceful and merciful nature which is not presented as a contradiction, but as a means to sustain this very lifestyle. Embedded in a religious worldview, the fighting men are shown as heroic because they are not fighting for their own interest or a grander political scheme, but for the maintenance of their collective identity.

The illustrations which accompany the article stress this very identity and peacefulness.[39] Rather than depicting battle action, a full-page illustration (cf. ibid., 228) shows a print of Franz von Defregger's 1879 painting "Andreas Hofer with His Advisers in the Hofburg at Innsbruck", which shows Hofer and a group of his men in plain clothes that stand out in their simplicity against the magnanimity of the surroundings. Interestingly, the illustration's caption alters the painting's title and reads "Andreas Hofer receiving the Presents of the Emperor of Austria at Innsbruck". This alteration re-interprets the scene depicted. Where the original caption had identified the Austrian politicians as advisers of Hofer's, the

38 The faith referred to in the last quotation is interestingly not specified. Andreas Hofer and the Tyrolese fighting with him had been Catholic, however, the text does not refer to the group's religious denomination but utilises their religion in a more general way in order to portray a Christian form of fight for freedom and independence.

39 This study understands periodical illustrations, following Simon Cooke, as "dual texts" (Cooke: Illustrated Periodicals, p. 121) in which image and word form a "dynamic fusion" (ibid., p. 191). For further discussions of text/image relation and Victorian culture see for example Anderson: The Printed Image; Brake / Demooor (eds.): Illustration; Renate Brosch: Victorian Visual Culture, Heidelberg 2008; Goldman: Beyond Decoration; Brian Maidment: Reading Popular Prints, 1790–1870, Basingstoke 2001; Stuart Sillars: Visualisation in Popular Fiction, 1860–1960. Graphic Narratives, Fictional Images, London 1995; Peter W. Sinnema: Dynamics of the Pictured Page. Representing the Nation in the Illustrated London News, Aldershot 1998 or Julia Thomas: Pictorial Victorians. The Inscription of Values in Word and Image, Athens, OH 2004.

new caption changes the power dynamic of the scene and makes the Austrians seek Hofer to reward him with presents, rather than Hofer seeking their help. With the gifts coming from "The Emperor", the caption even inscribes the Emperor's presence into the image. Thereby, the illustration emphasises the otherness of Hofer and the peasants in relation to the more organised political and military parties.

A second, smaller illustration depicts "Hofer's Cottage in Tyrol" (cf. ibid., 230); it shows a cottage within a pastoral setting, meadows beneath the mountains and a river running through the scene. Completely devoid of people, with the cottage as the only sign of civilisation, the image projects the calmness and peacefulness which the Tyrolese were presented as fighting for in the text. Thus, the images can be seen as directing the readers' attention by emphasising certain aspects of the text visually.[40] By visually highlighting the peaceful nature and the otherness of the Tyrolese, other aspects, such as the violence depicted in the verbal representation, are counterbalanced.

Similarly, the article "A Visit to the Marshes of La Vendée" shows how "crowds of labourers and shepherds become, under the impulse of some strong excitement, mighty and heroic armies" (A Visit to the Marshes of La Vendée, *LH*, 7 Jun 1855, 353). The information was mediated in the form of a travel report, a genre which was frequently employed in *LH* to convey historical information to the reader. In a form both entertaining and immersive, its present tense narrative gives the reader the notion of accompanying the narrators on their journey. Just as the "shepherds" and "labourers" are shown only resorting to violent means out of necessity, the description of the present day inhabitants then reassures the reader that a peaceful group of people live there:

> In this district, which witnessed the extinction of five republican armies, he would naturally expect to find a fierce and warlike race, more accustomed to use the sword than the spade; but, on the contrary, he sees a population calm, silent, and peaceful, working as diligently, and apparently with as much apathy of spirit, as their own gigantic oxen. (ibid., 354)

Thus, the violent action is presented as a disruption, which does not change the peasants, but enables them to maintain their "calm, silent, and peaceful" life.

In the depiction of civilian uproar against superior powers,[41] *LH* does not foreground the military component of the presented heroism, but the mercy

---

40 Cf. Gabriele Rippl: Intermedialität. Text/Bild-Verhältnisse, in: Claudia Benthien / Brigitte Weingart (eds.): Handbuch Literatur und Visuelle Kultur, Berlin/Boston 2014, pp. 139–158, here p. 148. The German original, which uses the example of Charles Dickens, reads: "So lenken etwa die den Romanen von Charles Dickens beigegebenen Bilder die Aufmerksamkeit der Leserinnen und Leser, indem sie die Semantik wichtiger Textpassagen visuell verdichten." Ibid.

41 Other examples include The Negro Liberator of Hayti, *LH,* 31 Mar 1853, 218–221 which foregrounds the humaneness of François-Dominique Toussaint Louverture in the Haitian Revolution and emphasises the mercy he showed his opponents; The Kingdom of Sardinia

which the fighters showed their enemies. Thereby, the depiction concurs with the growing ideal of a Christian military man who would fight in a way which was as humane and merciful as possible and would avoid unnecessary violence.

The idea of a Christian soldier becomes more frequent in the journal as the century progresses and is most obvious in relation to conflicts in the colonies. In this context, texts can be found which openly support organised military action if conducted in the context of the Christian civilising mission which *LH* as a religiously oriented publication supported.[42] This becomes especially pronounced in the context of the Second Boer War at the turn of the century. In 1890, W. H. Swain remarks in "A March from Johannesburg" that amidst the "heroism of the long-draw-out sieges" (W. H. Swain: A March from Johannesburg, *LH*, May 1890, 631) the best features of humanity have been brought to the fore. This is, in his opinion, not exemplified by mere military success, but in the way in which the soldiers deal with the Boers after the fight. In a tone which clearly infantilises the South African native population, the author praises the fact that the soldiers showed the "vast crowd of simple, childlike, helpless natives" Christian mercy. Similarly, "Varieties", a miscellaneous section which dealt with current topics, quotes an American correspondent in South Africa who had "seen a wounded Boer with his head resting in a British soldier's lap, while another gave him water" (Varieties, *LH*, Jun 1900, 744). The acts of the soldiers are then not seen as acts of killing, as the war-critical poem of 1870 had expressed it, but as "incidents of heroism [...], acts of self-forgetfulness and quick self-sacrificing service" (ibid.). Whereas war had been criticised in other contexts, the military actions conducted in the context of a Christian mission are viewed as "a glorious page in English history" (ibid.) and display a "self-forgetful spirit which makes great things possible in both Church and State" (ibid.). The reference to the Church is the most significant in this context, since it is this connection to religious aims which seems to justify the violent actions which are otherwise condemned and turns them into heroic acts. The murderous acts thus become heroic in a war which can be considered Christian.

As this short overview has shown, *LH*, rooted in an ideal of altruism and pacifism, was generally opposed to violent military actions, an opinion which changed, however, if the violent actions could be justified in a religious context

---

and its Sovereign, *LH*, Jan 3 1856, 8–11 which shows the small nation as a "brave, hardy, and independent race" fighting against "overwhelming numbers" (ibid., 11); or Russia under Alexander and Nicholas, *LH*, 26 Oct 1854, 676–679 which praises the "heroic struggle" (ibid., 677) of Polish peasants against Czar Nicholas.

42 As MacKenzie has argued, colonialism was important for a new popularity of the British army and British war efforts in a Christian framework which turned violent acts into "imperial action by a divinely ordained might. [...] Church, intellectuals, educationalists and artists were reconciled to war through its role in the extension of Christendom, its moral purpose not only in the life of the state but in producing a new global order." MacKenzie: Popular Imperialism, p. 4.

and if the fighters showed mercy towards their enemies. While the periodical used the vocabulary of the heroic in relation to established military men of the (mythical) past such as King Arthur, Nelson or Wellington in a very unreflected manner, positive assessments through the attribution of heroic status can mostly be found in the narration of unequal fights (in line with the biblical tale of David against Goliath) in which civilians are forced to take up arms in order to defend their peaceful lifestyle, and in relation to colonial conflicts, which could be seen as fights for Christianity. Unlike *CJ*, however, *LH* did not re-interpret the idea of heroism and associated it with ideals they thought worth emulating by their readers, and identification beyond the religious was not encouraged.

Leadership and Disruptive Potential – Military Heroism in Fraser's Magazine

The coverage of war and its heroes in *FM* is fundamentally different from the depiction in *CJ* and *LH*. Unlike the other two journals, which both seemed to be uncomfortable with dealing with the war and Britain's involvement explicitly, *FM* discusses the war much more directly, as will become apparent in articles published in the context of the Crimean War. Interestingly, for the contributors to the magazine the war was defined much less by battle action than by politics and, unlike *CJ* and *LH*, they rarely discussed the human expense and the individual experience of soldiers in battle. Consequently, most of the articles are written in a very sober and matter-of-fact fashion, individual soldiers and sailors do not feature and the language of heroism is far less frequent than in the two periodicals examined above. The magazine takes much more of an interest in the reasons for Britain entering the war and the political implications than in the situation of the British fighting in the Crimea or the Baltic. In "Turkey and the East of Europe in Relation to England and the West" in 1853, *FM* displays a positive reaction to the fact that the British public was so interested in the events. However, it does not relate this back to the fact that many people might have relatives fighting in the war, a sense of threat to their own living conditions, or straightforward patriotic sentiment. Rather, the article sees the interest as a sign of a general improvement in the education and living standards of the population at large:

> During the period of the discussions on the Reform Bill now twenty years ago or more, it used to be complainingly said by independent liberal members, who took great interest in foreign politics, that it was impossible to excite the English middle and lower classes on the interesting subject of foreign affairs. [...] yet a great change has since taken place in English opinion and feeling. (Turkey and the East of Europe in Relation to England and the West, *FM*, May 1853, 562)

This "great change", the text sees in the increased mobility of the "middle and lower classes".[43] As a consequence, "[m]en in a very humble sphere of life have, during the last five years, taken an eager and anxious interest in the struggles of Hungary and Italy, in the politics of France and of Germany, and in the maintenance of the integrity and independence of Turkey" (ibid., 563). This "eager and anxious interest" in the fate of the Ottomans is explained by a very rational fact: "If the Sultan were removed from his seat of Empire to-morrow, or another power installed in Constantinople, that trade which English and Levantine merchants now so prosperously drive would be transferred to other channels – would be loaded with fetters and restrictions" (ibid., 564), which might lead to a Russian domination of global trade. The text thus gives a very logical political reason for Britain supporting the Ottoman troops in their fight against Russia, however it also points out that Britain itself is on a different civilisatory level than Turkey and that the choice between "Ottoman dominion" and the "Russian Czar" is a choice between "two evils" (ibid., 564). Subsequently, the Ottomans are called a "semi-civilized and warlike tribe" (ibid., 563), their culture is however also described as rich and exotic in relation to its natural resources with

> lands flowing with milk and honey, and producing rice, wheat, tobacco, hemp, cotton, silk, and the finest and most luscious fruits. [...] It is rich in marbles, alabasters, jaspers, and precious stones; in drugs and medicaments of great value. There are mines of copper and quicksilver; breeds of horses of exceeding value; flocks of buffaloes and sheep [...]. (ibid., 564)

In this description, the text implicitly links the existence of the "Turkish system" (ibid.) back to British interests; as Britain does not flow "with milk and honey" and does not possess the same precious natural resources, its trade supremacy is integral for *FM*'s readership to be able to enjoy colonial goods and exotic luxuries in the future.[44]

Different from the previously discussed periodicals, *FM* in this text clearly positions itself in favour of the war in the Crimea for merely political reasons, which do not seem to be influenced by humanitarian thoughts or moral doubts, for: "[s]o long as we desire to retain our Indian empire there is no question con-

---

43 The article argues that "[i]t is a well ascertained fact, that travellers can now reach Paris in less time than they could reach Calais and Boulogne in 1830, and that the cost of the whole trip is less than the fares taken by the steamboats plying between London and Calais three-and-twenty years ago. As a consequence of this increased communication, for every one Englishman and woman who crossed the Straits to Dover in 1829, there are one hundred who cross it in 1853." Turkey and the East of Europe in Relation to England and the West, *FM*, May 1853, 563. It is highly questionable though that this increase of travel to Europe was in significant part made up by the "lower classes", yet this perception might also depend on the point of view and the "lower classes" defined by the upper class might be something different as defined by the middle or working classes.

44 This is further stressed by the explanation that "[f]or many years Great Britain, including her possessions of Malta and the Ionian Islands, has driven a larger import and export trade with Turkey than any three of the European powers together." Ibid., 567.

nected with the East or the Echelles du Levant that is not of paramount importance to us" (ibid., 568).

Significantly, then, the vocabulary of heroism in this text is not used in relation to British soldiers or officers fighting against Russia, but denotes Britain's new ally in the war: Louis Napoleon, who is not called by his name, but in reference to the coup d'état of 2 November 1851 as "the hero of December" (ibid., 572 and 573). The text thus depicts the French emperor as a continuing threat to British supremacy despite the fact that the two countries were allied in the current war against Russia. Louis Napoleon's heroism in this context clearly refers to a disruptive quality and can be related to the ideas of men like Carlyle, who had identified heroism as a way of replacing an existing order (which is subjectively perceived as deficient) with a new one (cf. chapter 2.1). Heroism, in this context, is a precarious concept with the power to destabilise existing order and hierarchies. Unlike *CJ* and *LH*, *FM* does not portray the French troops and their commander as an asset in the current war and additional security in the conflict, but as a still unpredictable political enemy. Articles looking into the military past of Britain, such as "Sketches of Campaigning Life" which in 1854 narrated Wellington's advance on Bajados, also remained clear in their definition of France as a threatening power within Europe. Large parts of the article were taken from William Francis Napier's *History of the War in the Peninsula* (1836). As a member of the British army during the Peninsular War, Napier's account could be presented as authentic,[45] but also made re-interpretation impossible and firmly situated the French as an opposing force, although allied in the present war. As an introductory note, the text professes its intention as follows:

> At a moment like the present, when all the nations of Europe are once more either engaged in, or on the brink of, hostilities, some sketches and details of personal adventure, exemplifying how matters were managed in the last stupendous war, may not prove unacceptable to the military or general reader. (Sketches of Campaigning Life, *FM*, Aug 1854, 223)

This comment on the account to follow not only gives the "military and general reader" the example of a successful war effort to boost confidence, but also reinforces a political opinion which is critical of France.[46] Subsequently, the

---

45 William Francis Napier had not been part of the siege of Bajados himself; he had only arrived after the city had fallen and the casualties among the officers gave him the opportunity to take command of a regiment himself. His historical account was, however, authenticated through the fact that he was given access to correspondence of the French military. John Sweetman notes that "Wellington refused use of his private papers, but gave Napier Joseph Bonaparte's correspondence with Napoleon, senior military figures, and politicians captured at Vitoria, and answered copious questions." John Sweetman: Napier, Sir William Francis Patrick (1785–1860), in: Lawrence Goldman (ed.): Oxford Dictionary of National Biography, 2008, DOI: 10.1093/ref:odnb/19772.

46 It is worth noting that the introduction neutrally refers to all European nations being "either engaged in, or on the brink of, hostilities" without qualifying the engagement as a joint one.

French are described as untiring, disciplined and skilled; the English, however, are still shown as superior and more enduring: "the enemy did their utmost, but at length retired" (ibid., 228). Interestingly, this text concerned with past events is the only one to appear during the Crimean War which describes actual battle action. Regarding the Crimean Campaign itself, the texts do not enter the battlefield in a narrative fashion but are kept in a matter-of-fact style, giving lists of equipment, analysing difficulties and expressing political beliefs. Thereby, an unemotional stance towards the war is adopted and a greater distance between the readers and the events created. Where publications like *CJ* had needed the description of soldiers' suffering to create the proximity and emotional involvement necessary for consumers to identify with the represented heroes, *FM* discusses the war as a part of politics and aims at a rational rather than an emotional response from its readership.

FM keeps this distanced style of reporting about the Crimea throughout its coverage. Additionally, it openly criticises other media, especially what it calls "graphic essayists" (Russian Ships and Russian Gunners, *FM*, Jun 1854, 613), which it believes lead their readership to wrong conclusions.[47] This, the text suggests, is often due to the fact that the presumed correspondents are not on site: "we will not, for instance, ask whether certain letters which last summer appeared, headed in showy capitals, 'From our own Correspondent, St. Petersburg,' were written from the Russian capital, or fabricated in London" (ibid., 624). *FM*'s own style of reporting was then decidedly not graphic in terms of wartime action, but very much so in terms of details which presumably should prove that their authors were not fabricating their stories "in London". In order to enable the reader "to arrive at a correct appreciation of the enemy's power of resistance by sea" (ibid., 613), the Russian, and later also the French and British ships, are described in great detail regarding their material, equipment, their speed, etc. In order to achieve a seemingly authentic picture of the situation in Russia, passages of the article are written in the style of travel writing. One sequence, for example, guides the reader on a tour through the docks of St. Petersburg:

> having now arrived in St. Petersburgh – and to steam the distance from Cronstat takes two and a quarter hours – we proceed to notice the building-yards of that capital. [...] The New Admiralty is on the left bank of the Neva, two miles above from the bar, and at the end of the well-known English quay. [...] Of the two larger ships no notion can be formed by persons whose ideas on the subjects are taken from what may be every day seen at Portsmouth and Plymouth. They are magnificent works [...]. (ibid., 614)

47 The *Daily News* (1846–1912) and *Morning Chronicle* (1770–1862) are excluded from this criticism, since they are said to have been "*comparatively* truthful" (Russian Ships and Russian Gunners, *FM*, Jun 1854, 625) in their reporting.

The Russian ships, in contrast, are described as inferior.[48] Similar to the previous text, heroism is in this context shown as a problematic concept, one which endangers an existing order and is unpredictable. Just like Napoleon was not to be trusted, this text sees the Russian emperor's "heroic dream of ambition and glory" (ibid., 631) as the root of the current military conflict. Heroism in this context is thus not something to aspire to or to be admired, but a danger to Britain's trade supremacy and its place in the world order. Interestingly, *FM*'s opinion on this form of authoritarian heroism is largely dependent on the context. In a situation where the existing order from which Britain benefited is threatened by this kind of heroism, it is denounced, called a mere "cover [for] a vain despot's wounded pride" (ibid.) in the face of his inferiority. In domestic issues related to class questions, however, *FM* often propagated just this form of leadership by heroic figures (cf. chapter 5.6).

Furthermore, the depiction of the Crimean War in *FM* seems to suggest that heroism on the British side was needless. Both the unpredictable form of heroism embodied by Louis Napoleon or the Russian Tsar as a reaction to a hopeless situation or a dangerous risk are never attributed to British soldiers or sailors. The war was rather presented as a necessary political measure achieved with military means and the magazine mostly presents the campaign as one which had already been won by the allied forces from the beginning. In September 1854, "The Garrisons of the Crimea" professes that "we trust and believe that the Allies are about to scour the hills of the Crimea in such effectual fashion that the Osmanli will henceforth be able to smoke his pipe in peace on the slopes of Haider Pasha" (The Garrisons of the Crimea, *FM*, Sep 1854, 356). Giving numbers of the Russian forces, the text is confident that British "superiority in mere numbers, would be, we repeat, immense, and may be added to, if necessary, by reinforcements from England and France, and from the Turkish army of the Danube" (ibid., 361). Although the text asserts that it does not "wish to convey that any of these movements are easy, or devoid of risk" (ibid.), a military victory for the allied forces is presented as a certainty. Having established that the British troops have no real enemy in this war, the vocabulary of the heroic is not ascribed to the British, but to an inferior group opposing Russia, which – unlike the British – runs the risk of being defeated, but nevertheless took up the fight: The Arnaouts, Albanians living in Syria, are attributed the status of heroes for beating back a Russian battery though being "ill-armed" (ibid.). However, the group of fighters is only elevated as such because of their weak position and the unlikeliness of their success. They are heroic for the very fact that their chances of beating the Russians in the specific situation were very slim. Britain, on the

[48] The contributor for example notes that "The first thing which strikes the European visitor to a Russian dockyard is, that the oak, a wood with us inseparable form the idea of maritime supremacy, is sometimes entirely, and always partially, replaced by materials which we should saw into kitchen tables and nursery doors." Ibid., 613.

other hand, does not seem to need such desperate heroism and is, at the close of the Crimean War, presented as a natural leader among the global powers: "setting aside our natural military superiority – which we will assert, without fear of contradiction, to be immense – we have all the advantages conferred on us by the position we have so long occupied as the vanguard of the civilization of the world" (ibid., 366–368). Unlike the Arnaouts, who need heroism in order to enhance their military prowess, Britain is depicted as such a leading power in both military and civil terms that heroism seems to be irrelevant for their success.

None of the texts dealing with the Crimean War refer to British casualties or the effects of the massive expenditure on Britain. The war was presented as political rather than as a military action that involved blood, suffering, living under bad conditions and death. Though the middle classes, the most educated of whom *FM* was targeting, would have been less directly involved in the war, the upper classes, which also made up the magazine's intended audience, would have been affected strongly by the war as most of the high ranks of the military came from this segment of society. In this light, it is interesting that *FM* did not praise or heroise the active involvement of their intended readers, but analysed the war as a de-individualised and to some extent also de-humanised political event.

In other contexts, instances of heroisation of specific military actors can be found. However, *FM* strongly differentiates between the military leaders and the mass of military men. While the latter are often depicted as having become heroes due to the circumstance of war and not due to individual prowess[49] (the labelling of military heroism as situational could also be observed in *CJ*, yet it was utilised in order to differentiate between military heroism and the heroic representation of a moral mindset), the leaders are frequently heroised for their vision and leadership qualities. In reasoning closely reminiscent of the idea of heroism as defined by Carlyle or Emerson, high-ranking prominent military men – mostly from the past – are commemorated. Furthermore, the potential of heroic military leaders to bring about societal change, if necessary by violent means, is stressed through examples such as Napoleon, William of Orange and Julius Caesar.

"Charles James Napier: A Study in Character"[50] by the contributor Shirley can serve as an exemplary article for the representation of military leaders as vision-

49 For example, "Kaye's History of the Indian Mutiny" says about the "heroic" British soldiers involved: "it happened to men who still walk about the streets, who have not yet reached middle age, and who have nothing after all very particular about them." Kaye's History of the Indian Mutiny, *FM*, Dec 1864, 757. Or "The Naval School on Board the 'Illustrious'" criticises the fact that "[a] seaman of the royal navy was, by courtesy, held to be a hero, though what was to make him such was rarely inquired into". The Naval School on Board the "Illustrious", *FM*, Apr 1855, 455.

50 The text refers to the army officer and governor in India Sir Charles James Napier (1782–1853), brother of the aforementioned William Francis Napier, not to be mistaken with the

ary heroes and objects of adoration in line with Thomas Carlyle's idea of a messianic hero-leader. Already the opening assertion that with Napier "[a]n authentic hero has been among us" (Shirley: Charles James Napier, *FM*, Feb 1858, 254) awards the British general an extraordinary position. As "one of her [England's] greatest and most strikingly original sons" (ibid.), he is estimated even higher than the widely admired Wellington. In a religiously inspired comparison, Napier is presented as the more timely and energetic of the two: "Not even *the* Duke was greater [...]. Wellington – massive and tranquil as a primeval god: Napier – bright and rapid as the lightning of Jove" (ibid.). Since Napier himself had fought under Wellington at Bussaco, the comparison is a very direct one. In public opinion, Napier had often been criticised for his harsh outspokenness[51] and problematic relation to authority. Especially during his time as commander of the British Army in India, Napier frequently criticised the leading figures, expressing

> his conviction of the stupidity and incompetence of the British rulers in India [...]. He expressed his views in the margins of his copy of Vincent Eyre's book on the war. Where Eyre wrote of the officers' bravery, Napier wrote "you were all a set of sons of bitches" (copy of V. Eyre, The Military Operations in Cabul, 1843, 227, BL OIOC). Eyre wrote, "It seemed as if we were under the ban of Heaven"; Napier crossed it out, writing, "Nonsense. These matters depend upon particular circumstances". (ibid., 127)[52]

With such wording, Napier alienated many of his contemporaries. Though criticising the authorities and their conduct, Napier nevertheless "argued that the only way to bring order to a disturbed area was through a leader" (ibid., 254). Given the previous observations on heroism in *FM*, it is not surprising then that the periodical, which believed in a heroic leader-figure of the same build, re-evaluated his importance. The text in *FM* re-attributes Dryden's *Absalom and Achitophel* to Napier:[53] "sagacious, bold, and turbulent of wit; / Restless, unfixed in principles and place; In power unpleased, impatient of disgrace; / A fiery soul, which worketh out its way, / [...] A daring pilot in extremity [...]" (ibid.). This

---

naval officer and politician Sir Charles Napier (1786–1860), a controversial figure who was widely considered "the common man's naval hero". Sweetman: Napier, n.p.

51 Ainslie T. Embree for example notes that Napier was full of criticism for his superiors: "After the battle of Talavera he wrote that Wellington was 'rash and imprudent ... his errors seem to be more of inexperience and vanity than want of talent' (Napier, Life, 1.127). [...] Napier's diaries and letters are full of complaints about his enemies in England, especially the Duke of York, whom he blamed for his non-promotion." Ibid. In his later career in India, Napier's open rivalry with General Sir James Outram caused much public attention. Ainslie T. Embree: Napier, Sir Charles James (1782–1853), in: Lawrence Goldman (ed.): Oxford Dictionary of National Biography, 2008, DOI: 10.1093/ref:odnb/19748.

52 Ibid.

53 The re-appropriation of Dryden's text is noteworthy; written as an answer to the religiously based exclusion crisis in the late 1670s, the quoted lines are used to describe the biblical Achitophel, a false advisor to David. In Dryden's work, Achitophel symbolises the Earl of Shaftesbury, who is depicted as one of the negative players in the intrigue. It is thus remarkable how the lines from *Absolom and Achitophel* are re-interpreted in a positive way.

recalls Carlyle's idea that heroic figures are not necessarily stabilisers of society, but through their visionary abilities and energy are able to disrupt existing structures in order to create something new. This fight against existing order is then attributed to Napier's military endeavours: "What better mission for a great captain than to lead his army into the provinces, release one of the fairest portions of the earth from foul misgovernment, and rescue the peaceful population of the great river from the domination of a worthless family of robbers?" (ibid., 257).

Not only this aspect is reminiscent of the contemporary model of a messianic hero and, in the emphasis on Napier's truthfulness and honesty, another feature of this type of hero is met. Thus, the text describes him as "inexorably honest" (ibid., 255), possessing a "stubborn truthfulness" and notes that "to him there was greater necessity to speak the truth out than to most men" (ibid., 256). Even if to his own disadvantage, Napier is shown articulating and defending his beliefs. Even a connection to the divine, which was stressed so persistently by Carlyle, is seen in him by the text, which states that he entertained "sentiments [...] as to the relations subsisting between man and the invisible world" (ibid., 261). The combination of these qualities then lead to the assertion that "[b]y nature he was intended for chief command" (ibid., 256).

Furthermore, the text attributes a poetic quality to Napier in both his military work and his writing.[54] About the latter, it notes that his "literary capacity was indeed most remarkable. [...] And the style of his writing is symptomatic of the style of his mind – strong, practical, terse, logical, with a dash of the finer sense we call 'genius'" (ibid., 255). A later passage then asserts that even "his military acts are *poetic*" (ibid., 265). The idea of literary and poetic talents again link Napier's heroism to the ideas of Thomas Carlyle, who had drawn direct links between a man's heroic qualities and his abilities to disseminate his ideas through print in his remarks on the "Hero as Man of Letters". Furthermore, the idea of poetic writing, in contrast to mediocre literature, had also been seen as the hero's link to the divine. In line with this presentation of Napier as a Carlylean hero, the text compares him to Mohammed and Napoleon (cf. ibid., 256 and 267), both of whom had been representatives of heroism for Thomas Carlyle.

Articles about military leaders depicted in the vein of the Carlylean messianic hero can be found throughout the runtime of *FM*. Almost always in the form of a biographical sketch or in the framework of a review of a biography,[55] all of the texts present high-ranking military men. As central elements of the men's hero-

---

54 It is said that his qualities can be seen "in his letters, journals, despatches; we see it in his conduct of war and government" (Charles Napier: A Study in Character, *FM*, Feb 1858, 255) and thereby connects the spheres of writing and his military and political endeavours.

55 Many of the texts include a critique of contemporary history writing for which Thomas Carlyle was referenced as the standard which other writers could not measure up to. Interestingly, it was most frequently criticised in a very subjective assessment that contemporary historians were not able to convey the 'truth' about a given period (cf. chapter 5.6 of this

ism, the texts always emphasise their ability to lead, their superior insight into the 'truth' and thus their superiority as individuals over the mass of society.[56]

As the analyses above have shown, the representation of military heroism and war are fundamentally different in the two periodicals. While *FM*, in line with its identity as a political paper intended for the elite, perceived war in political terms rather than in the more humane categories of life, death and suffering, *LH* was clearly opposed to war in general. Therefore, both periodicals abstained from depicting individual heroic acts of common soldiers in current war efforts – though for different reasons. *LH* in their pacifist approach did not seem to want their readers to identify with actions the periodical perceived as violent. *FM* on the other hand omitted depictions of rank-and-file soldiers and limited its veneration to military leaders. Thus, in its depiction of military heroism, the political publication *FM* clearly presented its worldview as one in which the few lead the many, in which it is heroic to lead the troops and come up with the tactics, but not heroic to execute those tactics. *FM* thus designed the military hero in line with Carlyle's thinking as a heroic leader-figure. *LH*, in its lack of heroic attribution to common soldiers, presents a fundamentally different view of the world: in decidedly *not* calling the military men heroic, it becomes obvious that the military profession is one which the periodical wants its readers *not* to enter. Therefore, it did not present any role models of this profession to its readers.

5.4 Heroes of Civilisation

Both *LH* and *FM* construct heroic figures whose achievements and works are praised as enhancing civilisation and society. In *LH* this is mostly played out in the domains of technology, exploration and missionary work, each of which displayed different types of heroes. While engineers in particular are presented to

study or Christiane Hadamitzky: The History of a Magazine Is But the Influence of a Great Man? Thomas Carlyle and the Decline of Fraser's Magazine, in: Ronald G. Asch / Michael Butter (eds.): Bewunderer, Verehrer, Zuschauer. Die Helden und ihr Publikum (Helden – Heroisierungen – Heroismen 2), Würzburg 2016, pp. 75–91 which analyses the connection between perceived inadequacy of history writing and the idea of a Carlylean hero in greater detail).

56 Prominent examples include Napoleon (e.g. Principal Campaigns in the Rise of Napoleon, *FM*, Feb–Nov 1848; Military Tableaux; or, Scenes from the Wars of Napoleon, Sketched in the Manner of Callot, *FM*, Apr 1844, 487–495), Wellington (e.g. The Duke of Wellington, *FM*, Oct 1852, 267–273), Henry Lawrence (Henry Lawrence, *FM*, Aug 1872, 251–264), Viscount Combermere (Field-Marshal Viscount Combermere, *FM*, Nov 1866, 564–587), Count Cavour (Count Cavour, *FM*, Feb 1878, 185–199), Frederick the Great (e.g. Carlyle's Frederick the Great, *FM*, Dec 1858, 631–649 and *FM*, May 1864, 539–550. In this specific case, the link to the Carlylean concept of heroism would have been even stronger as it reviewed, very favourably, Carlyle's biography of Frederick the Great). Texts which positively emphasise the socially disruptive quality of heroism include William the Silent: A Study in Character, *FM*, Apr 1860, 463–474; Motley's John Barneveld, *FM*, Aug 1874, 223–245 or Julius Caesar, *FM*, Jul 1867, 1–15 and Froude's Julius Caesar, *FM*, Sep 1879, 315–337.

the readers as possible role models, a greater distance is placed between the audience and the missionaries. Contrary to what one might expect from the didactic periodical, the work of (secular) educators – which was heroised in *CJ* – is not depicted in the language of the heroic in *LH*. Though *FM* occasionally portrays scientists and explorers in the vocabulary of the heroic, the periodical's idea of the heroism of civilisation is played out on a different field: politics. As the following sections will illustrate, the two periodicals in their representation of civilising heroism display fundamentally different concepts that emphasise their different intended readerships and ideas of the individual in relation to the collective.

Science and Technology in Leisure Hour

In the era of scientific and technological progress, *LH*, with its aim not only to entertain but to instruct, provided a large number of articles on popular science and technology. Different from *CJ*, the periodical quite frequently used the vocabulary of the heroic to describe the representatives of those men (for women, once again, do not feature prominently in that domain) whom the journal saw as contributing to the development of civilisation. Whereas military endeavour was perceived as societally destructive, science and technology were shown as means to enhance society and also to disseminate Christianity. This distinction is, for example, voiced in a poem inspired by the death of arctic explorer John Franklin and his crew. The poem states:

> Not on the battle-field they fell, with victory's laurels crowned,
> With trumpet-blast and cannon's roar, and clash of arms around!
> Heroes of higher grade were they – slain in a noble strife;
> Who sacrificed in science's cause – home, country, friends, and life! (Poetry, *LH*, 8 Feb 1855, 95)

This excerpt illustrates the opposition between the military and scientific realm and emphasises the speaker's opinion that military heroics are awarded too much attention.[57] The efforts by Franklin and his crew to explore the world in order to enlarge humankind's knowledge, however, are considered an act of a "higher grade". Though both actions can be seen as selfless and result in death, being metaphorically slain in the name of science is considered the higher form of heroics.

---

57 This fits Christine MacLeod's assessment that the depiction of inventors "personified their [the industrial classes'] claim that it was not military prowess that made Great Britain great, but the ingenuity and enterprise of its 'industrious' citizens: the country's strength and global influence rested on the prosperity generated by manufacturing and trade; peaceful competition was a more secure route than war to individual happiness and national supremacy". MacLeod: Invention, p. 1.

In that vein, the periodical praised many men of invention, exploration and industry as heroes in their contribution to society at large. However, the focus, as the following examples will illustrate, lay strongly on the practical fields of engineering and industry and less on the more abstract natural sciences. One can argue that this reflects the periodical's intended readership; with an emphasis on technology, it dealt with products and processes which the working classes would have been familiar with since they were the ones actually working with the newly invented machinery. The journal in the thematic emphasis made an identificatory offer to its readers, who could not only relate to the technology depicted, but also to the general ideas of industriousness and the work ethic represented by the engineers. Thus, the stories of men such as George Stephenson, William Fairbairn or the French Weaver Marie Joseph Jaquard were also stories of personal and moral progress which were intended to spark similar ambitions in the working men among the readership. At the same time, the relatively scarce heroisation of scientists compared to engineers or explorers also reflects the periodical's policy and the regulations that their financial supporters implicitly put on them. Though having toned down their strong religious orientation in order to reach more readers from the working classes, much of the funding for *LH* was coming from strongly religious members of the middle classes[58] who, from the mid-century onwards, were often unsettled by the scientific findings in the wake of Darwinism which contradicted their religious beliefs. Invention and technological development could be framed in a philanthropic and religious narrative and were much closer to the experience of the intended audience of the working classes; the new machinery used in many fields of production made working life easier for many and the work of the individual engineers could be seen as work for the whole of the community. Furthermore, as the following examples will illustrate, the new developments and inventions could be related to the grace of god and did not contradict biblical ideas, while scientific ideas such as the theory of evolution fundamentally challenged religious beliefs.[59]

Engineering and Industry

All of the articles start the narration with the protagonists' childhood and show them as being marked out as extraordinary from their earliest days. In this standard form of hero-narrative, the Frenchman Jacques Fontaine, who would invent a new kind of fabric-making, is depicted as "gifted with a robust constitution and more than ordinary force of character" (Story of a Forgotten Benefactor, *LH*, 27

58 Fyfe: Commerce, p. 171.

59 For scholarship on the relation between science and religion in the nineteenth century see chapter 3, Fn. 46.

Sep 1855, 621) from birth. Marie Joseph Jacquard[60] already in his youth showed "his taste for mechanics [...] by a number of curious little inventions" (The Lyonese Weaver, *LH*, 5 Feb 1852, 85) and Bernard Palissy, the discoverer of enamel, is shown as superior to his surroundings from childhood onwards:

> [...] we picture to ourselves the boy Bernard fingering his father's drugs, and asking puzzling questions concerning them; and failing to elicit satisfactory replies, rambling forth into the wood to think over, or ask again of nature, of whose teachings he was ever a diligent student. (An Artist in Earth, *LH*, 11 Nov 1852, 730)

This narratorial strategy, which was common to nineteenth-century didactic reading material, is pursued in the depiction of George Stephenson, who is the focus of a number of articles in *LH* through the decades. A two-part biographical text published in December 1857 serves as a good example of this. Drawing heavily on Samuel Smiles's *Life of George Stephenson* which had appeared in the same year, the text also turns to Stephenson's childhood. It professes the goal to show Stephenson's life "from the time when he was a poor cow-boy on the fields of Northumberland until he reached one of the highest and most distinguished positions to which honourable labour can attain, we shall see that 'to persevere' in a good cause meant with him, as it may mean with all others, 'to succeed'" (George Stephenson. Part I, *LH*, 17 Dec 1857, 811). Stephenson, who is frequently referred to by his childhood nick-name "Geordie Stevie" (ibid.) in the text, is established as coming from a poor yet pious and industrious family. His development into one of Britain's foremost engineers, foreshadowed in broad strokes in the above excerpt, then emphasises the fact that his humble origin could not hold him back. Similar to the above examples, his talent is already visible in his early self: "in little Geordie Stevie's essays in modellings [...], may we trace the birth of that mechanical ingenuity for which the future railway engineer was so eminently distinguished" (ibid., 811–812). The use of the term "mechanical" is worth noting in this context, as it can be seen as a term used to relate the prominent engineer to the everyday life of the intended readers, many of whom

60 It is worth noting that prominent examples of heroic engineers in *LH* come from the textile industry (such as Fontaine or Jacquard), which was of crucial importance both for British industrialisation as a whole as well as for the formation of the notion of the working class and as a major field of employment for women. As Jenkins notes, "textiles played the major role in initial industrial transition in terms of technique and organization". David T. Jenkins: The Textile Industries, Oxford 1994, p. IX–X. As the major consumer good after food, "the textile industry formed a significant part of manufacturing activity and participated in the expansion of the industrial sector". Ibid., p. XXXIV. However, the industry also had socio-political importance. The Factory Act of 1833, which was enacted in relation to the "desire to improve the health and education of child workers" (Robert Glen: Textile Industry, in: Sally Mitchell (ed.): Victorian Britain, New York/London 1988, p. 794), was first only applied to textile factories; furthermore, the industry was at the forefront of the trade union movement and "many factories became centres of social and cultural events for workers. [...] In myriad ways, therefore, the Victorian textile industry provided an important symbol for the new industrial age." Ibid.

would have been manual labourers or mechanics. This connection, even likeness, between engineer and working class man is, in the introduction of the biographical sketch, emphasised even more strongly. Here, the text quotes Stephenson himself speaking to the Leeds Mechanics' Institution in 1847 as a "fellow mechanic" (ibid., 811) and saying: "'I stand among you but as a humble mechanic. I have risen from a lower level than the meanest person here, and all that I have been enabled to accomplish in the course of my life has been done through Perseverance'" (ibid.).[61] Thereby, the text depicts Stephenson as being akin to the workers he addresses yet having progressed through the exertion of perseverance. This virtue is stressed throughout the articles and drawn on as the reason for Stephenson's ultimate success[62] but also implies that the "struggling hero" (George Stephenson. Part II, *LH*, 24 Dec 1857, 829) had to overcome obstacles.[63] Thus, he is shown as working in the local colliery from an early age, accomplishing his goal of becoming an engine-man through "perseverance and industry" (George Stephenson. Part I, *LH*, 17 Dec 1857, 812), which "far from causing him to relax in his habits of industry, only served to stimulate him to fresh exertion" (ibid.). However, not only his professional life is depicted as affected by his discipline, but also his private life: "while too many of his companions were spending their spare time and money in drinking-bouts, gambling, and dog and cock-fighting, Geordie Stevie was busy mastering the next step of his onward progress" (ibid.). In the description of Stephenson's success, his diligence and hard-working nature are emphasised, yet also the fact that he did not work on his railway designs for his own benefit and the want of fame, but first and foremost for the good of his community as he wanted to make the work processes in Killingworth easier. His final success in bringing the steam-locomotive to wide-spread use and setting the subsequent transportation revolution in motion is then dealt with only briefly.

Thus, the text's main emphasis is clearly on the didactic message which could best be illustrated through Stephenson's years before fame: through diligent work, temperance and perseverance, anyone can improve. Its intent to inspire readers of the working classes to similar efforts also surfaces in the frequent connections the text draws to the working reality of the past and the present: his untiring effort to teach himself is called a "weary and laborious task, and one whose

61 This is further stressed in the following excerpt: "In his retirement, his thoughts were often with the workers, from whom he had ascended. He was always ready to aid in the formation of a mechanics' institution, or to give advice to individual members of his class." George Stephenson. Part II, *LH*, 24 Dec 1857, 831.

62 This notion, however, contradicts to a certain degree the legend-like build-up of Stephenson's childhood narration which also heavily draws on him being extraordinarily talented.

63 The idea of a frustrating journey towards success of scientists and inventors can be seen in many of the other texts as well. One example is the aforementioned Bernard Palissy, who is shown as being marked by "trails and heroic sufferings" (An Artist in Earth, *LH*, 11 Nov 1852, 732) on his way towards his final discovery.

difficulties a working man of the present days might find it hard to estimate" (ibid., 814). Not only does this stress Stephenson's persevering nature, but also indicates to the reader that the text considers their own working environment less harsh. This notion is then authenticated through Stephenson himself, who "before he died, was able with pleasure to point to the unspeakable advantages which the mechanic of to-day possesses compared with the workman of his youth" (ibid.). Implicitly referring to Mechanics' Institutes and their libraries, but perhaps also to informational tracts published by the RTS, the text, through the example of the "struggling hero" Stephenson, clearly offers the engineer as a role model to its readership. The comparison between ordinary mechanics and Stephenson thus establishes a common identity which could possibly motivate the workers among *LH*'s readership to emulate Stephenson's behaviour, or at least his attitude towards self-improvement and work. The final paragraph of the text illustrates this fittingly, and adds a religious component to the narration, which had thus far been missing from Stephenson's biography:

> We do not promise to all working men who shall husband their resources and apply their power as he did, a similar social elevation, but 'by aiming' – to use a proverbial phrase – 'at a silk gown, they will gain a sleeve of it.' Perseverance and intelligent industry will certainly procure a working man a better status than he previously enjoyed, and will at all events advance him to the front rank of his own class. Now, in the attainment of such an object there is no better help than true piety. The self-denial, temperance, and industry which religion inspires, often become powerful levers and helps to a man's success in this world; for godliness has great gain, having the promise of the life that now is, as well as of that which is to come. (George Stephenson. Part II, *LH*, 24 Dec 1857, 831)

These final sentences add a notion of religious devotion to Stephenson's biography,[64] which is not present in Smiles's text, yet seems to be indispensable for its didactic message, which calls for the readers to be industrious, temperate and pious.[65]

---

64 A similar addition can be found in Bertie Orr's "The Requiem of George Stephenson", a poem which appeared in February 1899. The poem is written from the perspective of a steam train that thanks Stephenson who "gave us life and strength, speed and power and fame". The Requiem of George Stephenson, *LH*, Feb 1899, 261. This line is repeated in every stanza with slight alterations thanking the engineer for "patience" and "riches" (ibid.) as well. However, not only Stephenson, the engine's "creator" is praised, but ultimately "our creator's God". Ibid. This reference to god, which appears in every stanza, emphasises that the work conducted by Stephenson, though extraordinary in its own form of 'creation', is ultimately only possible within the framework of god's creation.

65 In a subsequent number of *LH* in May 1858, an article refers back to this text and its source material, Smiles's biography of Stephenson, and distinctly criticises the fact that Smiles does not incorporate religion into his depiction of Stephenson: "[W]e could have wished something more to have been added as to his hopes for the eternal world, and their foundation. He who gains a crown of life, and access to that river of holy pleasures which shall roll on for ever, is, after all, the only truly successful man; all success short of this is failure." Lessons from the Life of George Stephenson, *LH*, 12 May 1858, 301.

The focus on the process of self-improvement, on the character and selfless nature of the work of engineers rather than the final outcome, can be seen in the other articles in *LH* which portray heroes of industry. Many of the texts were unillustrated and those which contained illustrations showed the engineers as established public figures rather than in their early career, which was the focus of the narration of the texts. The Scottish inventor William Fairbairn is, for example, shown in a formal portrait adapted "from a photograph by H.J. Whitlock" (cf. The Late Sir William Fairbairn, *LH*, 28 Apr 1877, 264) and an article about Watt shows the illustration of his monument in Westminster Abbey (cf. Watt and the Steam Engine, *LH*, 30 April 1854, 760). While the texts emphasise the likeness of the men to other manual labourers, the illustration emphasises their public achievements. This disruption of the narrative can however also be seen as giving the readers something to aspire to.

On the whole, the depiction of "the great heroes of modern industry" (The Late Sir William Fairbairn, *LH*, 28 Apr 1877, 262) are shown, as the example of Stephenson has illustrated, as "fellow mechanics", as men who can be compared to the common worker, at least in the way they started out their careers. Thereby, *LH* closely aligns itself with the idea of industrious heroism as brought forth most prominently by Samuel Smiles, and propagates individual self-improvement as a means of contributing to a greater collective. At the same time, *LH* frequently tries to add religious piety as an integral feature to industriousness, a facet which could not be found in Smiles's original considerations. Furthermore, the heroism of science and industry is often constructed directly in contrast to established military heroism as in the following excerpt:

> Whenever it happens that anything worth gaining is to be gained by labour and peril, it is sure to happen also that the man who will perform the labour and dare the peril makes his appearance and enters upon his *mission.* [...] there is probably no walk of life which has not produced its heroes and its *martyrs*, who have exercised as much courage and self-devotion in the pursuit of their object as the *soldier* who marches cooly against the cannon of the foe. There is a chivalry with which warfare has nothing to do; it may be a *nobler* and meaner kind, according to the motive which incites it to action and the end it proposes to itself [...]. (The Story of the First English Silk-Mill, *LH*, 18 Dec 1856, 806, emphases mine)

The image of soldiers "march[ing] cooly" juxtaposed with the "nobler" kind of heroism of industry implies different qualities. While the soldiers are bound to situational heroism and seem to be facing inevitable death, the industrious heroism presented in the text seems to be less singular, more of a general attitude and future-oriented. Furthermore, the choice of words also roots this form of heroism in religion. Invention and technological developments are called a "mission", the field produces "heroes and [...] martyrs".

By adding a religious level, *LH* thus presents the heroism of science and technology as a collective form of heroism, which is rooted in piety and god-givenness ("our creator's god", Orr: The Requiem of George Stephenson, *LH*, Feb

1899, 261). At the same time, the domain offers a potential for identification to the audience and can be read as a didactic means to motivate readers to educate themselves, whether through Mechanics' Institutes (as hinted at in the biographical text about George Stephenson), or independently following the examples of many of the presented industrious heroes. The periodical can thus be seen as locating itself within this realm of self-improvement with the texts and the role models it presents as educating means.

"Great Sacrifices" – the Heroic Explorer in Leisure Hour

While the domain of industry and technology in *LH* can be seen as one representing a form of collective work for society as a whole, the field of exploration displayed individual commitment to the progress of society and mankind. In the depiction of explorers such as John Franklin, who features as the foremost example, it is selflessness and suffering which are emphasised as the central characteristics of heroism. The fact that scientists exploring unknown areas of the globe were putting their own lives at risk in order to gain insight into the world, increase the knowledge of mankind at large and further the spread of civilisation was seen as "generous heroism" (Sir John Franklin's First Journey in the Polar Regions, *LH*, 1 Jan 1852, 11). Texts such as the one about "Franklin's First Journey in the Polar Regions" depicted the physical sacrifices the expedition teams had to make in great detail. One sequence, for example, describes in detail how the group, upon finding a musk-oxen after days of starvation, kills the animal and immediately starts to eat its intestines. The "hero" (ibid., 10) Franklin and his team are shown on a tour "of sufferings" (ibid.) in harsh weather, while the fact that, at that point in time, it was unclear whether or not the members of Franklin's last expedition were still alive elevates their suffering for a greater cause into the realm of spiritual heroism. The text strongly emphasises the expedition team's piety, informing the reader that "the party, previously to leaving London, had been furnished with a small collection of religious books […]" (ibid., 12). Through this reading material, it stresses that "[t]heir faith in Divine Providence had never forsaken them even in the depth of their miseries, and it proved a stimulus to exertion which nothing else could supply" (ibid.). The scientific expedition is thus almost presented as a religious mission and again depicts the belief in god – through providence – as the foundation to scientific endeavours.[66]

---

66 Other contributions depicting Franklin and his expedition as heroic are "Sir John Franklin and the Arctic Expeditions", *LH*, 26 Feb 1852; the poem "The Men that Have been Long Dead", which was subtitled "Lines Suggested by the Fate of Sir John Franklin and His Crews" and calls the expedition team "heroes of a higher grade […] slain in a noble strife" (The Men that Have been Long Dead, *LH*, 8 Feb 1855, 95); and "The Late Sir John Franklin" under "Varieties", *LH*, 25 Sep 1875.

The religious facet to exploration is emphasised even more strongly in texts which relate to expeditions in areas that might potentially be missionised. "Heroes of Australian Exploration", published in December 1886, serves as a valuable example for this. Again, the text stresses the "great sacrifices" (Heroes of Australian Exploration, *LH*, Dec 1886, 841) and the introductory paragraph points out that "[t]he records of success are saddened by many episodes of disaster and death" (ibid.). The "heroism and suffering" of the explorers which was conducted to "benefit mankind" (ibid.) is, in its representation in *LH*, mostly linked to the native population, which is depicted as uncivilised, hostile and violent. Among the examples in the text are the explorers Eyre, Leichardt, Bass and Flinders, Burke and Wills, and Kennedy. A clear line is drawn between those who act to "benefit mankind" and those who seek fame and money, such as John McDouall Stuart, whose expedition is prompted by a reward offered by the government of "two thousand pounds to the first person who should cross the continent" (ibid., 844). Stuart is said to have been "soon in the field to earn the money and to secure the fame" (ibid.). Those whose "heroism" the text praises, however, are men like Robert O'Hara Burke and William John Wills, who are described as possessing "dash and energy" but especially "talent and Christian fortitude" (ibid.). Set in a Christian context and contrasted with the representation of the natives as uncivilised, the death of men like Burke and Wills on their expedition almost converts their "heroism and suffering" into a form of martyrdom. The illustrations which accompany this specific article on Australian exploration again counterbalanced the narration. While the text focused on the hardship of the expeditions, the harsh natural conditions, lack of water, starvation and conflicts with the local population, the illustrations do not visualise these scenes.[67] Rather, the images are utilised to spread knowledge gained through the explorations and depict, for example, a "Grass Tree" (cf. ibid., 846) or "Silver-Stemmed Eucalypts" (cf. ibid., 843). Similarly, the monument erected in honour of Burke and Wills in Melbourne, which is depicted on the first page of the article (cf. ibid., 841), creates a tension with the discrediting of fame established in the text.

The representation of explorers in *LH* was firmly rooted in Christian faith and is thus established as a scientific form of mission. By emphasising the sufferings and sacrifices the explorers had to make, which often resulted in death, their heroism is shifted towards the realm of martyrdom. Similar strategies, if more pronounced, become visible in the representation of missionaries and their work.

67 Other publications for working and lower-middle class audiences had a different approach when it came to illustrating heroism visually. For example, *The Workman*, a large broadsheet publication set up and edited by the Methodist reformer and Temperance campaigner Thomas Bywater Smithies, confirmed the verbal representation of heroism visually with large illustrations of heroic acts (such as a miner saving others in a colliery accident). Cf. Christiane Hadamitzky / Barbara Korte: Everyday Heroism for the Victorian Industrial Classes, in: Simon Wendt (ed.): Extraordinary Ordinariness. Everyday Heroism in the United States, Germany, and Britain, 1800–2015, Frankfurt am Main 2016, pp. 53–78.

In the age of British colonial expansion, Christian missionary work played a central role. The idea of religious supremacy provided the colonists and missionaries with a sense of moral authority to conduct their work, turning their commanding and often cruel actions into humane acts of civilising aid. As Anna Johnston shows, the missionary activity was often involved in the first steps of imperial expansion and a "heightened sense of religiosity in Britain at this time ensured that Christianisation was seen as a crucial part of the colonising and civilising projects of the eighteenth and nineteenth centuries".[68] Since evangelicals were highly involved in missionary work, it is not surprising that *LH*, as a periodical published by an evangelical society, frequently featured articles on missionary work. As Law and Loyd note, *LH* had a "steady focus on overseas travel, colonial life and foreign mission fields".[69] In the context of this study with its focus on the semantics of the heroic, it is especially striking that the periodical so strongly emphasises these "initial steps of imperial expansion"[70] in its portrayal of missionary heroes. Those missionaries called heroic are less frequently men and women who work on established missions, but predominantly groups of missionaries in new mission fields and during initial – and often hostile – contact with the indigenous population. Thus, *LH* portrays missionary heroes predominantly at the stage of their work at which the potential for narratives of suffering and individual sacrifice was highest.

The missionaries, in significant contrast to the engineers discussed above, are seldom depicted as being similar to the readers, but are often presented in saintly terms. "The Surgeon Missionary", a text about Richard Williams, a missionary in Patagonia, describes its protagonist as showing "indications of the coming man" (The Surgeon Missinary, *LH*, 23 Mar 1854, 186) from an early age onwards. His true piety however, so the text, is only revealed later in life; he becomes a surgeon and "appear[s] to have been decidedly sceptical and undevout" (ibid.). However, Williams is then said to have had visitations both physical and spiritual which, as a form of godly influence, lead to his decision to take up missionary work. Subsequently, the text identifies his activities in the mission in Terra Del Fuego as "Christian heroism" (ibid., 190), which is characterised through "manly piety, unquenchable zeal, victorious faith, serene submission, unfaltering fidelity, and divine repose" (ibid.). Not only is the work of the medical man on his mission described as deeply religious, but it is also marked as a distinctly *male* action. This idea of devout manliness is based on faith in a higher power and acceptance of suffering in which life is beyond individual control, but lies in the

68 Anna Johnston: Missionary Writing and Empire 1800–1860, Cambridge 2003, p. 23.
69 Law / Loyd: Leisure Hour, p. 256.
70 Johnston: Missionary Writing, p. 13.

hand of god.[71] The situation in Argentina is described as hostile, the missionaries have to flee from the natives and constantly be on guard. Yet these hardships are presented as worthwhile, since the men perceive themselves to be performing god's work and believe that the civilising forces of Christianity will succeed in the end: "this region is certainly not more wild and barbarous than our own island was when first visited by Christian missionaries in the days of the Caesars; and had the early disciples reasoned as some do now, this land would never have been visited by the light of sacred and civilizing truth" (ibid., 189). By comparing Patagonia to the pre-Christian era of Britain, the text thus gives proof for the civilising effect of (Christian) religion and creates a connection to the reality of the readers. In depicting Britain as having been civilised – and having maintained this state – through collective piety, the readers themselves are implicitly included in this act of civilisatory maintenance.

As a civilising force, missionary work is then, in direct comparison, characterised as even superior to the work of explorers such as those discussed above; referring to a text published earlier in the year about French arctic explorer Joseph René Bellot, the article notes that "the present work contains the record of heroism and an enthusiasm equally ardent [to that of Bellot], but consecrated to far higher and nobler objects" (ibid., 186). Though both men venture into previously unknown territory, it is the distinct Christian mission which makes Williams's work "higher and nobler". Bellot, whose exploration implies an element of *curiositas* and also denotes a form of adventure spirit, lacks religious motivation as a layer of meaning.

The idea of nobility was also employed in a text about the mission in Terra del Fuego a year earlier. "A Three Months' Captivity among the Giants of Patagonia" refers to the last expedition of General Gardiner in 1850, a former naval officer who later in life became a missionary. Accompanied amongst others by the aforementioned Richard Williams, Gardiner was stranded on an island in the Terra del Fuego archipelago. Due to conflicts with the native population and sparse resources, none of the party survived in the end. The men's actions are then characterised as follows: "[T]here has been in all benevolent minds but one feeling of admiration inspired by the noble heroism, the pure unselfish devotion, the uncomplaining endurance, and the *victorious* faith exhibited by Captain Gardiner and his companions in tribulation" (A Three Months' Captivity among the Giants of Patagonia, *LH*, 26 May 1853, 347). Under "circumstances the most humiliating and awful that can be conceived", Gardiner and his men still showed "steady zeal and Christian bravery" (ibid., 347). The choice of words in both quotes is striking. All of the characteristics are additionally qualified; "heroism", "devotion", "endurance", "faith", "zeal" and "bravery" are not enough on their

[71] The faith in divine providence is a recurring theme in *LH*'s representation of the heroic and can be found in all domains.

own, they are qualified as "noble", "pure", "unselfish", "uncomplaining", "victorious", "steady" and "Christian". The last qualifier is especially pertinent since bravery, especially in the context of a military man like Gardiner (his naval career significantly is not alluded to in the text, but could have been known to the readers), might be associated with violence and self-defence. The qualifier "Christian" however, seems to differentiate the bravery from the more adventurous idea of 'pluck' and turns it into a passive quality in line with the other characteristics, which all seem to imply silent suffering rather than active involvement. Whereas devotion and endurance both indicate a submissive attitude, faith, in contrast, is depicted as very active, it is *victorious*. Especially given the fact that all members of the mission party die, the idea of a victory of the Christian faith is striking. The idea of a victorious death for the idea of Christianity thus places the "noble heroism" of the missionary expedition in the realm of martyrdom.

The missionaries presented in the language of the heroic are almost exclusively well-known male missionaries.[72] In their focus on the early stages of missionary contact with the indigenous population, the texts stress the danger the missionaries place themselves in and the acceptance of their 'fate'. Though this passivity in regard to their own fate does not comply with traditional ideas of manliness, this is presented as a distinctly male Christian heroism in the texts. Throughout the 1850s, 60s and 70s, texts on missionaries in all regions of the world can be found in *LH*. A text about Henry Martin's missionary efforts in India praises his "heroic composure" (Some Traces of Henry Martin, the Missionary, *LH*, 25 Nov 1858, 749) and a strong emphasis is put on him being "alone and unprotected [...] in the midst of fanatical and often ferocious heathens" (ibid.). Similarly, texts on Livingstone and his work in Africa stress the "heroic patience he manifested under the suffering and disappointment" (Dr. Livingstone, *LH*, 25 Jun 1868, 480). The strong emphasis on the missionaries' vulnerability and suffering in combination with vocabulary of the heroic then seems to turn the missionaries' very existence into heroism. The fact that they, in spite of this struggling existence, then perform their duty as disseminators of religion adds to their heroicity. One text thus praises "Livingstone's Heroic Spirit of Duty" (Varieties, *LH*, 27 Mar 1875, 208), another celebrates the "Christian labourer['s] [...] noble self-devotion and steadfastness of purpose" (Dr. Living-

72 As Jeffrey Cox shows, most missionary literature in the early nineteenth century focused on male missionaries. Even missionary wives were omitted in the representation of missionary life, although they were much more common than independent female missionaries. An emerging female presence in missionary writing was possible in relation to domestic issues from the middle of the century: "The male missionary hero was a central figure in all of this literature. Missionary wives were largely but not entirely absent from the genre until the mid-century, when they began to develop a niche for themselves in the literature on the Indian household." Jeffrey Cox: The British Missionary Enterprise Since 1700, London 2007, 112.

stone, *LH*, 25 Jun 1868, 480).[73] Similarly, Martin is valued for always putting "the objects of his mission" before everything else (Henry Martin, the Missionary, *LH*, 25 Nov 1858, 749).

The subjects of the missionaries' endeavours, the indigenous population of the various countries, only ever feature as stereotypes, as an uncivilised cultural other, which reaffirms the missionaries' heroism. The texts present them as hostile upon first contact, and among the texts about missionary heroes almost none can be found which narrate a development or a growing connection between the missionaries and the native population. In the rare instances in which a development is mentioned, it is never described in detail and the focus remains on the perceived savageness upon contact. Shortly after Fiji had been added to the British Empire in 1874, a text describes British missionary work as follows:

> As in New Zealand, so in this new possession, the dark rule of cannibalism was first broken by the advent of unarmed missionaries preaching the gospel of Christ in its simplicity. The conquest of Fiji from savagery to comparative civilisation will always remain among the most heroic chapters in the history of missions. (Fiji, *LH*, 16 Jan 1875, 39)

Though describing a positive development, the way it is phrased still emphasises the negative state, the "dark rule of cannibalism". Significantly, the missionaries are, again, shown as vulnerable, even more so in a cannibalistic environment, and seem to have broken the "dark rule" by the mere power of the gospel.

The overall focus on male missionaries is even strengthened by a singular exception. "The Missionary's Wife" in 1863 describes the effect that the death of Livingstone's wife had on him. Having established beforehand that Livingstone's "Christian heroism" (The Missionary's Wife, *LH*, 10 Jan 1863, 31) had been tested by many years of suffering and deprivation, the text quotes from one of Livingstone's letters:

> "[…] I must confess that this heavy stroke quite takes the heart out of me. Everything else that has happened only made me more determined to overcome, but with this sad stroke I feel crushed and void of strength. […] I try to bow to the blow as from our Heavenly Father, who orders all things for us. […] I shall do my duty still, but it is with a darkened horizon I set about it […]." (ibid., 32)

It seems that the loss of Livingstone's wife, though lamented in the article as well, is considered an unnecessary suffering put on the missionary whose profession has him suffering already. The text then significantly ends with an appeal to other wives of missionaries:

---

73 Livingstone has been described as "the supreme example of self-help". MacKenzie, Popular Imperialism, p. 121. The topos of self-improvement, which had been employed so heavily regarding engineers in *LH*, is not utilised in the same extent in relation to Livingstone and other missionaries. Though also stressing the importance of perseverance in his efforts, the Christian element is foregrounded and given as the motivation and foundation of Livingstone's heroism.

> We do not counsel the same perilous devotion to every woman who has a hero for a husband. For the majority, the fireside is not only the fittest, but the most honourable place; and certainly the rough trials of the explorer's life are not those to which a woman should rashly expose herself. (ibid.)

Obviously considering women to be not fit for work in the missionary field, the text reminds female readers that their place should be at the *domestic* fireside in Britain and explicitly discourages the women to join their husbands abroad.[74] This dismissal of female sufficiency for the missionary field is significant in two ways: on the one hand, it does not acknowledge the reality of missionary work, in which women took an active role. As Frank Trentmann notes: "While religion legitimized women's role in the missionary movement, the actual work performed by women and their expanding public roles eventually came to challenge the moral and social boundaries that religious doctrine and institutions sought to uphold."[75] On the other hand, the explicit exclusion of women is remarkable given the fact that the male missionaries themselves have been described in heroic terms through characteristics which at the time were associated with the feminine: submission, suffering, and acceptance of one's fate.

In conclusion, a striking contrast could be observed in the depiction of the different heroes of civilisation in *LH*. The more secular forms of civilisatory progress, such as the lives of engineers, were clearly designed to inspire the readers to emulate the represented behaviour. In stressing the similarities between the everyday lives of men of the working classes and the beginnings of well-known engineers, the periodical created role models for the readers to identify with and imitate. Thus, they were encouraged, in the vein of Samuel Smiles's idea of self-help, to use their individual progress to contribute to the development of society as a whole. The herorization of missionaries' lives, however, refers back to a different idea of heroism, which is established with a greater distance placed between the represented hero and the recipients. The missionaries, often presented as almost martyr-like in their suffering and death, are meant to be praised for their dissemination of Christianity and their work to civilise heathen regions of the world; however, their lives are not used didactically to inspire imitation. Presented as incarnations of the "coming man", the missionaries are clearly shown as different from the readers and thus nearer to the idea of a messianic hero who

74 The text does not consider the possibility of a woman independently working as a missionary without a husband. This might, however, be due to the context of the article dealing with a married couple.

75 Frank Trentmann: Paradoxes of Civil Society. New Perspectives on Modern German and British History, New York 2003, p. 215. For further information on the female involvement in missionary work see for example Rhonda Anne Semple: Missionary Women. Gender, Professionalism, and the Victorian Idea of Christian Mission, Woodbridge 2003; Cox: Missionary Enterprise (especially chapters 5, 8 and 9); Robert A. Bickers / Rosemary Seton: Missionary Encounters, London 2013 or Rosemary Seton: Western Daughters in Eastern Lands. British Missionary Women in Asia, Santa Barbara 2013.

can shape society and lead others – those others being the 'uncivilised' communities. Though both are presented as catalysts of civilisation, the different types of heroes of civilisation are constructed with a significantly dissimilar distance between hero and community. The missionaries, in their description as saint-like, are distanced from the readership, and this distance is strongly marked in terms of religion. Whereas a religious level had to be added somewhat artificially to the achievements of secular engineers and explorers, the martyr-like missionaries are moved into the higher realm and thus removed as potential identificatory role models for the readers. The focus on the early stages of missionary engagement, the removed foreign setting and the often fatal outcome for the missionaries allowed for a herorization which did not need to be concerned with the integration of the missionaries into the everyday world. Thus, the allocation of hero-status to missionaries fulfilled a decidedly religious didactic function. In the emphasis of the suffering and even death of the missionaries *for Christian civilisation* as a whole, it created a sense of obligation which also reflects on the relation between the represented heroes and the readers. Though for the benefit of the entire religious community, their heroic actions are not imitable ones in the environment of the readers and construct a hierarchical order. The heroic agency is exclusively on the side of the missionaries – though materialising in a passive suffering – while the readership is only present as a recipient.

Explorers in Fraser's Magazine

Considering the dissimilar readership that *FM* was aimed at, it is not surprising that scientists, missionaries and explorers are only rarely heroised on the pages of the magazine. In one of the few examples, Franklin is labelled the "arctic Hero" (Franklin's Fate, and the Voyage of the "Fox", *FM*, Feb 1860, 227), but detailed descriptions of heroic acts on expedition can seldom be found. In the following, I will briefly discuss one of the rare exceptions since it shows a strikingly different depiction of explorers than *LH*. In December 1880, *FM* published a biographical account of Jacques Cartier by Annie Walker under the headline "A Forgotten Hero". While *LH* had focused on the suffering of the explorers and missionaries and the harsh conditions of their mission, *FM* depicts Cartier's travels to Canada in an overwhelmingly positive light. The Frenchman is shown as a bold and confident man whose vision is to explore unknown territories. Having secured financial means for his expedition, he and his crew set out for Canada. While any description of the travels there and the possible hardships the journey might have entailed are omitted, the text describes impressions of the new country and praises the wonders of the Canadian landscape. While the interaction of missionaries with the local population represented in *LH* had always been hostile and dangerous for the religious explorers, Cartier and his men are welcomed by "some Friendly Indians" who even "entrust to him two boys (apparently of the chief's family) to be taken to France" (Walker: A Forgotten Hero, *FM*, Dec 1880, 776). Everywhere the crew travels, they are greeted with "presents of fruit, maize and fish" or "tremendous uproar of joy" (ibid., 777): "a thousand persons [...] were assembled, dancing and singing tumultuously" (ibid., 779). Though the natives are described as inferior, "almost childish *savages*, wild men" (ibid., 777), they are "friendly, hospitable, confiding" (ibid.).

Despite the allusion to a period of "suffering" (ibid., 782) during the winter months caused by the weather, this is only mentioned in passing and the emphasis of the text lies clearly on the successful civilisatory act which Cartier and his men accomplished in establishing "a little stronghold of European power and civilisation in the midst of the primitive region" (ibid., 778). This one example can, of course, not be seen as a representative comparison with the far larger number of texts about explorers and missionaries in *LH*, yet it is nevertheless striking that "A Forgotten Hero" in *FM* portrays a successful act of exploration and Christianisation, while the texts in the evangelical publication published at the same time focus much more strongly on the suffering and sometimes even martyrdom of the explorers and missionaries and never describe a successful civilisation effort in the vocabulary of the heroic.

Civilisation through Politics

Large portions of *FM*'s content were devoted to politics. As the addresses to the readers have already shown, the periodical saw the discussion of political topics as at the centre of its identity. It is not surprising then that the political domain also plays a central role in examining the semantics of heroism in the magazine. However, specific political actors are seldom heroised; most frequently, the heroic is employed as a theoretical concept in line with Thomas Carlyle's thoughts on the subject and many of the texts explicitly evoke Carlyle to support their arguments. Over the decades, the constructive but also destructive potential of Carlylean heroes in politics is debated.

In the discussion of heroism in the political realm, the periodical makes one basic distinction, namely that between practical politics and political philosophy. Political heroes of the magazine's liking are exclusively situated in the latter realm. Thomas Hare, one of the few contributors who published under their names, in an 1860 article-series on political representation shows this distinction and its relation to heroism. In the first article of the series, "Representation in Practice and in Theory", Hare asserts that "[i]n our own days a remarkable difference is to be found between the sentiments and opinions of the literary school of political thought and those of professional politicians" (Hare: Representation in Practice and in Theory, *FM*, Feb 1860, 188). Clearly favouring the "literary school", he further states that:

> It is in literature, poetry, and the other kindred arts, where at least a certain manliness of temper, and liberty to follow truth, prevails or might prevail, that the world's chosen souls do now chiefly take refuge, and attempt what 'worship of beautiful' may still be possible for them; and it is true that this external school have on many subjects adopted views as distinguished by their breadth, as those of the professional politicians are noticeable for their narrowness and technicality. (ibid., 188–189)

Highly reminiscent of Carlyle's *On Heroes*, the "professional politicians" are degraded to mere mechanics dealing with the "technicality", while the "literary school of political thought" possesses a deeper insight into the matters. They "follow truth" and "worship" the beautiful. Evoking the idea of the "Hero as Poet", Hare argues that, in the technicality of political life, the spiritual component has gone missing, the professional politicians do "not go beyond the mechanical" (ibid., 189), they lack ambition and a vision to further society. While Carlyle had depicted the poet as the only one still able to see the divine in the modern world, Hare transfers this to the political stage by calling the representatives of a literary school the true politicians, who can still see and appreciate the "beautiful". In the course of the article, Hare makes this transfer even more obvious when he argues that good politicians are required

> to be sincere. [...] The test of *reality* and *sincerity* of being what they pretend to be, and performing what they are designed to do, may be fairly and instructively applied to the momentous subject of our representative institutions, and to the amendments which they need. In the application of such tests we need the aid of minds that look beneath the surface of things and examine their spirit and tendencies. From the *light which these throw* upon the inquiry, it will appear that so far as the future can be contemplated, our hope lies in adherence far less to the outward and literal form, than to the true spirit of the institution. (ibid., 190, emphases mine)

Hare here clearly employs the rhetoric of Carlyle's own considerations on heroism and describes the politicians which the country needs as sincere, possessing superior insight, a connection to the "true spirit" (ibid.), as bringers of light. He further adds that the politician should understand his work not as a mere profession, but as a divine right and thus should perceive his work not only as practical, but spiritual as well.[76] In his critique of the contemporary political profession, he then directly calls for heroism. The problems, he believes, originate in the fact that practical politicians possess "[n]o vision in the head; heroism, faith, devout insight to discern what is needful, noble courage to do it" (ibid., 191). "Not seeing eyes [can be found] there, but spectacles constitutionally ground, which to the unwary, seem to see" (ibid.). In the following articles of Hare's "Representation" series, he continually draws on Carlyle's concept, citing from *On Heroes* (cf. Hare: Representation in Practice and in Theory, *FM*, Apr 1860,

[76] Again drawing on Carlyle, Hare argues that "[t]he Spiritual everywhere originates the Practical [...]. Everywhere the things which have had an existence among men have first of all had to have a truth and within them, and were not semblances but realities". Representation in Practice and in Theory, *FM*, Feb 1860, 189.

527), naming "sincerity the guide" to good politics (ibid., 535) or calling for a hero to unite the political chaos (cf. ibid.). However, Hare also sees that the concept faces problems, since parliament offers "no career [to the] noble hero" (Hare: Representation, Feb 1860, 194). He attributes the source of this problem to the secularisation of society which he, again in the direct words of Carlyle, fears does "not bid very fair to bring nations back to the ways of God" (ibid., 196). And so Hare closes one article by stating that "political as well as religious regeneration must be in the person" (ibid., 204) in order to adequately represent their country: "As he [the statesman] succeeds in his work, so his labours become beneficial to mankind; he develops and cultivates all their highest powers, and 'it is the noble people that make the noble government'" (ibid.).

Thus, one year after the publication of Darwin's *On the Origin of Species*, Hare argues in opposition to the developing division of secular and spiritual. In his demand for a hero-politician, a revolt against the new, secular and science-oriented way of conducting affairs, but also an attempt to fight the lack of orientation and guidance can be observed. The worldview of many had been shaken by the scientific theories of the mid-nineteenth century. After the realisation that "nature propagates species and is careless about individuals",[77] the disorientation led to many people looking even more desperately for a guiding figure, an individual, a hero who would unite the divided society and show the confused and disoriented people what the 'truth', what 'reality' was.[78]

This spiritual undertone can be observed in many other articles which relate politics and heroism. For example, "Working Men's Clubs and Institutes" in 1865 discusses how the situation of the working classes could be improved through political means. Again referring to Carlyle, the text finally resolves that this can only be achieved through

> *heroic perseverance*, against various forms of social, legal, and political evil. [...] Mr. Carlyle's [...] *prophet soul* will take from it, we trust, some of that comfort which he surely deserves, [...] for bringing about the improved state of affairs which we now invite our readers to perpend and promote, acknowledging, meanwhile, the existence of such improvement with humble thankfulness to the *Author of all Good.* (Working Men's Clubs, *FM*, Mar 1865, 395, emphases mine)

Heroic political acts, so the text argues, can only be achieved if rooted in a spiritual notion of society which needs to be mediated to the mass of society by a prophet-like hero figure. In this case embodied by Carlyle himself, the "prophet soul" is necessary as a political actor. Furthermore, the text positions itself against propagators of self-help such as Samuel Smiles and argues that working men need to be guided by someone more able than themselves.

---

77 Owen Chadwick: The Secularization of the European Mind in the Nineteenth Century, Cambridge 1975, p. 253.

78 In the sense of Schindler et al., this liminal guiding figure acts as a "meaning maker" (Schindler et al.: Admiration, p. 99) for the specific group.

In contrast to the idea of a hero-politician rooted in the spirit of political philosophy, practical politicians are depicted by many contributors in *FM* as decidedly non-heroic if compared to the idea of a visionary hero in the vein of Carlyle. "On the Comparative Stupidity of Politicians" – the title from the outset implies a rather critical view of the political personnel – states that "[t]he great majority of even prominent politicians have just the gifts which make a man conspicuous in a town council or a board of guardians; physical energy, moral persistency, and ideas on a level with those of their fellows" (On the Comparative Stupidity of Politicans, *FM*, Oct 1877, 486). What might have been considered heroic in *CJ*, the idea of being morally persistent and "on a level with those of their fellows", is depicted as decidedly non-heroic in the context of *FM* and interpreted as "second rate" (ibid., 489) mediocrity:

> It is chiefly the second-rate order of minds and characters that betake themselves now to politics in England [...]. For this reason, probably, whenever an occasion demands a hero in politics, he has been seldom found in the walks of *professional* statesmanship. The national crisis which asks for a *deliverer*, finds him not among those who have been deteriorated and dwarfed by the *ordinary* work, but in a man who has lived among *nobler ideas* and associations, and cultivated a larger and more liberal nature. (ibid., emphases mine)

Again, this quote illustrates the clear distinction between the "ordinary" and "professional" work of practical politicians and the "nobler" sphere in which the hero-politician seems to be situated. Whereas the former produces only "figure head[s]", it is the latter which can produce a real "leader" (ibid., 486). Proverbial size is also repeatedly used as a marker for political vision. The practical politicians are "dwarfed" or collectively called a "company of dwarfs"[79] (ibid., 486), while the ideal politician is called "great" (ibid., 487).

> The natural and almost necessary *inferiority of politicians* as a class, is compatible with the *unsurpassed intellectual and moral greatness of statesmanship* of the highest class. Men are not wanting in the history of any country, least of all in that of ours, and they have representatives among us now, who have found or made work for themselves to do which taxes the very highest gifts, and in the doing of which the very humblest and most commonplace allies and instruments acquire a sort of transfiguration. Their appearance and exertions mark the high-water point in the national life, an epoch of brief but fruitful work, an *epoch of civil heroism*. Even the men who counted for much when they followed a *great leader*, become mere cyphers when the figure which stood at their head is removed. (ibid., 490, emphases mine)

---

79 The idea of being in a company of proverbial dwarfs is then presented as a vicious circle: "In other rods, the finest man is habitually in the presence of its inferiors, whose ideas and impulses are to it what his daily beer was to Mr. Justice Maule, the instrumentality with which he brought himself down to the level of his work." On the Comparative Stupidity of Politicians, *FM*, Oct 1877, 488.

This statement sums up the argument of the text: while practical politicians are "inferior" and "commonplace", it is the "civil heroism" of great statesmen which shapes the history of a country and distinguishes it. A "great leader" can thus only be found in the realm of the great statesmen and not among the humbler ranks of the mass of common society.

However, the "mechanical" way in which practical politicians execute their duty is seen by many as just as necessary as the visionary ideas of the political hero. "Derbyism" in 1854 states that

> we do have a Government composed, not perhaps of heroes, but at least of competent men, versed in the business of state, raised to their present station by ability in their several departments, tolerably free from class interest, and bound, in some tolerable measure, to consider government as duty, not as a prize, and to govern for the good of the whole nation. This is a good deal short of the ideal of Carlyle, and perhaps even of attainable perfection. But it is, at all events, more respectable, and more likely to put down faction, curb selfish interest, and unite us for the common good than anything we have seen. (Derbyism, *FM*, Jan 1854, 126)

The text stresses the very practical qualities, expert knowledge and experience in the operational sequences of politics which contributors like Hare had criticised. This practical politician, though not even "of attainable perfection", does not perceive his work as either spiritual or a calling, but as a rational and practical duty which requires certain skills. Thus, the motivation of the practical politician as described in the article is a very different one from that of the hero-politician depicted above. Whereas the hero is concerned with ideas, the practical politician is concerned with implementable solutions and is much more a common man and part of a collective than an extraordinary individual. This idea of rational sufficiency as opposed to spiritual grandeur is also brought forth in other articles. One contributor for example states that it would be better to have rational, practically oriented politicians at whom "we must not laugh with Mr. Carlyle; [...] they may stand in the way of a rising hero, but they may also stand in the way of a usurping rogue" (Whitelocke's Embassy to Sweden, *FM*, Mar 1855, 351). Pointing to the ability of heroic figures to destabilise existing order, the practically oriented politician might be presented as inflexible or narrow-minded, but is also a stabilising force.

Similar to some of the texts in the context of the Crimean War, heroism and hero-worship in politics were sometimes considered a possibly dangerous tool which could be used in the destabilisation of order. In this way "Is Monarchy an Anachronism?", which discusses the advantages and disadvantages of both monarchy and democracy, states that it is a most difficult thing in practice to choose the fittest public servant on all occasions, and still more difficult for a

> prejudiced and divided community to approve your choice; [...]. The leading politicians [...] never dream of selecting their wisest and ablest man; all that they hope to do is to find a convenient hero who happens to be popular at the time, or else to pitch upon some respectable Brown, Wilson, or Walker who has no great amount of prejudice

to encounter, and will cause the least division in their ranks. (Is Monarchy an Anachronism, *FM*, Oct 1875, 411)

The human habit of choosing role models and following them can therefore, so the text, be utilised for one's own profit with no regard to the common good. The hero can, in this political context, be deprived of all of his attributes and characteristics and merely satisfy the needs of people to both identify and look up to someone "who happens to be popular at the time" (ibid.), which seems to be the only unique feature left for the hero. Thus, the fact that hero-worship, as Carlyle puts it "never dies, nor can die", can in the political realm be exploited for the profit of individual parties which choose and style their representatives as heroes whom they assume the voters will admire. Whereas the Carlylean hero makes himself known to others through his distinguishing features and actions, the political hero as described in the article is turned into a 'great man' by others for their purposes, because it is "convenient" (ibid.) for them. However, this does not necessarily mean that the text dismisses the idea of political heroism. The problem with "convenient heroes" does not lie in the nature of the Carlylean heroism so often employed in a political context, but in the danger of people worshipping the wrong kinds of heroes, being guided by popularity rather than by heroic attributes as identified by Carlyle.

Though the necessity of practical politicians for the execution of everyday tasks is shown and their importance for political stability and the danger of 'false heroes' is brought up, the text still propounds that the mass of practical politicians need a leader who possesses "natural superiority" (ibid.) to guide them. Thus, the initial question of whether monarchy or democracy should be implemented is answered in favour of monarchy:

> Whatever be their faults, there are at present none who can undertake this duty so well as those who are born to it – the men whose fathers led our fathers – and, however much they may be distrusted, we shall nowhere find others to command equal confidence. Our much-abused aristocracy [...] would, if encouraged in their duty by a *loyal, confiding people*, supply the most successful social reformers. (ibid., 436, emphasis mine)

In returning to the idea of an elite of the few who rule the mass of "a loyal, confiding people", the text in the end also returns to the idea of a heroic leader guiding the masses.

Similarly, ideas of the emancipation of the lower classes are discussed in regard to heroic leadership. While some texts, such as the above-discussed essays on representation by Thomas Hare, acknowledge the growing demand of the lower-middle and working classes to voice their opinion and make a difference politically, *FM* remained clear in its opinion that the few should lead the masses, compliant with the idea of heroic leadership as developed by Carlyle. The fact that the periodical remained firm in its representation of guiding hero-figures can provide an explanation why the journal lost so many readers over the decades. In a changing political climate, the periodical's strong alliance to elitism had lost touch with its time.

Quoting Mill, Thomas Hare thus believes that democracy does not have to equal universal suffrage and political inclusion: "the best government (need it be said?) must be the government of the wise, and these must always be a few" (Hare: Representation, *FM*, Feb 1860, 195). While acknowledging the need to change the condition of the lower classes, he is nevertheless of the opinion that the change has to be brought about with the intellectual capacity of the upper class. To effect change, he wants "to bring to bear on the condition of the largest class of their fellow men intellectual power of the first order" (ibid., 197). Thereby, the "largest class" is not only put into the position of followers to a minority of leaders, but also discredited in terms of their intellectual potential. "Present Aspects of the Labour Question" in 1873 presents a similar opinion:

> I am aware that any hint about heroism in the higher towards the lower, will expose one to the taunt of hankering after paternal aid; but we submit that although the most advanced and prescient among us cannot tell what precise form future civilisation should assume, yet there is ever a vanguard and a rearguard in human progress. That the strong should help the weak, the enlightened instruct the ignorant, is something loftier than doing what we will with our own, and leaving ignorance and depravity to maxims of self-help. (Present Aspects of the Labour Question, *FM*, May 1873, 603)

While heroism is clearly situated in the realm of the higher classes, with the idea of a "vanguard and a rearguard" this is presented as a natural division which determined a person's place to begin with. Those who are gifted with the heroic qualities of insight and leadership "help the weak" and "instruct the ignorant". Interestingly, this is clearly distanced from the "maxims of self-help", which in this line of thinking can only be considered to be inferior, as a form of the 'weak helping the weak'.

As this overview has shown, *FM* clearly propagated that the progress of civilisation can only be brought about through the leadership of an elite over the mass of the people. This could be perceived on two levels. In the domain of politics, the practical or professional politicians are considered to be this mass of "mechanic" people who can only execute but never envision or inspire truly great politics. For this kind of visionary progress, a leader-figure modelled after the idea of Carlylean hero is considered necessary. In relation to class questions, the political leadership of a social elite is propagated. Though the condition of the lower classes is identified as deficient and worthy of change, the political impulses, so the contributors' opinion, need to come from the upper classes who, in an act of "heroism in the higher towards the lower", guide them towards a better life. Though the periodical acknowledged the achievements of the working classes, self-help, as propagated by Smiles and taken up by publications such as *CJ* and *LH*, is not considered a contribution to society as a whole, but – again comparable with the work of the professional politicians – considered "thoroughly practical" (Hare: Representation, *FM*, Feb 1860, 197).

5.5 *Everyday Heroism in* Leisure Hour

Although not as prominent as in *CJ*, everyday heroism also features in *LH*. Acts of lifesaving, by professionals as well as non-professionals, are awarded heroic status in particular. Thereby, a notion of a specific professional heroic identity of certain groups such as miners or lifeboat men emerges. However, the ambiguity towards hero-worship, which had already been visible in the different representations of heroes of civilisation, resurfaces in this domain as well. While acts of selflessness and lifesaving are encouraged and rewarded,[80] the near-celebrity status of figures such as Grace Darling is criticised. Thus, the representation of acts of lifesaving – in the vocabulary of the heroic – does not present itself as a clear-cut picture; on the one hand, risking one's life for others is presented as a heroic model to be emulated by others; on the other hand, the admiration of such deeds is seen as problematic. This can to some extent be explained through the shared features of religious worship and hero worship. Traditional notions of hero-worship, such as those put forward by Carlyle or Emerson, had a strong spiritual connotation which might have seemed blasphemous to *LH* given its evangelical background. This is voiced more strongly in relation to heroism of private life, which will be discussed later in this section.

Saving Lives

As an island nation, the sea, its opportunities but also its dangers, were continuously present in the British public. Fictional and factual tales of deadly peril at sea could commonly be found in adventure tales, but also in literary works for moral instruction[81] and on the pages of periodicals.

"A Few Days at Dover", for example, praises the lifeboat men of the coastal town. Embedded in travel writing, which gave readers information on the Kent-

---

80 The reward in some cases is twofold: for one, the representation of acts of lifesaving in the public medium of the periodical can be seen as a public honouring; additionally, the journal often also depicted men and women who had already received a public reward. In the series "The Montyon Prize. Its Heroes and Heroines" between 1889 and 1891, numerous winners of the French Montyon Prize were introduced to the readers. Significantly, this series is the only one which presents prize-winners for civil heroism and no life stories of English awardees of, for example, the Albert Medal, can be found.

81 The work on hero gift books, jointly conducted with Barbara Korte, has shown a large number of gift and prize books especially for boys in which exemplary (moral) heroism is mediated in the form of sea adventures. The values most frequently mediated to the young readers in this context are courage in the face of danger, the execution of duty and selflessness. Cf. Hadamitzky / Korte (eds): Hero Books.

ish town, its surroundings, its history as well as practical information for travellers, the text praises the "boatmen and their heroic daring in the hour of danger when life is only to be saved at the risk of life" (A Few Days at Dover, *LH*, 19 Aug 1852, 535). The genre and its close ties to tourism implied in the practical information established a relationship to readers' lives. The praise of the lifeboat men's selflessness is thus not only a moral tale, but also an assurance that readers could travel the region safely and would be rescued in case of danger at sea. The property of selflessness, of regarding one's own life less than that of another, is at the heart of this form of heroism. According to the text, this is the "truest heroism of all" because it "dares death to save life" (ibid.). "A Hero in Humble Life" in 1858 presents such an instance of a civilian act of rescue. It tells the story of a boat stranded before the Irish coast which cannot be safely reached from the shore. The townspeople who are watching the accident from the shore remain inactive, but for one fisherman who wants to try and save the stranded passengers. However, the majority of men remain unwilling to help: "It was the struggle of one brave and generous man against the terrors of the multitude" (A Hero in Humble Life, *LH*, 7 Oct 1858, 635). In the end, the exceptional individual wins over the mass and the fisherman succeeds in persuading enough men to get to the boat; he does so by evoking the idea of divine providence: "'tis the will of God to bless us, and to bring us back safe" (ibid.), he tells his peers – and this holds true, the men reach the boat, all passengers are saved and all fishermen return to the shore safely.

The instance of heroic lifesaving presented in this text then fits the definition of everyday heroism John Price gives. In his definition, the "term everyday heroism refers to acts of life-risking bravery, undertaken by otherwise ordinary individuals, largely in the course of their daily lives, and within quotidian surroundings".[82] Price thereby clearly draws a distinction between "acts of life-risking bravery" as shown by professionals and those of "otherwise ordinary individuals". And interestingly, when the "poor Irish fisherman" is subsequently called a hero in the text, this is done in comparison to an established professionalised form of heroism. "[He] was, we fear not to assert, as true a hero as ever shed his blood on a far-famed battle-field" (ibid., 636). Through referring to the established idea of military heroism, which often surfaces in an unreflected manner in *LH*, the fisherman's actions of persuading his peers and risking his life for others seems elevated in comparison. On the one hand, this is founded on the fact that he *voluntarily* comes to the help of the endangered passengers (while a soldier in battle cannot *choose* to risk his life, but is forced by circumstance), on the other hand, the distinction can also be seen in the divine support for the fisherman's deed. His promise that god will "bless" and "bring us back safe" holds true, shows god's support and the reward for trusting in god's providence. Thus, as so

82 Price: Everyday Heroism, p. 2.

often in *LH*, the act of heroism is also a religious one, since it is the dependence on and faith in god which gives the men the strength to conduct their act of heroism.

However, there are also entire professions which seem to have been predisposed to heroic acts in everyday life. Like *CJ*, *LH* identifies the heroic potential of the mining professions, though it does not heroise miners and their working class ethos to the same extent as *CJ* did. Similar to the examples of lifesaving at sea, these incidents of everyday heroism are compared to 'established' forms of heroism as well as related to religious faith. A note in the "Varieties" section in late 1880, for example, compares the actions of miners during an accident at Seaham Colliery to the fight of the British army in India:

> Colliery Accidents. – Canon Fleming, preaching at York Cathedral after the Seaham disaster, said: Much of England's greatness has been won by the courage of her sons. Last week we heard with pride of the resistless courage of our army in India, which achieved a decisive victory with comparatively small loss. We must not omit from the roll of heroism those brave fellows who won for us so many of our material comforts by the constant risk of their own lives. (Varieties, *LH*, 11 Dec 1880, 779)

Again, the selfless risking of one's life is what earns the miners their place on "the roll of heroism". However, the comparison to military heroism in this instance is not used as a demarcation of 'higher' and 'lower' heroism, but as an additional support of the worthiness of the miners' actions. Since the military struggle in India could be placed in the civilising and Christianising framework[83] of the colonial effort, *LH* did not apply its usual peace-oriented approach. With the dissemination and defence of religion as a motivation, the colonial conflicts were seen in a different light than for example the Crimean War. Therefore, the juxtaposition of the religiously motivated military heroism in India and the heroic risking of their lives of miners is a mutual validation with both forms of heroism being directed at the benefit of the (Christian) collective.

Whereas the link between the miners' heroism and the Christian faith was only given through the juxtaposition in the short note, the text "The Miners of Cornwall" makes this connection more prominently. Presented in the form of travel writing, as are many of the examples in *LH*, the text states: "A glance at the past history of Cornwall, had we time to devote to it, would show us […] the marked religious character of so large a section of the population" (The Miners of Cornwall, *LH*, 9 Feb 1860, 94). It is in this heightened *religious character* that the text sees the potential for heroism: "Among such a people we might be prepared for instances of heroism and self-denial, and many such are on record" (ibid.). With selflessness as the core virtue in the text, information is given on the dangers which the mining profession poses to the health of the workers. The

---

83 In its effects, the miners' work can be seen as a form of a civilising act as well, as it results in a heightened "material comfort" for the majority of the population. Varieties, *LH*, 11 Dec 1880, 799.

religious nature of this form of heroic selflessness is stressed by the fact that the text focuses on a minister as its prime example: toiling underground besides his ministerial duties, he is offered an easier position with better pay above ground. However, not regarding his own comfort, the minister declines the offer and suggests one of his co-workers for the job, since his comrade is in weak health and would benefit more from the transfer (cf. ibid.). The mining minister's heroism is thus not founded on a professional identity as a working-class miner, but on altruism and a feeling of responsibility for others based on religious faith.

Though heroic acts such as those noted above are portrayed in a positive – and religiously charged – light, other celebrated instances of lifesaving are criticised in *LH*. In this respect, the periodical displays an ambiguous attitude towards the heroic; on the one hand, the publication utilises its potential to create exemplary role models for the readers to emulate; on the other hand, it often falls back onto a traditional idea of heroism which includes the practice of hero-*worship*. With the evangelical RTS and its mission behind the periodical, the idea of worship of human individuals is treated with suspicion. Therefore, celebrated lifesavers such as Grace Darling, whose public hero status turned her into a celebrity of the day, are exposed as mere constructions. In 1883 an article takes the Fisheries Exhibition at South Kensington as a starting point to re-evaluate the famous incident on the Northumberland coast in 1838. Looking at the boat which Darling and her father had rowed and which is on display in the exhibition, the text recalls the "heroic story, so often told" (Grace Darling, *LH*, Jul 1883, 442). The criticism of heroism which follows is complicated by gender norms. The text for one criticises the fact that Grace Darling's daring actions were idealised in hindsight through the many medial representations, that her "spirit of heroism was nurtured" (ibid., 444) through continuous mediation and re-mediation. In addition, her heroism is diminished by presenting facts about the incident which belittle her involvement with regard to her gender. Quoting from *Grace Darling: Her True Story, from Unpublished Papers in Possession of Her Family* (published in 1880 with Hamilton, Adams & Co), it is stated that

> [m]ost writers have made Grace Darling and her father row back their boat with all the saved nine at once; yet among the many endeavours to *magnify a deed* which has no need of fiction one thing has generally been left unrecorded, which, while it *lessens the work the two* had to accomplish, materially enhances the risk they ran. (ibid., 443, emphases mine)

Though noting that the new information "materially enhances the risk" of Darling and her father, the text stresses the fact that common renditions of the incident "magnify" their actions and "lesse[n] the work" they did. This is emphasised even more strongly in relation to Darling's physical abilities; while it was often stressed how she surpassed her physical limitations *as a female* when rowing to the wrecked ship, the text states that Darling only rowed the first leg of the way while "there were able *men* to take her place" (ibid., emphasis mine) afterwards.

In presenting the "unpublished papers", the text thus not only tries to uncover the myth around Grace Darling and her act of heroism, but also attempts to show how she, as a woman, would not have been able to do what she was reported to have done. The text authenticated their reading of Darling and her presumed heroism through the fact that the material came from Darling's family and pronounces: "Had the exploit of Grace Darling always been described as rationally as *in the letter of her own father*, perhaps travellers would less often have been surprised by a disposition among the *boatmen of the neighbouring coast* to depreciate it" (ibid., emphases mine). Through the reference to the "boatmen of the neighbouring coast" and the evidence given by Darling's father, the text tries to reinterpret the almost mythical elevation of Darling and her deed to a more human scale and creates an idea of a more modest heroism suitable for women.

The text thus not only reveals a clear-cut idea of the limitations of female agency,[84] but also shows *LH*'s ambiguity towards hero narratives in everyday life. While some instances can be found in which daring acts were framed in the context of religious belief, texts such as the one about Grace Darling display the magazine's unease towards hero-worship and the celebration of actual individuals as more than exemplars.

Private Heroism of Piety

> Hero-Worship. – [...] the instinct of man's worship may find a true man worthy the adoration of all, and who reigns over the nations as their God and King. Every other species of man-worship is a robbery of him. It is a worship that belongs of right to the man Christ Jesus alone; the God whose throne is for ever and ever, and whom all the angels of God worship. (Varieties, *LH*, 3 May 1860, 288)

Similar ambiguous tendencies can be observed regarding the domain of everyday heroism in the private realm. On the one hand, vocabulary of the heroic is used to create an appealing image of morally and religiously approved behaviour worthy of emulation; on the other hand, quotes like the one above clearly show a general renunciation of the practice of hero-worship. Thus, *LH*'s conception of heroism in private life displays a tension: while acknowledging the group-binding and motivating power of heroism, the practice of hero-worship which it

[84] On the whole, *LH* portrayed traditional gender boundaries throughout the century, though a small number of exceptions can – as can be expected in a heterogeneous medium like the periodical – be found: The Lady Traveller, *LH*, 29 Jan 1852, 69–72 depicts Ida Pfeiffer's unfearing travels as heroic (cf. ibid., 69); significantly, the article is succeeded by a biographical sketch of the writer Felicia Hemans, whose female sensibility and its effects on her writing are deemed of a "higher heroism" (Felicia Hemans, *LH*, 29 Jan 1852: 73) than the public acts of men. In the succession of the texts, Ida Pfeiffer's more transgressive and active heroism is balanced by the private and morally elevated act of writing of Hemans.

may give rise to clashes with the religious ideal of worshipping only god. *CJ*, which had – for non-religious reasons – also struggled with the idea of hero-worship, had tried to resolve the problem by stripping heroes of their worship. By propagating the virtue of silent and private heroism which seemingly did not require an audience, the secular publication had tried to navigate the issues it had with the idea of worship and public honours. *LH*, however, as could be observed in relation to military heroism as well, did not attempt to re-interpret heroism as a concept and imbue it with its own set of meanings, but uses the vocabulary in ambiguous ways, in some instances as an encouraging didactic tool, in others assessing heroism as inappropriate. In stark contrast to *CJ*, where heroism played a central role in the periodical's mediation of its didactic content, heroism does not seem to feature prominently in *LH*'s didactic concept. Relying more strongly on religious ideas as vehicles of moral education, heroism often features unreflectedly as a term of validation in a religious context or – if reflected – is criticised.

If heroism can be found as a validating term for private moral excellence, it is thus often integrated in a religious rhetoric and supported by a religious motivation. For example, "Self-Possession in Moments of Peril" in 1853 connects the idea of heroism with the belief in divine providence. The text narrates short episodes in which believing men and women were saved due to their unbroken faith. Emphasising an example of female heroism, the text states that "[r]arely has there been a more striking instance of heroism, calmness, and presence of mind, *inspired and sustained by Christian faith*, than in the conduct of a peasant's wife in the Peak of Derbyshire" (Self-Possession in Moments of Peril, *LH*, 16 Jun 1853, 395, emphasis mine); this "conduct" of a farmer's wife, who is home alone and victim of a burglary, is described as follows:

> At the first view of him [the burglar], as she afterwards said, she felt ready to drop; but being naturally courageous, and of a deeply religious disposition, she soon recovered sufficient self-possession to suppress the cry which was rising to her lips, to walk with apparent firmness to a chair which stood on one side of the fire-place, and seat herself in it. The marauder immediately seated himself in another chair [...]. Her courage was almost spent; [...] she put up a prayer to the Almighty for protection and threw herself on his providence [...]. (ibid.)

Subsequently, the woman continues to "sit calmly, calling earnestly upon God" (ibid.) while the man draws a knife from his pocket. However, her calmness and her trust in god seem to have got to the burglar who simply gets up and escapes, leaving the home and the woman unharmed. The woman's heroism is constituted by two things: firstly, by suppressing the 'feminine' impulse "to drop" and "cry" and secondly by her unbroken faith in god, despite the immediate threat the burglar poses. The second feature is, however, the decisive one, since it is her religious faith which enables her to maintain her physical strength. In accordance with the article's headline, it is precisely "self-possession" which makes the woman heroic in the eyes of the text. Enabled by god, not doing what would be expected of a woman in this kind of situation is then the woman's heroic act – or rather non-act.

Similarly, a number of other texts construct private heroism of everyday life as a concept rooted in piety, examples of which can be used as role models and guides. "Bible Lessons for Everyday Life" asserts that "[a] nation, a whole nation, is raised and blessed by its heroes and saints. They give it a character by their own virtue, and largely help their fellows to be better than they would have been without their example and influence" (Bible Lessons for Everyday Life, *LH*, 25 Sep 1880, 614). The juxtaposition of "heroes and saints" in relation with "everyday life" in the article's title seems to construct heroism as an everyday – yet not a secular – form of sainthood. Clearly identifying the potential of these figures as role models, heroes are put to didactic use in the formation of a national identity and community. Their accomplishment lies in the influence they exert on their community, of which they seem to be ordinary members, as the phrase "help their fellows" suggests. However, this influence is, in the closing of the article, again appropriated in religious terms: "Take the knowledge and performance of His will as the *real motive* of our lives; for thus, and thus only, can we realise the true ends and aims of life. Then life rises out of the dull plains of *selfishness*, rises to its *true meaning* and purpose" (ibid. 615, emphases mine). Heroes' "true meaning" and "real motive" is then founded on their faith in god, and the communal act of helping "their fellows" is not based on a humanist moral ideal of selflessness, but on a religious belief in altruism.

The idea of altruism and the exertion of positive influence in everyday life are also exemplified in the poem "Heroines", which appeared in *LH* in 1887. The poem praises the everyday life of working-class women, its "heroines" being those "who work from dawn to starlight / that their children may be fed, / rendering up their very life-blood / For the scanty daily bread" (Heroines, *LH*, Aug 1887, 524). The women's effort is clearly directed at the wellbeing of others: "There are some who lie and suffer / All their lives in weary pain, / Yet to these the sad and friendless / Never come for cheer in vain. / Some who help the struggling workers, / Working with them through the day, / Holding up the Hands that falter, / Guiding feet too apt to stray" (ibid.). Toiling hard and suffering themselves, the "heroines" are shown to still have time for others whose lives they influence positively.[85] However, the heroines receive no immediate validation for their acts of altruism. Their reward is otherworldly and their heroism motivated religiously, as the last stanza suggests: "Many whom we pass unnoticed, / Angels watch with wondering eyes; / Some we have despised, forgot-

85 The poem not only evokes the women's families as beneficiaries of their kindness, but in its mentioning of the workers with feet "too apt to stray" (Heroines, *LH*, Aug 1887, 524) also hints at the temperance movement, in which female influence was often considered crucial for those prone to drink.

ten, / Shine like stars in Paradise. / For our heroines live among us, / In our city, at our gate, / None have told them they are noble, / They can suffer still – and *wait!*" (ibid.).[86]

The above examples of heroism in the private life of the everyday have shown a high degree of self-forgetfulness and suffering in their protagonists.[87] Through the juxtaposition with saints and the promise of remuneration in the afterlife, this idea of silent suffering is strengthened even further and the religious motivation emphasised. A note in the "Varieties" section summarises this idea of private heroism to the point where it states that even a hero is nothing if he tries to rely on himself instead of on god: "Nothing but faith in the one perfect sacrifice of Christ will enable men to draw near to God" (Varieties, *LH*, 27 Sep 1860, 624). Trying to follow this idea of Christ, the "true hero" can only be "the man who conquers himself" (A True Hero, *LH*, Jun 1881, 364).

This attempt to follow Christ can then also be seen as the point which complicates *LH*'s attitude towards heroism in ordinary people in everyday life. Though in a religious context Christ is *the* exemplar to aspire to and follow, any tendency to see a likeness in a common man and Christ can only be seen as blasphemous, since Jesus, as a part of the holy trinity, would have been considered a part of god. A belief in Christ, who had been the ideal which Thomas Carlyle had in mind when conceptualising his messiah-like hero, thus makes any human heroics of that kind virtually impossible for a believer. This belief then turns admiration of heroes into a form of idolatry. Coming back to the initial quote about "Hero Worship", the precarious position of the hero between role model and presumptuous figure in a religious context becomes evident. While admiring and aspiring to a hero as a role model was not problematic in a secular context, it becomes problematic in a religious setting:

> [W]e dislike hero worship. We deem it a sad misapplication of an inherent disposition of the mind, imparted for the most solemnly important of purposes. […] But the sentiment thus active, and expatiating in false directions, has a true direction in which to expatiate, and a worthy object on which to fix. […] It is a worship that belongs of right to the man Christ Jesus alone; the God whose throne is for ever and ever, and whom all the angels of God worship. (Varieties, *LH*, 3 May 1860, 228)

Thus, it has become apparent that in its didactic mission *LH* relies much more strongly on religious rhetoric, which is only in some instances accompanied by

86 A similar poem was published two years earlier for male heroes. Under the title "A True Hero", "true" male heroism is distinguished from established forms of heroics ("never braving special danger / Nor wearing laurel crown", A True Hero, *LH*, Jun 1881, 364). Similarly, remuneration beyond "glory" (ibid.) is promised to the hero who "conquers himself". Ibid.

87 Other examples of selfless private heroism in *LH* include "Heroes in Humble Rank", published as Varieties, *LH*, 12 Jul 1855, 448; Introductory Lessons on Morals: Second Series. Chapter VII: Easier and Harder Duties, *LH*, 1 Nov 1855, 694–696; The Floods in France, *LH*, 29 Jan 1876, 68–72; The Power of "Good Spirits", *LH*, May 1880, 335–336 or The Story of the English Shires. Durham II, *LH*, Oct 1885, 666–672.

vocabulary of the heroic. In these cases, heroism identifies selfless behaviour worthy of emulation, yet it is not utilised widely as an identificatory offer for the everyday lives of the readers. If reflected upon, as in the example above, the idea of heroism and the hero-worship it entailed for the periodical is criticised on the grounds of religious propriety.

5.6 *"In these Unheroic Days"* – Fraser's Magazine *and Its Engagement with a Heroic Past*

As could be seen above, *LH* shows inconsistencies and tensions in its use of the vocabulary of the heroic and the heroic does not seem to have played a decisive role in the periodical's (didactic) publishing agenda. In *FM*, on the other hand, a very specific concept of heroism is presented throughout its runtime. The periodical – in correspondence with its distinct political and conservative identity – puts forth a concept of heroism which is modelled after Thomas Carlyle's ideas. Thus, *FM* uses the idea of heroism as a vehicle for a worldview in which knowledge, expertise and reputation are in the hands of a few who use their heroic agency to lead the mass of society. The notion of a hero as a role model or the concept of everyday or private heroism rarely surfaces in the periodical and the idea is mocked in the few instances in which it does.[88] However, the worldview which the magazine evoked no longer represented contemporary societal realities. The class for which *FM* was writing – upper-class, male, intellectual conservatives – might still have been in the fore in Parliament, but had had to accept that they could not act as a leading class which the rest of the country would follow anymore. The middle classes had been growing in importance politically and through their increasing power on the consumer market. It is no wonder then that *FM*'s references to heroism are increasingly directed at a (mythical)

88 For example, the satirical text "A Week in Bed" ridicules the idea of the didactic use of heroism. The article gives instruction on what to do if one had to stay in bed for a week (for example due to a broken leg) and comments: "It would be a step, gained, surely, to acquire the habit of reflecting every night before we go to sleep on something noble, and loving, and good – on some rare instance of heroism – some glorious effort of self-sacrifice – some great example, superior to, yet in perfect sympathy with the ordinary tape of mankind. Such thought, repeated night after night, and persisted in, would gradually raise the mind into a purer atmosphere, would gather at length into an ideal which we might strive to imitate, though to its perfection we could never hope to attain. [...] A week in bed, you see, makes you ponder over many things which escape you in the hurry and turmoil of every-day work. [...] It probably originates many good resolutions, some of which are to be ignored, some broken, and some altogether forgotten." A Week in Bed, *FM*, Mar 1864, 334. Mockingly, the text depicts role-model heroism – a "glorious effort of self-sacrifice [...] yet in perfect sympathy with the ordinary tape of mankind" – as a waste of effort which is "altogether forgotten" soon after. Furthermore, the text at its outset already reveals its upper-class audience, since the very idea of fantasising about what one might do with an idle week in bed would not have been a major concern of an audience dependent on their daily work efforts.

past. In accordance with Carlyle's belief that the nineteenth century was an unheroic age, the periodical often referred to past ages as "heroic" in contrast to the present day.

As an expression of the scepticism towards the heroic potential of the present, a large number of articles can be found throughout the last decades of the periodical which lament an often unspecified mythical heroic past from the perspective of an unheroic present. Once again, *FM* is in agreement with Thomas Carlyle in this respect, who had professed that contemporary society (along with the eighteenth century) was a hostile environment for heroes. A further connection to *On Heroes* can be found in that fact that most of the articles evoke the idea of a heroic past in relation to epic literature or myths. This links heroism with important aspects of Carlyle's concept: the idea of literary mediation as a crucial tool of heroic agency and the idea of a supernatural entity which resonates in the vision of ancient myths.

This is voiced clearly in "Some Notices of Shakspearian Drama" which speaks about the times of Shakespeare and Homer as follows:

> [I]t was the fortune of the Englishman as well as of the Greek to put forth his inspirations in an *heroic age*, when every 'form of many-coloured life' lay open to observation – when superstition was rife – when *fables were accepted* by the multitudes as *realities*, and received by the few as things they were neither *free to believe* nor to be declared impossible [...]. (Some Notices of Shakspearian Drama, *FM*, Jun 1842, 645, emphases mine)

Both the early modern period and Greek antiquity are thus presented as a more favourable environment for the heroic; this is explained by the higher degree of superstition and freedom "to believe". It is this heightened spiritual freedom in the "heroic age" which enabled the two writers to produce their extraordinary literary works. In an implicit comparison, the present day of the article is constructed as a time with more clear-cut boundaries, a clearer notion of what is possible and impossible. Thus, the text reflects Carlyle's argument that the eighteenth century, and especially the "sceptics" (*OH* 153) of the Enlightenment, had introduced a thinking which was too rational and pragmatic to allow for the poetic and spiritual freedom which heroism needed. This striking similarity to Carlyle's line of argumentation makes sense in its temporal closeness to the lectures and publication of *On Heroes* (1840 and 1841) and the personal connection between the periodical and the thinker; however, the same line of argument can be found in many other texts throughout the decades up until the final issues of *FM*.

This idea of a heroic past is often related to Greek antiquity with texts evoking the idea of "ancient and heroic times" (Hare: Representation, *FM*, Feb 1860, 203) or longing for "the bright heroic days when Perseus wooed Andromeda"

(Thalatta! Thalatta!, *FM*, Apr 1862, 427).[89] Referencing Greek mythology, Celtic epics or the writers of romanticism, all of the articles which refer back to a past heroic age do so with reference to literary tradition. Whether "The Teutonic and the Celtic Epic" which sees the last traces of a "heroic age in Ireland" in the country's epic tradition (The Teutonic and the Celtic Epic, *FM*, Mar 1874, 336) or an autobiographical text about Arthur Hugh Clough which identifies his inspiration "in the heroic days" (Arthur Hugh Clough, *FM*, Apr 1862, 536) of Plutarch – true poetic art seems only possible in referring back to a heroic past. At a time of perceived loss of meaning and spirituality, one article finds hope in the fact that "[s]till, there is the heroic past whereof to sing" (Poems by Matthew Arnold, *FM*, Feb 1854, 141).[90] Great art in the vein of the "Hero as Poet", as many of the articles argue, is only possible when going back to a heroic past for inspiration.[91]

History Writing and the Historian as Messianic Hero

FM not only discusses the idea of a heroic past in relation to poetic literary production. Establishing the past as an important reference point for meaning making and identity formation, the mediation of the past is also at the centre of many articles in the periodical and historians, as mediators, are heroised. As a text concerned with the "heroic ag[es]" of English history notes: "Few things are more difficult than to compose an epitome of history, and few are more useful" (Revolutions in English History, *FM*, Apr 1860, 485). As mediators between the highly regarded past and the present day, *FM* frequently discusses the state of history writing in Britain. In the context of heroism, historians are considered of grave importance since they are the ones who not only shape their audience's view on history in general, but select history's heroes. It is those heroes who, after Carlyle, determine history and thus, the historians who construct them are

89 Other texts which compare the Homeric age as a heroic time to the present include: Notes on the National Drama of Spain, *FM*, Sep 1859, 324; Homer and the Homeric Age, *FM*, Jan 1859, 50 (in this text, the connection to Carlyle's *On Heroes* is drawn explicitly by connecting Homeric antiquity to Muhammad's times as "heroic ag[es]", ibid.); Matthew Arnold's "Merope", *FM*, Jun 1858, 698; or The Principle of the Grecian Mythology, or, How the Greeks Made Their Gods, *FM*, Jan 1854, 79.

90 It is worth noting that this statement appears in a text about Matthew Arnold, who, in his considerations about art and culture, though trying to do away with class distinctions, was still struggling to reconcile the elitist realm of art and the reality of mass culture.

91 Other examples for this argumentation with the use of phrases such as "heroic past" or "heroic times" include Heinrich Heine, *FM*, Nov 1866, 588–609 (which evokes German romanticists such as Heine, Tieck or Schlegel as desperately trying to "resuscitate" the heroic past for their own unheroic present [cf. ibid., 588]); A. H. A. Hamilton: Quarter Sessions under Queen Elizabeth, *FM*, Jun 1876, 733–746; The Past and Future of the High Church Party, *FM*, Feb 1878, 240–249; Annie Walker: A Forgotten Hero, *FM*, Dec 1880, 755–783 or English Satire in the Nineteenth Century, *FM*, Dec 1881, 753–761.

crucial. In the texts discussed in the following, it is mostly the subjects of historians' works that are called "heroes". Interestingly though, through attribution of Carlylean terms, most of the texts additionally identify a second type of hero: the historians themselves in a quasi-supernatural form of engagement with the heroic past.[92] Similar to the previously discussed notion of a lost heroic past, most texts about history writing in *FM* are united by a feeling of insufficiency and inadequacy and the demand which unites all articles on historiography is a demand for truth.[93] The emphasis on the truthfulness of the 'perfect' historian's account reoccurs in all articles dealing with contemporary history writing and is turned into *the* key characteristic. Nevertheless, it is never specified what the standard for the truthfulness of a historical account is and how a 'true' historian could be recognised. The term is simply used as an abstract concept which distinguishes the 'good' from the 'bad'. Unanimously, the texts agree that it is this truthfulness that constitutes the ideal historian and that it is this quality which accounts for their writing showing the 'real past'. The contributor Shirley contrasts an incompetent and a good historian and states:

> [A good historian] is an infinitely truer student of life, an infinitely more reliable observer of the past. [...] the one paints with inimitable grace the face; the other, though in a somewhat rough way, dissects the heart. The one is superficially accurate and picturesque, the other is true to the core. The one stops outside, and, microscope in hand, examines with immense attention the coat: the other pierces into the life. (Shirley: The Sphinx, *FM*, Jul 1861, 68–69)

While the mediocre historian will only look at the "outside", the ideal historian will "pierce into" life. While the one account is "accurate", yet only "superficially", the other one is "true to the core" and "dissects the heart". It seems not only to be a question of getting the facts right, but good historians' abilities apparently lie in their relation to the past, or even in their relationship to the past. Thus, the ideal historian seems to stand in direct contact to the time he describes and therefore, following the argument of Leopold von Ranke, able to paint a picture of how "things actually were".[94]

Here the connection to Carlyle and his considerations on heroism can be found, as the ability of seeing, knowing and conveying the truth to others was

92 The following considerations draw on my findings published in Hadamitzky: Decline, which offers a closer reading of much of the material presented in the following.

93 Of course, there are also reviews of history books to be found which show contemporary historical works in a favourable light, but nevertheless they always include points of criticism and whenever history writing is discussed in general, on a theoretical level, discontent is the driving force. The only exceptions are reviews of history books written by James Froude and Arthur Helps, both of whom were writing for *FM*, Froude even being its editor between 1860 and 1874. Notably, however, their books are not dealt with theoretically and are not used as an example for a general standard or design an ideal.

94 Leopold von Ranke: Sämmtliche Werke, Vol. 33, Leipzig 1885, p. 7, translation mine. The German original reads: "wie es eigentlich gewesen".

one of the key characteristics of a Carlylean hero. This central argument of Carlyle, as well as the attributes of 'his' heroes, are taken up and used by the contributors to describe their ideal historian: the model historian is "truthful" (Carlyle's Frederick the Great, *FM*, Dec 1858, 631), he possesses "marvellous insight" (Thoughts on Modern English Literature, *FM*, Jul 1859, 97), is "a seer" (Shirley: The Sphinx, *FM*, Jul 1861, 67), in short a "genius" (Carlyle's Frederick the Great, *FM*, Dec 1858, 631). Not only are the keywords for the description of the hero utilised for the description of the ideal historian in *FM*, but the correlation of their function also becomes obvious: while the Carlylean hero acts as a "bringer back of men to reality" (*OH* 119) for the present time, the historian performs the same function for the past.

Carlyle himself also features in the articles on history writing and it is not surprising that many of the contributors not only fashion their ideal historian after the Carlylean hero, but also give him a name: Thomas Carlyle. The connection to Carlyle's works and views is thus established by making him the prime example and representative of an ideal historian. By bringing up Carlyle again and again as *the* ideal historian and describing him with the categories of his own work, his lectures on heroism are indirectly evoked. Carlyle's views are thus, in connection to contemporary history writing, reaffirmed twice, on the one hand by designing the ideal historian as the Carlylean hero, on the other by turning Carlyle himself into a hero of his own kind.

Furthermore, this offers a glimpse at what the contributors would expect their audience to know. It can be presumed that the audience was assumed to understand the reference to Carlyle's *On Heroes*, thereby strongly emphasising its cultural significance.[95] The demand for the hero-historian can thus be seen as a revolt against the new, secular, science-oriented, and increasingly democratised way of conducting affairs which developed in the second half of the nineteenth century. Though the Chartists' efforts in the 1840s did not result in an effective change, the idea of granting political rights to members of all classes of society continued to circulate in public discussion and led to a parliament reform in 1867. The Second Reform Act extended the right to vote to all householders, as well as lodgers who paid rent of £10 a year or more. Although this change would only have affected middle-class men, it led to a change in public perception and continuing political demands from the working classes. After almost two more decades, in 1884, the Third Reform Act finally granted a near universal franchise – to men. It is into this climate of political change and the increasing voice of the middle and working classes that the articles discussed above fell. Apart from

95 Interestingly, the commercial aspect of history writing is not dealt with in any of the articles. Though Carlyle himself points to this issue when speaking about the "Man of Letters" as a hero, the contributors to *FM* do not reflect upon the mechanisms of the print market in which both the authors of history books as well as the periodical writers themselves are involved.

this opposition, the articles can also be read as an attempt to fight the lack of orientation after Darwin – by placing modern society in a longer historical narrative. The disorientation caused by the scientific developments led in some parts of society to a growing demand for a guiding figure, an individual, a hero who would unite the divided society and show the confused and disoriented people what *truth*, what *reality* really was. Similarly, the magazine in general had lost touch with the demands of the readers: having started out in the 1830s as a periodical which was designed *against* other competitors on the market, this 'being other than'-mentality was at the heart of the magazine's self-conception.

The articles discussed above serve as examples of this: by maintaining the format of long, political, conservative, and essentially elitist essays, the magazine set itself against contemporary society and tried to evoke a worldview which did not correlate with the public's predominant perception of the world anymore. The publication's high point in circulation numbers had been 8,000 copies in the 1840s, a success at the time but a number that could not stand up to those of popular magazines whose circulation numbers were often between 100,000 and 500,000 copies. *FM* clung to the idea of elitist specialised content at a high price for an exclusive readership, while other journals provided substantiated information as well as entertainment at cheap prices and, importantly, recognised the middle classes as a target group with both monetary as well as societal and political potential. Interestingly, this more democratised and egalitarian view of society also resulted in a different representation of the heroic in other periodicals of the time (which can be called 'popular' due to their high circulation numbers). In publications such as *LH*, *CJ* or other family magazines such as *All the Year Round*, heroism is not only something to be admired by the middle and working classes, but also something they can achieve themselves. Just as the middle classes in society seem to have taken up a portion of the upper classes' dominance, the concept of the Carlylean hero has been replaced by a more 'common' hero who serves as a role model and inspiration for others rather than a messiah.

FM, then, came to experience the regulatory power of their audience – they stopped consuming the periodical. Thus, the magazine was down to a run of 500 copies in 1880 and was finally discontinued in 1882. It had become too intellectual, theoretical and backwards-looking and, interestingly, the very last issue of the magazine programmatically contains almost only articles which look back at the past: texts about the history of agricultural terms, of the art of biography writing, or English philology. All of those state clearly that the past should be favoured over the present and the essay on English philology, which opens the last number, closes with the statement that the work of a real "Man of Letters" has its retribution beyond "mention in a price-list and market value" (English: Its Ancestors Its Progeny, *FM*, Oct 1882, 457). Thus, until its very last issue, the periodical shows a partiality for the past over the present, which is also evident in its depiction of heroism. At a time when the democratic movement was gaining momentum and the mass was gaining more and more power politically but especially as consumers, *FM* still predominantly stuck to the belief that the majority should be guided by a heroic leader figure.

6. Three Periodicals – Three Heroic Profiles

The analysis of the three periodicals confirms that fundamentally different configurations of heroism could exist side by side in their representation on the Victorian print market. Depending on a periodical's orientation and intended readership, different qualities of heroism were highlighted and perpetuated through repetition over the decades, which also reveals distinctive functionalisations of the heroic for their intended audiences. Particularly in the cases of *CJ* and *FM*, the vocabulary of heroism was – given the polylithic nature of periodicals as a medium – used surprisingly consistently and resulted in the emergence of distinct heroic profiles in the analysis of the material.

The idea of heroism that materialised in *FM* was closely linked to the works of Thomas Carlyle. A writer who had contributed to the magazine's distinct identity as a medium of controversial political thought, his idea of a messianic leader for the mass of the people reoccurs throughout the periodical's existence until 1882. With a strong focus on the political realm, the magazine called for charismatic heroes with strong individual agency and leadership abilities. In the vein of Carlyle's *On Heroes*, hero figures in *FM* were often established as 'seers'.

Although this superior vision was not always related to the spiritual realm, as it had been in Carlyle's considerations, heroes' deeper insight clearly marked them as 'other' than the average man and constituted a transgression of social boundaries. As extraordinary figures, heroes in *FM* were seen as part of an intellectual elite which was defined against the majority of the population. This was also in line with the intended readership of the periodical, which was directed at an exclusively male and formally educated audience. Thus, the opposition of the intellectual and the 'mechanical' worker is emphasised in all domains of heroism. This became most apparent in the depiction of heroic historians, whose almost supernatural connection to their field of study was contrasted with the uninspired mediation of facts which the periodical perceived as more mechanical. In the field of politics, which the periodical propounded to be the most important field for social and civilisatory advancement, it praised politicians whose actions were inspired by philosophical thought, while dismissing so-called 'practical politicians' for their pragmatism and lack of higher inspiration. Regarding militarism, which *FM* mainly discussed in terms of politics, only high-ranking military officials – as the decision-makers who linked the military to the political realm – were heroised. In this heroisation, the periodical praised first and foremost their individual agency that also included the possibility of overstepping rules and conventions in order to succeed in the pursuit of a political goal. Although *FM* occasionally referred to contemporary (political or military) figures as heroes, its notion of heroism was predominantly situated in the past. In line with Carlyle's diagnosis that the nineteenth century was a hostile environment for heroism, the periodical often referred to the mythical past of Greek or Celtic mythology or the early modern period. The text thus referenced points in history at which the hegemony of the elite had not been yet challenged and the rule of the few over the masses was still undisputed.

Directed at an intellectual, conservative, male audience, the usage of the semantics of heroism in *FM* can clearly be read as an attempt to stabilise the identity of the periodical's consumers as a social elite. Although the periodical – like *CJ* and, to a lesser extent, *LH* – emphasised the likeness of its heroic figures to its audience, this audience and the worldview which its heroes symbolised were fundamentally different. In its depiction of heroism, *FM* presented a worldview which was strongly opposed to democratisation and the enlargement of the franchise, which would have meant extending political power to the lower classes. At a time when the social power of the middle and lower classes was also growing steadily due to the emergence of mass consumerism, the idea of social hegemony which *FM* disseminated was increasingly marginalised. The periodical had to be discontinued in 1882 and was succeeded in the same year, under the same editorship, by *Longman's Magazine,* a fundamentally different publication, which was adapted to the tastes of the middle classes. This shows that the periodical had not been able to adapt to the requirements of the consumer market and that its heroes, and the worldview which they symbolised, were not compatible with contemporary society. Having established that heroism can function as an indicator for social questions and collective needs, the discontinuation of *FM* can be read as a negative measure in that it reveals a need that no longer persists.

In contrast to the distinct heroic profile which emerged for *FM*, *LH* displayed a more complicated attitude towards the heroic. This can be related to the periodical's production background and the religious orientation it entailed. The publication's aim to mediate Christian values to its readership made the depiction of heroes more multi-layered in different contexts. In this regard, the treatment of the military is particularly indicative. On the one hand, the military was, when discussed explicitly, not regarded as a possible field of heroic conduct, since it implied violence, which could not be reconciled with Christian values. Especially in the 1850s and 1860s, *LH* took a strong anti-war stance, emphasising the losses military actions entailed. The act of killing on the battlefield was explicitly referred to as murder. On the other hand, as conflicts in colonial regions turned violent, the periodical changed its attitude towards military heroics and, justified as a Christianising mission, heroised the form of 'muscular Christianity' in the context of imperialism. With a focus on self-sacrifice, *LH* displayed a reassignment of moral value to militarism. What had been so strongly criticised in relation to the Crimean War could later be understood as an "imperial action by a divinely ordained might. [...] Thus the soldierly became the instrument of a moral purpose in the world."[1] The depiction of military heroes in a colonial context served the dissemination of Christian values such as selflessness or altruism, but did not invite the readers to imitate the heroes' behaviour. Although these abstract values could have served as a means of identification for the readers, the heroes were not presented as role models.

A different strategy can be found in relation to the industrial field, in which the periodical located a number of heroic role models for the readers to emulate. At a time of rapid scientific and technological progress, *LH* emphasised the importance of industrial and mechanical work as a heroic deed. Omitting the field of science, the new findings of which continued to be precarious for a religious publication, the periodical acknowledged contemporary developments in the field of technology. In close alignment with the narrative strategies of Samuel Smiles, the periodical presented the biographies of well-known men of industry, such as George Stephenson, and emphasised their likeness to the readers' lives. In assigning hero-status to the famous engineers, not only in their achievements but especially in their enduring work at the beginning of their careers, the vocabulary of heroism was utilised to validate the audience's lives as well. Additionally, the biographies of engineers and explorers were given a layer of religious meaning, in order to inspire both persevering work ethos and piety. As representatives of the advancement of civilisation, these heroic figures were thus implicitly disseminators of religious belief.

Although *LH* on the whole stressed the likeness between its readership and the represented heroes, for example in the fields of industry and exploration or in the representation of pious everyday life, the idea of heroes as exemplars could not be found consistently in the periodical. This can also be traced back to the periodical's religious orientation, which resulted in a struggle with the general idea of hero worship. Since worship could, in a religious sense, only ever apply to god, the idea of worshipping heroes was discussed in *LH* with great unease and often evaluated as idolatry. This can also serve as an explanation for the periodical's inconsistent use of the term. Hero status was attributed quite unreflectedly to acts deemed noteworthy in regard to industry, exploration or lifesaving. In these cases, the term marks behaviour and values which the readers could closely relate to and were encouraged to emulate. However, if the acts themselves were within the realm of religion, such as stories about missionaries, this form of exemplary heroism became precarious in its intersection with divine power. Therefore, heroes of Christianity – in contrast to 'mere' heroes with a Christian motivation – were often presented as unattainable saintly figures with a greater distance to the audience. In their suffering to the Christian community, their heroic acts created a sense of (Christian) obligation and a clear hierarchical struc-

1 MacKenzie: Popular Imperialism, p. 4.

ture. On the whole, however, heroism, as a potentially problematic concept in a religious context, did not seem to be central in the didactic mission of *LH*.

Whereas both *FM* and *CJ* – due to their specific editorial situation – presented a very consistent image of the heroic throughout the period under examination, *LH* did not. This is partially due to the fact that periodical literature is in itself not monolithic and the large number of contributors can result in competing and opposing usages of a term such as 'heroism' surfacing on the pages of the same publication over time. However, the fact that specific domains, such as the field of industry and the realm of missionary work, were referring to different conceptualisations of the heroic and domains such as science were lacking heroic attributions can clearly be traced back to the periodical's evangelical background.

As the periodical with the strongest editorial leadership out of the three, *CJ* displayed the most coherent heroic profile. Unlike *LH*, which intended to reach a similar readership, *CJ* – as a secular publication – showed surprisingly little disruption in its representation of heroism and heroic acts. With courage, selflessness and perseverance at its core, the majority of texts about heroism in the publication evoked a heroic imaginary built on moral conduct rather than individual agency. The vocabulary of heroism was an integral part of the implementation of the periodical's didactic goal for the working and lower-middle classes. This intended readership was also reflected in the heroic personnel, which came almost exclusively from the lower ranks of society. With a communal focus, the periodical presented examples of selfless heroism in dangerous situations as well as in everyday life. Since heroism was predominantly shown as something which required neither extraordinary physical strength nor formal education or exceptional intellect, it became accessible to all for identification. Therefore, it could be, and was, applied to almost every domain of life from the work of miners to medical work or the normality of domestic life. These representations of the heroic were united in their orientation towards the wellbeing of something larger than the individual, representing the central value of heroism in *CJ*: selflessness. Significantly, the domain of science and industry was rarely described in the vocabulary of the heroic, emphasising how heroism was utilised as a tool in the *moral* education of the readers. Articles about scientific and technological developments, on the other hand, were often written in a very sober style and focused on factual instruction. This divide between moral education, factual instruction and pure entertainment also emerged in the analysis of other Chambers publications which showed that the vocabulary of the heroic was most frequently employed in reference to middle- and working-class personnel in texts with a moral didactic goal and intended for private consumption. Depiction of heroic leaders and well-known figures, which is almost completely missing from *CJ*, was predominantly used in texts which aimed only at amusement and entertainment.

The periodical clearly reacted to the contemporary political and social realities. This becomes most pronounced in times of war: While *CJ* generally took a peace-oriented stance, it subdued this message in times of war. In order to support public morale but nevertheless maintain its middle-class values, it employed transferral strategies in the depiction of military heroics. Depictions of heroic military men became more frequent as the century progressed and the periodical focused on rank-and-file soldiers rather than military leaders and decidedly did not portray their violent actions, but focused on their moral (patriotic and domestic) motivation. Hamilton argues regarding the public perception of the Victorian military that "[i]t was more and more the outward man, the active rather than the contemplative hero who seemed necessary in an increasingly troubled world."[2] This does not hold true for the depiction in *CJ*, which displayed a turn *away* from the active and military hero, and often specifically regarded this type of heroism as inferior to moral heroics as it was believed to be more situational. This could also be seen in the depiction of heroic everyday life. The heroisation of working-class communities, domestic women or acts of lifesaving on the one hand acknowledged the democratisation processes in late Victorian Britain and the growing public recognition for 'common' heroes through institutions like the Royal Humane Society and the Albert Medal. On the other hand, however, these acts of validation in the medium of the periodical also acted as a re-enforcement of hegemonic social structures. In the heroisation of the current status quo and particularly the selfless behaviour of the working classes for the whole of society, *CJ* encouraged the readers not to attempt social change.

Thus, *CJ* offered a very clear-cut idea of heroism on the pages of the periodical which was seldom disrupted and which emphasised the likeness and proximity between its readership and the represented heroes. This was further stressed through instances of precarious heroicity, for example in the figure of the 'hero of romance', which was considered dangerous for the very fact that such a great distance lay between the object of adoration and the adorer. The status-difference implied in the idea of adoration was, in these texts, clearly gendered female. *CJ*'s heroic imaginary was based on the assumption that heroic recognition could be realised as a *private* act. This reveals the central problem of the notion of heroism which the periodical offered: in its meta-heroic reflections, the publications demanded an *unmediated* form of private heroism, while at the same time mediating this idea in a public and commercial product. With the focus on fictional characters, the periodical tried to circumvent contributing to public celebrity of attested human beings and tell the stories of 'unsung heroes'. However, this can only be described as an unsatisfying strategy for a problem which remained unsolved.

However, in the analysis of the different heroic profiles, similarities could be perceived as well: All periodicals struggled with the representation of heroic

[2] C. I. Hamilton: Naval Hagiography and the Victorian Hero, The Historical Journal 23.2, 1980, p. 397.

women. Clearly displaying the contemporary idea of separate spheres for men and women, female heroes, as Edwards notes, were "an emblem of patriarchal instability and insecurity".[3] *CJ* and *LH* tried to solve this problem by transferring female heroism to the domestic and private sphere, thereby subduing women's agency and reinforcing patriarchal structures. Active female heroism was only ever displayed in foreign contexts. A spatial removal from the world of the readers seemed to ensure that emulation was not considered by the female audience and thus allowed for a larger degree of transgressivity in the heroic characters. On the whole, all three periodicals placed their heroism predominantly within Britain or assigned it to Britons in colonial contexts. Instances of other ethnicities showing heroic behaviour were so rare in all three periodicals that they could be seen as singular exceptions.[4] Also, more disruptive and violent forms of heroism were occasionally transferred to foreign figures, thereby distancing the readership from this type of heroics.[5] In this respect, heroism in the periodicals also embodied a specific *national* identity, which could be detected in particular in times of national insecurity such as the Crimean War or the Boer War at the turn of the century.

Similarly, the different periodicals displayed specific genres which they deemed most appropriate for the discussion and representation of the heroic. While *FM* dealt with heroism predominantly in (political) essays, *LH* often used short essays, tales or travel writing, which more often than not referred to actual human beings. *CJ* on the other hand played out most of its discussions of heroism in fictional texts with fictional characters, in order to prevent public hero-worship. While the texts which invited the readers to emulate the protagonists' behaviour were mostly fictional narratives, more abstract meta-reflections of heroism were discussed in essays and drew on history and contemporary culture for examples. It seems that fictional texts were better suited for a functionalisation of the heroic as a guiding role-model, while factual genres were better suited to attempts to define and discuss heroism more generally. Texts which reflect on heroism on a theoretical level appeared in all three periodicals. Thus, the publications pointed to the fact that heroism and hero-worship was not something which Victorian culture practiced naïvely, but something that was publicly debated. While *FM* discussed the way in which singular leaders could be established in contemporary society and deliberated over the disruptive potential, which such figures could entail, both *CJ* and *LH* displayed an unease to blindly

3 Edwards: Psyche, p. 4.

4 Cf. e.g. The Negro Liberator of Hayti, *LH*, 31 Mar 1853, 218–221; A Long Swim, *CJ*, 17 Nov 1866, 721–724; or Poccahontas, *LH*, 9–30 Sept 1852.

5 These instances of disruptive heroic energy are also among the few examples of negative heroism. On the whole, few articles could be found in which counter-heroes were constructed. Similarly, demonisation, de-heroisation or ridicule is seldom used in the representation of heroism. This again stresses the fact that heroism was utilised as an affirmative concept to stabilise identities.

follow heroes. Thus, a growing tendency to doubt grand public gestures and question celebrity could be observed.

Hero and Collective

The three periodicals not only represent different strands of thinking about heroes and heroism, but also illustrate different ways of relating to heroes and different ideas of collective and individual. The hero figures which *FM* disseminated possessed strong individual agency and were presented as charismatic and highly autonomous. Thus, they embodied an 'other' in relation to the mass of society, which could not be integrated into ordinary classifications. In their autonomy, they also incorporated a potential for social disruption and connoted power.[6] This form of heroism constituted a large distance between heroes and the community that related to them in adoration. While the exceptional intellectuals and politicians in *FM* might have served as a means of identification for the social elite the periodical was addressing, this form of heroism clearly valued the individual over the mass and showed the collective their limitations through the transgression of a singular individual. In agreement with Zink's considerations of adoration, this form of relating to an extraordinary hero figure was a strong manifestation of power.

In contrast to this, the other conception of heroism substituted distance with proximity. Heroism was here often depicted as communal, as directed at a common good which was greater than the individual. With a stress on the likeness between hero and collective and the focus on abstract virtues and motivation rather than heroic deeds and agency, it seemed to be a more socially integrative form of heroics which could be applied to almost everyone in the readership of the periodicals. Heroes thus functioned as a projection screen and presented on a larger scale the "heroic totality"[7] of features which were already present in the audience. By breaking heroism down to features which were deemed significant, the audience was enabled to emulate these features through their act of admiration. In this more immediate relation, heroes were, as Andrew Flescher describes it, turned into "exemplars of good human living".[8] In the didactic emphasis on the identificatory potential of heroes, they were differentiated from other figures such as the saint or the genius. While saints, as the analysis of *LH*

---

6 Cf. Veronika Zink: Von der Verehrung. Eine kultursoziologische Untersuchung, Frankfurt am Main 2014.

7 Cubitt: Heroic Reputations, p. 6.

8 Andrew M. Flescher: Heroes, Saints, and Ordinary Morality, Georgetown 2003, p. 110. While this assessment is productive in the analysis of heroism, Flescher's study as a whole is problematic in that it tries to define heroes and saints in an essentialist way and gives the reader instructions on how to relate to what the text supposes are 'real' heroes. Thereby, the book aligns itself with texts – such as the periodicals discussed in this study – that implement power structures rather than uncover them.

has shown, were too far removed from the audience's lives to act as role models for everyday life, the genius lacked the moral component and attainability. As a figure which was strongly based on talent, inspiration and intellectual superiority, the genius could not fulfil the communal function that the hero effected. The hero thus is one option from a wider spectrum of related figures, which could be chosen consciously for specific cultural or ideological reasons and would imply different cultural or ideological meaning. Thus, *CJ*'s choice to position the hero at the centre of its didactic message is just as revealing as *LH*'s decision to emphasise saints in their aim to provide religious education. In the construction of heroes as part of the collective, an attempt to symbolically validate 'the mass' and especially the lower ranks could be detected. However, while this created an identity of an 'acknowledged collective' it did not effect change within society. The power which the act of herorization connoted was merely symbolic and did not lead to an actual empowerment of the collective, but only to a private sense of appreciation.

It has become apparent that both conceptualisations of heroism were instrumentalised to (re-)enforce power: the form of heroism relying on distance between individual and collective revealed social boundaries through the heroes' liminality. In the representation of heroism as located within the community, a demarcation was made from outside, a boundary was drawn around the socially acceptable behaviour through the continuous repetition of the norms. Thus, though the relationship between the represented heroes and their audience was fundamentally different, both ways of relating perpetuated the social hegemony of the upper and increasingly established middle classes.

Victorian Periodicals and the Heroic

All in all, this study has shown that the periodical was an effective medium for the dissemination of ideas and is a rich source for the popular understanding of the heroic in Victorian society. As an ambiguous term which had no one definition, hero-status could be assigned to a broad range of figures and adapted to different worldviews and ideologies. Thus, the different periodicals could represent a form of heroism that was beneficial to the respective producers' vision of society and social order. In the act of continuous consumption of a periodical, the readers agreed upon a common identity with the editors and contributors which was also reflected in the depiction of heroism. While the discontinuation of *FM* could be seen as an indication of a decreasing relevance of elitist ideas of transgressive hero-leaders, the existence of the periodical up unto 1882 and the continued reference to Carlyle in other print publications also showed that different forms of heroism existed side by side in the Victorian public sphere.

When George Levine asserts that the Victorians related to heroism with a "quality of desperation"[9] and produced "at best, problematic heroes",[10] this study cannot affirm this regarding the periodical market. On the contrary, the growing dominance of heroes as role models in periodicals and other print products created a flood of distinctly *unproblematic* heroes. In their likeness to the reader, these heroes did not, as Ruskin's call for Grand Style had demanded, present "human character and form in their utmost, or heroic, strength and beauty",[11] but praised normality, favoured ordinariness over nobility. Though the heroisation of role-model figures could be complicated by other interests such as religion, the 'ordinary hero' possessed no disruptive potential and was thus socially unproblematic. This form of heroism was adaptable to a wider range of social groups and more gender-inclusive (the fallacy of including women into the heroic sphere has been elaborated on above). However, it was only egalitarian on the surface. In its public validation of existing social norms and structures, it took rather than gave agency to the underprivileged and stabilised existing power.

9 George L. Levine: "Not Like My Lancelot". The Disappearing Victorian Hero, in: Sara M. Putzell / David C. Leonard (eds.): Perspectives on Nineteenth-Century Heroism. Essays from the 1981 Conference of the Southeastern Nineteenth-Century Studies Association, Madrid 1982, p. 48.

10 Ibid., p. 50.

11 Ruskin: Modern Painters, p. 15.

Works Cited

Periodical Sources

The Adventures of Johann Gottfried Seume, Leisure Hour, 7 October 1852, pp. 650–655.

Address of the Editor, Chambers's Journal, 25 January 1840, p. 8.

After an Explosion, Chambers's Journal, 7 August 1886, pp. 510–511.

The Age of Iron, Chambers's Journal, 20 August 1864, pp. 533–536.

An Artist in Earth, Leisure Hour, 11 November 1852, pp. 729–733.

All the World Over, Chambers's Journal, 11 May 1861, pp. 297–300.

Grant Allen: Dumaresq's Daughter, Chambers's Journal, 3 January, 1891, pp. 1–7.

–: Dumaresq's Daughter, Chambers's Journal, 10 January 1891, pp. 18–21.

–: Dumaresq's Daughter, Chambers's Journal, 17 January 1891, pp. 35–39.

–: Dumaresq's Daughter, Chambers's Journal, 24 January 1891, pp. 52–55.

–: Dumaresq's Daughter, Chambers's Journal, 31 January 1891, pp. 67–70.

–: Dumaresq's Daughter, Chambers's Journal, 7 February 1891, pp. 83–86.

–: Dumaresq's Daughter, Chambers's Journal, 7 March 1891, pp. 148–151.

–: Dumaresq's Daughter, Chambers's Journal, 14 March 1891, pp. 163–165.

American National Songs, Leisure Hour, 5 February 1876, pp. 90–92.

An Anecdote of the Russian Police, Leisure Hour, 18 May 1854, p. 318.

The Art of Fireside Story-Telling, Chambers's Journal, 19 February 1881, pp. 120–123.

Arthur and the Round Table, Leisure Hour, 13 December 1860, pp. 790–794.

Arthur Hugh Clough, Fraser's Magazine, April 1862, pp. 527–536.

The Babes in the Woods, Chambers's Journal, 12 August 1848, pp. 110–111.

The Baltic, and the Russian Towns on its Coasts, Leisure Hour, 18 May 1854, pp. 311–314.

The Battle of Waterloo, Leisure Hour, June 1890, pp. 531–541.

Beggar My Neighbour, Chambers's Journal, 10 August 1861, pp. 81–85.

The Bells of Yarrick, Chambers's Journal, 3 April 1880, pp. 217–221.

The Bells of Yarrick, Chambers's Journal, 10 April 1880, pp. 233–235.

The Bells of Yarrick, Chambers's Journal, 17 April 1880, pp. 250–252.

Bible Lessons for Everyday Life, Leisure Hour, 25 September 1880, pp. 614–615.

Blanchette. A Fairy Tale, Chambers's Journal, 4 February 1854, pp. 77–80.

Books of Remembrance, Leisure Hour, September 1884, pp. 553–557.

Boyish Freaks, Chambers's Journal, 21 April 1888, 252–255.

The Bravest Briton at Waterloo, Chambers's Journal, 25 May 1901, pp. 401–405.

British Amazons, Chambers's Journal, 13 May 1893, pp. 298–300.

The British Navy, As it Was, Chambers's Journal, 17 March 1877, pp. 161–164.

The British Navy. From Coracle to the Line of Battle, Chambers's Journal, 8 April 1854, pp. 217–219.
Bushranging Yarns, Chambers's Journal, 20 September 1890, pp. 593–596.
Carlyle's Frederick the Great, Fraser's Magazine, December 1858, pp. 631–649.
Carlyle's Frederick the Great, Fraser's Magazine, May 1864, pp. 539–550.
The Clyffards of Clyffe, Chambers's Journal, 19 August 1865, pp. 516–519.
The "Coming Man", Chambers's Journal, 5 April 1851, pp. 216–218.
Common-Place People, Chambers's Journal, 10 January 1857, pp. 17–18.
Continental Courts Sixty Years Ago, Chambers's Journal, 24 August 1861, pp. 123–125.
Chivalry, Chambers's Journal, 9 August 1862, p. 96.
Count Cavour, Fraser's Magazine, February 1878, pp. 185–199.
M. Creighton: The Story of the English Shires. Durham II, Leisure Hour, October 1885, pp. 666–672.
The Crown of Life, Chambers's Journal, 24 June 1876, pp. 401–403.
Cultivation of Minds Amongst Artizans, Chambers's Journal, 25 January 1851, p. 64.
Darwin, Chambers's Journal, 28 January 1888, pp. 49–52.
A Day in Ancient Athens, B.C., 470, Leisure Hour, July 1890, pp. 615–618.
The Deadly Art of War, Leisure Hour, 10 August 1854, pp. 503–508.
The Deadly Art of War, Leisure Hour, 31 August 1854, pp. 551–557.
Derbyism, Fraser's Magazine, January 1854, pp. 118–126.
Domestic Help and Hindrances, Chambers's Journal, 9 December 1899, pp. 17–21.
Dr. Livingstone, Leisure Hour, 25 July 1868, pp. 479–480.
The Duke's Funeral, Leisure Hour, 9 December 1852, pp. 788–790.
The Duke of Wellington, Fraser's Magazine, October 1852, pp. 267–273.
The Duke of Wellington, Leisure Hour, 4 November 1852, pp. 713–718.
Early English Intercourse with Russia, Leisure Hour, 18 January 1855, pp. 45–46.
The Editor's Address to His Readers, Chambers's Journal, 4 February 1832, pp. 1–2.
The Eighteenth of November, Leisure Hour, 1 January 1853, pp. 13–16.
Eliza Warick. A Heroine in Ordinary Life, Chambers's Journal, 12 December 1874, pp. 785–787.
English Heroes and French Honours, Chambers's Journal, 6 September 1856, pp. 155–157.
English Satire in the Nineteenth Century, Fraser's Magazine, December 1881, pp. 753–761.
English: Its Ancestors Its Progeny, Fraser's Magazine, October 1882, pp. 429–457.
An Escape, Chambers's Journal, 6 October 1900, p. 719.

Expense of the War, Chambers's Journal, 20 September 1856, p. 192.
The Fairy Queen, Chambers's Journal, 11 January 1851, pp. 19–22.
The Family Scapegrace, Chambers's Journal, 12 January 1861, pp. 21–26.
Felicia Hemans, Leisure Hour, 29 January 1852, pp. 72–76.
Female Heroism, Chambers's Journal, 12 August 1848, pp. 108–110.
A Few Days at Dover, Leisure Hour, 19 August 1852, pp. 535–540.
A Few Days in Copenhagen, Leisure Hour, 30 January 1864, pp. 70–74.
A Few Words About Heroes, Chambers's Journal, 4 October 1856, pp. 222–223.
A Few Words About the Guides, Chambers's Journal, 3 January 1880, pp. 9–11.
Field-Marshal Viscount Combermere, Fraser's Magazine, November 1866, pp. 564–587.
The Fight with Lotters, Chambers's Journal, 22 March 1902, pp. 240–244.
Fighting for Life. A Story of a Welsh Coal-Mine, Chambers's Journal, 18 August 1877, pp. 526–528.
Fiji, Leisure Hour, 16 January 1875, pp. 39–44.
Filling Little Pitchers, Chambers's Journal, 20 August 1881, pp. 533–535.
The Floods in France, Leisure Hour, 29 January 1876, pp. 68–72.
Footprints of Frederick the Great, Leisure Hour, 11 March 1858, pp. 151–158.
The Fortress of St. Petersburg, Leisure Hour, 27 September 1855, pp. 616–168.
The Fortune of Bertram Oakley, Chambers's Journal, 23 April 1881, pp. 260–261.
Franklin's Fate, and the Voyage of the "Fox", Fraser's Magazine, February 1860, pp. 221–227.
Froude's Julius Caesar, Fraser's Magazine, September 1879, pp. 315–337.
The Funeral of Lord Nelson, Leisure Hour, 25 November 1852, pp. 753–757.
C. G. Furley: The Ring and the Bird, Chambers's Journal, 7 February 1891, pp. 89–92.
The Garrisons of the Crimea, Fraser's Magazine, September 1854, pp. 356–368.
George Stephenson. Part I, Leisure Hour, 17 December 1857, pp. 811–814.
George Stephenson. Part II, Leisure Hour, 24 December 1857, pp. 829–931.
George Stephenson, Chambers's Journal, 22 August 1857, pp. 125–128.
German Heroes, Chambers's Journal, 15 February 1879, pp. 111–112.
A Glance at Sebastopol, Leisure Hour, 16 February 1854, pp. 104–106.
The Glove, Chambers's Journal, 22 December 1860, pp. 398–400.
Good Form, Chambers's Journal, 3 January 1891, pp. 7–9.
The Great Teaboard School, Chambers's Journal, 16 July 1870, pp. 462–464.
Grace Darling, Leisure Hour, July 1883, pp. 442–444.
A. H. A. Hamilton: Quarter Sessions under Queen Elizabeth, Fraser's Magazine, June 1876, pp. 733–746.
Thomas Hare: Representation in Practice and in Theory, Fraser's Magazine, February 1860, 188–204.

Thomas Hare: Representation of Every Locality and Intelligence, Fraser's Magazine, April 1860, pp. 527–543.
R. Heath: Andreas Hofer, Leisure Hour, February 1894, pp. 225–230.
Heinrich Heine, Fraser's Magazine, November 1866, pp. 588–609.
Helps's Conquest in America, Fraser's Magazine, September 1855, pp. 243–256.
A Hero in Humble Life, Leisure Hour, 7 October 1858, pp. 635–636.
Heroes of Australian Exploration, Leisure Hour, December 1886, pp. 841–846.
Heroes of Peace, Chambers's Journal, 6 June 1885, pp. 353–355.
A Heroine at the Diggings, Chambers's Journal, 29 August 1874, pp. 560.
The Heroine of Lydenberg. An Episode in the Transvaal War of 1880–81, Chambers's Journal, 18 November 1899, pp. 801–803.
Heroines, Chambers's Journal, 2 August 1882, pp. 492–494.
Heroines, Leisure Hour, August 1887, p. 524.
Hero-Worship, Chambers's Journal, 1 September 1849, pp. 129–131.
A Homely Heroine, Chambers's Journal, 31 January 1874, pp. 65–68.
Homer and the Homeric Age, Fraser's Magazine, January 1859, pp. 50–65.
A Hospital Hero, Chambers's Journal, 25 June 1859, pp. 144–145.
A Hundred Years Ago, Leisure Hour, 16 December 1865, pp. 795–796.
The Ideal and Real, Afloat and Ashore, Chambers's Journal, 18 February 1854, pp. 103–105.
An Incident of War, Chambers's Journal, 6 March 1880, pp. 158–159.
In Kimberley During the Siege, Chambers's Journal, 19 March 1900, pp. 385–388.
Introductory Lessons on Morals: Second Series. Chapter VII: Easier and Harder Duties, Leisure Hour, 1 November 1855, pp. 694–696.
The Iron Duke, Leisure Hour, March 1900, pp. 405–414.
Is Monarchy an Anachronism?, Fraser's Magazine, October 1875, pp. 411–436.
Jeanne D'Arc. A Holiday Discovery, Leisure Hour, March 1893, pp. 343–344.
Joseph de Maistre, Fraser's Magazine, April 1849, pp. 383–396.
The Jubilee Singers, Chambers's Journal, 12 January 1878, pp. 17–20.
Julius Caesar, Fraser's Magazine, July 1867, pp. 1–15.
Kaye's History of the Indian Mutiny, Fraser's Magazine, December 1864, pp. 757–774.
The Kembles, Chambers's Journal, 22 November 1871, 717–720.
The Kingdom of Sardinia and its Sovereign, Leisure Hour, 3 January 1856, pp. 8–11.
The Lady Traveller, Leisure Hour, 29 January 1852, pp. 69–72.
Lambert, the "Hero and Martyr", Chambers's Journal, 26 August 1876, pp. 545–546.
Lamp Oils, Chambers's Journal, 20 June 1891, pp. 389–391.
The Late Sir William Fairbairn, Leisure Hour, 28 April 1877, pp. 282–267.

William Le Queux: Of Royal Blood. A Story of the Secret Service, Chambers's Journal, 2 December 1899, pp. 1–5.
–: Of Royal Blood. A Story of the Secret Service, Chambers's Journal, 16 December 1899, pp. 35–37.
–: Of Royal Blood. A Story of the Secret Service, Chambers's Journal, 6 January 1900, pp. 87–90.
–: Of Royal Blood. A Story of the Secret Service, Chambers's Journal, 13 January 1900, pp. 101–104.
–: Of Royal Blood. A Story of the Secret Service, Chambers's Journal, 20 January 1900, pp. 115–118.
–: Of Royal Blood. A Story of the Secret Service, Chambers's Journal, 27 January 1900, pp. 131–133.
–: Of Royal Blood. A Story of the Secret Service, Chambers's Journal, 3 February 1900, pp. 150–154.
–: Of Royal Blood. A Story of the Secret Service, Chambers's Journal, 17 February 1900, pp. 180–183.
–: Of Royal Blood. A Story of the Secret Service, Chambers's Journal, 24 February 1900, pp. 196–200.
–: Of Royal Blood. A Story of the Secret Service, Chambers's Journal, 3 March 1900, pp. 216–218.
–: Of Royal Blood. A Story of the Secret Service, Chambers's Journal, 17 March 1900, pp. 244–247.
–: Of Royal Blood. A Story of the Secret Service, Chambers's Journal, 14 April 1900, pp. 307–311.
–: Of Royal Blood. A Story of the Secret Service, Chambers's Journal, 28 April 1900, pp. 338–340.
A Leap For Life, Chambers's Journal, 30 June 1883, pp. 406–408.
Leniency: Why and How it Failed in South Africa, Chambers's Journal, 9 March 1901, pp. 226–230.
Lessons from the Life of George Stephenson, Leisure Hour, 12 May 1858, pp. 298–301.
Little Heroes, Chambers's Journal, 16 December 1882, pp. 806–807.
Livingstonia Mission and Central Africa, Chambers's Journal, 6 January 1900, pp. 90–93.
London in the Streets, Leisure Hour, 17 November 1877, pp. 725–728.
A Long Swim, Chambers's Journal, 17 November 1866, pp. 721–724.
Looting a Boer Camp, Chambers's Journal, 5 January 1901, pp. 94–96.
Lyell's Second Visit to the United State, Chambers's Journal, 21 July 1849, pp. 38–40.
Lyell's Second Visit to the United States, Chambers's Journal, 28 July 1849, pp. 53–55.

The Lyonese Weaver, Leisure Hour, 5 February 1852, pp. 85–87.
William Maginn: A Wind-up for our Seventh Volume, Literary, Political and Anti-Peelish, Fraser's Magazine, June 1833, pp. 750–752.
Matthew Arnold's "Merope", Fraser's Magazine, June 1858, pp. 691–701.
Mechanisms of Chambers's Journal, Leisure Hour, 6 June 1835, pp. 149–151.
Medals and Medal-Collecting, Chambers's Journal, 20 February 1892, pp. 124–126.
Meliboeus Has a Fish-Dinner At Greenwich, Chambers's Journal, 5 October 1861, pp. 218–221.
Men of the Time, Chambers's Journal, 22 March 1856, pp. 183–186.
The Men that Have Been Long Dead, Leisure Hour, 8 February 1855, p. 95.
Military Prisoners, Chambers's Journal, 13 April 1901, pp. 318–320.
Military Tableaux; or, Scenes from the Wars of Napoleon, Sketched in the Manner of Callot, Fraser's Magazine, April 1844, pp. 487–495.
The Miners of Cornwall, Leisure Hour, 9 February 1860, pp. 91–95.
Miss Winter's Hero, Chambers's Journal, 30 May 1891, pp. 344–347.
The Missionary Surgeon, Leisure Hour, 23 March 1854, pp. 186–190.
The Missionary's Wife, Leisure Hour, 10 January 1863, pp. 31–32.
Modern Spartans, Chambers's Journal, 29 April 1871, pp. 257–259.
The Month: Science and the Arts, Chambers's Journal, 28 July 1900, pp. 556–560.
Montyon Prize, Leisure Hour, November 1889, pp. 40–48.
Montyon Prize, Leisure Hour, December 1889, pp. 127–133.
Montyon Prize, Leisure Hour, February 1890, pp. 247–253.
Montyon Prize, Leisure Hour, May 1890, pp. 461–468.
Montyon Prize, Leisure Hour, July 1890, pp. 597–602.
Montyon Prize, Leisure Hour, September 1890, pp. 740–745.
Montyon Prize, Leisure Hour, October 1890, pp. 823–828.
Montyon Prize, Leisure Hour, July 1891, pp. 605–611.
Montyon Prize, Leisure Hour, August 1891, pp. 701–706.
Montyon Prize, Leisure Hour, September 1891, pp. 780–783.
Moral Without Physical Courage, Chambers's Journal, 24 February 1849, p. 128.
The Mother of the Czar, Leisure Hour, 21 December 1854, pp. 811–813.
Motley's John Barneveld, Fraser's Magazine, August 1874, pp. 223–245.
Mr Thackeray's Ballads, Chambers's Journal, 2 February 1856, pp. 73–76.
Mrs. Chisholm, Chambers's Journal, 25 September 1852, pp. 193–196.
My Coming Out, Chambers's Journal, 15 December 1860, pp. 369–371.
My Heroine, Chambers's Journal, 29 November 1879, p. 768.
My Midnight Visitor. A South African Story, Chambers's Journal, 21 June 1902, pp. 456–459.

My Midnight Visitor. A South African Story, Chambers's Journal, 28 June 1902, pp. 473–476.
Myself and My Relative, Chambers's Journal, 6 July 1861, pp. 1–5.
Naval Badges and Crests, Leisure Hour, 10 March 1877, pp. 152–154.
The Naval School on Board the "Illustrious", Fraser's Magazine, April 1855, pp. 455–466.
The Negro Liberator of Hayti, Leisure Hour, 31 March 1853, pp. 218–221.
Newton, Chambers's Journal, 13 September 1856, pp. 168–170.
Newton, Chambers's Journal, 20 September 1856, pp. 179–182.
A Non-Combatant Hero, Chambers's Journal, 8 March 1862, pp. 158–160.
Notes on the National Drama of Spain, Fraser's Magazine, September 1859, pp. 314–330.
Old Inventions of New Discoverie, Chambers's Journal, 17 November 1860, pp. 306–309.
On Autographs, Leisure Hour, February 1882, pp. 93–99.
On Board Nelson's Ship, Leisure Hour, February 1887, pp. 135–137.
On the Comparative Stupidity of Politicians, Fraser's Magazine, October 1877, pp. 486–490.
On the Rock with Garibaldi, Chambers's Journal, 29 June 1861, pp. 401–404.
One of Nelson's Captains, Leisure Hour, October 1899, pp. 58–60.
Bertie Orr: The Requiem of George Stephenson, Leisure Hour, February 1899, p. 261.
Our Confession of Faith, Fraser's Magazine, February 1830, pp. 1–7.
Our New Ally. In Two Parts. – Part I, Chambers's Journal, 21 July 1855, p. 40.
Our New Ally. In Two Parts. – Part II, Chambers's Journal, 28 July 1855, p. 40.
Over the Var, Chambers's Journal, 29 September 1860, pp. 193–197.
A Parcel of Anecdotes, Leisure Hour, July 1899, pp. 595–598.
John Parker: A Happy New Year, Fraser's Magazine, January 1849, pp. 1–3.
The Past and Future of the High Church Party, Fraser's Magazine, February 1878, pp. 240–249.
Patriot and Traitor, Chambers's Journal, 31 March 1900, pp. 283–284.
The Perkin Warbeck of Russian History, Leisure Hour, 22 March 1855, pp. 182–183.
Peter Mackenzie the Naturalist, Chambers's Journal, 11 May 1850, pp. 299–300.
Pitmen, Past and Present, Chambers's Journal, 30 October 1886, pp. 696–699.
Poccahontas, Leisure Hour, 9 September 1852, pp. 577–582.
Poccahontas, Leisure Hour, 16 September 1852, pp. 593–597.
Poccahontas, Leisure Hour, 23 September 1852, pp. 609–612.
Poccahontas, Leisure Hour, September, pp. 625–627.
Poems by Matthew Arnold, Fraser's Magazine, February 1854, pp. 140–149.
Poetry, Leisure Hour, 8 February 1855, p. 95.

Popular Heroes, Chambers's Journal, 24 October 1863, pp. 264–266.
Popular Medicine in Russia, Chambers's Journal, 5 March 1881, pp. 159–160.
Portland Prison, Chambers's Journal, 23 March 1861, pp. 190–192.
The Power of "Good Spirits", Leisure Hour, May 1880, pp. 335–336.
Presence of Mind, Chambers's Journal, 30 April 1870, pp. 273–276.
Present Aspects of the Labour Question, Fraser's Magazine, May 1873, pp. 597–604.
Prince Michael Woronzoff, Leisure Hour, 28 December 1854, pp. 820–823.
Principal Campaigns in the Rise of Napoleon, Fraser's Magazine, February 1846, pp. 157–179.
Principal Campaigns in the Rise of Napoleon, Fraser's Magazine, March 1846, pp. 276–287.
Principal Campaigns in the Rise of Napoleon, Fraser's Magazine, April 1846, pp. 413–433.
Principal Campaigns in the Rise of Napoleon, Fraser's Magazine, May 1846, pp. 545–560.
Principal Campaigns in the Rise of Napoleon, Fraser's Magazine, June 1846, pp. 649–665.
Principal Campaigns in the Rise of Napoleon, Fraser's Magazine, July 1846, pp. 49–66.
Principal Campaigns in the Rise of Napoleon, Fraser's Magazine, August 1846, pp. 182–197.
Principal Campaigns in the Rise of Napoleon, Fraser's Magazine, September 1846, pp. 283–300.
Principal Campaigns in the Rise of Napoleon, Fraser's Magazine, October 1846, pp. 428–435.
Principal Campaigns in the Rise of Napoleon, Fraser's Magazine, November 1846, pp. 551–566.
The Principle of the Grecian Mythology, or, How the Greeks Made Their Gods, Fraser's Magazine, January 1854, pp. 69–79.
Printing By Magic, Leisure Hour, 4 February 1854, pp. 68–70.
The Printing Office – a Visit to Clowes's, Chambers's Journal, 11 April 1840, pp. 94–95.
Privateers and Privateering, Chambers's Journal, 8 July 1854, pp. 29–31.
The Professor's Wife, Chambers's Journal, 26 May 1860, pp. 326–330.
The Prophetic Thought, Chambers's Journal, 6 September 1851, pp. 145–146.
The Proudest Moment of My Life, Chambers's Journal, 4 January 1862, pp. 9–12.
Quarantinem, Chambers's Journal, 16 November 1889, pp. 731–733.
Railway Literature, Leisure Hour, 22 March 1845, pp. 177–180.

Recollections of an Anglo-Indian Chaplain, Chambers's Journal, 19 June 1880, pp. 390–391.
Remarkable Naval Duels, Chambers's Journal, 2 September 1854, pp. 153–155.
A Remarkable Rogue, Chambers's Journal, 8 January 1881, pp. 30–32.
Revolutions in English History, Fraser's Magazine, April 1860, pp. 485–500.
A Russian Aesop, Leisure Hour, 28 September 1854, pp. 619–620.
Russia as I Saw it Forty Years Ago, Leisure Hour, 15 November 1855, pp. 726–728.
Russia as I Saw it Forty Years Ago, Leisure Hour, 22 November 1855, pp. 742–743.
Russia as I Saw it Forty Years Ago, Leisure Hour, 29 November 1855, pp. 758–759.
Russian Campaigns in Turkey 1828 and 1829, Leisure Hour, 20 June 1854, pp. 455–458.
Russia under Alexander and Nicholas, Leisure Hour, 26 October 1854, pp. 676–679.
Russia under Catherine II and Paul, Leisure Hour, 18 October 1854, pp. 660–663.
Russia under Peter the Great, Leisure Hour, 12 October 1854, pp. 650–653.
Russian Ships and Russian Gunners, Fraser's Magazine, June 1854, pp. 613–631.
Scrambles Up the Hill of Life, Chambers's Journal, 23 April 1881, pp. 267–269.
A Seaside Story, Chambers's Journal, 27 February 1858, pp. 129–132.
Sedan, Chambers's Journal, 2 February 1901, pp. 158–160.
Self-Possession in Moments of Peril, Leisure Hour, 16 June 1853, pp. 394–396.
Shirley: Charles James Napier: A Study in Character, Fraser's Magazine, February 1858, pp. 254–268.
Shirley: The Sphynx. A Discourse on the Importance of History, Fraser's Magazine, July 1861, pp. 54–70.
Sir Henry Havelock, Leisure Hour, 31 May 1860, pp. 250–252.
Sir Henry Lawrence, Fraser's Magazine, August 1872, pp. 251–264.
Sir John Franklin and the Arctic Expeditions, Leisure Hour, 26 February 1852, pp. 135–139.
Sir John Franklin's First Journey in the Polar Regions, Leisure Hour, 1 January 1852, pp. 10–12.
Sketches of Campaigning Life, Fraser's Magazine, August 1854, pp. 223–237.
Sketches of the Crimea, Leisure Hour, 15 March 1855, pp. 169–172.
Sketches of the Crimea, Leisure Hour, 22 March 1855, pp. 183–187.
Sketches of the Crimea, Leisure Hour, 12 April 1855, pp. 232–236.
Sketches of the Crimea, Leisure Hour, 26 April 1855, pp. 264–268.
Sketches of the Crimea, Leisure Hour, 10 May 1855, pp. 295–299.

Soiree to Working People By Their Employers, Chambers's Journal, 7 August 1841, pp. 231–232.
Some Brave Women, Chambers's Journal, 18 September 1880, pp. 606–608.
Some Episodes of the Afghan War of 1880, Chambers's Journal, 19 January 1901, pp. 113–115.
Some Notices of the Shakspearian Drama, Shakspeare, and His Commentators, Fraser's Magazine, June 1842, pp. 645–653.
Some of the Men of the Great Reform Bill, Leisure Hour, September 1883, pp. 554–559.
Some of the Men of the Great Reform Bill, Leisure Hour, November 1883, pp. 663–668.
Some Traces of Henry Martin, the Missionary, Leisure Hour, 25 November 1858, pp. 749–751.
Storm Warriors, Chambers's Journal, 28 October 1876, pp. 689–692.
Story of a Dramatist, Chambers's Journal, 25 July 1851, pp. 63–64.
Story of a Forgotten Benefactor, Leisure Hour, 27 September 1855, pp. 621–623.
The Story of a Hero, Chambers's Journal, 15 October 1859, pp. 243–246.
The Story of the First English Silk-Mill, Leisure Hour, 18 December 1856, pp. 606–608.
A Strange Wedding, Chambers's Journal, 28 August 1880, pp. 553–557.
Stray Thoughts in a Library, Chambers's Journal, 5 June 1880, pp. 365–366.
Street Ballads of the War, Chambers's Journal, 17 May 1856, pp. 305–309.
The Street News-Boys of London, Chambers's Journal, 21 February 1874, pp. 113–115.
The Subsidence of Land in the Salt Districts of Cheshire, Chambers's Journal, 22 January 1881, pp. 59–61.
The Surgeon Missionary, Leisure Hour, 23 March 1854, pp. 186–190.
W. H. A. Swain: March from Johannesburg, Leisure Hour, May 1890, pp. 630–631.
A Swim for Life, Chambers's Journal, 26 March 1859, pp. 207–208.
A Tale, Entitled Myself and My Relative, Chambers's Journal, 15 June 1861, p. 384.
A Tale, Entitled Myself and My Relative, Chambers's Journal, 29 June 1861, p. 416.
The Teutonic and the Celtic Epic, Fraser's Magazine, March 1874, pp. 336–354.
Thalatta! Thalatta!, Fraser's Magazine, April 1862, pp. 415–431.
Things Talked of in London, Chambers's Journal, 27 November 1852, pp. 350–352.
Thirty Years of the Reign of Victoria, Leisure Hour, 27 July 1872, pp. 471–472.
This Ought Ye to Have Done, Chambers's Journal, 11 August 1900, p. 592.

Thought on Modern English Literature, Fraser's Magazine, July 1859, pp. 97–110.
A Three Months' Captivity among the Giants of Patagonia, Leisure Hour, 26 May 1853, pp. 347–351.
Three Visits to the Hotel des Invalides. 1705, 1806, 1840, Leisure Hour, 2 August 1854, pp. 481–484.
The True Amazon, Chambers's Journal, 25 June 1859, p. 416.
True Chivalry, Chambers's Journal, 29 June 1850, p. 416.
True Chivalry, Chambers's Journal, 15 September 1866, pp. 592.
A True Hero, Leisure Hour, June 1881, p. 364.
Turkey and the East of Europe in Relation to England and the West, Fraser's Magazine, May 1853, pp. 562–573.
The Twin Brothers, Chambers's Journal, 3 January 1851, p. 16.
The Ugly Duckling Theory, Chambers's Journal, 15 January 1881, pp. 46–48.
An Umbrella Eclogue, Chambers's Journal, 7 November 1863, pp. 294–296.
Universal Hero-Worship Company (Limited), Punch, 4 June 1864, p. 236.
Unsung Heroes, Chambers's Journal, 21 July 1888, pp. 464–464.
Up and Down Regent Street, Chambers's Journal, 16 June 1860, pp. 369–371.
A Vaal River Adventure, Chambers's Journal, 23 November 1901, pp. 820–824.
Varieties, Leisure Hour, 12 July 1855, p. 448.
Varieties, Leisure Hour, 3 May 1860, p. 288
Varieties, Leisure Hour, 27 September 1860, p. 624.
Varieties, Leisure Hour, 24 September 1870, p. 624.
Varieties, Leisure Hour, 27 March 1875, p. 208.
Varieties, Leisure Hour, 25 September 1875, p. 624.
Varieties, Leisure Hour, 11 December 1880, pp. 779–780.
Varieties, Leisure Hour, June 1900, pp. 774–776.
Visit of Peter the Great to the Prussian Court, Leisure Hour, 8 February 1855, pp. 93–95.
A Visit of Sebastopol in the Time of Peace, Leisure Hour, 31 May 1855, pp. 350–351.
A Visit to the Marshes of La Vendée, Leisure Hour, 7 June 1855, pp. 353–357.
A Visit to Walmer Castle in November, 1852, Leisure Hour, 10 February 1853, pp. 105–107.
Annie Walker: A Forgotten Hero, Fraser's Magazine, December 1880, pp. 755–783.
Watt and the Steam Engine, Leisure Hour, 30 April 1854, pp. 758–562.
A Week in Bed, Fraser's Magazine, March 1864, pp. 327–334.
What Is Heroism, Chambers's Journal, 9 May 1857, pp. 297–298.
What to Do in the Meantime, Chambers's Journal, 6 December 1851, pp. 353–355.

Whitelocke's Embassy to Sweden, Fraser's Magazine, March 1855, pp. 345–354.
The Wild Huntress, Chambers's Journal, 21 July 1860, pp. 38–44.
William the Silent: A Study in Character, Fraser's Magazine, April 1860, pp. 463–474.
Won – Not Wooed, Chambers's Journal, 11 February 1871, pp. 82–87.
Won – Not Wooed, Chambers's Journal, 18 February 1871, pp. 102–107.
Woolwich Arsenal, Leisure Hour, 3 August 1854, pp. 487–490.
A Word With Our Readers, Leisure Hour, 1 January 1852, pp. 8–10.
Working Men's Clubs and Institutions, Fraser's Magazine, March 1865, pp. 282–295.
Working-Men, Chambers's Journal, 18 May 1867, pp. 317–320.

Archival Material

Charles Chambers: Letter to Grant Allen, 1885, Dep 341/165: No 822, National Library of Scotland, Edinburgh.
Charles Chambers: Letter to William Le Queux, 1900, Dep 341/167: No 355, National Library of Scotland, Edinburgh.
Correspondence, 1854-1855, Dep. 341/129: unnumbered, National Library of Scotland, Edinburgh.
Anna Maria Hall: Letter to Chambers's Journal., n.d., Dep 341/121: No 17, National Library of Scotland, Edinburgh.
Hawke: Letter to Chambers's Journal, 1854, Dep 341/129: unnumbered, National Library of Scotland, Edinburgh.
Charles Martel: Letter to Chambers's Journal, 1854, Dep 341/131, unnumbered, National Library of Scotland, Edinburgh.
William Le Queux: Letter to Charles Chambers, 1900, Dep 341/143: No 36, National Library of Scotland, Edinburgh.
William Le Queux: Letter to Charles Chambers, 1899, Dep 341/143: No 37, National Library of Scotland, Edinburgh.
Paper sent in by Readers, 1854, Dept 341/131: unnumbered, National Library of Scotland, Edinburgh.
Payment Records 1871–1879, Dep 341/368: unnumbered, National Library of Scotland, Edinburgh.
Payment Records 1888–1893, Dep 341/370: unnumbered, National Library of Scotland, Edinburgh.
Payment Records 1893–1903, Dep 341/371: unnumbered, National Library of Scotland, Edinburgh.
Reverend: Letter to Chambers's Journal, 1883, Dep 341/139: unnumbered, National Library of Scotland, Edinburgh.

W. B. Adams: Leading Events in English History. Adapted to the Requirements of the Educational Code, London/Edinburgh 1880.
Matthew Arnold: On the Study of Celtic Literature and on Translating Homer, New York 1970 [1861].
Charles Booth: Labour and Life of the People, London 1902 [1889].
Thomas Carlyle: On Heroes, Hero-Worship, and the Heroic in History. Six Lectures. Reported With Emendations and Additions, Ann Arbor 2006 [1841].
Robert Chambers: A Biographical Dictionary of Eminent Scotsmen. With a Supplement Continuing the Biographies to the Present Time, Glasgow 1875.
–: Vestiges of the Natural History of Creation, London 1860 [1844].
Robert Chambers / William Chambers (eds.): Exemplary and Instructive Biography. For the Study of Youth, Edinburgh 1836.
–: Exemplary and Instructive Biography, Edinburgh 1846.
–: Entertaining Biography. From Chambers's Repository, Edinburgh 1855.
–: Chambers's Supplementary Reader, Edinburgh 1872.
–: Chambers's National Reading-Books, Edinburgh 1873.
–: Chambers's British Science-Biographies, Natural History, Edinburgh 1886.
–: Chambers's Story Readers, Edinburgh 1899.
–: Chambers's Summary of English History, Edinburgh 1904.
William Chambers: Jubilee Year of Chambers's Journal. Reminiscences of a Long and Busy Life, Edinburgh 1882.
–: Memoir of William and Robert Chambers, Edinburgh 1883.
– (ed.): Famous Men. Being Biographical Sketches from Chambers's Miscellany, Edinburgh 1886.
– (ed.): Social Science Tracts, Edinburgh 1860.
Robert Cochrane: Great Thinkers and Workers, Edinburgh 1888.
–: Lives of Good and Great Women, Edinburgh 1888.
Auguste Comte: The New Calendar of Great Men. Biographies of the 559 Worthies of All Ages and Nations, London 1920 [1849].
T. Darling: Grace Darling, Her True Story. From Unpublished Papers in Possession of Her Family, London 1880.
Ralph Waldo Emerson: The Collected Works of Ralph Waldo Emerson, vol. 4: Representative Men. Seven Lectures, Cambridge 1987 [1850].
Eliza Greenup: Friendly Advice to Pupil-Teachers, Edinburgh 1877.
George Jacob Holyoake: Sixty Years of an Agitator's Life, London 1892.
Joseph Johnson: Clever Boys of Our Time and How They Became Famous Men, London 1879 [1860].
–: Clever Girls Of Our Time Who Became Famous Women, London 1862.
Charles Kingsley: The Heroes, Hildesheim 1968 [1856].

William Linwood: Great Men, Their Characteristics, Influence and Destiny. A Lecture Occasioned by the Death of the Rev. E.W. Channing, London 1843.
John Stuart Mill: Utilitarianism, Oxford 1998 [1861].
H. Alleyne Nicholson (ed.): Chambers's British Science-Biographies. Natural History, Edinburgh 1886.
Henry Parnell: On Financial Reform, London 1830.
David Patrick / Francis Hindes Groome: Chambers's Biographical Dictionary. The Great of All Times and Nations, London/Edinburgh 1897.
Leopold von Ranke: Sämmtliche Werke, Vol. 33, Leipzig 1885.
John Ruskin: Modern Painters, New York 1863 [1860].
George Saintsbury: A History of Nineteenth Century Literature 1780–1895, London 1896.
Samuel Smiles: Self-Help, London 1997 [1859].
–: Brief Biographies, New York 1881.
Thomas Wright: Some Habits and Customs of the Working Classes, London 1867.
Charlotte M. Yonge: A Book of Golden Deeds, London 1864.

Secondary Sources

Brian Abel-Smith: History of the Nursing Profession, London 1960.
Amrollah Abjadian: Ruskin and the School of "Grand Style", in: Etudes Anglaises. Grande-Bretagne, Etats-Unis 29, 1976, pp. 15–26.
Lynn Abrams: Ideals of Womanhood in Victorian Britain, in: BBC History 9, 2001, pp. 1–9.
James Eli Adams: The Hero as Spectacle. Carlyle and the Persistence of Dandyism, in: Carol T. Christ / John O. Jordan (eds.): Victorian Literature and the Victorian Visual Imagination, Berkeley 1995, pp. 213–232.
Thomas R. Adams / Nicolas Barker: A New Model for the Study of the Book, in: Nicolas Barker (ed.): A Potencie of Life. Books in Society, London 1993, pp. 5–43.
G. A. Aitkin: Chambers, Robert (1832–1888), in: Lawrence Goldman (ed.): Oxford Dictionary of National Biography, 2014, DOI: 10.1093/ref:odnb/5080.
Edward Alexander: Matthew Arnold and John Stuart Mill, London 2010 [1965].
–: Matthew Arnold, John Ruskin, and the Modern Temper, Columbus 1973.
Sally Alexander: St. Giles's Fair, 1830–1914. Popular Culture and the Industrial Revolution in the 19th Century, Oxford 1970.
Richard Altick: The English Common Reader, Columbus 1998 [1957].
–: The Presence of the Present. Topics of the Day in the Victorian Novel, Columbus 1991.
Benedict Anderson: Imagined Communities. Reflections on the Origin and Spread of Nationalism, London 2006.

Dennis R. Alexander: The Implications of Evolutionary Biology for Religious Belief, in: Kostas Kampourakis (ed.): The Philosophy of Biology, Dordrecht 2013, pp. 179–204.

Olive Anderson: The Growth of Christian Militarism in Mid-Victorian Britain, in: The English Historical Review 86.338, 1971, pp. 46–72.

Patricia Anderson: The Printed Image and the Transformation of Popular Culture 1790–1860, Oxford 1991.

R. D. Anderson: Education and the Scottish People 1750–1918, Oxford 1995.

R. D. Anderson et al. (eds.): The Edinburgh History of Education in Scotland, Edinburgh 2015.

Juliette Atkinson: Victorian Biography Reconsidered, Oxford 2010.

Janet Badia et al. (eds.): Reading Women. Literary Figures and Cultural Icons from the Victorian Age to the Present, Toronto 2005.

Chris Baggs: "In the Separate Reading Room for Ladies Are Provided Those Publications Specially Interesting to Them". Ladies' Reading Rooms and British Public Libraries 1850–1914, in: Victorian Periodicals Review 38.3, 2005, pp. 280–306.

Tracey Alison Baker: The Figure of the Nurse. Struggles for Wholeness in the Novels of Jane Austen, Anne, Charlotte, Emily Bronte, and George Eliot, in: Dissertation Abstracts International 46.2, 1985, pp. 427a–428a.

Chris Barker: Cultural Studies. Theory and Practice, London 2012 [2000].

Derek Beales: Garibaldi in England. The Politics of Italian Enthusiasm, in: John A. Davis / Paul Ginsborg (eds.): Society and Politics in the Age of the Risorgimento. Essays in Honour of Denis Mack Smith, Cambridge 2002, pp. 184–216.

Margaret Beetham: Open and Closed. The Periodical as a Publishing Genre, in: Victorian Periodicals Review 22.3, 1989, pp. 96–100.

–: Towards a Theory of the Periodical as a Publishing Genre, in: Laurel Brake et al. (eds.): Investigating Victorian Journalism, New York 1990, pp. 19–32.

–: A Magazine of Her Own?, London 1996.

–: Women and the Consumption of Print, in: Joanne Shattock (ed.): Women and Literature in Britain, 1800–1900, Cambridge 2001, pp. 55–77.

–: Magazines, in: Laurel Brake / Marysa Demoor (eds.): Dictionary of Nineteenth Century Journalism in Great Britain and Ireland, Ghent/London 2009, pp. 391–392.

–: Time. Periodicals and the Time of the Now, Victorian Periodicals Review 48.3, 2015, pp. 323–342.

Scott Bennett: Revolutions in Thought. Serial Publication and the Mass Market for Reading, in: Joanne Shattock / Michael Wolff (eds.): The Victorian Periodical Press. Samplings and Soundings, Leicester/Toronto 1982, pp. 225–257.

Eric Bentley: The Cult of the Superman, Gloucester 1969.

Robert A. Bickers / Rosemary Seton: Missionary Encounters, London 2013.

Sarah Bilston. "It Is Not What We Read, But How We Read". Maternal Counsel on Girls' Reading Practices in Mid-Victorian Literature, in: Nineteenth-Century Contexts 30.1, 2008, pp. 1–20.

Alistair Black: Lost Worlds of Culture. Victorian Libraries, Library History, and Prospects for a History of Information, in: Journal of Victorian Culture 2.1, 1997, pp. 95–112.

Jeremy Black: The Victorian Maritime Empire in Its Global Context, in: Miles Taylor (ed.): The Victorian Empire and Britain's Maritime World, 1837–1901, Basingstoke 2013, pp. 167–188.

Maurice Blanchot: The End of the Hero, in: id. (ed.): The Infinite Conversation, Minneapolis 1993, pp. 368–378.

Frank Bösch: Zwischen Populärkultur und Politik. Britische und deutsche Printmedien im 19. Jahrhundert, in: Archiv für Sozialgeschichte 45, 2005, pp. 549–584.

Pierre Bourdieu: Distinction. A Social Critique of the Judgement of Taste, Cambridge 1984.

Peter J. Bowler: Evolution. The History of an Idea, Berkeley 1989.

Laurel Brake: The "Popular Weeklies", in: Bill Bell (ed.): The Edinburgh History of the Book in Scotland, vol. 3, Edinburgh 2007, pp. 358–369.

–: The Advantage of Fiction. The Novel and the "Success" of the Victorian Periodical, in: Beth Palmer (ed.): A Return to the Common Reader, Farnham 2011, pp. 9–21.

–: The Lure of Illustration in the Nineteenth Century. Picture and Press, Basingstoke 2009.

Laurel Brake et al. (eds.): Nineteenth-Century Media and the Construction of Identities, Basingstoke 2000.

Laurel Brake / Marysa Demoor (eds.): Dictionary of Nineteenth-Century Journalism in Great Britain and Ireland, Ghent/London 2009.

Lucien Braun: Polysémie du concept de héros, in: Noémie Hepp / Georges Livet (eds.): Héroïsme et création littéraire sous les règnes d'Henri IV et de Louis XIII, Paris 1974, pp. 19–28.

Asa Briggs: Iron Bridge to Crystal Palace. Impact and Images of the Industrial Revolution, London 1979.

–: Victorian Things, London 1988.

Charles Frederick Briggs / August Maverick: The Story of the Telegraph and a History of the Great Atlantic Cable, Ann Arbor 2006 [1958].

Ulrich Broich: On Heroes and Hero-Worship, Especially in English Romanticism, in: Anglistik 16.2, 2005, pp. 49–62.

John Hedley Brooke: Religious Belief and the Content of the Sciences, in: Osiris 16, 2001, pp. 3–28.

Renate Brosch: Victorian Visual Culture, Heidelberg 2008.

Anthony Burton: The Railway Empire, London 1994.

Dennis Butts / Pat Garrett (eds.): From the Dairyman's Daughter to Worrals of the WAAF. The Religious Tract Society, Lutterworth Press and Children's Literature, Cambridge 2006.

Barbara Caine: English Feminism 1780–1980, Oxford 1997.

–: Feminism, Journalism and Public Debate, in: Joanne Shattock (ed.): Women and Literature in Britain 1800–1900, Cambridge 2001, pp. 99–118.

–: Victorian Feminists, Oxford 1992.

Jason Camlot: Style and the Nineteenth-Century British Critic. Sincere Mannerisms, Aldershot 2008.

Colin Campbell: The Romantic Ethics and the Spirit of Modern Consumerism, Oxford 1987.

John Angus Campbell: Scientific Revolution and the Grammar of Culture. The Case of Darwin's Origin, in: Quarterly Journal of Speech 72.4, 1986, pp. 351–376.

Geoffrey Cantor et al. (eds.): Introduction, in: Louise Henson (ed.): Culture and Science in the Nineteenth-Century Media, Aldershot 2004, pp. xvii–xxv.

Nick Carter: Britain, Ireland and the Italian Risorgimento, Basingstoke 2015.

Cornelius Castoriadis: The Imaginary Institution of Society, Cambridge, MA 1998.

Martin Ceadel: The Origins of War Prevention. The British Peace Movement and International Relations 1730–1854, Oxford 1996.

Owen Chadwick: The Secularization of the European Mind in the Nineteenth Century, Cambridge 1975.

Chambers's Edinburgh Journal, in: The Waterloo Directory of English Newspapers and Periodicals. 1800–1900, www.victorianperiodicals.com/series2/default.asp, 22 January 2020.

Malcom Chase: Chartism. A New History, Manchester 2008.

Edward H. Cohen: Henley Among the Nightingales, in: Nineteenth-Century Studies 8, 1994, pp. 23–43.

James B. Conacher: Britain and the Crimea 1855–56. Problems of War and Peace, Basingstoke 1987.

Sondra Miley Cooney: Chambers, Robert (1802–1871), in: Lawrence Goldman (ed.): Oxford Dictionary of National Biography, 2014, DOI: 10.1093/ref:odnb/5079.

Simon Cooke: Illustrated Periodicals of the 1860s, London 2010.

Courage, in: OED Online, Oxford University Press, December 2019, www.oed.com/view/Entry/43146?rskey=aDwFNN&result=1#eid.

Jeffrey Cox: The British Missionary Enterprise since 1700, London 2007.

Christina Crosby: The Ends of History. Victorians and "the Woman Question", London 1991.

Geoffrey Cubitt: Introduction, in: Geoffrey Cubitt / Allen Warren (eds.): Heroic Reputations and Exemplary Lives, Manchester 2000, pp. 1–26.

Nicholas John Cull et al. (eds.): Propaganda and Mass Persuasion. A Historical Encyclopedia 1500 to the Present, Santa Barbara 2003.

Hugh Cunningham: Grace Darling. Victorian Heroine, London 2007.

Cynthia Curran: Private Women, Public Needs. Middle-Class Widows in Victorian England, in: Albion. A Quarterly Journal Concerned with British Studies, 1993, pp. 217–236.

H. Dagnall: The Taxes on Knowledge. Excise Duty on Paper, in: The Library 6.4, 1998, pp. 347–363.

Robert Darnton: What Is the History of Books, in: Daedalus 111.3, 1982, pp. 65–83.

Leonore Davidoff: Gender and the "Great Divide": Public and Private in British Gender History, in: Journal of Women's History 15.1, 2003, pp. 11–27.

Leonore Davidoff / Catherine Hall (eds.): Family Fortunes. Men and Women of the English Middle Class 1780–1850, London 2002.

Catherine Delafield: Serialization and the Novel in Mid-Victorian Magazines, Farnham 2015.

Thomas Dixon: The Invention of Altruism. Making Moral Meanings in Victorian Britain, Oxford 2008.

Allen Douglas / Paul F. Anderson: Consumption and Social Stratification. Bourdieu's Distinction, in: Advances in Consumer Research 21, 1994, pp. 70–74.

Patrick A. Dunae: Penny Dreadfuls. Late Nineteenth-Century Boys' Literature and Crime, in: Victorian Studies. A Journal of the Humanities, Arts and Sciences 22, 1979, pp. 133–150.

Marie Alexis Easley: Longman's Magazine, in: Laurel Brake / Marysa Demoor (eds.): Dictionary of Nineteenth Century Journalism, Ghent/London 2009, pp. 378–379.

Cecil D. Eby: The Road to Armageddon. The Martial Spirit in English Popular Literature 1870–1914, Durham, NC 1987.

David Edgerton: Science, Technology and the British Industrial "Decline" 1870–1970, Cambridge 1996.

Lee R. Edwards: Psyche as Hero. Female Heroism and Fictional Form, Middletown 1984.

Elizabeth L. Eisenstein: The Printing Press as an Agent of Change, Cambridge 1982.

Alvar Ellergård: The Readership of the Periodical Press in Mid-Victorian Britain. II. Directory, in: Victorian Periodicals Newsletter 13, 1971, pp. 3–22.

Simon Eliot: Some Patterns and Trends in British Publishing 1800–1919, London 1993.

Ainslie T. Embree: Napier, Sir Charles James (1782–1853), in: Lawrence Goldman (ed.): Oxford Dictionary of National Biography, 2008, DOI: 10.1093/ref:odnb/19748.

Rainer Emig: Eccentricity Begins at Home. Carlyle's Centrality in Victorian Thought, in: Textual Practice 17.2, 2003, pp. 379–390.

Mark Engel: Collating Carlyle. Patterns of Revision in Heroes, Sartor Resartus, and The French Revolution, in: Davis R. Sorensen et al. (eds.): The Carlyles at Home and Abroad, Aldershot 2004, pp. 240–247.

Lee Erickson: The Economy of Literary Form. English Literature and the Industrialization of Publishing 1800–1850, Baltimore 1995.

Robert Escarpit: Book Revolution, London 1966.

John Feather: A History of British Publishing, London 2005 [1988].

W.H. Fevyer / Craig P. Barclay: Acts of Gallantry, vol. 3, Luton 2013.

Gary B. Ferngren: Science and Religion. A Historical Introduction, Baltimore 2002.

Orlando Figes: Crimea. The Last Crusade, London 2010.

S. E. Finer: The Life and Times of Sir Edwin Chadwick, London 1952.

David Finkelstein: Publishing and the Materiality of the Book, in: Kate Flint (ed.): The Cambridge History of Victorian Literature, Cambridge 2012, pp. 13–33.

Margot C. Finn: After Chartism. Class and Nation in English Radical Politics 1848–1874, Cambridge 1993.

Judith Flanders: The Victorian City. Everyday Life in Dickens' London, London 2012.

Andrew M. Flescher: Heroes, Saints, and Ordinary Morality, Georgetown 2003.

Kate Flint: Reading, Prohibition and Transgression, in: Robert L. Patten: Dickens and Victorian Print Cultures, Surrey 2012, pp. 249–258.

Josef Früchtl: Das unverschämte Ich. Eine Heldengeschichte der Moderne, Frankfurt am Main 2004.

Aileen Fyfe: Commerce and Philanthropy. The Religious Tract Society and the Business of Publishing, in: Journal of Victorian Culture 9.2, 2004, pp. 164–188.

–: Periodicals and Book Series. Complementary Aspects of a Publisher's Mission, in: Louise Henson (ed.): Culture and Science in the Nineteenth-Century Media, Aldershot 2004, pp. 71–82.

–: Science and Religion in Popular Publishing in 19th-Century Britain, in: Peter Meusburger et al. (eds.): Clashes of Knowledge, Dordrecht 2009, pp. 121–132.

–: Science and Salvation. Evangelical Popular Science Publishing in Victorian Britain, Chicago 2004.

–: Steam-Powered Knowledge, Chicago 2012.

Paul du Gay et al.: Doing Cultural Studies. The Story of the Sony Walkman, London 1997.

Ranjan Ghosh: Carlyle's "Hero as Poet" and Sri Aurobindo's Poetic Theory. Reconfiguring Few Dimensions of Creativity, in: Angelaki 11.1, 2006, pp. 35–44.

Bernhard Giesen: Triumph and Trauma, Boulder 2004.

–: Zwischenlagen. Das Außerordentliche als Grund der sozialen Wirklichkeit, Weilerswist 2010.

Mark Girouard: The Return to Camelot. Chivalry and the English Gentleman, New Haven 1981.

Robert Glen: Textile Industry, in: Sally Mitchell (ed.): Victorian Britain, New York/London 1988, pp. 793–794.

Lawrence Goldman: Science, Reform, and Politics in Victorian Britain. The Social Science Association 1857–1886, Cambridge 2007.

Paul Goldman: Beyond Decoration. The Illustrations of John Everett Millais, London 2005.

Eleanor Gordon / Gwyneth Nair: Public Lives. Women, Family, and Society in Victorian Britain, New Haven 2003.

Guinevere L. Griest: A Victorian Leviathan. Mudie's Select Library, in: Nineteenth-Century Fiction 20.2, 1965, pp. 103–126.

–: Mudie's Circulating Library and the Victorian Novel, Bloomington, IN 1970.

Jürgen Habermas: Between Facts and Norms. Contributions to a Discourse Theory of Law and Democracy, Cambridge 1996.

Christiane Hadamitzky: The History of a Magazine Is But the Influence of a Great Man? – Thomas Carlyle and the Decline of Fraser's Magazine, in: Ronald G. Asch / Michael Butter (eds.): Bewunderer, Verehrer, Zuschauer. Die Helden und ihr Publikum (Helden – Heroisierungen – Heroismen 2), Würzburg 2016, pp. 75–91.

–: Public vs. Private Honour. The Precarious Case of Victorian Modest Heroism in Chambers's Journal and The Leisure Hour, in: helden. heroes. héros. E-Journal zu Kulturen des Heroischen, special issue 2, 2016, pp. 56–60. DOI: 10.6094/helden.heroes.heros./2016/QMR/10.

–: "Your Fathers, Where Are They?" The Representation of Communal Heroism During Times of War in Chambers's Journal and The Leisure Hour, Life and Death in the 19th Century, RSVP Conference, Ghent University, 11 July 2015.

Christiane Hadamitzky / Barbara Korte: Everyday Heroism for the Victorian Industrial Classes, in: Simon Wendt (ed.): Extraordinary Ordinariness. Everyday Heroism in the United States, Germany, and Britain, 1800–2015, Frankfurt am Main 2016, pp. 53–78.

Christiane Hadamitzky / Barbara Korte (eds): Hero Books on the Victorian and Edwardian Print Market. Commented Bibliography, 2016, www.heroic-as-gift.uni-freiburg.de/.

Monroe Z. Hafter: Heroism in Alas and Carlyle's On Heroes, in: MLN 95.2, 1980, pp. 312–334.

N. John Hall: Trollope and His Illustrators, New York 1980.

Stuart Hall: Questions of Cultural Identity, London 2002.

Stuart Hall (ed.): Modernity and Its Futures, Cambridge 1992.

C. I. Hamilton: Naval Hagiography and the Victorian Hero, in: The Historical Journal 23.2, 1980, pp. 381–398.

Peter Harrison: "Science" and "Religion". Constructing the Boundaries, in: The Journal of Religion 86.1, 2006, pp. 81–106.

Katherine Haskins: The Art-Journal and Fine Art Publishing in Victorian England 1850–1880, Farnham/Burlington 2012.

Charles H. Haws: Carlyle's Concept of History in Heroes and Hero-Worship, in: John Morrow (ed.): Thomas Carlyle 1981. Papers Given at the International Thomas Carlyle Centenary Symposium, Frankfurt am Main 1983, pp. 153–163.

Kevin J. Hayes: Maggie in the Hospital, in: Notes and Queries 259.4, 2014, pp. 582–583.

Jennifer Poole Hayward: Consuming Pleasures. Active Audiences and Serial Fictions from Dickens to Soap Opera, Lexington 1997.

Ian Haywood: The Revolution in Popular Literature. Print, Politics and the People 1790–1860, Cambridge 2004.

Sheila Herstein: The Langham Place Circle and Feminist Periodicals of the 1860s, in: Victorian Periodicals Review 26.1, 1993, pp. 24–27.

Martin Hewitt: The Dawn of the Cheap Press in Victorian Britain. The End of the "Taxes of Knowledge" 1849–1869, London 2014.

Geraldine Higgins: Heroic Revivals from Carlyle to Yeats, Basingstoke 2012.

Linda Hughes / Michael Lund: The Victorian Serial, Charlottesville 1991.

Ralf von den Hoff et al.: Heroes – Heroizations – Heroisms. Transformations and Conjunctures from Antiquity to Modernity. Foundational Concepts of the Collaborative Research Centre SFB 948, in: helden. heroes. héros. E-Journal zu Kulturen des Heroischen, special issue 5: Analyzing Processes of Heroization. Theories, Methods, Histories, 2019, pp. 9–16, DOI: 10.6094/helden.heroes.heros./2019/APH/01.

Patricia Hollis: Women in Public 1850–1900. Documents of the Victorian Women's Movement, London 2013.

Heather Holmes (ed.): Scottish Life and Society. A Compendium of Scottish Ethnology, vol. 11, Edinburgh 2000.

Stephen Mark Holmes: Education in the Century of Reformation, in: R. D. Anderson et al. (eds.): The Edinburgh History of Education in Scotland, Edinburgh 2015, pp. 57–78.

Pamela Horn: Pleasures and Pastimes in Victorian Britain, Stroud 1999.

Walter Houghton: Periodical Literature and the Articulate Classes, in: Joanne Shattock (ed.): The Victorian Periodical Press. Samplings and Soundings, Leicester/Toronto 1982, pp. 3–27.

–: The Victorian Frame of Mind 1830–1870, New Haven 1957.

–: The Wellesley Index to Victorian Periodicals 1824–1900, vol. 2, Toronto 1972.

R. A. Houston: Scottish Literacy and the Scottish Identity. Illiteracy and Society in Scotland and Northern England 1600–1800, Cambridge 2002.

W. M. Humes: Leadership Class in Scottish Education, Edinburgh 1986.

W. M. Humes / Hamish M. Paterson: Scottish Culture and Scottish Education 1800–1980, Edinburgh 1983.

Nikolas Immer: Der inszenierte Held. Schillers dramenpoetische Anthropologie, Heidelberg 2008.

Wolfgang Iser: The Fictive and the Imaginary. Charting Literary Anthropology, Baltimore 1993.

David T. Jenkins: The Textile Industries, Oxford 1994.

Anna Johnston: Missionary Writing and Empire 1800–1860, Cambridge 2003.

John O. Jordan / Robert L. Platten (eds.): Literature in the Marketplace. Nineteenth-Century British Publishing and Reading Practices, Cambridge 1995.

Catherine Anne Judd: Hygienic Aesthetics. Sick Nursing and Social Reform in the Victorian Novel 1845–1880, in: Dissertation Abstracts International 53.10, 1993, pp. 3537a–3537a.

James G. Kellas: Modern Scotland, London/Boston [2]1980.

Christopher A. Kent: Higher Journalism and the Promotion of Comtism, in: Victorian Periodicals Review 25.2, 1992, pp. 51–56.

Susan Kingsley Kent: Sex and Suffrage in Britain 1860–1914, Princeton 1987.

Linda K. Kerber: Separate Spheres, Female Worlds, Woman's Place. The Rhetoric of Women's History, in: The Journal of American History 75.1, 1988, pp. 9–39.

Paul E. Kerry: The Outsider at the Gates of Victorian Society. Thomas Carlyle's *On Heroes, Hero-Worship, and the Heroic in History*, in: Steven Wright (ed.): The Image of the Outsider in Literature, Media, and Society, Pueblo 2002, pp. 369–373.

Jeffrey L. Kieve: The Electric Telegraph. A Social and Economic History, Newton Abbot 1973.

Andrew King / John Plunkett (eds.): Victorian Print Media. A Reader, New York 2006.

Robert J. Kirkpatrick: From the Penny Dreadful to the Ha'penny Dreadfuller, London 2013.

Barbara Korte: Krimkrieg und „Indian Mutiny“ als Anlass zum Kulturvergleich in viktorianischen Publikumszeitschriften, in: Angelika Epple / Walter Erhart (eds.): Die Welt beobachten. Praktiken des Vergleichens, Frankfurt am Main 2016.

–: Viele Helden für viele Leser. Das Heroische in viktorianischen Publikumszeitschriften, in: Ronald G. Asch / Michael Butter (eds.): Bewunderer, Verehrer, Zuschauer. Die Helden und ihr Publikum (Helden – Heroisierungen – Heroismen 2), Würzburg 2016, pp. 93–114.

Albrecht Koschorke: Zur Funktionsweise kultureller Peripherien, in: Susi K. Frank et al. (eds.): Explosion und Peripherie. Jurij Lotmans Semiotik der kulturellen Dynamik revisited, Berlin/Boston 2012, pp. 27–40.

Andrew Lambert: Napier, Sir Charles (1786–1860), in: Lawrence Goldman (ed.): Oxford Dictionary of National Biography, May 2011, DOI: 10.1093/ref:odnb/19747.

George P. Landow: Aesthetic and Critical Theory of John Ruskin, Princeton 1971.

Edward Larson: Evolution. The Remarkable History of a Scientific Theory, New York 2006.

Graham Law: Serializing Fiction in the Victorian Press, Basingstoke 2000.

Graham Law / Amy Loyd: The Leisure Hour, in: Laurel Brake / Marysa Demoor (eds.): Dictionary of Nineteenth Century Journalism, Ghent/London 2009, pp. 356–357.

Patrick Leary: Fraser's Magazine and the Literary Life 1830–1847, in: Victorian Periodicals Review 27.2, 1994, pp. 105–126.

Doris Lechner: Histories for the Many. The Victorian Family Magazine and Popular Representations of the Past, Bielefeld 2016.

George L. Levine "Not Like My Lancelot". The Disappearing Victorian Hero, in: Sara M. Putzell / David C. Leonard (eds.): Perspectives on Nineteenth-Century Heroism. Essays from the 1981 Conference of the Southeastern Nineteenth-Century Studies Association, Madrid 1982, pp. 47–72.

David C. Lindberg / Ronald L. Numbers: Beyond War and Peace. A Reappraisal of the Encounter between Christianity and Science, in: Church History. Studies in Christianity and Culture 55.3, 1986, pp. 338–354.

Ruth Livesey: Reading for Character. Women Social Reformers and Narratives of the Urban Poor in Late Victorian and Edwardian London, in: Journal of Victorian Culture 9.1, 2004, pp. 43–67.

Jurij M. Lotman: Die Struktur literarischer Texte, Munich 1993.

John M. MacKenzie: Popular Imperialism and the Military 1850–1950, Manchester 1992.

Christine MacLeod: Heroes of Invention. Technology, Liberalism and British Identity 1750–1914, Cambridge 2007.

Brian Maidment: Comedy, Caricature and the Social Order 1820–50, Manchester/New York 2013.

Brian Maidment: Reading Popular Prints: 1790–1870, Basingstoke 2001.

Brian Maidment / Aled Jones: Illustration, in: Laurel Brake / Marysa Demoor (eds.): Dictionary of Nineteenth-Century Journalism in Great Britain and Ireland, Ghent/London 2009, pp. 304–305.

J. A. Mangan: "Muscular, militaristic and manly". The British Middle-Class Hero as Moral Messenger, in: The International Journal of the History of Sport 13.1, 1996, pp. 28–47.

Alberto Manguel: A History of Reading, New York 2014 [1996].

H. C. G. Matthew: Darling, Grace Horsley (1815–1842), in: Lawrence Goldman (ed.): Oxford Dictionary of National Biography, 2010, DOI: 10.1093/ref:odnb/7155.

Jane McDermid: Education and Society in the Era of the School Boards 1872–1918, in: R. D. Anderson et al. (eds.): The Edinburgh History of Education in Scotland, Edinburgh 2015, pp. 190–208.

Sheila McIntosh: Two Victorian Heroes, in: Rivista di Studi Vittoriani 2.3, 1997, pp. 59–79.

Rohan McWilliam: The Melodramatic Seamstress. Interpreting a Victorian Penny Dreadful, in: Beth Harris (ed.): Famine and Fashion. Needlewomen in the Nineteenth Century, Aldershot 2005, pp. 99–114.

David F. Mitch: The Rise of Popular Literacy in Victorian England, Philadelphia 1992.

Jan Mohr: Männer mit Äxten. Heroismus in der Populärkultur, das Imaginäre und Hard Rock. Ein Versuch, in: KulturPoetik. Journal for Cultural Poetics 12.2, 2012, pp. 208–232.

Karina Momm: Der Begriff des Helden in Thomas Carlyles *On Heroes, Hero-Worship and the Heroic in History*, Freiburg 1986.

James Moore: The Historiography of Science and Religion, in: Gary B. Ferngren (ed.): Science and Religion. A Historical Introduction, Baltimore 2002, pp. 208–218.

Kenneth Morgan: The Birth of Industrial Britain. 1750–1850, Harlow 2011.

Patricia Morton: Wars and Military Engagements, in: Sally Mitchell (ed.): Victorian Britain. An Encyclopedia, New York 1988, pp. 844–845.

James Mussel: New Journalism, in: Laurel Brake / Marysa Demoor (eds.): Dictionary of Nineteenth Century Journalism in Great Britain and Ireland, Ghent/London 2009, p. 443.

Bob Nicholson: Counting Culture; Or, How to Read Victorian Newspapers from a Distance, in: Journal of Victorian Culture 17.2, 2012, pp. 238–246.

Robert Nisbet: History of the Idea of Progress, New York 1980.

Ronald L. Numbers: Science and Religion, in: Osiris 1, 1985, pp. 59–80.

Francis O'Gorman (ed.): The Cambridge Companion to Victorian Culture, Cambridge/New York 2010.

John W. Osborne: The Silent Revolution. The Industrial Revolution in England as a Source of Cultural Change, New York 1970.

Ian Ousby: Carlyle, Thackeray, and Victorian Heroism, in: Yearbook of English Studies 12, 1982, pp. 152–168.

Thomas Pakenham: The Boer War, London 1980.

E. M. Palmegiano: The First Common Market. The British Press on Nineteenth-Century European Journalism, in: Media History Monography 11.1, 2009, pp. 1–44.

Beth Palmer / Adelene Buckland (eds.): A Return to the Common Reader. Print Culture and the Novel 1850–1900, Farnham 2011.

James Paradis: Victorian Science and Victorian Values. Literary Perspective, New Brunswick 1985.

David Payne: The Reenchantment of Nineteenth-Century Fiction, Basingstoke 2005.

Morse Peckham: Victorian Revolutionaries. Speculations on Some Heroes of a Cultural Crisis, New York 1970.

Elizabeth Penner: "The Squire of Boyhood". G. A. Hutchison and the *Boy's Own Paper*, Victorian Periodicals Review 47.4, 2014, pp. 631–647.

Harold James Perkin: The Origins of the Popular Press, History Today 7.7, 1957, pp. 425–435.

Jennifer Phegley: Educating the Proper Woman Reader. Victorian Family Literary Magazines and the Cultural Health of the Nation, Columbus 2004.

Melanie Phillips: The Ascent of Woman. A History of the Suffragette Movement and the Ideas Behind It, London 2004.

Matthew Philpotts: A Return to Theory, in: Victorian Periodicals Review 48.3, 2015, pp. 307–311.

John Plunkett: Queen Victoria. First Media Monarch, Oxford 2003.

Ed Podesta / Pam Canning: Enquiring History. Italian Unification 1815–1871, London 2015.

Branwen Bailey Pratt: Carlyle and Dickens. Heroes and Hero-Worshippers, in: Dickens Studies Annual. Essays on Victorian Fiction 12, 1983, pp. 233–246.

Leah Price: How to Do Things with Books in Victorian Britain, Princeton 2013.

John Price: Everyday Heroism. Victorian Constructions of the Heroic Civilian, London 2014.

Lyn Pykett: Reading the Periodical Press. Text and Context, in: Victorian Periodicals Review 22.3, 1989, pp. 100–108.

Reality, in: OED Online, Oxford University Press 2015, Dezember 2019, www.oed.com/view/Entry/158934?redirectedFrom=reality#eid.

Jane Rendall: Langham Place Group, in: Lawrence Goldman (ed.): Oxford Dictionary of National Biography, 2015, DOI: 10.1093/ref:odnb/93708.

John R. Reed: The Army and Navy in 19th-Century British Literature, New York 2011.

Lucy Riall: Garibaldi. Invention of a Hero, New Haven 2008.

Gabriele Rippl: Intermedialität: Text/Bild-Verhältnisse, in: Claudia Benthien / Brigitte Weingart (eds.): Handbuch Literatur und Visuelle Kultur, Berlin/ Boston 2014, pp. 139–158.

Bronwyn Rivers: Reforming the Angel. Morality, Language and Mid-Victorian Nursing Heroines, Australasian Victorian Studies Journal 8, 2002, pp. 60–76.

George Robb: British Culture and the First World War, Basingstoke 2002.

Lewis Roberts: Disciplining and Disinfecting Working-Class Readers in the Victorian Public Library, in: Victorian Literature and Culture 26.1, 1998, pp. 105–132.

–: Trafficking in Literary Authority. Mudie's Select Library and the Commodification of the Victorian Novel, in: Victorian Literature and Culture 34.1, 2006, pp. 1–25.

Solveig C. Robinson: "Amazed at Our Success". The Langham Place Editors and the Emergence of a Feminist Critical Tradition, Victorian Periodicals Review 29.2, 1996, pp. 159–172.

Mary Beth Rose: Gender and Heroism in Early Modern English Literature, Chicago 2002.

Edward Royle: Chartism, London 2006 [1996].

Matthew Rubery: Journalism, in: Francis O'Gorman (ed.): The Cambridge Companion to Victorian Culture, Cambridge 2011, pp. 177–194.

Colin A. Russell: The Conflict of Science and Religion, in: Gary B. Ferngren (ed.): Science and Religion. A Historical Introduction, Baltimore 2002, pp. 3–12.

Richard Salmon: "The Unaccredited Hero". Alton Locke, Thomas Carlyle, and the Formation of the Working-Class Intellectual, in: Aruna Krishnamurthy (ed.): The Working-Class Intellectual in Eighteenth- and Nineteenth-Century Britain, Surrey 2009, pp. 167–193.

–: Thomas Carlyle and the Idolatry of the Man of Letters, in: Journal of Victorian Culture 7.1, 2002, pp. 1–22.

Valerie Sander: Women, Fiction and the Marketplace, in: Joanne Shattock (ed.): Women and Literature in Britain 1800–1900, Cambridge 2001, pp. 142–161.

Ines Schindler et al.: Admiration and Adoration. Their Different Ways of Showing and Shaping Who We Are, in: Cognition and Emotion 27.1, 2013, pp. 85–118.

Christian Schneider: Wozu Helden?, in: Mittelweg 36. Zeitschrift des Hamburger Instituts für Sozialforschung 18.1, 2009, pp. 91–102.

Alfonso Scirocco: Garibaldi. Citizen of the World, Princeton 2007.

John R. Searle: The Construction of Social Reality, New York 1997.

James A. Secord: Victorian Sensation. The Extraordinary Publication, Reception, and Secret Authorship of Vestiges of the Natural History of Creation, Chicago 2003.

Selfless, in: OED Online, Oxford University Press, Dezember 2019, www.oed.com/view/Entry/175323?redirectedFrom=selfless#eid.

Rhonda Anne Semple: Missionary Women. Gender, Professionalism, and the Victorian Idea of Christian Mission, Woodbridge 2003.

Rosemary Seton: Western Daughters in Eastern Lands. British Missionary Women in Asia, Santa Barbara 2013.

Joanne Shattock (ed.): Women and Literature in Britain 1800–1900, Cambridge 2001.

David Shaw: Gerald Massey. Chartist, Poet, Radical and Freethinker, London 1995.

Robert B. Shoemaker: Gender in English Society 1650–1850. The Emergence of Separate Spheres, London 2014.

Stuart Sillars: Visualisation in Popular Fiction, 1860–1960. Graphic Narratives, Fictional Images, London 1995.

Jack Simmons / Gordon Biddle: The Oxford Companion to British Railway History. From 1603 to the 1990s, Oxford/New York 1997.

Peter W. Sinnema: Dynamics of the Pictured Page. Representing the Nation in the Illustrated London News, Aldershot 1998.

L. D. Smith: Carpet Weavers and Carpet Masters. The Handloom Carpet Industry of Kidderminster 1780–1850, Kidderminster 1986.

Myron J. Smith / Terry White: Cloak and Dagger Fiction. An Annotated Guide to Spy Thrillers, Westport 1995.

David Smurthwaite: The Boer War 1899–1902, London 1999.

David Sonstroem: The Double Vortex in Carlyle's *On Heroes and Hero Worship*, Philological Quarterly 59.4, 1980, pp. 531–540.

Edward Spiers: War, in: Francis O'Gorman (ed.): The Cambridge Companion to Victorian Culture, Cambridge 2010, pp. 80–100.

John Springhall: "A Life Story for the People?" Edwin J. Brett and the London "Low-Life" Penny Dreadfuls of the 1860, in: Victorian Studies. A Journal of the Humanities, Arts and Sciences 33.2, 1990, pp. 223–246.

–: "Pernicious Reading?" The Penny Dreadful as Scapegoat for Late-Victorian Juvenile Crime, in: Victorian Periodicals Review 27.4, 1994, pp. 326–349.

–: "The Mysteries of Midnight". Low-Life London "Penny Dreadfuls" as Unrespectable Reading from the 1860s, in: Martin Hewitt (ed.): Unrespectable Recreations, Leeds 2001, pp. 160–175.

Ilia Stambler: Heroic Power in Thomas Carlyle and Leo Tolstoy, in: European Legacy. Toward New Paradigms 11.7, 2006, pp. 737–751.

Tom Standage: The Victorian Internet. The Remarkable Story of the Telegraph and the Nineteenth Century's Online Pioneers, London 1999.

E. D. Steele: Palmerston and Liberalism 1855–1865, Cambridge 1991.

Claudia Strauss: The Imaginary, in: Anthropological Theory 6.3, 2006, pp. 322–344.

John Sugden: Nelson. A Dream of Glory, London 2005.

–: Nelson. The Sword of Albion, London 2012.

Marcella Pellegrino Sutcliffe: Garibaldi in London, in: History Today 64.4, 2014, pp. 42–49.

John Sutherland: Victorian Fiction. Writers, Publishers, Readers, New York 2005.

John Sweetman: Napier, Sir William Francis Patrick (1785–1860), in: Lawrence Goldman (ed.): Oxford Dictionary of National Biography, 2008, DOI: 10.1093/ref:odnb/19772.

John S. Tanner: When God Is Hero. Worshipping God as Hero in Carlyle and Hopkins, in: The Hopkins Quarterly 10.4, 1984, pp. 145–163.

Charles Taylor: A Secular Age, Cambridge, MA 2007.

–: Modern Social Imaginaries, Durham, NC 2004.

Miles Taylor (ed.): The Victorian Empire and Britain's Maritime World 1837–1901. The Sea and Global History, Basingstoke 2013.

Julia Thomas: Pictorial Victorians. The Inscription of Values in Word and Image, Athens, OH 2004.

Nicola Diane Thompson: Reviewing Sex. Gender and the Reception of Victorian Novels, New York 1996.

Miriam M. H. Thrall: Rebellious Fraser's. Nol Yorke's Magazine in the Days of Maginn, Thackeray, and Carlyle, New York 1934.

Michael Timko: Thomas Carlyle. Chaotic Man, Inarticulate Hero, in: Carlyle Studies Annual 14, 1994, pp. 55–69.

John Tosh: A Man's Place. Masculinity and the Middle-Class Home in Victorian England, New Haven 2007.

–: Home and Away. The Flight from Domesticity in Late-Nineteenth-Century England Re-Visited, in: Gender and History 27.3, 2015, pp. 561–575.

D. J. Trela / Rodger L. Tarr: The Critical Response to Thomas Carlyle's Major Works, Westport 1997.

Frank Trentmann: Paradoxes of Civil Society. New Perspectives on Modern German and British History, New York 2003.

Frank M. Turner: Between Science and Religion. The Reaction to Scientific Naturalism in Late Victorian England, New Haven 1974.

Keaghan Kane Turner: In Perfect Sympathy. Representations of Nursing in New Woman Fiction, in: Dissertation Abstracts International 68.4, 2007, pp. 1472a–1472a.

Mark W. Turner: Fraser's Magazine, in: Laurel Brake / Marysa Demoor (eds.): Dictionary of Nineteenth Century Journalism, Ghent/London 2009, pp. 229–230.

J. Don Vann: Victorian Novels in Serial, New York 1985.

Amanda Vickery: Golden Age to Separate Spheres? A Review of the Categories and Chronology of English Women's History, in: The Historical Journal 36.2, 1993, pp. 383–414.

Max Weber: The Theory of Social and Economic Organization, New York 2009 [1947].

Toni Weller: Preserving Knowledge through Popular Victorian Periodicals. An Examination of *The Penny Magazine* and the *Illustrated London News* 1842–1843, in: Library History 24.3, 2008, pp. 200–207.

Roland Wenzlhuemer: Connecting the Nineteenth-Century World. The Telegraph and Globalization, Cambridge 2015.

Edwin G. West: Education and the Industrial Revolution, London 1975.

Lara Baker Whelan: Class, Culture and Suburban Anxieties in the Victorian Era, London 2010.

Martin Wiener: English Culture and the Decline of the Industrial Spirit 1850–1980, Cambridge/New York 2004.

David Sloan Wilson: Darwin's Cathedral. Evolution, Religion, and the Nature of Society, Chicago 2010.

Worship, in: OED Online, Oxford University Press, Dezember 2019, www.oed.com/view/Entry/230345?isAdvanced=false&result=1&rskey=WORcPD&.

Jane Wright: Sincerity's Repetition. Carlyle, Tennyson and Other Repetitive Victorians, in: Timothy Milnes / Kerry Sinanan (eds.): Romanticism, Sincerity, and Authenticity, New York 2010, pp. 162–181.

Deborah Wynne: The Sensation Novel and the Victorian Family Magazine, Houndsmill 2001.

Arlene Young: "Entirely a Woman's Question". Class, Gender, and the Victorian Nurse, in: Journal of Victorian Culture 13.1, 2008, pp. 18–41.

Veronika Zink: Von der Verehrung. Eine kultursoziologische Untersuchung, Frankfurt am Main 2014.

Index